# Religion and the Subtle Body in Asia and the West

D0551631

Subtle-body practices are found particularly in Indian, Indo-Tibetan and East Asian societies, but have become increasingly familiar in Western societies, especially through the various healing and yogic techniques and exercises associated with them. This book explores subtle-body practices from a variety of perspectives, and includes both studies of these practices in Asian and Western contexts.

The book discusses how subtle-body practices assume a quasi-material level of human existence that is intermediate between conventional concepts of body and mind. Often, this level is conceived of in terms of an invisible structure of channels, associated with the human body, through which flows of quasi-material substance take place. Contributors look at how subtle-body concepts form the basic explanatory structure for a wide range of practices. These include forms of healing, modes of exercise and martial arts as well as religious practices aimed at the refinement and transformation of the human mind–body complex.

By highlighting how subtle-body practices of many kinds have been introduced into Western societies in recent years, the book explores the possibilities for new models of understanding which these concepts open up. It is a useful contribution to studies on Asian religion and philosophy.

**Geoffrey Samuel** is Professor of Anthropology in the School of History, Archaeology and Religion at Cardiff University, UK, and Honorary Associate in the Department of Indian and Subcontinental Studies, University of Sydney, Australia.

**Jay Johnston** is Senior Lecturer in the Department of Studies in Religion at the University of Sydney, Australia, and Senior Lecturer in the School of Art History and Art Education, College of Fine Arts at the University of New South Wales, Australia.

# Routledge Studies in Asian Religion and Philosophy

# Religion and the Subtle Body in Asia and the West

Between mind and body

**Edited by Geoffrey Samuel and Jay Johnston**

Routledge
Taylor & Francis Group

LONDON AND NEW YORK

the context of healing and medicine but developing into a variety of spiritual and interpersonal modalities. To the extent that these sensitivities can be shown to be objectively valid, they raise philosophical issues about the nature of the senses and of the person. Healing techniques associated with the subtle body also raise issues of both practical and philosophical interest. At the same time, the progressive incorporation of these practices into Western societies is in itself a cultural phenomenon of considerable interest.

Sophisticated versions of subtle-body practices have also existed in Western thought (including Neoplatonism, Islam and Judaism) though they have been historically marginalized and for many centuries have been associated primarily with mystical, occult and esoteric traditions. Outside these sophisticated and literary contexts, similar concepts and practices are staples of folk healing and shamanic practices around the world.

Subtle-body practices of many kinds have been introduced, or reintroduced, into Western societies in recent years, and hundreds of thousands of people today are engaged with them in one way or another. It no longer makes sense simply to dismiss these practices as unscientific or nonsensical, but it is far from easy to know how we might understand them. This book explores subtle-body practices from a variety of perspectives. It includes studies of these practices in Asian and Western contexts, and explorations of the possibilities for new models of understanding which these concepts open up. It also considers some of the ways in which subtle-body practices may be of use within the complementary and alternative health context. We hope that the book will help to establish this field as an area of serious and systematic scholarly enquiry, and also suggest some of the lines along which that enquiry might proceed.

The editors thank Dorothea Schaefter, Jillian Morrison and Leanne Hinves of Routledge for their encouragement and support for this project, despite the considerable delays that have ensued in bringing it to completion. We thank all our contributors, and acknowledge the convenors of the 2nd International Conference on Religions and Cultures in the Indic Civilization conference, which took place in Delhi in December 2005, for providing the initial impetus for this book. Jay Johnston would especially like to thank Geoffrey Samuel for initiating this project and his subsequent enthusiasm and patience with its development, Barbara Maré for meticulous proofreading assistance and Iain Gardner and Lili Kamala Johnston for all manner of sustenance and support. Geoffrey Samuel equally would like to thank Jay for her ongoing energy and commitment, without which this book would certainly never have reached completion and Santi Rozario, whose encouragement and support was vital to this book, as to all his work.

# General introduction

*Geoffrey Samuel and Jay Johnston*

As this book demonstrates, ideas and practices relating to what we term here 'subtle bodies' have been around for many centuries, and they can be found in many parts of the world. While they are most often associated with Asian cultures, particularly Indic and Chinese, ideas and practices of this general kind have been found in a very wide range of societies, and form part of many religious traditions, at both elite and vernacular levels. Much of the contemporary literature regarding them, however, is popular rather than academic. This is a major omission, which we hope that this book will go some way to remedy. There have been academic studies of specific subtle-body traditions within particular cultures, but the present volume is, as far as we know, the first strictly academic book that attempts to survey and make some sense of subtle-body concepts and practices over a wide range of societies. Whether or not we regard these concepts as referring in some way to real phenomena within human experience, the wide range of time and space within which they have been evidenced surely implies that there is something there worth studying.

## What are subtle-body concepts and practices?
## The Theosophical connection

To start with, though, what do we mean in this book by subtle-body concepts and practices? The key idea here is that of concepts that assume a common basis or substance for both mind and matter. Often, they are phrased in terms of an inter-mediate level (or series of levels) *between* 'mind' (spirit, consciousness) and matter. Thus, if the mainstream of Western thought, going back to the Cartesian distinction, treats mind and matter as radically different in nature, subtle-body concepts and practices treat them as continuous. Consciousness, in this picture, has a material aspect, if often thought of as more 'subtle' (finer, less solidly material) than ordinary physical matter. Such subtle material levels of consciousness are then conceived of as interacting with material reality in various ways. They provide both an explanatory model for phenomena which cannot easily be encompassed by theories based on a rigid mind–matter dichotomy, and also, and perhaps crucially, they form the basis of techniques by which one can learn to operate with these finer or more subtle levels of thought and consciousness.

The term 'subtle body' became established in English usage in large part through scholars and writers influenced by the Theosophical Society, an influential organization founded in the USA in 1875 and dedicated to the pursuit of esoteric knowledge. The Theosophical Society's members saw themselves as involved in a restating of 'Eastern wisdom' (mainly Hindu, also Buddhist) for contemporary (mainly Western) consumption. Initially 'subtle body' served as a translation of the Vedantic term *sūkṣmaśarīra*, a key concept in Vedanta philosophy, for example in the work of the great Indian philosopher Śaṃkara, who lived perhaps in around 800 CE. The *sūkṣmaśarīra*, in the context of Śaṃkara's work, forms part of a series of three bodies, the material or physical body (*sthūlaśarīra*), subtle body (*sūkṣmaśarīra*) and causal body (*kāraṇaśarīra*). Beyond these three bodies lies identity with the ultimate self, itself identical with Brahman (see Chapter 2).

The terms used here – physical body, subtle body, causal body – have been found problematic by more recent scholars, in part because of their close association with the work and teachings of the Theosophical Society. Ideas regarding the subtle body already appeared in the works of the founding figure of Theosophy, Helena Blavatsky (1831–91), and they were developed further in the works of Theosophical writers such as C. W. Leadbeater (1854–1934), Annie Besant (1847–1933), and of Rudolf Steiner (1861–1925), initially a Theosophist and after his breakaway from the Theosophical Society the founder of another influential esoteric movement, Anthroposophy. The Theosophical writers assumed, with some variations, a series of 'higher bodies' coexistent with the physical body, typically including astral, mental, causal and etheric bodies, and corresponding to successive higher planes of existence of progressively finer materiality (see Introduction to Part Four for further details).

While the initial impetus here came from Indian thought, and many early Indologists were influenced by Theosophical thought, the Theosophists developed their concepts further on the basis of psychic and clairvoyant insights, and their usage of Sanskrit terminology differs in many respects from the meanings of these terms in their Indian context. Neither Theosophy nor Anthroposophy was part of the scientific and scholarly mainstream of Western thought, although they had many influential followers, including some significant scholars. Thus ideas about the subtle body became linked within Western societies with currents of thought that have historically been regarded by many scholars as questionable, even as unworthy of serious consideration.

Many contemporary Indological scholars are uncomfortable with the Theosophical-derived terminology, and the translation of *sūkṣmaśarīra* as 'subtle body' has itself been contested in recent years.[1] Indeed, the continuing association of the 'subtle body' with Theosophical thought remains a problem for viewing this area clearly, and the revival of Theosophically-derived ideas in contemporary society within New Age and alternative medical circles has if anything intensified the difficulties. As far as the editors of this book are concerned, we feel that it is important to maintain a critical perspective towards Theosophically-inspired interpretations in relation to subtle-body concepts and to be wary of the continued dominance of such interpretations in popular discourse.

However, a blanket dismissal of subtle-body concepts because of the Theosophical associations of the term would be unfortunate. Subtle-body concepts and practices existed long before Theosophy came along, and the need for a coherent and systematic approach to them remains, irrespective of the value one places on the specifically Theosophical versions of these ideas.

We are left with the questionable nature of the term 'subtle body' itself. Our intention in this work is to use it as a generic term, while being aware of the possible difficulties that this may cause. Certainly there is a need for a generic term to cover the various concepts, practices and phenomena discussed in this book. They have in common their interstitial positioning between mind and matter, as well as a series of established or possible historical relationships, some of which will be explored in the following chapters. 'Subtle body' is not ideal, but it at least conveys a general sense of the area we are considering, and we have decided, with some reservations, to retain it. As noted above, in this book we use the term 'subtle body' generically, to include not only concepts such as the Vedic *sūkṣmaśarīra* and related ideas, but a variety of aspects of Indian and Tibetan yogic and tantric practices, and a range of similar conceptualizations found in East Asia and elsewhere in the world. We will explore a variety of these in Parts One to Three of this book. We will be also looking, in Part Four, at ideas and practices relating to the subtle body in the contemporary world, and at the possible contributions of subtle-body concepts to contemporary thought.

## Between mind and body

Virtually all human cultures known to us have some kind of concept of mind, spirit or soul as distinct from the physical body, if only to explain experiences such as sleep and dreaming. Those human cultures that historically developed systematic philosophical understandings of human consciousness have taken such concepts in a variety of different directions. As we have already noted, the tendency of European thought from the seventeenth and eighteenth centuries onwards has been to treat mind and body as fundamentally different phenomena that operate at quite different levels and can be related to each other only with considerable difficulty. This tendency, while often associated with the French philosopher René Descartes, has deep roots in Western, and specifically Christian, thought, with its characteristic opposition of spiritual and material concerns. Such dichotomizing tends to lead to a materialist reduction on the one side, an idealist rejection of the world on the other, and leaves little room for a messy and complex reality that arguably includes not only the extremes, but much in between.

Thus the Christian moral was, by and large, that everyday material or physical reality was of little value, except for what it might contribute to the life of the spirit. Spirit was seen as an entirely separate realm from the body, and the human task was understood as involving a continuous purification and refinement of spirit until the confines of the body were finally left behind at death. Modern Western science, particularly bioscience and biomedicine, has taken the opposite direction, treating material reality as primary and consciousness as a secondary and derivative phenomenon. Thus most contemporary scientific thought is strongest on the materialist reduction and finds itself in considerable difficulties when faced with phenomena where mind cannot easily be reduced to the physical.

Some of these issues have been discussed by one of us elsewhere in relation to the field of medicine, where dogmatic materialism often makes it difficult to understand modes of healing that operate with the body-mind as an integrated field (see Samuel 2005a, 2006a, 2006b, 2007, 2010). While Western medical scientists have made an enormously important contribution to human well-being, their frequent inability to construe, and their consequent tendency to reject, other modes of healing is a major problem in an increasingly pluralistic world. The conflicts here are, of course, economic and political as well as intellectual, since biomedicine and the other modes of healing are competing both for patients and for other material resources. If, however, we had a better understanding at the intellectual level of concepts such as the subtle body which have an important role in many non-biomedical approaches to healing, that would surely help in understanding these conflicts and reaching a fairer resolution.

If Western science has tended to devalue and dismiss the mind and spirit, and Christian religion to take the opposite tack, many Western contexts, both religious and secular, still involve an uneasy coexistence of mental and physical factors. Many of the typical Western intellectual dilemmas (nature or nurture? freewill or determinism?) owe their specific form, if not their essential nature, to the difficulty of making sense of the mind–body relationship in a dichotomized conceptual framework.

As the following chapters evidence, conceptualizations of the subtle body complicate concepts of the physical self (matter) and ideas of the soul and/or spirit in interesting and significant ways. They open up possibilities for new modes of analysis that may be worth pursuing in strictly scientific terms, as well as for developing and understanding practical applications. At the same time, while some subtle-body traditions have highly developed conceptual structures, definitions of the substance(s) of which subtle bodies are thought to be comprised are not necessarily clear-cut. As a form of embodiment, subtle bodies slip not only between sharp matter–spirit dualisms, but also among concepts of soul, spirit and self.

If Western thought, with important exceptions, has been marked by a dichotomy between mind and body, we should not assume that non-Western philosophers have always regarded the entire mind-body field as a unity, or mind and body as of equal value and significance. Both materialism and idealism in their extreme forms can also be found in Indic thought. Many Indic religions, particularly in their textual expressions, exhibit a noted cultural partiality for imagery of purity and transcendence, so valuing the higher realms of spirit over more material levels. The interest of the area of subtle-body concepts, however, is that it lies between the materialistic and idealistic extremes, and recognizes a complex interplay between matter and spirit. Indic religious thought has been particularly strong in developing a practical understanding of this area. Much of the history of yoga and tantra within Indic religious traditions can be seen as a sustained series of attempts to bridge the gap between materialist and idealist extremes, to draw 'mind' and 'body', 'consciousness' and 'material reality', 'matter' and 'spirit', within the same field of discourse.

While such developments were by no means unknown in the Western tradition, they have tended to be marginalized into residual categories of mystical, occult or poetic (see Uberoi 1984; Samuel 2005b; and Chapters 10, 11 and 13 in this volume). Subtle bodies nevertheless came to feature strongly in Western mystical and esoteric traditions, often on the basis of borrowings from the Jewish mystical tradition of the Kabbalah, which itself had close associations with the Islamic mystical tradition of Sufism. In this respect the founders of the Theosophical Society were continuing a long-established tradition of 'esoteric' thought, although choosing to find their inspiration in an alternative and South Asian cultural context. In contemporary esotericism, subtle levels of consciousness continue to feature, for example in the practice of ritual magic, where they provide the mediating yet invisible substance that enables a spell, charm or ritual to work. In general, for such practices, the 'intent' (mind) of the practitioner is directed to manipulating subtle matter.

Chinese thought has also developed its own modes of understanding subtle-body phenomena, as have many of the preliterate traditions found in small-scale societies around the world. Indian philosophical schools, with their partiality for non-dualist approaches, have nevertheless probably provided the most complex and intellectually sophisticated descriptions of subtle-body processes. Buddhist varieties of non-dualism in particular, such as the Madhyamaka philosophy of Nāgārjuna and his followers, can be read as a systematic refusal to avoid closure to one side or the other, and this refusal led naturally, as in the Cittamatrā or 'Mind-Only' schools, to many centuries of intellectual speculation and practical enquiry into what might lie between.

## The internal physiology of Tantra

An important subset of subtle-body practices, found particularly in Indian and Tibetan Tantric traditions, and in similar Chinese practices, involves the idea of an internal 'subtle physiology' of the body (or rather of the body-mind complex) made up of channels through which substances of some kind flow, and points of intersection at which these channels come together. In the Indian tradition the channels are known as *nāḍī* and the points of intersection as *cakra*. When it comes to describing what is going on in the space between mind and body, these internal physiologies of channels and meeting-points are of particular interest.

A critical question for the linkage between mind and body is how one understands the substance that is flowing through the *nāḍī* or channels. In Indic thought, this is seen primarily as a form of *prāṇa* or 'breath'. *Prāṇa* covers a considerably wider area than the English terms 'breathing' or 'respiration', with, for example, five internal forms of *prāṇa* classically associated with specific bodily functions.[2] *Prāṇa* is also closely associated with mind and with emotion, including sexual energy (*vīrya*). This is part of the logic behind the use of breathing practices as a way to control the mind and emotions. Thus the circulation of *prāṇa* becomes at once a matter of breath, mind, mood and emotion, and also, one might add, motivation to action.[3]

It is important to note here that matters such as mind, mood and emotion have a strongly interpersonal component. We learn to think in dialogue with others, and we learn to feel in relation to others. One of the more significant aspects of the subtle body language is the way in which it can open our picture of the individual out to include the relationship with others. These issues have been explored at considerable length by one of us elsewhere (see Johnston 2008, 2010a, 2010b; also Chapter 13 in this volume). This interpersonal dimension is particularly relevant to any consideration of subtle body practices in the context of healing, since healing is always at some level about relationships between people. Western medicine tends to minimize these aspects, while subtle-body approaches highlight them (cf. Johnston 2010c; Samuel 2010).

Subtle-body concepts in the Tantric tradition are practical more than theoretical. The aim is not for the most part simply to understand but to use, primarily, though not only, for the purpose of physical and spiritual transformation. Thus Buddhist Tantric understandings of the circulation of *prāṇa* through the *nāḍī* and *cakra* of the subtle body are linked to a series of physical and meditative exercises aimed at working with the flows through the channels and wheels. In the course of these processes, knots or tangles in the flows through the channels are untied, and the substances flowing through them are concentrated in a central channel, a process homologous with the progress towards spiritual awakening.

The substances flowing through the channels in these practices again have both physical and mental or emotional correlates. They are at one level identified with male and female sexual substances, but they are also identified with *bodhicitta*, the central motivational state cultivated within Mahāyāna Buddhist practice, the desire to attain Buddhahood in order to relieve the suffering of sentient beings. There is a close linkage or identification here of flows of internal substances with emotional states or states of bodily excitation. The whole series of processes becomes both a way of achieving the optimal functioning of the human organism, and of going beyond it to achieve the goal seen as implicit within that organism, Buddhahood itself (Samuel 1989).

Analogous developments are found in China (with flows of a substance referred to as *qi* through channels known as *mai*, most familiar outside China as the acupuncture meridians). In China, the practices are generally associated with the Daoist tradition, and again are essentially part of processes aimed at physical and spiritual transformation.

## The subtle body in modern Western thought

Both Indo-Tibetan and Chinese versions of subtle-body concepts and practices have been incorporated in recent years into alternative healing and New Age contexts within Western societies. In the Western context, subtle-body practices tend to be given a psychological reading. Here, specific *cakra*-s may be identified with various aspects of psychological functioning, untying knots in psychic channels may be seen as releasing emotional blockages, and so on. Much of this goes back to the development of *cakra* concepts within the Theosophical tradition from the 1920s onwards. A key figure here was Charles Webster Leadbeater, whose book *The Chakras*, first published in 1927, has been particularly influential (Leadbeater 1972). In addition to the work of Blavatsky, Leadbeater and other Theosophists of his time relied extensively on the translations and other writings of Sir John Woodroffe (Arthur Avalon), particularly *The Serpent Power*, first published in 1919 (Woodroffe 1953). This modern Western history of the subtle body underlies several of the chapters in Part Four.

Indic, Chinese and for that matter 'New Age' subtle-body practices can also be seen as part of a wider range of concepts and phenomena, including soul and spirit concepts, synaesthesia and other apparently anomalous sensory processes, 'shamanic' forms of healing and religion, and non-dualistic modes of understanding more generally. It is tempting to interpret much of this material in psychological terms, especially since many of the practices have been incorporated into a general field of therapy oriented around individual self-improvement. However, we should be cautious about Western psychological readings, particularly in relation to earlier Indic and Chinese concepts and practices. Western psychology tends to take for granted much of the mind–body dichotomizing endemic in contemporary Western thought, and psychological readings of subtle-body concepts may be partial, simplistic or simply irrelevant. In fact, much of the contemporary value of subtle-body concepts may lie in their potential to generate a critique of Western psychology (cf. Samuel 1990, and Chapter 14 in this volume). Subtle-body processes do not fit neatly into the Western categories of mind (consciousness) or body, but hint at the need for models and modes of understanding that go beyond these divisions.

Western medical science accepts the interaction of mind and body within an essentially materialistic framework, and subtle-body practices have been studied scientifically in terms of the yogic control over physiological and neurological processes associated with consciousness (electrical impulses, temperature, etc.; see Chapter 14). However, the subtle body and similar ideas strain the limits of such reductionisms. A full understanding of subtle-body processes is likely to encompass humanities and social sciences as well as natural sciences. It is also likely to require some degree of openness to the experiences of those who have or claim to have worked with subtle-body processes. We hope that this book will stimulate further work in these areas.

## The structure of the book

The book is divided into four parts. Part One looks at subtle bodies in China and India, including the existence of subtle-body-like concepts in the folk practices of Indian *dai* (midwives). Part Two consists of three chapters on subtle-body concepts and practices in Tibet, including an exploration of their contemporary medical applications. Part Three looks at subtle-body practices in European history and in Islam, and Part Four, 'Subtle Bodies and Modernity', examines subtle-body practices in modern Western societies (Chapters 10 to 12), and discusses the possibilities for understanding the subtle body in Western terms (Chapters 13 and 14). The Introductions to each part discuss further issues relating to the subject area and introduce the individual chapters in more detail.

There are no easy equivalences to be made between Asian and Western propositions regarding the subtle body, and both editors would wish to stress the importance of respecting cultural difference in the exploration of the schemas. However, such respect does not need to shut down cross-cultural dialogue on the topic. Indeed, it should open it out with reference to particularity and the ethics of 'lived' subtle-body relations. We hope that the book as a whole will serve to bring into closer focus an important area of human thought and activity in many lands and over many centuries, and encourage others to give it the serious attention that we believe it deserves.

## Notes

1  Thus Dominik Wujastyk comments that the time is long overdue to drop 'subtle' as a translation for *sūkṣma* in *sūkṣmaśarīra*, both because of its Theosophical associations and because the word 'subtle' has itself changed significantly in sense since the nineteenth century (personal communication, 2 August 2012).
2  The exact associations vary: e.g. *prāṇa* proper with inhalation and intake of food, *samāna* with digestion, *apāna* with exhalation and excretion, *vyāna* with circulation, *udāna* with upwards movement, as with speech.
3  Further references on subtle-body concepts in India include Hartzell 1997, Flood 2006 and Samuel 2008.

## References

Flood, G. (2006) *The Tantric Body: The Secret Tradition of Hindu Religion.* London and New York: I.B. Tauris.

Hartzell, J. F. (1997) 'Tantric Yoga: a study of the Vedic precursors, historical evolution, literatures, cultures, doctrines, and practices of the 11th century Kaśmīri Śaivite and Buddhist unexcelled Tantric Yogas,' unpublished PhD dissertation, Columbia University. UMI No. 9723798.

Johnston, J. (2008) *Angels of Desire: Esoteric Bodies, Aesthetics and Ethics*, Gnostica Series. London and Oakville: Equinox.

—— (2010a) 'Hermetic embodiment: angels and intersubjectivity', in M. T. Mjaaland, S. Fiorgeirsdóttir and O. Sigurdson (eds) *The Body Unbound: Philosophical Perspectives on Embodiment, Politics and Religion.* Newcastle upon Tyne: Cambridge Scholars Press.

—— (2010b) 'Cyborgs and chakras: intersubjectivity in spiritual and scientific somatechnics', in C. Cusack and C. Hartney (eds) *Religion and Retributive Logic: Essays in Honour of Professor Garry W. Trompf.* Leiden: Brill.

—— (2010c) 'Subtle anatomy: the bio-metaphysics of alternative therapies', in E. B. Coleman and K. White (eds) *Medicine, Religion and the Body.* Leiden: Brill.

Leadbeater, C. W. (1972) *The Chakras.* Wheaton, IL: Theosophical Publishing House.

Samuel, G. (1989) 'The body in Buddhist and Hindu Tantra: some notes', *Religion* 19: 197–210.

—— (1990) *Mind, Body and Culture: Anthropology and the Biological Interface.* Cambridge and New York: Cambridge University Press.

——(2005a) 'Beyond biomedical assimilation?', paper for ACHRN Conference, Diversity and Debate in Alternative and Complementary Medicine, Nottingham University, 29 June–1 July.

—— (2005b) 'The attractions of Tantra: two historical moments', in Samuel, *Tantric Revisionings*. Delhi: Motilal Banarsidass and London: Ashgate.

—— (2006a) 'Healing and the mind-body complex: childbirth and medical pluralism in South Asia', in H. Johannessen and I. Lázár (eds) *Multiple Medical Realities: Patients and Healers in Biomedical, Alternative and Traditional Medicine.* New York and London: Berghahn Books.

—— (2006b) 'Tibetan medicine and biomedicine: epistemological conflicts, practical solutions', *Asian Medicine: Tradition and Modernity* 2: 72–85.

—— (2007) 'Spirit causation and illness in Tibetan medicine', in M. Schrempf (ed.) *Soundings in Tibetan Medicine: Anthropological and Historical Perspectives.* Leiden: Brill.

—— (2008) *The Origins of Yoga and Tantra: Indic Religions to the Thirteenth Century.* Cambridge and New York: Cambridge University Press.

—— (2010) 'Healing, efficacy and the spirits', *Journal of Ritual Studies* 24(2): 7–20 (special issue, *The Efficacy of Rituals Part II*, ed. W. S. Sax and J. Quack).

Uberoi, J. P. S. (2004) *The Other Mind of Europe: Goethe as a Scientist.* Delhi, Oxford and New York: Oxford University Press.

Woodroffe, Sir J. (Arthur Avalon) (1953) *The Serpent Power: Being the Shat-Chakra-Nirūpana and Pādukā-Panchaka, Two Works on Laya-Yoga*, translated from the Sanskrit, with introduction and commentary, by A. Avalon, 5th enlarged edn. Madras: Ganesh.

# Part One
# Subtle bodies in China and India

# Introduction to Part One

*Geoffrey Samuel*

As noted in the Introduction above, subtle-body-type concepts can be found all over the world, and developed versions exist in most major world cultures. If the concept of 'subtle bodies' has saliency around the world today, however, it is primarily owing to its development in two Asian traditions, the Chinese and Indian, and their offshoots, including Tibetan Buddhism (see Part Two).

Subtle-body concepts and practices can already be identified in China in the second century BCE in manuscripts and images uncovered in the Mawangdui tombs, which present medical and sexual practices aimed at preserving and restoring health (Harper 1987, 1997; Lo 1998). These texts and images already describe structures of channels within the body, and physical exercises aimed at promoting proper flow of substances through the channels.

Early medical and Daoist texts preserved by the literary tradition include material that goes back to the same period, and these texts show that these practices also developed a cosmological and soteriological significance. A central goal was the attainment of immortality through ascetic practices, which were premised on the cultivation and transformation of the subtle substance known as *qi*. Livia Kohn, who provides an account of these practices in their mature form in Chapter 1, has written a historical anthology of these texts (Kohn 1993) and edited a number of collections dealing with Daoist transformative practices (e.g. Kohn and Sakade 1989; Kohn and Wang 2009).[1]

Subtle-body concepts were evidently present in some form in Indian material from the late Vedic period (fourth to first century BCE) but a developed conceptual structure comparable to that found within the Chinese material is first attested in surviving materials from the seventh and eighth centuries onwards, as part of a series of developments within all the main Indian religious traditions (Hindu, Buddhist and Jain) which is now generally termed Tantra (Hartzell 1997; Samuel 2008). Tantric religion was enormously influential, but its authority and legitimacy was often contested within Indian society. Today Hindu Tantra is no longer the mainstream of Indian religion, but it survives in a wide variety of forms, including the practices of various traditions of ascetic renunciates, among lay Tantrics such as the Nāths and Bauls, and hereditary Tantric ritualists who serve as temple priests. Buddhist Tantra (Vajrayāna), while developed to a high level of sophistication by both lay tantric practitioners and the scholars of the great monastic universities of Northeast India, disappeared from the Indian mainland, with the exception of the Newars of the Kathmandu Valley in Nepal, but was transmitted to China, Korea, Japan and Tibet.

Part One presents material from China and India, and consists of three chapters. The first, by Livia Kohn, introduces the body of ideas within which the Chinese system of concepts regarding subtle bodies are framed. As Kohn notes, Daoist concepts of the body are located between Daoist cosmology and traditional Chinese medicine. *Qi*, a central concept within Daoist conceptualizations of the subtle body, occurs from early times both in texts on spiritual and sexual self-cultivation and in medical writings. In the developed structure of ideas presented by Kohn, it is a central term in a complex and fully developed set of ideas regarding the functioning of the body and its relationship to the wider universe. These ideas have remained as important for medical practice as for Daoist traditions of self-cultivation.

Chapter 2, by Geoffrey Samuel, sketches developments in India. Early Indian sources are difficult to date. Terms suggestive of subtle-body concepts can be found in late Vedic texts, including the Upaniṣads. A fully developed set of ideas and practices regarding the subtle body, comparable to that found in China, is not attested until the 'Tantric' literature of the eighth and ninth centuries. The associated practices became central to the Indian traditions of asceticism and self-cultivation, and were exported to Southeast and East Asia and to Tibet.

Chapter 3, by Janet Chawla, is included as representative of the important presence of subtle-body-type concepts within vernacular and non-literary contexts. It strongly makes the point that subtle-body-type concepts are not just about intellectual understanding, they are also about doing. The context here is that of childbirth in contemporary India, which is still largely handled by midwives or birth attendants (*dais*) whose knowledge comes from family or folk tradition rather than biomedical training (cf. Rozario and Samuel 2002). Chawla shows how Indian midwives today employ subtle-body concepts in their work. The example is particularly significant because, as Samuel notes in Chapter 2, subtle-body concepts may well have arisen in India in large part as a way of understanding childbirth and the coming into existence of new human life.

Readers might note that Indian concepts of the subtle body are explored elsewhere in this volume in Chapter 7, which develops a comparison between ideas of physical and spiritual cultivation in India and in ancient Greece.

## Note

1  Other useful studies include Schipper 1994 and Mayor and Micozzi 2011. The latter includes a range of studies analysing *qi*-type processes in scientific terms.

## References

Harper, D. (1987) 'The sexual arts of ancient China as described in a manuscript of the second century B.C.', *Harvard Journal of Asiatic Studies* 47: 539–92.

—— (1997) *Early Chinese Medical Literature: The Mawangdui Medical Manuscripts*. London: Kegan Paul International and New York: Columbia University Press.

Hartzell, J. F. (1997) 'Tantric Yoga: a study of the Vedic precursors, historical evolution, literatures, cultures, doctrines, and practices of the 11th century Kaśmīri Śaivite and Buddhist unexcelled Tantric Yogas,' unpublished PhD dissertation, Columbia University. UMI No. 9723798.

Kohn, L. (1993) *The Taoist Experience: An Anthology*. Albany: State University of New York Press.

Kohn, L. and Sakade, Y. (eds) (1989) *Taoist Meditation and Longevity Techniques*. Ann Arbor: University of Michigan Press.

Kohn, L. and Wang, R. R. (eds) (2009) *Internal Alchemy: Self, Society and the Quest for Immortality*. Dunedin, FL: Three Pines Press.

Lo, V. (1998) 'The Influence of Yangsheng 養生 Culture on Early Chinese Medical Theory,' unpublished PhD thesis, University of London, School of Oriental and African Studies.

Mayor, D. F. and Micozzi, M. S. (2011) *Energy Medicine East and West: A Natural History of Qi*. Edinburgh: Churchill Livingstone.

Rozario, S. and Samuel, G. (eds) (2002) *Daughters of Hariti: Childbirth and Female Healers in South and Southeast Asia*. London: Routledge.

Samuel, G. (2008) *The Origins of Yoga and Tantra: Indic Religions to the Thirteenth Century*. Cambridge and New York: Cambridge University Press.

Schipper, K. (1994) *The Taoist Body*. Berkeley and Los Angeles: University of California Press.

# 1   The Daoist body of *qi*

## *Livia Kohn*

The body in Daoism is both a central concept and the main location of cultivation practice. It is located between Daoist cosmology and traditional Chinese medicine, integrating both universal concepts such as *dao* 道 and the various technical aspects of the energy body to culminate in a complete different complex: the body as the residence of deities and the location of energetic centres of alchemical transformation.

While concepts of Dao go back to before the Common Era to the period commonly known as philosophical Daoism, part of the formative period of Chinese thought, concepts of vital energy and body cosmology (yin-yang, the five phases) were formulated first in the Han dynasty and are documented both in philosophical and medical classics from this period. Both underlying dimensions of Daoist body conceptions have remained relevant throughout the ages to the present day – despite differing interpretations and modifications in various schools and contextual settings.

The formulation of the Daoist body as inhabited by body gods and as the root of cosmic visualization practice occurred in the early centuries of the Common Era, notably around the year 300, at a time when Chinese religion was in great flux and new schools and lineages developed. The school within Daoism that made most ample use of this body vision and became responsible for placing it firmly at the core of Daoist body practice is known as Highest Clarity (Shangqing). It emerged through a series of revelations in the mid-fourth century and remained dominant throughout the medieval period.[1] The understanding of the Daoist body as described below is thus based on classical, early sources and reflects what is still current in the religion today.

## Daoist cosmology

The fundamental concept underlying Daoist cosmology is Dao, literally 'the way'. The term indicates the way things develop naturally, the way nature moves along and living beings grow and decline. The concept of Dao is not limited to Daoism, although the latter takes its name from it. Rather, it is part of the general Chinese understanding of the world, which appears in all different philosophical schools – albeit in slightly varying interpretations. This is why A. C. Graham calls his book on early Chinese philosophy *Disputers of the Dao* (1989). Dao in this general sense is the one power underlying all. It makes things what they are and causes the world to come into being and decay. It is the fundamental ground of all: the motivation of evolution and the source of universal being.

The *Daode jing* 道德經 (Book of the Dao and Its Virtue) says, 'The Dao that can be told is not the eternal Dao' (ch. 1). Still, it is possible to create a working definition. In *The World of Thought in Ancient China*, Benjamin Schwartz describes the Dao as 'organic order' (1985), organic in the sense that it is not wilful, not a conscious, active creator or personal entity but an organic process that just moves along. But beyond this, Dao is also order – clearly manifest in the rhythmic changes and patterned processes of the natural world. As such it is predictable in its developments and can be discerned and described. Its patterns are what the Chinese call 'self-so' or 'nature' (*ziran* 自然), the spontaneous and observable way things are naturally (Liu 1998). Yet, while Dao is nature, it is also more than nature – its deepest essence, the inner quality that makes things what they are. It is governed by laws of nature, yet it is also these laws itself.

In other words, it is possible to explain the nature of the Dao in terms of a twofold structure: the 'Dao that can be told' and the 'eternal Dao'. One is the mysterious, ineffable Dao at the centre of the cosmos; the other is the Dao at the periphery, visible and tangible in the natural cycles of the known world. About the eternal Dao, the *Daode jing* says (ch. 14):[2]

> Look at it and do not see it: we call it invisible.
> Listen to it and do not hear it: we call it inaudible.
> Touch it and do not feel it: we call it subtle ...
> Infinite and boundless, it cannot be named;
> It belongs to where there are no beings.
> It may be called the shape of no-shape,
> It may be called the form of no-form.
> Call it vague and obscure.
> Meet it, yet you cannot see its head,
> Follow it, yet you cannot see its back.

This Dao, although the ground and inherent power of the human being, is entirely beyond ordinary perception. Vague and obscure, it is beyond all knowing and analysis; we cannot grasp it however hard we try. The human body, senses and intellect are not equipped to deal with it. The only way a person can ever get in touch with it is by forgetting and transcending ordinary human faculties, by becoming subtler and finer and more potent, more like the Dao itself.

The Dao at the periphery, on the other hand, is characterized as the give and take of various pairs of complementary opposites, as the natural ebb and flow of things as they rise and fall, come and go, grow and decline, emerge and die. The *Daode jing* (ch. 36) has:

> To contract, there must first be expansion.
> To weaken, there must first be strengthening.
> To destroy, there must first be promotion.
> To grasp, there must first be giving.
> This is called the subtle pattern.

Things develop in alternating movements as long as they live. It is the nature of life to be in constant motion. Things always move in one direction or the other: up or down, towards lightness or heaviness, brightness or darkness. Nature is a continuous flow of becoming, whether latent or manifest, described as the alternation of complementary characteristics and directions that cannot exist without each other. This becoming can be rhythmic and circular, or it can move back towards the source of life in the ineffable Dao, which at the same time is a forward movement towards a new level of cosmic oneness.

## Vital energy

The way the Dao manifests in the human body is through a vital energy known as *qi* 氣, which is the concrete aspect, the material potency of the universe, the basic stuff of nature. In ancient sources, *qi* is associated with mist, fog and moving clouds. The character as it appears in the oracle bones of the Shang dynasty (1766–1122 BCE) consists of two parts: an image of someone eating and grain in a pot. Combined, these parts signal *qi*, the quality which nourishes, warms, transforms and rises. *Qi*, therefore, is contained in the foods we eat and the air we breathe. But more subtly it is also the life force in the human body and as such is the basis of all physical vitality.

By extension, *qi* also denotes anything perceptible but intangible: atmosphere, smoke, aroma, vapour, a sense of intuition, foreboding, or even ghosts. There is only one *qi*, just as there is only one Dao. But it, too, appears on different levels of subtlety and in different modes. At the centre there is primordial *qi*, prenatal *qi*, or true, perfect *qi*; at the periphery there is postnatal *qi* or earthly *qi* – like the measurable Dao it is in constant motion and divided according to categories such as temperature, density, speed of flow, and impact on human life.

*Qi* is the basic material of all that exists. It animates life and furnishes the functional power of events. *Qi* is the root of the human body; its quality and movement determine human health. *Qi* can be discussed in terms of quantity, since having more means stronger metabolic function. This, however, does not mean that health is a by-product of storing large quantities of *qi*. Rather, there is a normal or healthy amount of *qi* in every person, and health manifests in its balance and harmony, its moderation and smoothness of flow. This flow is envisioned in the texts as a complex system of waterways with the 'Ocean of *Qi*' in the abdomen; rivers of *qi* flowing through the upper torso, arms and legs; springs of *qi* reaching to the wrists and ankles; and wells of *qi* found in the fingers and toes. Even a small spot in this complex system can thus influence the whole, so that overall balance and smoothness are the general goal.

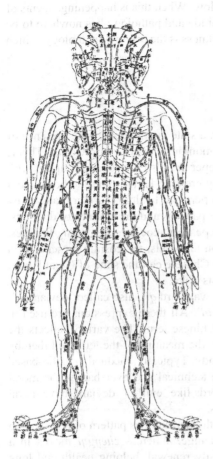

*Figure 1.1* The meridians in the body (from *Leijing*).

Human life is the accumulation of *qi*; death is its dispersal. After receiving a core potential of primordial *qi* at birth, people throughout life need to sustain it. They do so by drawing postnatal *qi* into the body from air and food, as well as from other people through sexual, emotional and social interaction. But they also lose *qi* through breathing bad air, overburdening their bodies with food and drink, and getting involved in negative emotions and excessive sexual or social interactions.

It is thus best to breathe deeply and to eat moderately in accordance with the seasons, to move smoothly, exercise without exertion, and match activities to the body's needs. This is how one keeps balance and creates health. As the *Lüshi chunqiu* (Spring and Autumn Annals of Master Lü), a text from about 260 BCE, has it (ch. 4):

One wants the skin to be tight, the blood vessels to allow unimpeded motion; the sinews to be firm and the bones hard; the heart, mind, and will to be concordant; and the vital energies to flow. When this is happening, agents of disorder [sickness] have nowhere to abide and pathology has nowhere to be produced. The abiding of agents of sickness is the origin of pathology, which is blocking the flow of *qi*.

## Health and disease

The Daoist *qi*-body is meant to be healthy, a state guaranteed by the presence of a strong vital energy and of a smooth, harmonious and active flow of *qi*. This is known as the state of *zhengqi* 正氣 or 'proper *qi*', also translated as 'upright *qi*'. The ideal is to have *qi* flow freely, thereby creating harmony in the body and a balanced state of being in the person. This personal health is further matched by health in nature, defined as regular weather patterns and the absence of disasters. It is also present as health in society in the peaceful coexistence among families, clans, villages and states. This harmony on all levels, the cosmic presence of a steady and pleasant flow of *qi*, is what the Chinese call the state of Great Peace, a state venerated by Confucians and Daoists alike.

The opposite of health is *xieqi* 邪氣 or 'wayward *qi*', also called 'deviant *qi*', 'pathogenic *qi*', 'heteropathic *qi*' or 'evil *qi*'. All these expressions are used in Western textbooks to translate the same Chinese term. The variety reflects the different views of the translators and shifts the meaning of the term and thereby the understanding of what goes on in the body. Typically, medical or Latin-based words like 'heteropathic' tend to be more technical and overshadow the moral implications of the original term, while words like 'evil' or 'deviant' have moral and social rather than medical implications.

*Xieqi* or 'wayward *qi*' is *qi* that has lost the harmonious pattern of flow and no longer supports the dynamic forces of change. Whereas *zhengqi* moves in a steady, harmonious rhythm and effects daily renewal, helping health and long life, *xieqi*, disorderly and dysfunctional, creates change that violates the normal order. When it becomes dominant, the *qi*-flow can turn upon itself and deplete the body's resources. The person no longer operates as part of a universal system and is not in tune with the basic life force around him or her. *Xieqi* appears when *qi* begins to move either too fast or too slow, is excessive or depleted, or creates rushes or obstructions. It disturbs the regular flow and causes ailments.

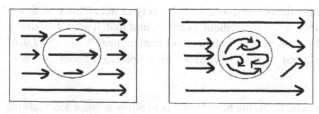

*Figure 1.2* The proper and wayward flow of *qi*.

*Qi* can become excessive through outside influences such as too much heat or cold or through inside patterns such as too much emotion or stimulation. Excessive *qi* can be moving too fast or be very sluggish, as in the case of excessive dampness. Whatever the case, from a universal perspective there is no extra or new *qi* created, but localized disharmonies have arisen because existing *qi* has become excessive and thus harmful. Still, even describing it in this way we are thinking in terms of *qi* as an energetic substance, which it really is not. A better way to speak of it would be to say that the process itself of turning hot or angry is *qi*, that the way things move and change is what constitutes our being *qi*.

Similarly, *qi* can be in depletion. This may mean that there is a tense flow of *qi* due to nervousness or anxiety, or that the volume and density of *qi* have decreased, which is the case in serious prolonged illness. However, more commonly it means that the *qi* activity level is lower, that its flow is not quite up to standard, that there is a lower than normal concentration of *qi* in one or the other body part. In the same vein, perfection of *qi* means the optimal functioning of energy in the body, while control of *qi* means the power to guide the energetic process to one or the other part.

To conceptualize *qi* in the body, imagine a fluid-filled sack under water. The sack has a semi-permeable membrane: it can absorb the external fluid and excrete fluid out. The water surrounding the sack has waves that also influence its inner fluids. Viewed from a bird's-eye perspective as an integrated system, every wave and eddy in both sack and water are 'upright' or 'correct', because that is just how things are. However, within the smaller system of the sack there is a microcosm of flow which can be out of balance. This imbalance can come from exposure to certain aspects of the greater flow which causes the internal flow to become overly committed to one specific pattern. Or it could be that the fluid in the sack has too much or too little internal substance, and is thus unable to keep up with external patterns. Whichever it is, the uncooperative flow within the smaller sack is *xieqi* or 'wayward *qi*'. From a universal perspective, any flow is just flow. From the perspective of the individual body, some flow may be wayward because correctness (health) is the desired state.

It is important in this context to realize that *qi* functions in subtle forms and activities and that it should not be described in terms of substance or as a limited 'energy'. Rather, the way *qi* works should be expressed in terms of relationships and correspondences, as what it does and how it impacts cosmos and self. *Qi* is process. The way to describe human life as subtle body accordingly is by speaking not about an existing quality but about the way things function. In other words, rather than saying that we 'have' *qi*, it is correct to say that we 'are' *qi*, which, moreover, appears in a variety of different forms.

## Qi *dimensions*

The different forms *qi* takes in the human body are described as bodily forces and fluids, typically divided into yin and yang, depending on whether they are grosser or subtler and flow more on the surface or in the interior of the body.

The most basic yang force is personal *qi*. It constitutes health and sickness and determines how we move, eat, sleep, and function in the world. Flowing through meridians that have not been matched with anything in Western anatomy, it is the source of movement in and of the body, present in continuous circulation. Also, through breath, food, drink, physical contact, sexuality and emotions, this *qi* is in constant exchange with the outside world. As noted earlier, it can be proper, well aligned, harmonious, right in amount and timing and activity, or wayward, heteropathic, misaligned, off-track and harmful.

The yin counterpart of personal *qi* is *xue*, often translated as 'blood'. It passes through veins that run deep in the body and includes various fluids known from Western anatomy, such as blood and lymph, but also carries internal life-force and is considered the matrix of the mind. Problems in respect to *xue* tend to involve deficiencies or obstructions, presenting in paleness and lacklustre dry skin, or in sharp pains, tumours, cysts and swellings.

*Xue* is closely connected to *qi*, often described as the wagon drawn by the horse of *qi*. Both are metabolized from the interaction of 'grain-*qi*' (*guqi*, food) in the stomach and small intestine and 'empty *qi*' (*kongqi*, air) in the lungs under the impact of the transformative power of heart-fire. This produces internal *qi*, which is further differentiated into the various bodily forces. This metabolism is the work of the triple heater (*sanjiao*三焦), sometimes also called the triple burner. A uniquely Chinese entity, it is described in the main medical classic *Huangdi neijing suwen* 黃帝內經素問 (Yellow Emperor's Inner Classic: Simple Questions), which goes back to the Han dynasty (206 BCE–220 CE),[3] as providing a connection between Heaven (upper heater), Humanity (middle heater), and Earth (lower heater). Over time the triple heater came to be associated with the aspects of the body cavity: thoracic, abdominal and pelvic – i.e. the lungs, small intestine and bladder. Commencing its function immediately after birth, the triple heater system takes the place of the integrated nourishment from primordial and mother *qi* in the womb and controls the transport, utilization and excretion of the body's energies. Its functioning can be schematized as shown in Figure 1.3.

The triple heater is also responsible for the production of another yin-yang pair of energies, the protectors (*weiying* 衛營). They are forms of *qi* that pulsate through the body at different levels to defend and nurture it. *Wei* is yang in quality and commonly called protective or defensive *qi*. It moves next to the meridians and travels widely around the body, nourishing and strengthening the skin. It regulates the sweat glands, moistens the skin and hair, nourishes the tissues, and controls the opening and closing of the skin's pores. Its main job is to form a defence against harmful outside influences and pathogenic stress. It maintains the stability of the body, somewhat like the immune system in Western medicine.

*Ying*, the other protector in the body, is yin in nature and usually called constructive or nutritive *qi*. It is associated with the *xue*-blood and moves with it. It nourishes the muscles and the organs and ensures that the body's tissues remain strong. *Wei* and *ying* are a complementary pair, like *qi* and blood. They are characterized similarly in that their yin aspect is thicker and heavier and stays

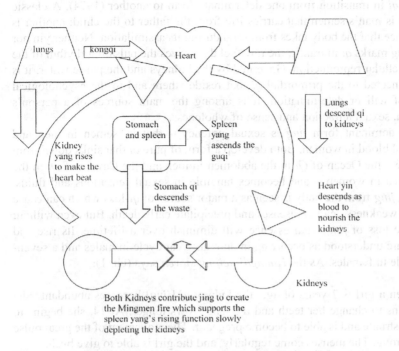

*Figure 1.3* Postnatal metabolism (courtesy of Stephen Jackowicz).

deep within the body, while its yang counterpart is thinner and lighter and moves at the surface of the body, interfacing with the outside world.

The same also holds true for the body fluids (*jinye* 津液). They are defined as nutritive substances, formed when food in the digestive process is subjected to the functions of the stomach, spleen, lungs, and so on. Among them, *jin* are yang in nature. They appear as light, clear fluids that come to the body's surface due to internal processes. Examples include saliva (associated with the kidneys), tears (liver), sweat (heart), nasal mucus (lungs), and oral mucus (spleen). They lubricate the skin and the flesh. *Ye*, on the other hand, are yin. They are heavy, thick fluids diffused internally due to body movement, as for example lymph and internal mucus. They lubricate the joints and tendons, protect the brain and fill the spine. The fluids, when produced in their appropriate amounts, serve as protectors and lubricants of the body. When they are deficient or excessive, however, they can be useful diagnostic tools. For example, a person with continuous dryness in the nose may well be suffering from chronic hay fever which affects his *qi*-flow even when it is not acute.

### Essence and spirit

Functioning between these various yin and yang energies is *jing* 精, often translated as 'essence'. As Manfred Porkert defines it, *jing* is the indeterminate aspect of *qi* or *qi* in transition from one determinate form to another (1974). A classic example is man's semen that carries life from the father to the child; another is the essence that the body takes from food during its assimilation. Neither yin nor yang, *jing* marks *qi* in transit, the raw fuel that drives the pulsating rhythm of the body's cellular reproduction. Governed by the kidneys and the phase water, it is also connected to the primordial *qi* that resides there and to the psychological power of will or determination. It is among the main sources of a person's charisma, sexual attraction and sense of wholeness.

In its dominant form *jing* is sexual potency – that is, semen in men and menstrual blood in women. Both develop a form of pure *qi* that sinks down from its centre – the Ocean of *Qi* in the abdomen in men and the Cavern of *Qi* in the breast area in women – and becomes tangible in sexual sensations and fluids. Emitting *jing* from the body is seen as a major source of *qi*-loss which can cause physical weakness, lead to diseases and precipitate early death. But even without excessive loss of *jing*, vital essence will diminish over a lifetime. Its rise and decline are understood as occurring in an eight-year cycle in males and a seven-year cycle in females. As the *Huangdi neijing suwen* says (ch. 1):

> When a girl is 7 years of age, the kidney *qi* [*jing*] becomes abundant. She begins to change her teeth and the hair grows longer. At 14, she begins to menstruate and is able to become pregnant. The movement of the great pulse is strong. The menses come regularly, and the girl is able to give birth.
>
> At age 21, the energy is steady, the last tooth has come out, and she is fully grown. When she reaches the age of 28, her tendons and bones are strong, her hair has reached its full length, and her body is flourishing and fertile. At 35, her yang brightness pulse begins to slacken, her face begins to wrinkle, her hair starts falling out.
>
> When she reaches the age of 42, the pulse of the three yang regions deteriorates in the upper part of her body, her entire face is wrinkled, and her hair turns gray. At age 49, she can no longer become pregnant, and the circulation of the great pulse is decreased. Her menstruation is exhausted, and the gates of blood are no longer open. Her body declines, and she is no longer able to bear children.

To regulate and possibly slow down this process, there are various medical, longevity and Daoist practices that control sexual energies and teach people to retain and strengthen their *jing*, even cause it to revert back to *qi* and thus renew life. They commonly involve both physical disciplines and meditation practices, allowing the *qi* to sink down and transform into *jing*, rendering it tangible as sexual arousal, but then preventing it from being emitted and instead reverting it back to *qi*.

Beyond the more tangible, fluid forms of *qi* in the body, there is also a pair of yin and yang energies that are more elusive and more psychological or spiritual in nature, yet are seen as forms of cosmic *qi*. They are spirit (*shen* 神) and numen (*ling* 靈). Spirit is classified as yang and understood as the guiding vitality behind the various other forces. In Daoism reinterpreted to indicate a multitude of 'spirits', the so-called body-gods who simultaneously reside in the stars, it is the active, organizing configurative force and transformative influence in the person, connecting him to Heaven and original destiny. It manifests as individual consciousness and constitutes the individual's awareness and mental direction. Associated with the upper heater, it resides in the heart and is related to the mind and the emotions. It is an important cause of sickness, since much *qi*-exchange with the outside world happens through the emotions. Impossible to be perceived directly and physically, spirit is a vitalizing force that exerts transformative influence on all other aspects of the human being (Kaptchuk 1983: 58).

Numen is the yin counterpart of spirit. Largely ignored by practitioners in Communist China, it is sometimes translated as 'soul' and designates the inherent spiritual self-nature of beings, the numinous power behind their physical presence. Supplementary to spirit, it is more internal and less obvious in interaction with the outside world, but appears in the names of five acupuncture points. It comes to the fore in death, when the remaining spiritual aspect of the person is called 'numen'. In fact, both spirit and numen are very much religious terms in traditional China. *Shen* also means 'divine', god' and 'ancestral spirit'; *ling* indicates 'numinous', 'ghostly', 'soul' and 'supernatural entity'. Both can best be understood as the potential in human beings that works behind the scenes, either active and moving (spirit) or organizing and latent (numen). The central aspect of religious cultivation, *shen* is both the foundation and the goal of Daoist practice, the subtlest of *qi*-levels from which the body evolves and to which it ultimately returns.

## The five organs

The body as *qi* in its various forms is further managed by five organ-complexes, which – in close link with related cosmic and bodily forces – maintain it in a constant flow of movement and exchange. Based on the system of yin and yang as they transform into each other in rhythmic flow, the five organs come in two lists of yin or storing organs (1) and yang or transformative intestines (2) and are linked with the five phases (often also called 'elements') and their cosmic correlates (see Table 1.1)

*Table 1.1* Correspondences of the five phases

| Yin/yang | Phase | Direction | Colour | Season | Organ 1 | Organ 2 | Emotion | Sense |
|---|---|---|---|---|---|---|---|---|
| Minor yang | Wood | East | Green | Spring | Liver | Gall | Anger | Vision |
| Major yang | Fire | South | Red | Summer | Heart | Small intestine | Euphoria | Touch |
| Yin-yang | Earth | Centre | Yellow | | Spleen | Stomach | Worry | Taste |
| Minor yin | Metal | West | White | Fall | Lungs | Large intestine | Sadness | Small |
| Major yin | Water | North | Black | Winter | Kidneys | Bladder | Fear | Hearing |

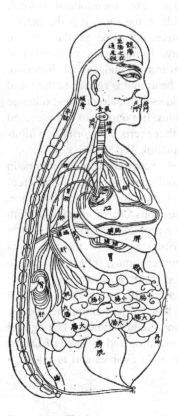

*Figure 1.4* The inner organs in the body (from *Leijing*).

To describe them individually, the 'spleen' (*pi* 脾) is not just one organ but part of the phase earth and all the cosmic connections that implies: the colour yellow, the season of late or Indian summer, the direction of the centre, and in general with stability and centredness. Further connected with muscles and sinews, mouth and lips, the sense of taste, and the body fluid of oral mucus, its key emotion is worry, which includes thoughtfulness, planning and overanalysing, leading to the fact that many brain-workers tend towards spleen issues. Among virtues, it represents honesty: trust in oneself and others, faithfulness and confidence. Most closely associated with *qi* proper, together with its yang partner, the stomach, it is 'the primary organ of digestion, the crucial link by which food is transformed into *qi* and *xue*-blood' (Kaptchuk 1983: 79).

The spleen is the root of the person's acquired constitution, the seat of nutritive *qi*, and the place where both *qi* and *xue* originate. It distributes active fluids throughout the body, firms up tissues, and stabilizes the internal fluid system. Its main function is to divide clear from turbid *qi* after food and drink have been ingested through the mouth, its associated sense of taste providing a first indication of what to expect energetically. Its channel runs along the inside of the leg and through the abdomen. The spleen has two major aspects, an active dimension known as spleen *qi* and a warming power called spleen yang (fire). Both have warming and drying powers needed in food processing to eliminate extraneous liquids. Should these aspects go astray, some liquids are not processed but remain as a kind of slush to create condition known as 'dampness' which eventually may grow into phlegm and lead to serious obstructions (Engelhardt and Hempen 1997: 421).

The spleen's matching yang organ is the stomach (*wei* 胃). It serves as an intermediate and balancing centre in food processing, taking care to properly cool and moisturize the various substances. Its favoured flavours are neutral and slightly sour, while its desired temperature is cooling rather than warming.

The lungs (*fei* 肺), next, are the organ associated with the phase metal: fall, white, and west. It is also linked with the large intestine as its yang partner and in charge of the skin as main body part. This explains why people with chronic digestive dysfunction often develop asthma and skin problems, which – in reversal of the disease's unfolding – tend to clear up with a lung-supportive diet. They are in charge of transforming air into ancestral *qi* by mixing empty *qi* with the grain *qi* of the spleen. They then distribute it all over the body through the exterior body fluids (*jin*) and the defensive *qi*. Their related sense organ is the nose, matching the body fluid of nasal mucus and connecting them to the common cold. In general, the lungs are easily harmed by cold and wind, favouring warms and dryness, which connects to their flavour of pungent or spicy.

The emotion of the lungs is sadness – pensiveness, melancholy and reluctance to let go – while its virtue is righteousness, impartial justice or integrity, and the ability to accept gain and loss, success and failure as they come (Kaptchuk 1983: 91). The related *qi*-channel starts in the chest, moves through the armpit and along the inner side of the arm, and ends at the top of the thumb. It has eleven acupuncture points, used to treat symptoms of colds and cough as well as cases of shoulder and back pain (Kaptchuk 1983: 112; Kohn 2005: 53).

Receiving ancestral *qi* from the lungs and transporting it into the body's channels, next, is the heart (*xin* 心), the organ linked with the phase fire, the colour red, the season of the summer, and the direction of the south. It also manages the constructive *qi*, which transports *xue*, and the workings of the blood vessels. Among senses, it corresponds to touch; among body fluids it connects to sweat (a precious entity that contains many important substances); among emotions it relates to joy (enthusiasm, euphoria, or hatred); its virtue is propriety – appropriate behaviour, timely interactions, and behaving suitably in a given context.

The heart is also the seat of the spirit, ensuring that internal consciousness, awareness, thought and reflection intersect properly with the world of time and space (Kaptchuk 1983: 88). It is very much in charge of the person in general and takes care of proper rest by providing sufficient sleep. As already the *Suwen* says: 'The heart is the residence of the ruler: spirit and clarity originate here.' Its channel begins in the armpit and, with an internal branch connecting to the heart itself, passes through the chest and lungs. After moving along the side of the throat and through the inner side of the arm, it ends at the tip of the little finger (Kaptchuk 1983: 118; Kohn 2005: 54).

Complementing the heart in the scheme of the five phases is the kidney complex (*shen* 腎), which belongs to the phase water, the season winter, and the colour black. The most yin among organs, it is also the most potent, being in charge of essence (*jing*), a core form of concentrated *qi* that forms bones, teeth and brain, and is key to hard work, endurance and perseverance. Essence also rules birth, development and maturation and is the primordial seat of the life process, often associated with sexuality and procreation (Kaptchuk 1983: 83–4).

The body fluid of the kidneys is the saliva; their related sense organ are the ears – described in Daoist literature as the 'Dark Towers', the name also given to the kidneys. The related emotion is fear (caution, anxiety, panic), counteracted effectively by the virtue of wisdom, a sense of life and its unfolding, the intuitive knowledge when to move and when to rest. The *Suwen* notes: 'The kidneys are the residence of the business men: activity and care originate here' (3.1b). The related channel begins at Bubbling Well (Yongquan 湧泉) in the centre of the sole, then runs through the instep, circles around the medial ankle, moves up the inner leg and through the abdomen to the chest (Kaptchuk 1983: 122–3; Kohn 2005: 55).

The kidney system warms the centre and supplies *qi* to the heart as well as running the entire water-system of the body. The kidneys being so important to the overall functioning of the body, and salty being its key flavour, such foods play a large role in dietetics and food preparation. It also explains the ubiquity of soy sauce, the great all-spice of Chinese cooking (Kohn 2010: 58). Its matching yang partner is the bladder (*pang* 膀) with the longest of the channels that runs down the back in two parallel lines as well as across the head and along the outside of the legs. Its main task is to transform body fluids and lead them towards elimination.

The last of the five organ systems is the liver (*gan* 肝), associated with the phase wood: spring, east and green. The moderator of the entire system, its main task is to control the overall flow of *qi* and to store the *xue*. In terms of its wider associations, it is linked with the working of joints and tendons and corresponds to the sense of vision and the eyes (Porkert 1974: 117–19). Among body fluids, liver means tears, among emotions it relates to anger (aggression, courage, or lack thereof), while in the virtues it matches benevolence or kindness.

The liver is also indicative of the repetitive cycles of human life, curtailing extremes and ensuring the smooth movement of *qi* (Kaptchuk 1983: 81–2). Its channel begins at the tip of the big toe, then moves up the instep to the inner side of the leg, crosses the pubic region, lower abdomen, liver, and lungs to end in the rib cage. An internal branch ends at the liver. Its most important point is Too Fast (Taichong 太衝; Li-3) on the top of the foot near the ankle. It is a strong point for moving *qi* and helps with numerous ailments (Kaptchuk 1983: 128; Kohn 2005: 57).

Its matching yang organ is the gall bladder (*dan* 膽), the main recipient of fluids from the liver and provider of *qi* for the stomach. Also associated with decision-making, courage and initiative, it suffers mostly from dampness and should be kept warm both externally through clothing and internally through food.

## Cosmic vision

Daoists further connect this energy body of Chinese medicine to the larger cosmos. The oldest relevant description appears in the *Huainanzi* 淮南子 (Writings of the Prince of Huainan) of the first century BCE (see Major 1984, 1993). Here the human body is likened to the entire cosmos, the head resembling Heaven, the feet looking like Earth, and all the various cosmological agents actively engaged:

> The roundness of the head is an image of Heaven, the square of Earth is the pattern of Earth. Heaven has four seasons, five agents, nine directions, and 360 days. Human beings have accordingly four limbs, five inner organs, nine orifices, and 360 joints. Heaven has wind, rain, cold, and heat. Human beings have accordingly the actions of giving, taking, joy, and anger. The gall bladder corresponds to the clouds, the lungs to the breath, the liver to the wind, the kidneys to the rain, and the spleen to the thunder.
>
> (ch. 7)

In addition, the five organs and various body parts are seen to interrelate like different administrative agencies of the state. An early description appears in the *Huangdi neijing suwen*:

> The heart is the residence of the ruler; spirit and clarity originate here. The lungs are the residence of the high ministers of state; order and division originate here. The liver is the residence of the strategists; planning and organization originate here. The gall bladder is residence of the judges; judgments and decisions originate here.
>
> The center of the breast is the residence of a special task-force; joy and pleasure originate here. The stomach is the residence of the granary administration; the various kinds of taste originate here. The large intestine is the residence of the teachers of the Dao; development and transformations originate here … The kidneys are the residence of the business men; activity and care originate here.
>
> (3.1ab; Veith 1972: 133)[4]

Among Daoist scriptures, especially the *Laozi zhongjing* 老子中經 (Central Scripture of Laozi, DZ 1168), one of the earliest texts on visualization methods that may go back as far as the second century CE (see Schipper 1979), uses the same basic administrative structure:

> The eight gods of the lungs are the masters of Great Harmony. They are also called the 'Secretaries of the Palace of Jade Purity'. They govern 3,600 minor officials. They ride in carriages of white energy, drawn by white tigers. Occasionally they will also ride on white dragons.
>
> The eight gods of the heart are the strategists and military generals. They are also called the 'Original Luminant Ones' or the 'Old Ones from the South

Pole' or 'of the Scarlet Palace'. They equally govern 3,600 minor officials. They ride in carriages of red energy of which red birds furnish the canopies and cinnabar-coloured snakes serve as the handles. The carriage is drawn by red birds. Occasionally these gods will also ride on red dragons.

The seven gods of the liver are the gods of Lord Lao. They are also called 'Officials of the Blue Terrace of the Hall of Light'. They govern 3,600 minor officials. They ride in carriages of green energy, drawn by green dragons. Occasionally they will also ride on white deer.

The five gods of the gall are the Dao-Masters of the Great One. They reside in the Palace of the Purple Chamber. They ride in carriages of jade-coloured energy, covered by a five-coloured canopy and drawn by six flying dragons. They also govern 3,600 minor officials.

(Homann 1971: 35–6)

For Daoist meditation practices, this means that a key effort is to be extended to activate the various body gods within and transform the internal organs from energetic functioning to advanced wisdom and the cultivation of virtues. To this end, practitioners begin by visualizing the organs with their respective colours in an exercise traditionally called the Five Sprouts and today known as the Inner Smile (see Chia and Chia 1993), exhale with their proper mouth positions and breaths (the so-called six healing sounds; see Despeux 2006), consciously let go of negative emotions and tensions, and actively invite the main virtues to come to stay (see Table 1.2).

Once the organs are sublimated to an energetically subtler level, the body gods are actively visualized and the body becomes a cosmic constellation rather than an individual entity. Eventually adepts join the celestials they have harboured within and go off to transcend all in ecstatic pervasion. This state is described as an increase in energetic subtlety, an enhancement of motion, openness, joy, light, even ecstasy, until the successful adept of immortality takes up a position next to the Jade Emperor of the Great Dao. The imagery tends to be shamanistic: the flight into higher realms, the experience of an altered state of consciousness, the freedom from the limits of this world. The process is one of attaining ultimate freedom; it is depicted as one of getting lighter and brighter; the higher one ascends, the purer the spirit becomes, the more light one will radiate. By attaining

*Table 1.2* The six healing sounds

| Yin Organ | Yang Organ | Sound | Colour | Emotion | Virtue |
|---|---|---|---|---|---|
| lungs | large intestine | sss | white | sadness | righteousness |
| kidneys | bladder | chooi | black | fear | compassion |
| liver | gall bladder | shhh | green | anger | benevolence |
| heart | small intestine | haw | red | excitement | joy |
| spleen | stomach | ho | yellow | worry | wisdom |
| pericardium | triple heater | hsee | | | letting go |

this level, the Daoist graduates to immortality, becomes one with Dao in all its aspects, as underlying power of all and as the creative power of the world, continuously moving and forever transforming.

## Notes

1 For details on Highest Clarity, see Robinet 2000; Miller 2008.
2 There are numerous translations of this important text, e.g. Chan 1963; Addiss and Lombardo 1993. For a comparative discussion, see LaFargue and Pas 1998.
3 This text, too, has been translated variously. See Veith 1972; Ki 1985; Lu 1987; Ni 1995.
4 The same statement is also contained in the Daoist meditation manual *Huangting jing* (Yellow Court Scriptures). See Homann 1971: 29.

## References

Addiss, S. and Lombardo, S. (1993) *Tao Te Ching*. Indianapolis: Hackett Publishing Company.

Chan, W. (1963) *A Source Book in Chinese Philosophy*. Princeton: Princeton University Press.

Chia, M. and Chia, M. (1993) *Awaken Healing Light of the Tao*. Huntington, NY: Healing Tao Books.

Despeux, C. (2006) 'The six healing breaths', in L. Kohn (ed.) *Daoist Body Cultivation*. Magdalena, NM: Three Pines Press.

Engelhardt, U. and Hempen, C.-H. (1997) *Chinesische Diätetik*. Munich: Urban & Schwarzenberg.

Graham, A. C. (1989) *Disputers of the Tao: Philosophical Argument in Ancient China*. La Salle, IL: Open Court Publishing Company.

Homann, R. (1971) *Die wichtigsten Körpergottheiten im Huang-t'ing-ching*. Göppingen: Alfred Kümmerle.

Kaptchuk, T. J. (1983) *The Web that Has No Weaver: Understanding Chinese Medicine*. New York: Congdon & Weed.

Ki, S. (1985) *The Canon of Acupuncture: Huangti Nei Ching Ling Shu*, Los Angeles: Yuin University Press.

Kohn, L. (2005) *Health and Long Life: The Chinese Way*. Cambridge, MA: Three Pines Press.

—— (2010) *Daoist Dietetics: Food for Immortality*. Dunedin, FL: Three Pines Press.

LaFargue, M. and Pas, J. (1998) 'On translating the *Tao-te-ching*', in L. Kohn and M.LaFargue (eds) *Lao-tzu and the Tao-te-ching*. Albany: State University of New York Press.

Liu, X. (1998) 'Naturalness (Tzu-jan), the core value in Taoism: its ancient meaning and its significance today', in L. Kohn and M.LaFargue (eds) *Lao-tzu and the Tao-te-ching*. Albany: State University of New York Press.

Lu, H. C. (1987) *The Yellow Emperor's Book of Acupuncture*. Blaine, WA: Academy of Oriental Heritage.

Major, J. S. (1984) 'The five phases, magic squares, and schematic cosmography', in H. Rosemont (ed.) *Explorations in Early Chinese Cosmology*. Chico, CA: Scholars Press, American Academy of Religion.

—— (1993) *Heaven and Earth in Early Han Thought: Chapters Three, Four, and Five of the Huainanzi*. Albany: State University of New York Press.

Miller, J. (2008) *The Way of Highest Clarity: Nature, Vision and Revelation in Medieval Daoism*. Magdalena, NM: Three Pines Press.

Ni, M. (1995) *The Yellow Emperor's Classic of Medicine*. Boston, MA: Shambhala.

Porkert, M. (1974) *The Theoretical Foundations of Chinese Medicine*, Cambridge, MA: MIT Press.

Robinet, I. (2000) 'Shangqing – Highest Clarity', in L. Kohn (ed.) *Daoism Handbook*. Leiden: Brill.

Schipper, K. M. (1979) 'Le calendrier de jade: note sur *le Laozi zhongjing*', *Nachrichten der deutschen Gesellschaft für Natur- und Völkerkunde Ostasiens* 125: 75–80.

Schwartz, B. (1985) *The World of Thought in Ancient China*. Cambridge, MA: Harvard University Press.

Veith, I. (1972) *The Yellow Emperor's Classic of Internal Medicine*. Berkeley, CA: University of California Press.

# 2 The subtle body in India and beyond

*Geoffrey Samuel*

This chapter sketches the history of subtle-body concepts in India, beginning with the early indications of subtle-body and *prāṇa*-concepts in the Upaniṣads and the Yoga-Sūtras of Patañjali, through to the complex internal structure of *cakras* and *nāḍīs* in the Kaula, Tantra and Haṭha Yoga texts. Both Śaiva (Hindu) and Buddhist Tantric traditions are discussed, and I also look briefly at the contrasting construction of the subtle body found in texts associated with Śaṃkara and the Advaita Vedānta school. The closing section comments briefly on the ways in which Tantric subtle-body concepts were taken up and developed in Tibet and in East Asia.

## Early subtle-body-type concepts in India

The first major appearance of subtle-body concepts within the Indic textual tradition occurs in the Upaniṣads. Specifically, the *Taittirīya Upaniṣad* includes a well-known discussion (II.1–5) of five bodies or selves, starting from the physical body formed by food (*anna-maya*) and proceeding through a series of other, finer or subtler bodies or selves, each one shaped like a human being and pervading the one before: the body or self made of vital breath (*prāṇa-maya*); the body or self made of mind (*mano-maya*); the body or self made of consciousness or intellect (*vijñāna-maya*), and finally the body or self made of bliss (*ananda-maya*). This set of progressively finer bodies is a classic example of what we are referring to in this book as a subtle-body concept.

The *Taittirīya Upaniṣad* is generally regarded as one of the earliest Upaniṣads; a plausible dating would be the fourth or fifth century BCE, though this is far from certain (Olivelle 1996: xxxvi).[1] Apart from the discussion of the five bodies, the *Taittirīya Upaniṣad* also includes a passage (I.6) suggestive of ideas regarding an internal anatomy of the subtle body, with a central channel through the body and the possibility of movement in different directions from that central channel. Similar ideas can be found in other probably early texts in the Upaniṣadic corpus (Hartzell 1997: 70–127); as well as in Greek thought at what was perhaps around the same time (McEvilley 2002).[2] As is apparent from Livia Kohn's description in Chapter 1, there are also similarities to early Chinese material here, which can be found in a developed form in texts recovered from tombs from the second and first centuries BCE (Harper 1987, 1997; Lo 1998).

I comment further on these connections later in the chapter. It seems clear from the Upaniṣadic evidence, however, that thought about these issues had been present in India from at least the fourth and fifth century BCE, and had presumably developed in early yogic and ascetic circles which were active by this time (Samuel 2008: 119–72). Although detailed evidence is limited and scattered, we can assume that both practical experimentation and conceptual speculation continued in such circles over the following centuries.

In the late Vedic texts known as the *saṃhitā*-s and *brāhmaṇa*-s, we find the enumeration of various bodily 'winds' or 'breaths' (*prāṇa*). These gradually settle down into a list of five kinds of *prāṇa*, given also in the Praśna and Maitri Upaniṣads (perhaps first century BCE; Zysk 1993, 2007; Connolly 1997). These are individually named *prāṇa*, *apāna*, *vyāna*, *samāna* and *udāna*. Their precise definition is the subject of considerable speculation, but in general terms they are respectively associated with inhalation, exhalation, distribution of breath within the body, digestion, and excretion of waste products. *Prāṇa* already had aspects of a cosmic principle as well as a physiological one in Indian thought, with close links to the *ātman* or self, and this association between physiological and cosmological elements, which was taken up in both religious and medical thought, was a significant component in later Indic ideas about subtle bodies. By the time of the *Yogasūtra* text attributed to Patañjali, perhaps the fourth century CE (Larson 2009: 488), there are indications of a localization of yogic processes in various parts of the body that may foreshadow the later *cakras* of Tantra and *haṭha-yoga* (2009: 493).

## Vedanta and Tantra

The classical Vedantic perspective on these matters, perhaps a millennium after the *Taittiriya Upaniṣad*, involved an adaptation or reworking of the five-body or five-self scheme in which the five bodies of the *Taittiriya* become a series of five 'sheaths' (*kośa*) that cover and obscure the inner self.[3] Reference was made in the Introduction to the Vedantic sequence of three bodies (*sthūlaśarīra, sūkṣmaśarīra, kāraṇaśarīra*); four bodies if the ultimate *atman* is included. The first of these, the material or physical body (*sthūlaśarīra*), is implicitly or explicitly identified with the first sheath or body, the *kośa* made of food of the *Taittiriya*, the *sūkṣmaśarīra* with the next three *kośa*-s, and the *kāraṇaśarīra* with the fifth *kośa*, the body or sheath made of bliss. Texts such as Śaṃkara's *Vivekacūḍāmaṇi* show a certain amount of interest in how these various *śarīra*-s and *kośa*-s function, but the Vedantic concern with such matters is primarily negative. The various subtle bodies and sheaths, like the physical body but at a more subtle or refined level, are significant mainly as obstacles to the achievement of union with Brahman.

The Tantric tradition, both Hindu and Buddhist, takes a different approach here, since it sees the subtle bodies as offering potentiality for yogic practices leading to spiritual transformation. In other words, a tension developed within Indic traditions regarding the degree of significance given to the subtle bodies.

This reflects a wider, and no doubt in part political, struggle about what were regarded during this period as valid religious approaches. While it is hard to reconstruct Śaṃkara's life in any detail, he came in later periods to represent the triumph of a certain kind of puritanical Hindu orthodoxy over both Buddhist and Tantric heterodoxies (see below, also Samuel 2008: 322). Tantra itself, while remaining closely associated with the power of the state in many if not most Hindu kingdoms (2008: 291–323), became increasingly marginalized and looked down upon by orthodox Hindus.

Speaking at all of Tantra, of course, raises a whole host of definitional problems to do with delimiting and defining what one is talking about. These problems need to be approached separately within the Hindu and Buddhist contexts.[4]

In the Hindu context, Gerald Larson has argued for the primary meaning of *tantra* in the third to fifth centuries CE being 'science', meaning a learned system arising from tradition of empirical investigation. There were parallel *tantra*s of yogic practice (the study of self), of medicine and of grammar, all the product of 'an elite intellectual milieu, made up of literate *paṇḍita* communities, most likely in north and northwestern South Asia' (Larson 2009: 489). The usage of the term *tantra* to refer to a style of spiritual practice came about only gradually, particularly on the Hindu side, where it is most closely associated with the Śaiva and Śākta traditions (worshippers of the god Śiva and various forms of the goddess, generically *Śakti*), including the so-called Kula and Kaula lineages that developed from perhaps the sixth and seventh centuries onwards (White 1998, 2003; Sanderson 1988).

Tantra was viewed with disfavour by many scholars of the nineteenth and early twentieth centuries, and there is still a tendency to see it through a list of largely negative attributes. Thus, for example, Gerald Larson lists some of the 'distinctive features' of *tantra* as:

(a) *bubhukṣu* (desire for worldly experience) rather than *mumukṣu* (desire for release); (b) focus on the modalities of 'desire' (*kāma*); (c) liberation while living (*jīvanmukti*); (d) quest for extraordinary 'powers' (*siddhis*); (e) transgressive or antinomian ritual practices (either in fantasy or literally) involving onanism, coitus, cunnilingus, and fellatio together with the exchange of sexual fluids; (f) what André Padoux has called a 'swarming pantheon with its fearsome deities' (both fearsome and benevolent, and both male and female); (g) meditation practices that link the body of the practitioner (microcosm) with the body of the cosmos (macrocosm); and (h) the use of sacred sounds, that is to say, phonemes, syllables, *mantras*, and other ritual utterances in the context of prayer and/or magic.

(Larson 2009: 491–2)

Larson sees *tantra* in this sense as emerging in India from the sixth century onwards. If his description still reflects much of the older negative stereotyping of Tantra as decadent and immoral, other contemporary scholars would select different lists of characteristics and place less emphasis on transgressive aspects (see Padoux 2002; Brown 2002; Lorenzen 2002 for some examples), arguing that Tantra was a serious spiritual path for at least some of its followers. Brown rightly notes that, *contra* Larson's first item, much of what has been traditionally defined as Tantric, both on the Hindu and Buddhist side, aims at enlightenment or liberation as well as worldly success (Brown 2002: 3).

On the Buddhist side, such negative stereotyping is less common, particularly in Tibet where Tantra is regarded as a highly elevated and spiritually profound tradition. In Tibet, the definition of Tantra (Tibetan *rgyud*), or of Mantra and Vajrayāna (*sngags, rdo rje theg pa*), which are in most respects equivalent terms, is, in one sense at least, quite uncontroversial. Tantras (at least as far as the 'New Tantras' are concerned) are simply the texts that are found in the 'Tantra' section of the Tibetan canon.

Of course, this begs the question of what these texts might have in common, other than being in the canon. In fact, much of what is classed as Tantric in the Tibetan context consists of straightforward rituals of worship of peaceful and benign deities without any significant antinomian or transgressive components. The kinds of Tibetan 'Tantra' that bear some relationship to Larson's definition above are a subset of what the Tibetans call Tantra, and consist primarily of texts and practices within the Mahāyoga category of the rNying-ma-pa or 'Old Tantra' tradition and the so-called Anuttarayoga category of the 'New Tantras'. It should be noted, though, that while worldly matters are certainly part of what these Tantras aim at, the major Tibetan Buddhist Tantric texts in these categories all clearly have their principal aim as Buddhahood; worldly aims are presented as secondary and accessory. Thus practitioners should aim to attain long life and control over health in order to provide the conditions to practise the Dharma better and so increase their ability to attain Buddhahood for the sake of all sentient beings.

It would seem that much the same was true in the Indian Buddhist material; texts such as the Guhyasamāja or Hevajra, despite their apparently antinomian tendencies, retain a clear orientation towards Buddhahood and towards the altruistic motivation through which it must be achieved. For the Tibetans at any rate, Tantra became the key technique for the attainment of Buddhahood, though it retained a sense, particularly for the dominant dGe lugs pa tradition, of being an advanced path for elite practitioners, to be preceded by a thorough training in the sūtra practices. Thus the Fourteenth Dalai Lama commented:

> A person who has practised the stages of sutra and wishes to attain quickly the state of a blessed Buddha *should* enter into the Secret Mantra Vehicle that can easily bestow realization of Buddhahood [i.e. should practise Tantra]. However, you cannot seek Buddhahood for yourself, engaging in Mantra in order to become unusual. ... Not all persons can practise tantra, but someone who has performed good actions over many lifetimes, who even as a child possessed a strong thought to help, and who has good predispositions should seek the aid of a spiritual guide [and eventually practise Tantra].
>
> (1977: 17–18)

What the Dalai Lama means here by practising Tantra has little to do with the desire for worldly experience referred to by Larson. Nor does it involve the transgressive practices Larson mentions, although references to these remain, generally in symbolic form, in Tibetan Tantric ritual.

As Lorenzen observes, in making sense of Tantra it is also important to look beyond the Sanskrit texts to the wide range of affiliated popular beliefs and practices (Lorenzen 2002: 25–6). The fact remains, though, that Tantra is a problematic category, particularly in Hindu thought, and has been deployed in different ways both by writers in the past and by contemporary scholars within and outside India.

This reflects its complex history. In the Hindu context, Tantra was widely adopted by ruling elites throughout the subcontinent, becoming an essential part of the machinery of statecraft, and involving both defensive and aggressive ritual practices. The practice of Tantra was, however, criticized by rival forms of religion, especially by the proponents of the developing *bhakti* (devotional) cults. The figure who has become emblematic of this developing critique was the great philosopher Śaṃkara. The reforms associated with Śaṃkara and his successors propagated a primarily devotional form of religion for the masses, while reserving a cleaned-up version of what were seen as dangerous Tantric practices for the elite. This led to a split between so-called 'right hand' and 'left hand' approaches to Tantra, terms that are heavily loaded in India because of the polluting associations of the left hand with its association with defecation and bodily impurities. The 'right hand' approaches avoided polluting and transgressive practices, and could and were to be carried out by respectable members of high castes. 'Left hand' approaches retained transgressive elements, and their practice was for the most part confined to ascetics who were beyond the restrictions of the caste system, or lay practitioners, such as the Bauls in Bengal, who were willing to accept the low status that went along with such practices. In parts of India, however, the practice of 'left hand' approaches to Tantra, involving ritual sexuality, the consumption of meat and alcohol, and other problematic aspects, continued in secret among members of some high-caste groups.

Śaṃkara's own philosophical position, Advaita Vedanta, recognized subtle-body phenomena (as we have seen, the English term 'subtle body' originated primarily as a translation of the Vedantic usage of *sūkṣmaśarīra*), but had little interest in working with them. While much of the Indian ascetic tradition traces its origins to Śaṃkara, it was within this tradition that the 'internal' subtle-body practices of Tantra mostly continued (Alter 2005). Thus the powerful, dangerous forms of Tantra survived, but they were progressively pushed to the side or practised in secret. Lay Tantric practice became increasingly uncommon, though it never entirely disappeared (Samuel 2008: 335–7; White 2009). In Tibet, by contrast, Buddhist Tantra (Vajrayāna) became the dominant stream, although the more transgressive aspects were reduced or performed only symbolically, in part because of issues to do with monastic celibacy.

At any rate, it is within the texts of these two traditions, the Kaula texts of the Hindu Śaiva tradition and the Buddhist Tantric texts of the Mahāyoga and

Anuttarayoga Tantra, that we find the most complex and sophisticated descriptions of subtle-body processes within the Indic and Indo-Tibetan traditions, and it is within the Śaiva and Buddhist lineages that the associated practices have been continued into modern times. It is in these texts and practices that one finds, in particular, the well-known internal anatomy of channels (*nāḍī*) and wheels (*cakra*) through which circulate substances related variously to consciousness, energy or emotion, referred to in the General Introduction and at the start of this chapter. Such ideas became central to the soteriological process as understood in Vajrayāna Buddhism and also in the related Śaiva traditions (e.g. Silburn 1988). The achievement of enlightenment or liberation was held to take place through the cultivation and training of specific subtle-body processes, and the Completion Stage (*sampannakrama, rdzogs rim*) processes of Anuttara Yoga Tantra gives detailed instructions for these (Huntington and Bangdel 2003). The so-called Six Yogas of Nāropa are one of a number of sets of practices of this kind (Guenther 1963; Mullin 2006).

There are also physical exercises (*'phrul 'khor* or *'khrul 'khor* in Tibetan, sometimes called *yantra yoga* by modern Tibetan teachers) associated with the internal practices and visualizations (cf. Chaoul in this volume; Loseries-Leick 1997). Similar concepts and practices are important in Hindu tantric yoga, as with the so-called *kriyā yoga* practices, which again incorporate both physical movements and inner visualization.

The question of how all this became integrated into the practice of Buddhist yogic contemplatives is of some interest. We can perhaps suppose a historical sequence in which these techniques were progressively adopted by Buddhists as a supplement to the already existing ritual and meditational procedures of the sūtra texts, in part no doubt to meet the needs of their patrons for rituals to bring about the 'worldly ends' those patrons desired, such as health, prosperity and defence against hostile forces (Samuel 2008: 258–68; Sanderson 2009). The earlier stages of what, retrospectively at least, became known as the Buddhist Tantric tradition involved relatively straightforward offering rituals to benign deities already present within or little different from those of the later Mahāyāna Sūtras. While breathing practices were significant from the earliest days of the Buddhist tradition, they do not seem to have been theorized in terms such as those used in the Tantric tradition, or linked with concepts of the subtle body. The subtle-body practices seem to have come in at a much later stage, as part of the extensive sharing and mutual borrowing between Buddhist and Śaiva practices which led on the Buddhist side to the Anuttara Yoga Tantric lineages associated with deities such as Hevajra and Cakrasaṃvara.

The subtle-body practices remained somewhat separate from the deity-visualization side of Tantra. In the Anuttara Yoga Tantras, deity-yoga is primarily reserved for the Generation Stage, and subtle-body practices for the Completion Stage, although there is some overlap, and the Tibetan tradition in particular tends to use subtle-body practices more widely, just as it tends to draw everything possible into the framework of Tantric practice (Thurman 1985; Germano 1994).

## The *cakras* and the *nāḍīs*

The term *cakra* literally means 'circle' (as does its Tibetan translation, *'khor lo*) and it has at least a double reference, since the *cakra* were also the 'circles' in which tantric practitioners met to perform worship (*cakrapūjā, gaṇacakra*). These external *cakras*, as many of the Tantric texts explain, took place at the major Śākta pilgrimage sites (*pīṭha*) which were found throughout the Indian subcontinent, from Afghanistan in the far west to East Bengal in the east (Sircar 1973).

The main *cakras* within the body, points of focus in Tantric internal practice where the *nāḍīs* or channels meet, were associated with these external *cakra*, following a standard logic of internalization within Indic thought (e.g. Flood 2006: 113–17).

*Nāḍī* means stream or river; the *nāḍī* were conceived of as channels throughout the body along which flowed the breath-substance of early Indian thought, *prāṇa*. The major Tantric traditions, Śaiva and Buddhist, concur on there being three principal *nāḍī* – a central channel running down the back of the body, roughly following the spinal column, and two others to its left and right, winding around it and meeting with at the successive *cakra*. The central channel is usually called *suṣumnā* in Śaiva systems; in Buddhist systems it is sometimes referred to as *avadhūtī*. The left and right channels are called *iḍā* and *piṅgala* (*lalanā* and *rasanā* in Buddhist systems) and are associated with male and female, semen and blood, moon and sun (see Hartzell 1999: 116–17).

Further subsidiary channels emanate outwards from each *cakra*, enabling the *prāṇa* to be distributed around the body. The *cakra* are often depicted as lotus-like, with multiple petals from which channels emerge. These petals may also be the seats for a circle of deities associated with that particular *cakra*. As mentioned earlier, a set of five *prāṇa*, often extended to ten, had developed in earlier Indian thought, and this too was integrated into the *cakra-nāḍī* system (Wallace 2001: 57–8). The *cakra* and *nāḍī* can become the basis for elaborate series of correspondences; thus the last major Indian Buddhist Tantra, the *Kālacakra*, equates the six *cakra* in its system with the four *kāya* of the Buddha, the four *vajra*, the six elements, and the twelve links of dependent origination (Wallace 2001: 159), with the four *kāya* becoming the basis of a series of further correspondences (2001: 167; see also Hartzell 1997: 635ff.).

In Chinese thought, as Livia Kohn has shown in Chapter 1, *qi*, which fills a similar role to *prāṇa*, derives from the digestion of food, and is progressively purified in a healthy metabolism into *jing* or essence, corresponding also to male and female sexual potency, and onwards into higher and more refined forms (*shen, ling*). Indian medical theory incorporates a similar series of transformations, in which food is transformed into *ojas*, a refined form of vital energy. This process, however, is not usually closely integrated into systems of Tantric theory and practice, again suggesting somewhat distinct origins to the Tantric and medical systems. While the later Tibetan Tantric practices developed a health dimension in the form of *tshe sgrub*, which are Tantric practices aimed at the cultivation of health and long life, the stress in these practices is on drawing in the pure essence of the external universe (phrased as *bcud*, 'juice, essence' or *bdud rtsi*, corresponding to Sanskrit *rāsa, amṛta*) rather than on internal transformations (Samuel 2012).

The number of *cakra* and *nāḍī* varies between different Tantric traditions. The set of six or seven main *cakra* familiar from modern Hindu, yogic and New Age contexts only gradually became the norm within the Hindu tradition. This set consists of *mūladhāra* (base or anal *cakra*), *svādhisthāna* (at the genitals), *maṇipura* (at the navel), *anahāta* (at the heart), *viṣuddha* (at the throat) and *ājñā* (between the eyebrows); the seventh when included is at the crown of the head (*sahasrāra*). The first appearance of this system seems to have been in the eleventh-century *Kubjikāmata Tantra* (Flood 2006: 158). Gavin Flood describes some of the earlier variants, including the six-*cakra* system of the *Netra Tantra* and the eight-*cakra* system of the *Kaulajñāna-nirṇaya* (2006: 158–60; see also White 2003: 225). The Buddhist Tantras generally operate with four or five *cakra*, and this system can already be found in the *Hevajra Tantra*, dating probably to the eighth century:

> In the Centre [i.e. *cakra*] of Creation [at the sexual organ] a sixty-four petal lotus. In the Centre of Essential Nature [at the heart] an eight petal lotus. In the Centre of Enjoyment [at the throat] a sixteen petal lotus. In the Centre of Great Bliss [at the top of the head] a thirty-two petal lotus.
>
> (Farrow and Menon 1992: 15; *Hevajra Tantra* 1,1,23)

The names of these four *cakra* are derived from the names of one of the standard sets of four *kāya* or bodies of the Buddha[5] (*nirmāṇa* = Creation, *dharma* = Essential Nature, *saṃbhoga* = Enjoyment, *mahāsukha* = Great Bliss). These are then correlated with the four moments of actualization, the four noble truths, four *tattva*, four joys and the four main doctrinal schools (1,1,26–30). The main Sanskrit commentary, the *Yogaratnamalā*, adds a further and more detailed set of correlations with the four consecrations that form a standard part of Tantric Buddhist empowerments for tantras such as the Hevajra (Farrow and Menon 1992: 15–21). The *Hevajra* lists 32 *nāḍī*, including the three main *nāḍī*, given their usual names in Buddhist Tantra of *lalanā, rasanā* and *avadhūtī* (1,1,14). Table 2.1 correlates the four Buddhist *cakra* with the most usual system of seven Śaiva *cakra*.

*Table 2.1* Typical Śaiva and Buddhist *cakra* systems

| Śaiva | Buddhist | Position in body |
|---|---|---|
| sahasrāra | mahāsukha | crown of head |
| ājñā | – | eyebrows |
| viṣuddha | saṃbhoga | throat |
| anahāta | dharma | heart |
| maṇipura | – | navel |
| svādhisthāna | nirmāṇa | genitals |
| mūladhāra | – | anus |

The question of how far these centres are seen as physically existing at specific points within the body is difficult to answer. They probably were, in the early texts, although different texts give different lists of *cakra* and also different arrangements of the *nāḍī* around them. Thus, as Tibetan scholars noted, the knots formed by the two outer *nāḍī* around the central *nāḍī* have to be visualized differently in the *Kālacakra* system from in other tantras:

> In other tantras it is often said that when the side channels form knots around the central channel, they do so very tightly, leaving no space whatsoever in the coils. In Kalachakra, however, one visualizes the knots as being loose and having space between the coils.
>
> (Dalai Lama 1982: 132)

The point here is not that other tantras are wrong and the *Kālacakra* is correct but that when performing the other tantras one visualizes in one way, for the *Kālacakra* in another. As this suggests, the material existence of the *cakra* and *nāḍī* is not the central issue for Tantric practitioners, although it became a matter of concern for Tibetan medical scholars (Gyatso 2004; see also Gerke, this volume). The central issue for Tantric practitioners is how one uses a particular system as a meditational device for personal transformation or other ritual ends. This issue is discussed further in Chapter 14.

The details of how the subtle body is employed within Tantric practice vary between the specific Tantric systems, both Buddhist and Śaiva. David White suggests that there was a transformation over time from what he refers to as the Kula and Kaula systems, where the emphasis is on the production of dangerous and powerful sexual fluids for magical purposes, to 'High Hindu Tantra' where the emphasis is on inner experience and transformation, and where the subtle body concepts become central. The use of sexual secretions and sexual practices in early Śaiva Tantra seems to have been motivated primarily by their value as being polluting, dangerous and so magically potent. In addition, White argues, the ingestion of sexual fluids was central to initiation, since it was seen as transmitting the essence of the lineage from teacher to student (White 1998, 2003). In the later versions of Śaiva Tantra (White's 'High Hindu Tantra'), which correspond broadly to those in which the *cakra-nāḍī* structure is employed, sexual practice acts primarily as a mode of access to states of enlightened consciousness (White 1998, 2003; Muller-Ortega 2002).

White suggests that the same transition took place within the Buddhist Tantras (2003: 109). While the consumption of sexual fluids is certainly described in the early Buddhist Tantric texts, in modern practice it is performed symbolically, and the primary purpose of the exercise is inner transformation. The key process in Buddhist Tantra is already described elliptically in the last verse of chapter 1 of the *Hevajra Tantra*:

> Caṇḍālī blazes up in the navel. She burns the Five Buddhas. She burns Locanā and the others. Ahaṃ is burnt and the Moon flows down.
>
> (Farrow and Menon 1992: 21)

Caṇḍālī ('the fierce one'; Tibetan *gtum mo*), like her equivalent in the Śaiva system, Kuṇḍalinī, is a goddess visualized in the lowest *cakra*. Awakened, she blazes up through the successive *cakra*, and in so doing destroys the apparent world (symbolized by the five Buddhas and their consorts) and destroys attachment to the ordinary self (*ahaṃ*), allowing for the emergence of the Buddha-nature in the form of the Tantric deity. The Śaiva equivalent here would be the attainment of identity with Śiva in the form of Bhairava or an equivalent fierce Tantric manifestation (Muller-Ortega 2002).

In the Buddhist system, the underlying premise is the opposition between ordinary or conventional truth (*samvṛtti sātya*) and the ultimate reality of Buddhahood (*paramārtha sātya*). The central assumption here is that in the experience of ordinary reality, the breath (*prāṇa*) flows primarily through the two side channels, circulating from there into the subsidiary channels. The experience of ultimate reality corresponds to the concentration of the breath in the central channel. Normally this does not take place, because the 'knots' where the side channels meet the central channel at each *cakra* are blocked by various 'obscurations' corresponding to negative emotions and karmic obscurations of various kinds. By gradually concentrating the *prāṇa* in the central channel, the practitioner creates the *vajra*-body through which he or she can awaken the transformative process (Huntington and Bangdel 2003: 230–1, 248–51).

## Sexual practices in Buddhist Tantra

The male and female sexual substances retain a central role in the Buddhist Tantric version of this process, but rather than being lost to the body and consumed externally, they are retained and transformed internally (hence the avoidance of male ejaculation). The assumption here is that both men and women contain the male and female sexual substances, so that the practices can be done by both men and women. These substances correspond at one level to semen and menstrual blood, but at another level they are described as white and red *bodhicitta*. *Bodhicitta* is a key term in Mahāyāna Buddhist practice, and it refers to the motivational state that is a necessary precondition for the attainment of Buddhahood. This is the urgent desire to free all living beings from the sufferings of ordinary reality (*saṃsāra*). This desire has to become a central and irreversible part of one's being as part of the process of Buddhist awakening or Enlightenment. In the Tantric version of this process, the accumulation of drops (*bindu*) of white and red *bodhicitta* in the central channel is homologized with the building-up of the *vajra*-body, itself an essential prerequisite for the attainment of Buddhahood.

The connection of subtle body practices with sexual yoga here is notable. At one level, sexual practice is parallel to other yogic practices associated with dreaming and with the after-death state, in that the aim is to maintain balance and self-control over the processes of the subtle body in an emotionally intense situation. However, the simultaneous identification of the substance being concentrated in the central channel with male and female sexual secretions and with *bodhicitta* adds another level of significance to the sexual practices. One could say that the erotic impulse as aroused in the practice is consciously sublimated and redirected into the universal love and compassion that leads to Buddhahood. In later Tibetan tradition, while the sexual practices were frequently performed symbolically, with a visualized rather than a physical sexual partner, they were seen in many traditions as essential to the attainment of Buddhahood (Samuel 1993: 276).

Both Buddhist and Śaiva traditions developed a set of physical yogic exercises intended to prepare the mind-body complex for the sexual practices. The Śaiva versions of these exercises were the origin of the *haṭha yoga* and similar traditions that gave rise to modern postural yoga (Alter 2005).

The Tibetan versions of these exercises, generally known as *rtsa rlung* (Skt. *nāḍī-prāṇa*) and *'phrul 'khor* (Skt. *yantra*) are still practised, but generally only in closed communities of yogic practitioners (Loseries-Leick 1997). Two non-Tantric versions of these practices, from the Buddhist and Bon-po rDzogs-chen traditions, have been taught publicly to Western students in recent years by the lamas Namkhai Norbu Rinpoche and Tenzin Wangyal; one of these forms the basis of the adaptation of *rtsa rlung* practice for modern medical purposes discussed by Alejandro Chaoul in Chapter 6.

## Relationship to Chinese practices

Historically, Tantric internal practices and the associated *cakra-nāḍī* concepts are first attested in India in the seventh and eighth centuries (Samuel 2008: 276). However, the combination of subtle-body practices with sexual cultivation can be found in China at a considerably earlier date, certainly by 150–100 BCE, when it survives in texts preserved in Han-dynasty tombs. This early Chinese material is more explicit and detailed about what we could call the internal yogic structure of the subtle body and its connection with sexual practices than anything found in India until many centuries later, which raises the possibility that these practices may have been imported from China (White 1996: 53–5, 61–5; Samuel 2008: 278–82).

The strong association of Indian Tantric practices with the achievement of immortality (e.g. Schaeffer 2003), or at least a greatly extended life-span, is also a Chinese theme from early times; as we saw in Chapter 1, Chinese subtle-body concepts are intimately linked to medical and health concerns, and the attainment of a long life. In relation to sexual practice, India, of course, has its own sophisticated tradition of erotics, with the oldest surviving and most famous of its texts, the *Kāma Sūtra*, generally dated to around the third century CE. There is nothing whatsoever in the *Kāma Sūtra*, however, and little in the later *kāmaśastra* tradition, to suggest that sexual techniques were seen as of spiritual value, nor does the connection with longevity occur in the *kāmaśastra* tradition. The earliest suggestions of meditational practices of this kind can perhaps be found, as David Snellgrove noted many years ago, in the *Mahāyānasūtrālaṃkāra*, a Buddhist text that probably dates from the fifth century (Snellgrove 1987: 126–8; Samuel 2008: 274–6).[6]

All this raises quite a few interesting questions, on which I have speculated a little in other places (e.g. Samuel 2008: 271–90). Whatever the precise history here, it is clear that the subtle-body practices became viewed primarily in terms of their providing a powerful technique to assist in the attainment of Buddhist enlightenment. Indeed, in Tibetan tradition, they came to form part of the normative path to Buddhahood.

## The spread of Tantra within and beyond India

In India, Tantra became part of state technology, and it was exported in that form. Much of the point appears to have been the aggressive or defensive use of Tantric technology for military purposes, which encouraged rulers to establish colleges of Tantric ritual practitioners, Śaiva or Buddhist, and to translate Tantric texts into local languages (Samuel 2008: 291–323). In this they continued a long-standing interest of Indian and other Asian states in state-defensive ritual and in rituals to promote success in military engagements (Samuel 2008; Willis 2009). The connections between Tantra and martial arts have remained in many areas (see Alter, this volume for India; Mohan 2001 for Korea; Connor 1995 for Bali). Buddhist Tantric rituals were regularly used for state-defending purposes in East Asia and doubtless elsewhere in the Buddhist world (Samuel 2008).

This is not to suggest that the interest in Tantra was entirely military. Other aspects of Tantra, such as Tantric practices for health and longevity, were undoubtedly also attractive to rulers and other people in authority, and there are cases where substantial numbers of the ruling elite received Tantric empower-ments and perhaps engaged in Tantric practice. This took place in Kashmir and among the Mongols (Samuel 2008: 334). According to Tibetan tradition, the late eighth century Tibetan emperor Khri srong lde'u btsan became an advanced Tantric practitioner and close associate of the Tantric guru Padmasambhava. While much of the story is probably legend, the association between royalty and Tantric practice may well have been genuine.

How far the Śaiva export versions of Tantric ritual included versions of the subtle-body technology, and how extensively they were practised if so, is not clear. The Buddhist ones certainly did, as part of advanced yogic training, and have particularly been preserved in Tibet. We will see more of this in Part Two, which discusses various aspects of the Tibetan versions of these practices.

In modern usage, the *haṭha yoga* practices have generally been divested of their Tantric and sexual associations, although these are still present in various Indian ascetic traditions. This process can already be seen in the *Haṭhayoga-Pradīpikā*, dating perhaps from the fifteenth century, and one of the foundational texts for modern postural yoga. It was taken much further in the twentieth century by a series of modern Indian 'reformers' who progressively eliminated the central focus of the tradition on the attainment of enlightenment. As Joe Alter has noted, this process has generated a yoga that is essentially a set of techniques whose central goal has vanished (Alter 2005).

There have been similar attempts to 'clean up' Śaiva Tantra itself and to play down its associations with sexual practice and other problematic elements. It now seems clear that the works published by the British High Court judge Sir John Woodroffe, along with his Indian collaborator A. B. Ghose, under the name 'Arthur Avalon' represent an attempt of this kind (Taylor 1996, 2001). This is of some significance, since these books were very influential in forming Western images of Tantra in the early twentieth century. Woodroffe and Ghose did, however, give a basically accurate description of the role of the *cakra* and internal *prāṇa* flows within Tantric practice. Their work thus enabled Western scholars and others to gain their first fairly clear account of Tantra as practice, rather than as negative stereotype, as well as providing a description of the associated subtle-body practices. Over the subsequent century or so, it has become increasingly evident that we cannot make sense of modern physical yoga, or of Tantric practice more generally, without a full recognition and understanding of the role of the internal subtle-body practices within the tradition.

## Notes

1  Olivelle actually gives the date as fifth or sixth century, but he notes (1996: xxxvi n.21) that this is assuming the old chronology for the Buddha's death, and that he in fact supports the revised chronology, according to which the Buddha's death is moved a century or so later. This revised chronology seems increasingly likely, and would require moving the probable date of the *Taittirīya Upaniṣad* forward by a similar amount.
2  See McEvilley 2002, who cites the *Chāndogya* and *Maitri Upaniṣads*, Plato's *Timaeus*, and the early Greek medical tradition (2002: 93–6). I should add that I do not endorse some of the later, more speculative sections of McEvilley's article.
3  I am not too certain exactly when this happened. The *kośa*-s are described in Śaṃkara's *Vivekacūḍāmaṇi*, vv.159–213. They are also alluded to in his *Ātmabodha*, v.14.
4  There was also a Jain tradition of Tantra, but the sophisticated subtle-body techniques do not appear to have formed part of it. The versions of these techniques discussed by the twelfth-century Jain author in his *Yogaśāstra* appear to derive from Nāth (i.e. Śaiva) sources (see Samuel 2008: 332–3). Similarly the Vaiṣṇava Tantric tradition of the Pāñcarātra seems not to have taken up the subtle-body practices.
5  The three *kāya* (*dharmakāya*, *sambhogakāya*, *nirmāṇakāya*) familiar from non-Tantric Mahāyāna contexts are frequently expanded to four in Buddhist Tantric contexts through the addition of the self-existent body (*svābhāvikakāya*) or, as here, the Body of Great Bliss (*mahāsukhakāya*).
6  Rituals involving sexual practices aimed at pragmatic, this-worldly ends, as distinct from meditational practices with an explicitly soteriological goal, have a much longer history in Indian societies, and can be found in Vedic and Upaniṣadic contexts.

## References

Alter, J. S. (2005) 'Modern medical yoga: struggling with a history of magic, alchemy and sex', *Asian Medicine: Tradition and Modernity* 1: 119–46.
Brown, R. L. (2002) 'Introduction', in K. A. Harper and R. L. Brown (eds) *The Roots of Tantra*. Albany: State University of New York Press.

Connolly, P. (1997) 'The vitalistic antecedents of the ātman-Brahman concept', in P. Connolly and S. Hamilton (eds) *Indian Insights: Buddhism, Brahmanism and Bhakti: Papers from the Annual Spalding Symposium on Indian Religions*. London: Luzac Oriental.

Connor, L. H. (1995) 'Acquiring invisible strength: a Balinese discourse of harm and well-being', *Indonesia Circle* 66: 124–53.

Dalai Lama I, Gendun Drub (1982) *Bridging the Sutras and Tantras: A Collection of Ten Minor Works*, comp. and trans. G. H. Mullin. Ithaca, NY: Gabriel/Snow Lion.

Dalai Lama XIV, Tenzin Gyatso (1977) 'Introduction', in *Tantra in Tibet: The Great Exposition of Secret Mantra, by Tsong-Ka-Pa*, trans. and ed. J. Hopkins. London: George Allen and Unwin.

Farrow, G. W. and Menon, I. (1992) *The Concealed Essence of the Hevajra Tantra With the Commentary* Yogaratnamālā. Delhi: Motilal Banarsidass.

Flood, G. (2006) *The Tantric Body: The Secret Tradition of Hindu Religion*. London and New York: I.B. Tauris.

Germano, D. F. (1994) 'Architecture and absence in the secret Tantric history of rDzogs Chen', *Journal of the International Association of Buddhist Studies* 17(2): 203–335.

Guenther, H. V. (1963) *The Life and Teaching of Nāropa*. Oxford: Clarendon Press.

Gyatso, J. (2004) 'The authority of empiricism and the empiricism of authority: medicine and Buddhism in Tibet on the eve of modernity', *Comparative Studies of South Asia, Africa and the Middle East* 24: 83–96.

Harper, D. (1987) 'The sexual arts of ancient China as described in a manuscript of the second century B.C.', *Harvard Journal of Asiatic Studies* 47: 539–92.

—— (1997) *Early Chinese Medical Literature: The Mawangdui Medical Manuscripts*. London: Kegan Paul International and New York: Columbia University Press.

Hartzell, J. F. (1997) 'Tantric Yoga: a study of the Vedic precursors, historical evolution, literatures, cultures, doctrines, and practices of the 11th century Kaśmīri Śaivite and Buddhist unexcelled Tantric Yogas', unpublished PhD dissertation, Columbia University. UMI No. 9723798.

Huntington, J. C. and Bangdel, D. (2003) *The Circle of Bliss: Buddhist Meditational Art*. Columbus, OH: Columbus Museum of Art and Chicago: Serindia Publications.

Larson, G. J. (2009) 'Differentiating the concepts of "yoga" and "tantra" in Sanskrit literary history', *Journal of the American Oriental Society* 129: 487–98.

Lo, V. (1998) 'The Influence of Yangsheng 養生 Culture on Early Chinese Medical Theory,' unpublished PhD thesis, University of London, School of Oriental and African Studies.

Lorenzen, D. N. (2002) 'Early evidence for Tantric religion', in K. A. Harper and R. L. Brown (eds) *The Roots of Tantra*. Albany: State University of New York Press.

Loseries-Leick, A. (1997) 'Psychic sports: a living tradition in contemporary Tibet?', in H. Krasser, M. T. Much, E. Steinkellner and H. Tauscher (eds) *Tibetan Studies: Proceedings of the 7th Seminar of the International Association for Tibetan Studies, Graz 1995*, Vol. 2. Wien: Österreichische Akademie der Wissenschaften.

McEvilley, T. (2002) 'The spinal serpent', in K. A. Harper and R. L. Brown (eds) *The Roots of Tantra*. Albany: State University of New York Press.

Mohan, P. N. (2001) 'Maitreya cult in early Shilla: focusing on Hwarang as Maitreya-incarnate', *Seoul Journal of Korean Studies* 14: 149–73.

Muller-Ortega, P. E. (2002) 'Becoming Bhairava: meditative vision in Abhinavagupta's *Parātriśikā-Laghuvrtti*', in K. A. Harper and R. L. Brown (eds) *The Roots of Tantra*. Albany: State University of New York Press.

Mullin, G. H. (2006) *The Practice of the Six Yogas of Naropa*. Ithaca, NY and Boulder, CO: Snow Lion.

Olivelle, P. (1998) *Upaniṣads, translated from the Original Sanskrit*. Oxford and New York: Oxford University Press.

Padoux, A. (2002) 'What do we mean by Tantrism?', in K. A. Harper and R. L. Brown (eds) *The Roots of Tantra*. Albany: State University of New York Press.

Samuel, G. (1993) *Civilized Shamans: Buddhism in Tibetan Societies*. Washington and London: Smithsonian Institution Press.

—— (2008) *The Origins of Yoga and Tantra: Indic Religions to the Thirteenth Century*. Cambridge and New York: Cambridge University Press.

—— (2012) 'Amitāyus and the development of Tantric practices for longevity and health in Tibet', in I. Keul (ed.) *Transformations and Transfer of Tantra in Asia and Beyond*. Berlin and New York: Walter de Gruyter.

Sanderson, A. (1988) 'Śaivism and the Tantric traditions', in S. Sutherland, L. Houlden, P. Clarke and F. Hardy (eds) *The World's Religions*. London: Routledge.

—— (2009) 'The Śaiva age: the rise and dominance of Śaivism during the early mediaeval period', in S. Einoo (ed.) *Genesis and Development of Tantrism*. Tokyo: Institute of Oriental Culture, University of Tokyo.

Schaeffer, K. R. (2003) '*The Attainment of Immortality*: from Nāthas in India to Buddhists in Tibet', *Journal of Indian Philosophy* 30: 515–33.

Silburn, L. (1988) *Kuṇḍalinī: The Energy of the Depths. A Comprehensive Study Based on the Scriptures of Nondualistic Kaśmir Śaivism*. Albany: State University of New York Press.

Sircar, D. C. (1973) *The Śākta Pīṭhas* (2nd rev. edn). Delhi: Motilal Banarsidass.

Snellgrove, D. L. (1987) *Indo-Tibetan Buddhism: Indian Buddhists and Their Tibetan Successors*. London: Serindia.

Taylor, K. (1996) 'Arthur Avalon: the creation of a legendary orientalist', in J. Leslie (ed.) *Myth and Mythmaking*. Richmond: Curzon.

—— *Sir John Woodroffe, Tantra and Bengal: An Indian Soul in a European Body?* London: Routledge.

Thurman, R. A. F. (1985) 'Tsoṅ-kha-pa's integration of sūtra and tantra', in B. N. Aziz and M. Kapstein (eds) *Soundings in Tibetan Civilization*. New Delhi: Manohar.

Wallace, V. A. (2001) *The Inner Kālacakratantra: A Buddhist Tantric View of the Individual*. New York and Oxford: Oxford University Press.

White, D. G. (1996) *The Alchemical Body: Siddha Traditions in Medieval India*. Chicago and London: University of Chicago Press.

—— (1998) 'Transformations in the art of love: Kāmakalā practices in Hindu Tantric and Kaula traditions', *History of Religions* 38(4): 172–98.

—— (2003) *Kiss of the Yoginī: 'Tantric Sex' In Its South Asian Contexts*. Chicago: University of Chicago Press.

—— (2009) *Sinister Yogis*. Chicago and London: University of Chicago Press.

Willis, M. D. (2009) *The Archaeology of Hindu Ritual*. Cambridge and New York: Cambridge University Press.

Zysk, K. G. (1993) 'The science of respiration and the doctrine of the bodily winds in Ancient India', *Journal of the American Oriental Society* 113: 198–213.

—— (2007) 'The bodily winds in ancient India revisited', *Journal of the Royal Anthropological Institute*: S105–16 (special issue, *Wind, Life, Health: Anthropological and Historical Perspectives*, ed. C. Low and E. Hsu).

# 3    The life-bearing body in *dais'* birth imagery

*Janet Chawla*

In the Indian subcontinent childbirth is rarely associated with religion, spirituality or for that matter medical knowledge or aesthetics. This is despite the fact that explicit sculptural renderings of the birth process have found their way to the *śikharas* of south Indian temples, and from the earliest Upaniṣads, sacred texts are often replete with, to use Eliade's phrase, 'sexual and gynaecological' symbolism.[1] This chapter focuses on the body mappings, representational and ritual imagery and birth knowledge of *dais*, the traditional handlers of birth – who operate both as ethno-medical and ritual practitioners.

I have devoted myself, in the last fifteen years, to documentations and reclamations of the religio-cultural and indigenous medical worlds of these usually low and outcaste women. They increasingly serve the poorest of the poor – but retain an exquisite sense of the birth process and aesthetic heritages within which to understand it. A caveat is needed here: a *dai* is one who helps, supports at birth. The health establishment calls them TBAs or traditional birth attendants and considers them unskilled. The data presented here is drawn from *dais* who are older, experienced, custodians of tradition and recognized as experts by the communities they serve.

*Dais'* imaging of the body and their use of the expression *naari* serve them in their roles as midwives, hands-on practitioners of indigenous birth knowledge and skills. Their concerns are the well-being of the mother and the baby, not yogic prowess or enlightenment. Today in India *dais* still attend more childbirths than any other category of care-givers.[2] This term *naari*, however (corresponding to Sanskrit *nāḍī*, 'channel' or 'flow'), is more conventionally associated with the concepts of 'subtle body', used by practitioners and textual traditions of Ayurveda and Yoga – both of which are masculine-dominated systems. Conversely, although occasionally one finds a male *dai* in a tribal area, *dais* are female.

In this chapter I explore NGO[3] data from the field, and some scholarly material, from the perspective of notions of the subtle body – using that term in its broadest sense. Body imagery and its use in ritual and birthing practices not only facilitate parturition but also give meaning to childbearing for women, their families and communities. I attempt to establish that *dais*, and the communities they serve, have traditionally viewed the *jachcha* (parturient woman) as fertile and perhaps polluted, but more essentially a 'life-bearing body' full of *jee* or life-force. (Here I do not accept nor utilize the mind–body dichotomy common in biomedical and modernist language.) The woman-centred nature of my work is intended to challenge prevalent hierarchies that privilege the subtle body over the gross body and consequently the male 'spiritual' body over the female material, reproductive and maternal body. Furthermore, I explore tentative correlations between the yogic and Ayurvedic subtle-body term *prāṇa* and that of *dais'* terms *saans* (breath) and *jee* (life).

In Indian imagistic traditions the female body and the earth (body) have been abidingly conflated. This is not a symbolic relationship. The earth is not a symbol of woman, nor is woman a symbol of the earth. Rather song, image, myth and birthing practice have all celebrated the fertility of both, in the same breath, so to speak. The Sāṃkhya philosophical system is foundational to this imagery in which *prakṛti* represents the entire phenomenal world, and *puruṣa*, consciousness. Strictly speaking, the *prakṛti-puruṣa* dyad is conceptual, abstract and ungendered. But in fact its exoteric, popular and gendered manifestation has had disastrous consequences for what is commonly termed 'the status of women'. Woman is identified with the field/matter (*prakṛti*), and man with 'knowledge of the field' (*puruṣa*). Although in the Sāṃkhya philosophical system this 'knowledge of the field' is equivalent to 'consciousness', in social history it has played out as power, privilege and patriline. Perhaps a practitioner of yoga or meditation can experientially identify the terms field-knower and field as aspects of the inner *līlā* (play) of attention (*dhyān*) and objects towards which attention is directed. Society, however, is not composed exclusively of philosophers, *yogis* and meditators.

Sociologist Leela Dube's article 'Seed and earth: the symbolism of biological reproduction and sexual relations of production' (1986) exposes the sociopolitical consequences of this philosophic and folk homology. She quotes the *Nāradasmṛti*: 'Women are created for offsprings; a woman is the field and a man is the possessor of the seed' (1986: 24). Dube shows how this analogy functioned to legitimize male rights over female sexuality (the right to 'plough' the field), rights to both agricultural land and children ('the crop should belong to him who has sown the seed').

Furthermore, the assumption is that the earth/woman can 'bear' or support life – that women can suffer or bear pain in the support of life (i.e. children, family, domestic and agricultural responsibilities). This image or conflation translates into the common perception that pain is somehow 'natural' to woman in other domains as well as childbirth – and feminist writers have roundly critiqued that assumption. This naturalization of female pain is similar to the biblical curse on Eve for eating the apple in the Garden of Paradise: 'To the woman he [Yahweh God] said I shall give you intense pain in childbearing, you will give birth to children in pain' (Genesis 3:16, *New Jerusalem Bible*). I argue that a review and reclamation of the woman-earth conflation need not valorize female suffering and victimization.

I have modified and elaborated on this essential equation of earth equals woman elsewhere. In 'The conflation of the female body and earth in Indian religious traditions: gendered representations of seed, earth and grain' (Chawla 2000) I nuance a distinction between 'earth' and 'field'. A scrutiny of many *dais'* traditional use of grain in a ritual performance facilitating birth displays a woman-centred conflation of earth body and female body, a conflation valorizing the fecundity of both earth and woman. The custom entails *atta* (moist flour) being placed on a *tali* (plate) in one mound and the woman separating that mound of *atta* into two with her hand, invoking the goddess Bemata and the help of the *dai*. 'With the power of Bemata, and the support of the *dai*, may the baby separate from me as easily as I separate this one mound into two.'

Foregrounding data from *dais* and birth traditions interrogates and challenges androcentric assumptions inherent in the dominant religious traditions and nuances the feminist analyses of Dube's paper. Data from *dais*, privileging their voices and customs, leads us to other ways of understanding female physiological processes. Their perceptions of birth-giving and the conflation of earth and female bodies require us to make an epistemological shift – allowing us empathetically to access their knowledge skills and lives. Data from *dais* provides imagistic mappings of reproductive bodies earthy, whole and sacred, which stands apart from the priestly, biomedical or 'new age' views.

Geoffrey Samuel has explored the use of subtle-body imagery and its power to situate the individual within culturally specific body praxis in both healing and birthing arenas (2006: 121–35).

> One of the more significant aspects of the subtle body language is the way in which it can open our picture of the individual out to include the relationship with others. It is particularly relevant to any consideration of subtle body practices in the context of healing, since healing is always at some level about relationships between people. Such an approach would involve looking at childbirth practices in South Asia *simultaneously in terms of physiology, and in terms of what these practices communicate to the birthing mother and other participants in the childbirth about how to make sense of the process of childbirth.*
>
> (2006: 123; my emphasis)

To paraphrase Samuel – as I have often stated in my childbirth preparation classes – 'What a woman has between her ears (i.e. her mind-culture-beliefs) has more to do with the process of her labour than does the width of her pelvis.' And, of course, who is supporting and accompanying her, midwifing her. (Here I must acknowledge that in circumstances of poverty her all too real deprivation of basic bodily needs profoundly and negatively affects her at the time of parturition.)

## Historical context: birth traditions as a contested site

Today *dais* serve the poorest of the poor – and have always been associated with embodiment and not enlightenment – thus negotiating the energy flowing through the mother's body (not to mention the family!); getting the baby born, and the survival of mother and baby, are their central concerns. Nevertheless, cosmological understandings and their subtle-body implications have emerged from our analysis of their indigenous medical imagery and ritual enactments.

Socio-political and economic realities, however, impinge on any consideration of birth attendants and practitioners. *Dais* and other birth workers in the informal sector still occupy the nether end of the caste hierarchy. Caste was a geographically varied social organization that was re-enforced by Western imperial interventions. Privileged Indians in proximity to colonial powers and attitudes reflected and often exaggerated colonial disdain for lower-caste birth work and women's health traditions. Katherine Mayo, in her now infamous but at the time very influential *Mother India* (1927) – a book Mahatma Gandhi referred to as 'a gutter inspector's report' – devotes a chapter to motherhood. She quotes a Dr N. N. Parikh: 'Ignorance and the purdah system have brought the women of India to the level of animals. They are unable to look after themselves, nor have they any will of their own. They are slaves to their masculine owners' (1927: 119). *Dais* and birth customs were a terrain for bitter ideological writings about 'backwardness' and 'filth'. Again to quote from Mayo:

> The first *dai* that I saw in action tossed upon this coal-pot, as I entered the room, a handful of some special vile-smelling stuff to ward off the evil eye – my evil eye. The smoke of it rose thick – also a tongue of flame. By that light one saw her Witch-of-Endor face through its vermin-infested elf-locks, her handing rags, her dirty claws, as she peered with festered and almost sightless eyes out over the stink-cloud she had raised.
>
> (1927: 93–4)

I would argue that colonial ideologies segue into the contemporary scene. Any reclamation of 'traditional' birth practices among middle- and upper-class women and their families is challenging because of attitudes and economics:

> the attack on *dais* was an aspect of the way in which the new middle class and upper caste elites were defining themselves and shaping their identity. Interwoven with this attack were questions of who were the high and the low of the society, and how spaces hitherto accessible to women and the lower castes were to be prized open and appropriated for middle class men and women.
>
> Further, the newly worked out concept of cleanliness was important for the definition of the middle class as well as the lower caste. The colonial state, entering the competitive world inhabited by a number of medical and semi-medical practitioners, picked on the 'dirt' and the 'filth' of the lower caste *dai* and the customs related to birthing to assert its hygienic, scientific and moral superiority. The colonial state used the notion of aseptic cleanliness as a weapon to introduce Western medicine, while for the Punjabi upper castes, sanitized cleanliness became an ideology for asserting middle class identity as it worked in tandem with notions of caste purity and pollution.
>
> (Malhotra 2006: 201)

Not only were *dais* and traditional birthing practices the 'dirty' aspect of low castes and classes, they were also harmful displays of female ignorance. Women and tradition needed to be revamped in the name of 'ideal motherhood'; that is, nationalist reconstruction involved imported Western notions of ideal motherhood.

> Lack of knowledge and education amongst women was seen as causing harm not only to the family but even to the nation. It was pointed out that women who were ignorant of the rules of the body would not only harm themselves, but by producing weak and deficient children, would also destroy the nation. Thus ... women were awarded a special augmented status in remodelling the private domain of the nation. In the twentieth-century reconstruction of ideal motherhood, and in the activities of women's organizations, we find a broadening of the class basis of future mothers of the nation and incorporation of the poorer classes as being in need of education in mothercraft.
>
> (Mukherjee 2001: 209)

These ideological constructions were pervasive and still exist. A bulwark of 'safe motherhood' trainings has been the 'Five Cleans', a continuing attempt to clean up Mayo's filthy midwife – a project totally devoid of the cultural awareness put forward in this chapter. The enterprise of 'development' extends these ideologies into domains of the modern and even the postmodern and globalization. Today *dais* are considered dirty, ignorant and superstitious by 'educated' Indians and held primarily responsible for high maternal-infant mortality and morbidity by global health establishments. Women who handle birth occupy the nether regions (pun intended) of all hierarchies – class, caste and even gender (thanks to the wholehearted acceptance by feminists of the biomedical delivery of services approach to women's health).

MATRIKA and Jeeva research methodologies and the analyses put forward in this chapter invert these hierarchies foregrounding the *dais'* world-view, philosophy and cosmology.[4] *Dais*, demeaned with the term TBAs (traditional birth attendants) by health establishments, are the inheritors of India's birth knowledge, ritual and hands-on skills. One woman Ayurvedic practitioner claimed, '*Dais* are the obstetricians of Ayurveda'.[5] Midwife literally means 'with woman' – being *with* her and mediating her own cultural understanding of the birth process.

I once conducted a workshop for an NGO in Koraput District of south Orissa, helping them document a remote and primitive tribe's birth practices. I was told by the doctor and nurses who had worked in the area for ten years that these women gave birth alone – because no system of *dais* and certainly no biomedical practitioners or facilities existed in the area. In a role-play on the first day, an older tribal woman grabbed hold of a curtain (simulating a rope) with her legs straight out in front of her. Soon a neighbour came in and sat behind her, spooning her body with her own, then another and another – a train of labouring women. I felt in my own body the energy that would flow from one into the other, the labouring woman's back leaning against this literal support system – and

I had been told that these women laboured alone! These were 'midwives' with labouring women. (I am not, however, making claims in this chapter about these tribal women's body knowledge.)

Unfortunately the enterprises of modernization and 'development' are effectively erasing a vast compendium of 'folk' and female-body knowledge and practice. I posit this site as contested – not in global, or even national public health discourse (where institutional birth is financially incentivized) – but rather by fact. Most births still occur at home especially in poor and rural areas. Contestation occurs not in high discourse but on the ground – where this knowledge base, cultural orientation and these indigenous practitioners are the only available resources.

## Maternal connections, dirty matters and 'subtle' bodies

When I first encountered the fact, confirmed in all our MATRIKA and Jeeva research locales, that traditional birth always involved severing the umbilical cord only after the placenta was delivered, I thought that such practice was so appropriate in this society that valued family bonds in general and the mother–child bond in particular. The *dais* reported their practical reasons for retaining this connection: they would stimulate the placenta with heat to revive a seemingly lifeless baby; the placenta was easier to deliver with the cord connected; and (illustrating the decentralized knowledge-culture system) the women attendants or family members would blame them if anything bad happened had they cut the cord!

On another level, the umbilical cord is understood by *dais* to contain channels/*naari* and it is through this thread that *jee* or life-force flows into the foetus. But the significance of this cord-connection is diverse. Some *dais* in Rajasthan and Jharkhand claimed to read the sex of women's subsequent progeny in the form and twists of the cord; one Punjabi *dai* said that she would never cut the cord of women in her own family, because that would be like cutting off her own roots (those of her family). Another very elderly *dai* claimed that it was said by others that cutting the umbilical cord was a great *paap* or sin.

None of the *dais* would have, of their own volition, cut the cord before the placenta emerged. As one *dai* said, 'The placenta and the baby have been together for nine months. What is the hurry to separate them?' All governmental and non-governmental '*dai* training' teaches them to cut the cord immediately. The biomedical approach is a totally functional one. The purpose of the cord/bond has been served – now cut it. Delayed cord-cutting displays comfort with the 'mess' of merger, birth and the process of the baby emerging slowly.

I have often speculated that the 'sin', filth, disdain and pollution associated with the cutting of the cord – and the extent of this 'traditional belief' cannot be exaggerated in my experience – involve problematizing a form of violence. One can imagine a razor blade (or bamboo slice, sickle or arrowhead) encountering the rubbery, fleshy cord-of-life connecting mother-placenta-newborn. One Rajasthani *dai* claimed:

The new mother can also cut the cord. If she is not fully conscious then *Dai* cuts it. *Dai Mai* (*Dai* mother) is as loveable as a mother ... but the *dai* is *Mai, Vaid, Kasai* (mother, Ayurvedic doctor, butcher). *Dai* cuts the cord, nobody else because it's a *dosh* (blemish, transgression). There is life in the *nala* (cord) equivalent to the life of a baby – it has 72 *naari* and by cutting one commits *paap* (sin).

(Manori)

The significance of this 'life of the baby' – *jee* – in the placenta and the cord is explored more fully below.

As Sara Pinto writes of her respondents in Uttar Pradesh:

> Even if they do not refer to their tasks as sinful, their work and silences speak of the cutting of the umbilical cord as a momentary and permanent violence in which bringing-into-life entails a small act of death, the severing of a channel for *jivan* and the bond between the earthly baby and not-quite-earthly placenta ... the placenta enters the realm of death and decay and the baby enters the world, becoming human, social, alive.

(2006: 228)

The 'stuff' of relationship and connection is often not visible or acknowledged. The placenta in polite parlance (even in biomedical, public health and safe motherhood discourses) is relegated to the domain of trash or the repulsive, the abject. It is the ultimate polluting substance in Brahmanical Hinduism.

## Cords, *phool* and *jee*

A common practice is the *dai*'s burial of the placenta in the house or the *angan* (inner courtyard), or even in the fields. I once heard of a resident of one village that had been swallowed up by Delhi whose younger brother challenged his right to inherit the family home because his placenta was not buried on that land, the man having been born in Safdarjang Hospital. Sometimes it is only the boy baby's placenta that will be buried, because he will stay (the land going to 'him who has the seed'), but the girl's placenta, in Pinto's research, was tossed on the trash heap, because she will move on to another family, to 'belong to' another place (Pinto 2006: 206).

On the other hand, our recent Jeeva pilot project study in Jharkhand found that in that area, burial of placenta was done for both male and female neonates by all communities.

> Regardless if a girl or a boy has been born, everybody buries the placenta in the earth. When a boy is born then does it come out from a particular side, and there is a different kind of pain? And when a girl is born, then does she come out from the other side and is there a different kind of pain? When there is no difference in all these things then why should there be a difference in

the *phool*? So this is the reason that the *phools* of both are all buried in the ground.

(Maithila)

However we interpret it, the act of severing that 'ma-babe' connection, and the handling of the placenta, is fraught with meaning in the subcontinent. Ayurveda provides us with a concept relevant to this exploration of the most primal of all relationships in nomenclature of the pregnant woman as *dauhṛdaya*, or the 'two-hearted one'. Anuradha Singh writes of this seeming paradox:

> In this enigmatic state (of being both one and two persons) the usual distinction between self and other is obliterated. The embryo is not 'other' nevertheless it is a different self. The umbilical cord that characterizes the one-who-is-two is said to have about 1600 *naari-s* or channels. Interestingly both dais and texts make this claim.

(2006: 155)

Singh describes the Ayurvedic view of the maternal body during parturition as 'a microcosmic workplace, the site of creation and regeneration. Here macrocosmic forces were transacted in microcosmic bodily form' (2006: 137).

## The social body

Some feminist slogans make absolutely no sense to me. 'My body is mine' is of limited value during parturition, not only because of the baby that occupies and grows within one's physical being, but also because of the support a mother often needs during that time. The following *sohar* or birth song, sung at one of our MATRIKA workshops, is blatantly proprietary of the *jachcha* (birth-giving woman). 'My *jachcha*' is the first line. We don't know the relationship of the singer to the *jachcha*, allowing everyone to claim her.

My *jachcha* is the full moon of *Sharad* [as round/full/bright/radiant/beautiful as]
Beneath the *mahal* the *dai* waits
With all that's needed for the *jachcha*.
Beneath the *mahal saas* (mother-in-law) waits
With all that's needed to make *charua*.
Beneath the *mahal jethani* (HBW) waits
With all that's needed to make *laddoos*.
Beneath the *mahal nandi* (HZ) waits
With all that's needed for *sathiya*.
Beneath the *mahal devar* (HB) waits
Ready to play the flute.

Not only is the pregnant woman conflated with the most beautiful 'full' moon of the year, but the activities of all her attendants are listed: the mother-in-law makes the herbal concoction; the older sister-in-law makes the celebratory sweets; the husband's sister prepares to draw the auspicious symbols on the walls – and the husband's younger brother is ready to play the flute – and they are all *beneath* the *mahal*/woman/*jachcha* (Rao 2006: 91).

This *sohar* exemplifies Samuel's notion of 'modal states' or ways of being (and modes of action) that are both individual and cultural. Samuel sees these emotive states as 'a repertoire of personal states ... internalized during their life-time' (2006: 123). Birth, especially if a son is born, is when the young wife reaps the benefits of her position in the family as mother.

> The young wife has specific relations of deference, service and compliance towards her husband, her mother-in-law, father-in-law, and other kinds of patterned relationships with her husband's elder brother and his wife, her husband's younger siblings and their spouses if any, and so on. Equally, she has expectations of specific forms of behaviour in response from each of these persons.
>
> (2006: 123)

Data from both MATRIKA and Jeeva is full of what we might term social or familial facilitations of birth. In one Bihar workshop we were told that a labouring woman might be made to drink a glass of water in which her mother-in-law's big toe was dipped. We were rather aghast at that until we learned that in Ayurveda the *nāḍī* for *prāṇ vāyu* (understood to be the carrier of knowledge and experience) exited the body through the big toe. Touching the feet of the elders may transmit wisdom; drinking the toe-water grants permission for the birth to proceed. As I have speculated elsewhere:

> The social hierarchy of mother-in-law/daughter-in-law is perhaps encoded in this rite, transmitting the respected female elder's permission for the birth to proceed – granting the status of maternity to the *bahu*, but at the same time asserting her authority and primacy.
>
> (Chawla 2002a: 152)

Another fascinating ritual I encountered in the once polyandrous mountain area of Jaunpur in the state of Uttaranchal was *Matri masaan ka puja*. If a young woman had signs of a threatened miscarriage she would walk back to her natal home (*maike*), accompanied by her male *sasural* (woman's married home) kins-men, dressed in a black blanket, to perform this *puja* at the water source, spring, river or tap where she herself had drawn water as a child. The understanding was that she had been afflicted by the figure *Matri masaan* who resided there and needed to be worshipped and relinquished. *Matri* means mother, and *masaan* means the ashes-bone remnants of a cremated body in the cremation grounds. The woman performed *puja*, took off her *shringar ka saman* – *bindi*, bangles, earrings, *kumkum* – which were offered; and she was not supposed to return to her *maike* throughout the pregnancy. I read the term *masaan* as referring to memories (now ashes) of life with mother in the natal home, before marriage – the girl's incomplete transfer emotionally to her *sasural*.

The emotionally and socially profound switch from her natal home to her married home is implicated here – 'out-married daughters' leave their maternal home and enter that of strangers (often at a very young age). Obeisance is paid to this entity (*bhūt*, *pret*, deity) and also the marks of feminine beauty are left here – speaking the transition not only from daughter to wife, but also that of wife to mother. The ritual performance of *Matri masaan ka puja* is a public display of the vulnerable state of the young woman. Wordlessly her anguish is showcased to family, neighbours, all in the vicinity, inviting their care and consideration.

Both mother-in-law's big toe ritual and *Matri masaan* can be read together insofar as each bestows permission on the new mother for the labour to proceed, and to carry the pregnancy to term. There are two kinds of female lineages, that of the *sasural* and of the *maike* 'mother's home' – which the new mother is betwixt and between. Reconciliation and relocation are ritually enacted; healing is effected.

## Cosmic moorings and earthly connection

*Matri masaan* and another female deity/demon, *Bemata*, whom we will now consider, signify complex and multiple realities in what I have come to think of as geo-mysticism. According to some *dais*, *Bemata* lives deep within the earth (*narak*). She rules that domain and is responsible for the conception, growth and birth of humans as well as all vegetation and animal life. *Bemata*, invoked at the onset of labour, must gradually leave the mother's body via the post-partum bleeding, lest she be responsible for problems for the mother. It seems that the *Bemata* figure functions as a tracking modality for women post-partum, in much the same way that the biomedical Apgar score is for the neonate.

*Narak*, a residence of *Bemata*, is commonly understood and translated as 'hell', one of the three worlds (*triloka*). Reclaiming *dais'* work involves inverting the valuation of these realms of *swarg-bhu-narak* or the celestial realms, the mundane earthly and visible, and the underground, unseen and chthonic. These are accepted categories of textual Hinduism, and of folk culture as well. *Dais* are associated with *narak ka samay* and are more comfortable with this 'dirty' and bodily world than the twice-born castes. Their concept of *narak* allows for a mapping of the unseen, inner world of the body, privileging senses and capacities other than the visual, primarily touch and intuition, as well as allowing for negotiation with the spirit world. And indeed, *dais* have practised non-invasive techniques that negotiate and affect the inner body without violating the integrity of the skin/body/life-force. Their holistic health modalities utilize touch (massage, pressure, manipulation) and natural resources (mud, baths and fomentation, herbs) and application of 'hot and cold' (in food and drink, fomentation, etc.) and isolation and protection (from domestic, maternal and sexual obligations) (Chawla 2002b: 176).

In our MATRIKA data the post-birth time, that of the 'closing' body, was inextricably entwined with conceptions of *narak*. What is normally closed (the vagina, cervix, psyche of the birthing woman), is now open, vulnerable and leaking bodily fluids along with new life. Women who attend birth are more comfortable with this openness and fluidity than the rest of us. *Narak ka samay*, the *narak* period, when voiced by *dais*, carries a totally different valence than that of the pundits. This is what I investigate here in terms of body/matter: mother, matrix and material – all etymologically connected in Indo-European languages.

The concept of *narak* structures gives meaning to the time, care and social relations of the mother post-partum – and in keeping with the phenomenon of the 'open' body, menstruation is included in this rubric. My intent here is to insert 'fertility' into health and healing debates and discourses rather than simply jettison the 'pollution' and uncleanness associated with menstruation and post-partum.

The common term for the ritual that progresses the mother post-partum from the time of *narak* back into the social world is *chatti* or sixth – though this may have traditionally fallen on different days with different castes and in different areas. In the passage below, one of a number of quotes given here from a MATRIKA workshop in Rajasthan, we see the infant handed to the women who will co-mother him or her!

> On *Chhati* day (after birth) the *narak* period ends. The *dai* checks if the umbilical cord has fallen off. Then she bathes the baby and beats a *thaali* (plate) and gives the baby to *Chachi* (husband's younger brother's wife). *Chachi* does *Namaskar* to God and gives the baby to *Jethani* (husband's elder brother's wife). Then the woman is bathed and she wears new clothes. The *dai* then cleans the room where the delivery took place and the mother was kept separately for six days.
>
> (Manori)

Also in Rajasthan, we heard that the place for dirt, blood, *narak* (and rest for the new mother) is located in her maternal home, whereas the post-partum well worship is only done when she returns to her married home.

> It's the *jachcha*'s mother's duty to have her daughter's birth in her *pihar* (father's home). Then her daughter gets rest. But *jalwa puja* (well worship) is done only in *sasural* no matter how long the *jachcha* spends in her *pihar*. This is because after delivery *nau mahene ka narak nikalta hai* (nine months of *narak* comes out). This is also called *narak ka kund* (reservoir of *narak*).
>
> (Rukma)

The phrase '*narak ka kund*' speaks the language of what I have called geo-mysticism. A *kund* is a spring-fed pond, so we again have a *dai* using an analogy between the earth-body and the maternal reproductive body. A spring-fed pond is structurally similar to the placenta's fountain-like action. Obviously these representations of bodily structures and processes differ radically from Mayo's 'filth'.

## 'The creating of a person is through its navel': *jee* and breath in the placenta

During recent research in Jharkhand with the Jeeva Project we obtained amazing insights into local *dai* concepts of the life-force, which they claim resides in the *phool* (placenta). It is this *jee* which is tapped during the heating of the placenta to revive a listless newborn. We were not 'fishing' for any correlation between 'breath' and life-force. Rather, the quotes cited below came from the *dais* spontaneously when talking of their practice of placental stimulation and understandings of the physiology of reproduction.

In the context of 'subtle-body imagery' it is very tempting to relate notions of *prāṇa* drawn from Ayurvedic and yogic texts and practices with *dai* reports of the breath/life in the placenta. For the sceptics – Jeeva researchers took photos of two children whom the *dai*, the mother, the family and neighbouring women all agreed had been revived by this method.

> When the *baccha* is inside [the mother's body], its breath (*saans*) reaches it through the cord (*naar*). In this way the *phool* keeps its life going. Even after coming out, the *baccha* still takes breath through the *naar*. The creating of a person is through its *navel*. And we keep the *phool* and the *baccha* at equal level. If this is not done then the *naar* will get pulled and the child's breath may be drawn back into the *phool*.
>
> (Burdhi)

> When the *baccha* doesn't breathe or open its eyes, when the heartbeat becomes slow, when the *phool* and *naar* slowly does *dhuk-dhuk*, then ... I don't cut the *naar*. When the *baccha* seems as if it is dead then we keep the *phool* along with the *baccha*. People say, 'cut the *naar*,' but I don't cut it. If the child can be saved then I save it.
>
> (Khooni)

In one report the placenta was not stimulated, but the baby-cord-placenta remained connected for two hours, during which time *jee* presumably kept transiting to the infant's body.

> After it was born the *baccha* looked like this [she went limp, as if she were unconscious]. So then I spread a blanket on the ground and placed the *baccha* and its *phool* upon it. And I covered both with a cloth. I didn't separate the *phool* because it has *jaan* (life) in it. After this I didn't do anything to the *phool*, I just kept it like that for two hours. The mother told me to look after her *baccha* as she was okay. The family members were telling me to cut the *naar* but I didn't. I splashed a bit of cold water and then the *baccha* slowly started to move and then it began to cry.
>
> (Budhni)

My hypothesis is that this *jaan* or *jee* is comparable to the *prāṇa* which we are more familiar with from yogic and Ayurvedic literature and practice. A thorough review of the literature in these areas is beyond the purview of this chapter. However, Zysk, in his textual mapping of *prāṇa*, 'The science of respiration and the doctrine of bodily winds', quotes the Atharvaveda: 'A human being breathes out (*ápānati*) and breathes in (*prāṇati*) when inside the womb (*gárbhe*). When you, O *Prāṇa,* urge him on he is born again' (AV 11.4(6).14, cited in Zysk 1993: 201). Whereas the Jharkhand *dais* would agree with this assertion, Zysk states that it is 'scientifically incorrect', and proceeds:

> As respiration was the primary life-force, it was natural for the Vedic Indians to imagine that it was present in the active foetus ready for birth and that the issuance of the foetus from the womb resulted from the functioning of the life breath … Moreover, this conceptual connection between bodily wind and the foetus could have resulted from the observation of the breathing patterns of women in labour.
>
> (Zysk 1993: 201)

I am not surprised that the *dais* of Jharkhand would be in agreement with the Atharva Veda concept. As Anuradha Singh points out, *dais* and Ayurveda possess similar understandings of body, mind, substances, health and disease as well as therapeutics.[6] Reflections, origins of Ayurveda can be found in earlier texts such as the Atharva Veda. Therapeutics similar to those of *dais*, herbs, charms, amulets, mantras, demonic beings, are all to be found in the classical Indian medical texts, *Charaka* and *Susruta*. Direct, measurable 'scientific' equivalences of '*prana* equals *jee*' cannot be made. And anatomical and physiological detailing cannot be scientifically established. The textual analyses (of Atharva Veda, Upanishads, Ayurvedic and yogic texts) of Zysk as well as some scholarly writings on modern yoga all corroborate that within the Indian context there is no single meaning of the term *prāṇa* over the millennia.

Furthermore, the seeming Brahmanic influence towards *prāṇa* as *ātman* or *brahman* or soul bears little relationship with our *dai* informants' ritual performances or childbirth knowledge. The *dais*' mention of 'breath' and 'life' seems closer to the concepts of vital force in homeopathy and to the geographically closer *qi* of China or *ki* of Japan, or to the generic and non-scholarly Indian usage of *prāṇa*.

The data also presents a tentative answer to Samuel's musing: 'I am particularly interested here in the widespread image of an internal "subtle physiology" of the body (or rather of the body-mind complex) made up of channels through which substances of some kind flow' (1995). The *dai* answers above (at least when speaking of the placenta and cord) would be *jee* and *saans* – or as Budhni simply states of the *phool*, 'it has *jaan* in it'.

## A gendered poetics of reproductive bodies

Martha Ann Selby's exploration of the Ayurvedic texts (2005) attends to the poetics of sexed bodies. The schema of maleness and femaleness she describes, especially the openness and susceptibility of the pregnant woman, is omnipresent in the MATRIKA data. Selby uses the word 'poetics' in a broad cultural sense, which she claims is grounded in texts as well as in practice, and which constitutes what she terms a 'cultural semiotics'.

Women and the 'feminine' are red; men and the 'masculine' are white. The redness of women and the whiteness of men are based on the colours of their observable sexual effluents: menstrual fluid in the case of women, and semen in the case of men. White and red exist in a dominant/subordinate relationship, both in the medical texts themselves and within the larger and more articulated contexts of quasi-Hindu social hierarchy. In general, white always predominates, with red and other colours ranked below it. White is the colour of coolness, celibacy, virility, purity and goodness, whereas red represents heat, sexuality, permeability, taint and energy (Selby 2005: 261).

Selby's writing contributes to our consideration of the relational body. The male body/self is more 'individual' and the female body/self is more permeable:

> White is 'male' and 'closed'; red is 'female' and 'open'. It is a woman's redness and openness that cause her susceptibility to all kinds of outside influences, both good and bad, and her porousness and fluidity allow for an exchange to occur in which elements in the environment – sights, sounds, and smells, as well as foods and medicines that are actually prescribed and ingested – all leave impressions in a woman's body that are incorporated into any embryo that she is actually carrying or might soon be carrying ...
>
> (2005: 261)

The valuation of white over red hearkens back to the gendered polarity of the 'field knower' and the field. Interestingly, in one of our Rajasthan workshops discussions turned towards death. We learned that, in accordance with common funereal practice, a stillborn baby or dead neonate was ushered into the next life according to this poetic. 'If a dead baby is born then we dig a place with a hoe and bury it and plant a bush there. If the baby is a boy then we cover him with a white cloth and if it is a baby girl, then a red cloth is used.' And touchingly, it was mentioned that if the family was very poor, just a little square patch of red or white fabric was buried along with the tiny body.

## Conclusion

In the civilizational traditions of India there has been an abiding merger between form and meaning; between the image and what is signified. In these conflations – the fertility of woman and earth, the red of the female, white of the male – there exists an aesthetics of representational meaning, a pattern of wholeness. The British colonizers perceived this as weakness, and this cultural semiotics of the body has been deeply disturbed by fragmentation and modernization.

Mayo's 'filth' and the colonial project of valorizing 'scientific' medicine seem to have succeeded. From our data and my own experiences in globalized 'Safe Motherhood' conferences it seems that concepts of 'development' have adopted the essentials of this project. Its ontological and epistemological under-pinnings mimic the colonial perspective on *dais*. Even the National Rural Health Mission, touted to address the health needs of the 'underserved' rural poor, has excluded *dais* from its purview.

Throughout India, *dais*, their female sacrality and birth rituals, are dying, literally and figuratively. Oxytocin injections are replacing rituals invoking *Bemata*, because the power to birth is increasingly understood by families, as well as doctors and policy-makers, not to reside in the mother's body but rather in 'science' – often the ritual use of 'scientific' medicine.

## Notes

1 'In fact, the initiatory symbolism of sacrifice is emphasized by its sexual and gyneco-logical symbolism. The texts are clear' (Eliade 2009: 110).
2 In the third round of the National Family Health Survey (NFHS-III: 2005–06 India Report, Vol. 1, Table 8.18), the data on 'Assistance at delivery' (all-India, all strata) shows the highest percentage for Dai (36.6%) compared to 35.2% for Doctor, 10.3% for ANM or Nurse-midwife, 16.2% Relative, 0.5% for No one (self-delivered) and 1.3% for Other/unknown.
3 Non-governmental organizations; here primarily MATRIKA and Jeeva.
4 MATRIKA (Motherhood and Traditional Research, Information, Knowledge and Action) was an NGO research project devoted to documenting traditional midwives' skills, knowledge and religio-cultural context. Workshops were conducted in four areas of north India: Bikaneer District, Rajasthan; Fategarh District, Punjab; Gomia District, Bihar; and the resettlement colonies of Delhi (see www.matrika-india.org). Jeeva, a collective of concerned health professionals, collected data from Chandankiari and Chas Blocks of Jharkhand in January and February of 2009. See 'Entering dais' world: Jeeva pilot project report, June 2010', available online.
5 Dr P. Girija, in a seminar, 'Back to the Future: Indigenous Medicine in Contemporary India', at Jawaharlal Nehru University, 2006.
6 'Indigenous systems of medicine: essential inputs for maternal health policies', paper presented by Janet Chawla and Anuradha Singh at Global Maternal Health Conference, 31 August 2010, New Delhi, India.

## References

Chawla, J. (2000) 'The conflation of the female body and earth in Indian religious tradi-tions: gendered representations of seed, earth and grain', in S. Marcos (ed.) *Gender / Bodies / Religions*. Mexico: ALER Publications.

—— (2002a) '*Hawa, gola* and mother-in-law's big toe: on understanding dais' imagery of the female body', in S. Rozario and G. Samuel (eds) *Daughters of Hariti: Childbirth and Female Healers in South and Southeast Asia*. London: Routledge.

—— (2002b) 'Negotiating Narak and writing destiny: the theology of Bemata in dais' handling of birth', in N. Chitgopetkar (ed.) *Invoking Goddesses, Gender Politics and Religion in India*. New Delhi: Har-Anand Publications.

Dube, L. (1986) 'Seed and earth: the symbolism of biological reproduction and sexual relations of production', in L. Dube, E. Leacock and S. Ardener (eds) *Visibility and Power: Essays on Women in Society and Development.* Delhi: Oxford University Press.

Eliade, M. (2009) *Yoga Immortality and Freedom.* Princeton and Oxford: Princeton University Press.

Malhotra, A. (2006) 'Of dais and midwives: "middle class" interventions in the management of women's reproductive health in colonial Punjab', in S. Hodges (ed.) *Reproductive Health in India: History, Politics, Controversies.* Hyderabad: Orient Longman.

Mayo, K. (1927) *Mother India,* 1977 edn. Delhi: Low Price Publications.

Mukherjee, S. (2001) 'Disciplining the body? Health care for women and children in early twentieth-century Bengal', in D. Kumar (ed.) *Disease and Medicine in India: A Historical Overview.* New Delhi: Tulika Books.

*New Jerusalem Bible* (1985) London: Darton, Longman and Todd.

Pinto, S. (2006) 'Divisions of labour: rethinking the "midwife" in rural Uttar Pradesh', in J. Chawla (ed.) *Birth and Birthgivers: The Power Behind the Shame.* New Delhi: Shakti Books.

Rao, V. (2006) 'Singing the female body', in J. Chawla (ed.) *Birth and Birthgivers: The Power Behind the Shame.* New Delhi: Shakti Books.

Samuel, G. (2005) 'Subtle bodies in Indian and Tibetan yoga: scientific and spiritual meanings', conference paper, 2nd International Conference on Religion and Cultures in the Indic Civilization, 17–20 December, Delhi.

—— (2006) 'Healing and the mind-body complex: childbirth and medical pluralism in South Asia', in H. Johannessen and I. Lázár (eds) *Multiple Medical Realities: Patients and Healers in Biomedical Alternative and Traditional Medicine.* New York and London: Berghahn Books.

Selby, M. A. (2005) 'Narratives of conception, gestation and labour in Sanskrit ̄ayurvedic texts', *Asian Medicine: Tradition and Modernity* 1: 254–74.

Singh, A. (2006) 'Her one foot is in this world and one in the other: Ayurveda, dais and maternity', in J. Chawla (ed.) *Birth and Birthgivers: The Power Behind the Shame.* New Delhi: Shakti Books.

Zysk, K. G. (1993) 'The science of respiration and the doctrine of the bodily winds in Ancient India', *Journal of the American Oriental Society* 113: 198–213.

## Part Two

# Subtle bodies in the Tibetan tradition

Part Two

# Subtle bodies in the Tibetan tradition

# Introduction to Part Two

## Geoffrey Samuel

The Tantric Buddhism of Tibet derived from Indian and perhaps also Central Asian sources. Buddhism was initially introduced into Tibetan society during the early empire (seventh to ninth centuries), with further Tantric lineages and practices being added during the tenth to twelfth centuries (Samuel 1993, 2012). These later lineages are distinguished as Sarmapa (*gsar ma pa*) or 'New' in contrast with the 'Old' tradition which claims origin in the early period. They are represented today by the Sakyapa, Kagyüpa and Gelugpa traditions, each deriving from a number of major teaching monasteries headed by high-status reincarnating lamas. The Bon tradition, which claims to go back to a pre-Buddhist teacher, Tönpa Shenrab, of Central Asian origin, preserves its own body of Tantric traditions, which are broadly similar to those of the Buddhist traditions. From the thirteenth century onwards, Mongolian populations in Central Asia were in contact with Tibetans, and Tibetan-style Buddhism was gradually established in Mongolia (Heissig 1980), where it competed and coexisted with indigenous shamanic traditions.

After the imposition of Chinese rule between 1949 and 1959, and the massive destruction associated with the Cultural Revolution in Tibet, Tibetan Buddhist yogic practices have mainly been preserved and continued in those borderland areas that remained outside Chinese control, and among refugee communities in India, Nepal and elsewhere. However, Tibetan Buddhism has gradually revived in Tibet, and has also been influential among mainland and overseas Chinese communities, and around the world.

Tibetan Buddhism incorporated the Tantric subtle-body practices from early on, and they became a central part of the training for a Tantric ritual practitioner or lama within Tibetan society.

Part Two consists of three chapters, all on themes relating to Tibetan Buddhism. Chapter 4, by Angela Sumegi, explores the relationship between shamanism and Buddhism. Shamanic-style discourse of lost or wandering 'souls' or 'spirits' is common in Tibetan and Mongolian Buddhist societies, but does not seem easily reconcilable with the classic Buddhist doctrine of 'no-soul' or 'no-self'. Sumegi suggests that neither world-view is as rigid s it might appear, and that the subtle-body concepts within Tantric Buddhism provide the scope to enable these apparently very different views of reality to coexist.

Barbara Gerke's discussion of subtle-body concepts in Tibetan medicine (Chapter 5) examines the difficult area of the overlap between Tantric and medical concepts. *Rtsa* (Skt. *nāḍī*), the term for the 'channels' of the subtle body, also refers in the medical context to the more straightforwardly material 'channels' that transfer blood, wind and water around the body, and Tibetan doctors have long been concerned about how the Tantric 'subtle body' relates to physical anatomy. Gerke questions what 'subtle' might actually mean in the medical context, and suggests caution about assuming that the medical 'channels' constitute a 'circulatory system'. Her chapter complicates our understanding of Tibetan ideas of the body in interesting and important ways.

Finally, Alejandro Chaoul (Chapter 6) looks at the application of Tibetan subtle-body (*rtsa rlung* or 'channel-breaths') practices from the Bön tradition in the contemporary Western medical context of cancer treatment. Here we can see some of the ways in which Tibetan approaches to health and human functioning can provide a practical complement to the approaches of Western biomedicine, and allow patients to participate actively in their own healing.

# References

Heissig, W. (1980) *The Religions of Mongolia*. London: Routledge and Kegan Paul and Berkeley and Los Angeles: University of California Press.

Samuel, G. (1993) *Civilized Shamans: Buddhism in Tibetan Societies*. Washington, DC: Smithsonian Institution Press.

—— (2012) *Introducing Tibetan Buddhism*. London and New York: Routledge.

# 4 On souls and subtle bodies

## A comparison of shamanic and Buddhist perspectives

*Angela Sumegi*

Meanwhile, when I was calling on my ongod, it seemed to me that something invisible embraced me suddenly and I became conscienceless [*sic*]. Afterwards it seemed very easy for me myself and I, riding on a nice horse, began to travel through unknown beautiful mountain, plain and river areas. During this time I met a lot of Grand-grand Fathers and Mothers (ongons) in a consecutive way. Unfortunately, I did not know what topics were they talking about. Only after their departure and my *return* I began to understand gradually, who were in my place, what they were talking or asking about etc.

(Quoted in Purev 2002: 129)

My mind expanded into a supremely blissful state, the essential nature of sheer lucidity in which I could not cling to anything as good or bad in the ordinary sense, like unborn space that is nothing at all in and of itself, yet with an absolutely unimpeded natural radiance ... I then had the sensation of climbing higher and higher into vaguely defined space, more swiftly than a wild white-tailed vulture soaring into the heavens ... I suddenly found myself in a place that I did not recognize ... In every direction were mountains ... Covering the ground in all directions were flowers of five lovely hues ... I experienced this realm as an actual place.

(Drolma 1995: 9–10)

The passages above are the recorded words of two twentieth-century women. The first describes the trance experience of Choin Dolgor (1902–51), a Mongolian female shaman. The second is taken from the account of Dawa Drolma (d. 1941), a devout Tibetan Buddhist who lay unconscious on her bed for five days in a state described as neither alive nor dead. Drolma's spirit journey as a *'das log* (one who has died and returned from the dead)[1] begins with a vision of four goddesses arriving on beams of rainbow light who carry her off in a litter. On her return to consciousness, she recounts experiences of beings and realms beyond this world, both wonderful and horrific.

Although the main features of these women's dream-like experiences are similar – an induced state of altered consciousness, preceded by a loss of consciousness (not regarded as ordinary sleep or a state of mere unconsciousness), and followed by sensations of travelling through strange landscapes and meeting various individuals that belong to their sacred worlds – the episodes are constructed within very different frameworks. From a shamanic perspective, the Mongolian shaman is simply reporting events that took place in the spirit world while her soul was separated from its body during trance. In the Buddhist environment of Dawa Drolma's account, her son, Lama Chagdud Rinpoché, interprets such experiences as 'the rich display of the nature of mind, experienced when meditation breaks through the limitations of ordinary perception' (Drolma 1995: x). Nevertheless, although his explanation situates her visions within the context of Buddhist theories of mind and meditation, her narration conforms to the shaman's account in that it purports to record an actual event. While her body lay as if dead, Drolma, like the shaman in trance, reported that 'she' was travelling in another world encountering particular places and persons.

Despite arguments that decry the analysis of a person in terms of radical body/mind or body/soul dualism, the idea of a fundamental duality underlying the complexities of human nature would appear common to cultures past and present. In her linguistic analysis of soul discourse among modern language speakers, Anna Wierzbicka (1989) offers evidence that soul concepts reflect a universal culture-independent belief that the visible material body is only one aspect of a person and that to be a person involves an immaterial counterpart, interpretations of which vary widely. Regardless of the way in which the counterpart is understood or analysed – whether as soul, mind, heart, life-force, or consciousness – and despite the permeability or interconnectedness of these categories, cross-culturally, the linguistic terms for 'person' or 'self' or 'I' assume a relationship between the purely physical body and that which is constituted as other than the body. In a shamanic complex, the activity of the shaman is predicated on belief in the distinction between body and soul. Contrary to shamanic discourse, the Buddhist doctrine of 'no-soul' or 'no-self' (*anātman*) denies any enduring substantial vitalistic essence as the basis of life or identity. Wherever Buddhism has encountered the beliefs and practices of shamanism, the canonical Buddhist negation of a soul entity has been challenged by the shamanistic affirmation of a soul that leaves the body. Yet, despite the difference in theory, Buddhists whose heritage includes ancestor veneration continue to make offerings to the souls of their dead ancestors, and shamanic practices of negotiating with evil spirits for the return of a lost or stolen soul appear in the Buddhist ritual repertoire.

Belief in a soul entity that endures beyond death is a common finding in Buddhist communities. In his analysis of Bön and Tibetan Buddhist rituals of recalling the soul, Samten Karmay (1998) concludes that the ritual of ransoming or repurchasing the soul (*bla bslu*) has its origins in the indigenous shamanic beliefs of Tibet; however, he also notes that the shamanic concept of soul implied in the ritual contradicts fundamental Buddhist doctrine. In a study of another Buddhist community, Nancy Eberhardt points out that among the Shan of Thailand, in order to allow for traditional soul belief, the *anātman* theory is popularly interpreted as 'having no control over oneself' or 'being unable to keep oneself from changing'. She goes on to say:

If questioned about it, a few people will be able to give a satisfactory account, but most will repeat an abbreviated version that they've been told and then direct you to the appropriate local specialist ... Meanwhile, they go about their lives, secure in the knowledge that someone, somewhere understands these things, while relying for their own needs on a less complicated and more intuitive understanding of the way things work.

(2006: 9)

The intuitive understanding is that there is some continuing aspect of the person that is responsible for the support of life and its departure signals death but not annihilation. Buddhist doctrine accords with this common feeling insofar as it accepts the idea of an individual mindstream that carries the karmic propensities and habit patterns of a person, and continues beyond death to be reborn in a different form. However, there are conflicting views regarding the ultimate nature of the one who continues from life to life. The *anātman* theory and its subsequent development in the Mahāyāna doctrine of *śūnyatā* (emptiness) represents the rejection of reification of any kind, especially of the type that shamanic soul theories present, but Tibetan Buddhist schools vary in their interpretations of what constitutes 'reification'. Although there is not space here to investigate the debates among Buddhists themselves regarding how the doctrine of emptiness is to be interpreted, we can note that in the attempt to negotiate a middle path between the danger of reification and the danger of nihilism, there are those Tibetan schools, like the Gelug, whose theories guard against the danger of reification, and those like the Nyingma, who guard against nihilism.[2]

My question is, considering the beliefs and rituals of ordinary Buddhists regarding the soul, as well as the yogic practices of adepts focused on the subtle energies of the body, do doctrine and experience, theory and practice ultimately diverge on this aspect of the interface between Buddhism and shamanism, or is there another perspective that can be brought to bear on the dichotomy between soul affirmation and soul negation? I suggest that one opportunity for resolution lies in the Buddhist concept of the subtle body. The notion of a complex psycho-physical body consisting of energy pathways and energy centres, adopted and adapted from a broader Indian yogic system,[3] is especially prominent in the Tibetan Vajrayāna form of Buddhism. Although the subtle body cannot be directly equated with the shamanic idea of soul, its description resonates with the dualistic and vitalistic language of shamanism and, therefore, suggests a basis for comparison through which one may identify possible points of overlap or resolution. In his discussions with Francisco Varela and the scientific community on the nature of subtle body forms, Tenzin Gyatso, the Fourteenth Dalai Lama, speaks of a 'special dream body [that] is able to disassociate entirely from the gross physical body and travel elsewhere' (Varela 1997: 39). He further asserts that 'it is possible in one's meditative practice to separate the very subtle energy-mind from the gross body and to bring it back' (1997: 207).

In this chapter, I am not concerned with whether or not phenomena such as spirits, souls, or subtle bodies actually exist or can wander about separated from the physical body; nor am I interested in their social or psychological features; my interest is in the ontological implications of such beliefs. In what follows, I compare the characteristics of soul in shamanism with subtle body in Vajrayāna Buddhism, and propose that the discourse related to both implies a shared belief in the ultimate and irreducible nature of personhood.

## A word on shamanism

On the contentious question of definitions, I follow the lead of scholars who have accepted an extended use of the terminology surrounding shamanism (Lewis 1971; Basilov 1999; Hoppál 1998; Samuel 1993), and who employ the category for analytic rather than descriptive purposes. As it is used here, 'shamanism' is a convenient label signifying a constellation of magico-religious beliefs and practices that appear cross-culturally in hunter-gatherer and small-scale agricultural communities. My working definition understands shamanism as grounded in an animistic world-view and involving distinctive practices that focus on the ability of certain individuals to induce and control various states of consciousness for the purpose of mediating between culturally accepted dimensions of the world in response to the needs of a particular group.

Shamanism thrives among diverse cultures that share certain beliefs – among them, the belief that humans coexist with all manner of non-human persons (animate and inanimate), that the world itself and its beings are constituted of visible and invisible dimensions, that intentional communication with the unseen aspect is dependent on the assistance of spirit persons, and that such communication takes place primarily through alternate states of consciousness ranging from trance and possession to dream or waking visions. Although shamanism is constellated differently among the societies in which it is found, certain basic elements imply that as a cultural category it can be treated with coherence. For exemplification, then, I will draw primarily from Mongolian shamanism with the understanding that there are many shamanisms that could illustrate the shamanic modalities highlighted in this chapter.

## Materiality and multiplicity

Anthropological research among animistic societies has identified a bewildering variety of soul concepts, yet from group to group, the descriptions exhibit a family resemblance – souls have shape and mobility, they experience suffering, are vulnerable to attack, illness and destruction, and can be of many types. Otgony Purev (2002: 153, 176), writing on the beliefs of Mongolian shamanism, reports that the souls of deceased shamans (*ongons*), although invisible, are said to have weight and are believed to be able to lift and transport physical objects weighing between five and eight kilograms within a ten-kilometre radius.[4] Like other spirits in the Mongolian shamanic environment such as the *lus* (water spirits),[5] *ongons* travel along well-defined pathways with rest stops along the way, often by a special tree or mountain pass. *Ongon* spirits are believed to be more active at night during the spring, and for ordinary people their movement manifests as the sound of drums or bells. Sleeping or hunting in such an area would be banned. *Ongons*, which are the deities invoked by shamans, are either spirits of the *lus* or souls of deceased human beings. They can be passed down from parent to child or from teacher to student, or even rented out for use by another (Purev 2002: 153–4). In Black shamanism,[6] upon death the souls of humans and animals pass from the light world of the living to the dark world of dead spirits, a gloomy place described as without destiny, thanks, happiness, attractiveness or life, where they exist by means of their own self-emanating light (Purev 2002: 128, 189). The dark world is invisible to ordinary people but accessible to shamans and it is understood that the spirits and *ongons* of the dark world include not only those who bring harm but those who protect and care for the world and its inhabitants.

With regard to different types of soul, shamanic societies generally identify more than one soul belonging to an individual; often these are linked with specific locations in the person's environment or with parts of the body. In Mongolian shamanism, there is the belief in three souls: two that eventually die, and an immortal one that continues after death. The flesh and bones of a living creature each have a mortal soul derived from the 'red seed of the mother' and the 'white seed of the father' respectively. In a brief article, Rinchen Yöngsiyebü describes them as follows:

> The host-souls are called *ejen sünesün* or shortly *ejen* – the host. The host-soul of the bones looks after them and secures their normal development. The aperture of the pelvis is its permanent seat and it lives after the death of the creature while the pelvis remains unbroken.[7] The host-soul of flesh cares for it and after the death of the creature guards its body and infects anyone who touches it. For three years it surveys the remains and dies after the full disappearance of the remains of flesh and sinews on the bones.
>
> (1984a: 25)

The third soul is the main soul, which is everlasting and which, after the death of its non-eternal body dwelling, wanders for three years existing on the scent offerings of food and drink offered by the family. Through subsequent death rituals that take place when the flesh has completely decayed from the bones, the souls of prominent clan chieftains or shamans become *ongons* and receive their *möngke bey-e* (Everlasting Bodies), represented by images made of felt, silk, wood, brass, horse-hair, clay or cotton. Such images were set up in the dwelling-place and worshipped with offerings and sacrifices. The soul of a commoner would not become an *ongon* but simply be joined to the communion of ancestral spirits (Yöngsiyebü 1984a: 25–6). In his 1846 essay, Dorji Banzarov claimed that *ongons* were the souls of shamans or people famous for good or evil deeds. Exactly who became an *ongon* was determined by the clan shaman. Good *ongons* lived peacefully on the earth with people but evil *ongons* were consigned to an intermediate region between this world and the next. They roamed around bringing illness and destroying children. Only the shaman could determine which *ongon* was causing the trouble and cast him out (Banzarov 1981: 78).

Caroline Humphrey's study (1999) of Mongolian death rituals in Ulaanbaatar in the 1980s reflects Buddhist elements as well as traditional shamanic or folk beliefs, as, for example, in the continued fear of the corpse and the souls that guard it. She notes that no one stays with the body, which is locked up in an empty yurt or in a room set apart for the dead person. When the time comes to transport the corpse to the burial place, the 'bone carrying person' (the one designated as the main escort for the corpse) wears his clothes and hat inside out or back to front, and at crossroads or streams sprinkles offerings of rice, millet, tea and coins along the route to the grave. The offerings are intended variously to prevent the soul from taking those paths or to pacify evil spirits who may follow the cortege (Humphrey 1999: 73). According to her research, among the preparatory rites related to the corpse is a simple shape or sign marked on the body with soot from a cooking pot. In the future, the sign would be looked for as a birthmark on a new baby signifying, in a Buddhist context, the rebirth of the dead person. This practice relates also to the notion in Mongol Black shamanism of a wandering or 'vagrant' soul, which is guided through such markings by the shaman to find its 'target body' (Purev 2002: 145).

Another belief of the Mongols that Humphrey studied is that upon death, the soul is thought to enter into an uncertain period where it possesses or takes up residence in some animal or insect. After 49 days, the soul is finally released from the animal form and finds its way to its next rebirth. Somewhat contradictory is the further belief that upon death, the soul is said to hide or take shelter in a certain object familiar to the dead person. This object needs to be discovered through divination and removed from the family home so that the soul can move on, let go of its attachments, and not disturb the family. Divination is required because no one knows what the object may be, not even the dying person, since it is not the person's conscious choice but the soul's choice (Humphrey 1999: 67–70).

Such beliefs indicate that in this and many other shamanic complexes, the quasi-material, multiple spirit-energies or 'souls' of an individual, although intrinsically linked to the physical body, frequently behave like separate persons themselves, in that they communicate, transform, and possess agency to act independently. The shamanic world is one in which the various powers or capacities of a person – to live, to dream, to move this or that limb, to heal – are constituted as beings in themselves with their own powers and limitations.

Despite the Buddhist rejection of the soul as a distinct vital or metaphysical entity that transmigrates from life to life, an idea comparable to the separable soul of shamanic belief can be found in the concept of a subtle mental body separable from the physical body. Learning how to actualize and work with a mental body formed part of the gradual training of a monk from the earliest days of the Buddhist monastic order. The successful practitioner is required to identify clearly the nature of and distinction between body and mind. Based on this knowledge, the monk further practises to create a mental body that is described, much like the shamanic soul, as having characteristics of form, shape, etc. According to the *Dīgha Nikāya*,

> And he, with mind concentrated ... having gained imperturbability, applies and directs his mind to the production of a mind-made body. And out of this body he produces another body, having a form, mind-made, complete in all its limbs and faculties.
>
> (Walshe 1987: 104)

The process is described as though one were to draw out a reed from its sheath or a sword from its scabbard. The monk is expected to distinguish unmistakably between the mental and the physical bodies – just as a person could say, 'This is the sword, this is the scabbard, sword and scabbard are different. Now the sword has been drawn from the scabbard' (Walshe 1987: 104).

In the Vajrayāna Buddhism of Tibet, one of the most well-known sources for the description of a subtle body is the *Bar do thos grol*. Popularly known in the West as the *Tibetan Book of the Dead*, it contains guidance for recognizing the nature of mind in daily practice, the signs and stages of dying, and instructions to be recited for the dead or dying to remind them of what to expect as the process unfolds. The text reminds the practitioner of the opportunity for enlightenment that now presents itself, of how to negotiate the terrors of death, and of how to choose a good rebirth. The *Bar do thos grol* describes the characteristics of a subtle body that exists after death in a series of intermediate states (*bar do*) between death and rebirth. The dead person is told, 'The body that you now have is called a "mental body", it is the product of [subtle] propensities and not a solid corporeal body of flesh and blood' (Dorje 2006: 236). Further:

> Your awareness is now separated from its [gross] physical support. Therefore, this is not a body of solid form. Accordingly, you now have the ability to move unobstructedly; penetrating to the core of all forms, you can pass through Mount Sumeru, and through dwellings, the earth, stones, boulders and mountains.
>
> (2006: 275)

In this subtle form, as in the ordinary physical body, the person experiences all the sense perceptions, and can even faint from overpowering emotions of fear and terror (2006: 255–6). The mental body also has a specific recognizable shape; at first it is said to look like the former physical body, but later it takes on the aspect of the future body of rebirth and the person is able to recognize others who are to be born in the same cosmological world (2006: 274–6). The *Bar do thos grol* also encompasses the shamanic belief that the seen and unseen dimensions of the world intersect. For example, the dead person, in a mental body form, sees the physical family gathered at the death bed and hears their cries (2006: 232). Interestingly, although the mental body of the *bar do* state is of the same type as the mental body of the dream state, in ordinary dreams there are sense perceptions but no material sense objects on which the perceptions are based, whereas the *bar do* state (and certain other special dream states) appears to be one in which material and immaterial dimensions function interactively without losing any of their characteristics.

Just as shamanic systems identify several kinds of soul, similarly, different kinds of subtle body are described in Vajrayāna Buddhism. Although the typology of the subtle body is very complex, for our purposes it is enough to have a sense of some basic divisions. The ordinary dream body or *bar do* body (*yid lus*) spontaneously arises in the dream or *bar do* state. The illusory body (*sgyu lus*) is generated by tantric practice related to the subtle channels and 'winds' or energies (*rtsa rlung*), and finally, the rainbow body (*'ja lus*), particular to the rDzogs chen (Great Perfection) tradition in the rNying ma School, is recognized by the total dissolution of the physical body at death, signifying buddhahood.[8]

Worth noting here is that in Buddhist thought, mind or consciousness is always linked with a corresponding support (ranging from gross to extremely subtle). With regard to the subtle body, the Dalai Lama uses the term 'energy-mind' to indicate the inseparable nature of mind and its support (Varela 1997: 92–5). Expanding on this correlation, a rNying ma scholar commented that the dream body or *bar do* body (*yid lus*) is spontaneously actualized by a mind that is still habituated to strong dualistic thought patterns and the sense of an inherently existing self. The illusory body (*sgyu lus*) related to the subtle channels and energies is actualized, through training, by a more subtle mind, more purified of dualistic habit patterns and self-conceptions, and the rDzogs chen rainbow body (*'ja lus*) is actualized by a mindstream that is completely purified of all karmic traces.[9]

The various types of subtle body, then, indicate the actualization of the person in a form that corresponds to the grossness or subtleness of the associated mental state as well as to the level of mental purification from karmic habits such as grasping onto the identity of self and other. The subtle body manifests either spontaneously and unintentionally (i.e. driven by karma), as in the dreams and death of ordinary people, or intentionally, by means of training through meditation and spiritual practice. Similarly, in shamanic traditions, the role of training and practice is crucial in the development of the shaman's ability to enter intentionally into spirit form.

## Transformation

The animistic perspective has been famously characterized by the Chukchi quote recorded by Bogoras (1904–09: 281): 'All that exists lives. The lamp walks around. The walls of the house have voices of their own.' However, an animistic world-view does not necessarily imply that life or soul is a given characteristic of inanimate things. In her book dealing with the beliefs and practices of the Daur Mongols, Caroline Humphrey (Humphrey and Onon 1996: 59) recounts a story in which an ordinary tree, chosen for its prominence in the landscape, which would make it suitable as a resting spot for *ongons*, began to be worshipped as a sacred tree. Subsequent to the rituals of worship, the tree was thought to be possessed of an in-dwelling spirit. In other words, the act of worship represents a process of interrelating through which both worshipper and worshipped are constituted as persons. In her consideration of Mongol death rituals and the meanings placed on grave goods and other things related to the dead, Humphrey points to the processes of 'objectification', through which persons and things are mutually constituted and transformed. 'Material things and living beings have surfaces, but they also have interiors, which are mysterious. The [dead person's] soul can in theory penetrate (*orshi-*) an object or animal and be inside it' (Humphrey 1999: 79). She concludes: 'there are various distinctive networks of associations that change the content of "persons" and "objects" through action' (1999: 80).

The status of the beings that populate the Mongol shamanic environment depends, then, on their involvement and interaction with others, and the interpretations placed on personal encounters. From a shamanic perspective, to say 'all that exists lives' is not to assign spirit life simplistically or automatically to inanimate objects but to recognize the independence and integrity of each thing and its capacity for interaction, interrelationship and transformation. So the Mongolians can say that a chipped cup is no more a cup, it is a dead soul and should not be used for living people (Purev 2002: 141). Similarly, among humans the permanent separation of the soul from the body results in death and a separate existence in another realm for the soul-person. The transformation from one state of being to another – human to spirit, life to death, or from unborn to birth – is a function of the activity of the soul. The soul is also the vehicle by which alternate or ecstatic states are accessed temporarily, as for example during the soul-journey trances of the shaman, during possession, or in dream.

Although Vajrayāna Buddhism upholds the denial of a substantial soul, the persistence of the personality beyond death is explained through the continuation of the person (characterized like all compounded phenomena as impermanent, essenceless, and subject to suffering) in a subtle body/mind form. The *Bar do thos grol* describes three *bar do* states associated with death and rebirth. The *chos nyid bar do* is the period of the disintegration and dissolution of the gross body/mind at death and the arising of a subtle body, which continues throughout the process. The *'chi kha'i bar do* is a period of visions or hallucinations both beautiful and horrific, and the *srid pa'i bar do* is the period when the person, exhausted by the fear and instability of existing in that mental body, seeks for a womb in which to be established. With regard to personal transformation, then, the subtle body is similar in function to the shamanic soul, since it is by means of the subtle body that the 'person' separates from the physical body at death, traverses the *bar do* states, and is born into another physical form. It is by means of the subtle body that the trained practitioner can travel to other realms in the Buddhist cosmology as shamans travel to the spirit world. Finally, in tantric practice, it is the subtle body that the practitioner must access and work with in order to achieve the ultimate spiritual transformation from an unenlightened to an enlightened state.

## Personhood

Shamanic souls and Buddhist subtle bodies are both described as having characteristics of materiality and mobility. They are regarded as vehicles of personal transformation, and in both cases training is required to intentionally actualize an invisible form of oneself in order to be able to act in that form, making use of its particular characteristics. The underlying concepts of personhood, however, which support the ideas of soul and subtle body, and are supported by them, would appear to be radically different. From a shamanic perspective, the spirit or soul of a thing signifies its most fundamental mode of existence, its 'being in relation'. Further, the interpenetration of material and spirit dimensions does not imply any ultimate eradication of difference. In shamanism, personhood and the integrity of separate things are irreducible. To be is to exist with the capacity for relationship – in other words, with the capacity to be a person.

In Mahāyāna Buddhism, the opposite would appear to be the case. The practitioner aims to realize the essenceless, illusory nature of persons and things. Self-identity along with conceptions of other-identity are regarded as convenient fictions. Moreover, the Tibetan rDzogs chen tradition of Vajrayāna Buddhism presents a cosmogony in which the fiction of existence extends into the physical world, which is said to evolve from manifestations of light into illusory experiences of solidity and materiality.[10] In the text commonly known as *sNang sbyang* ('Refining One's Perception') composed by the nineteenth-century rNying ma pa master bDud 'joms gling pa (Dudjom Lingpa), the transformation from light into solidity is described as unfolding stage by stage, dependent on the reifying mind and the appropriation of self and other as substantially, inherently existing entities (Dudjom Lingpa 2002: 95–6). According to rDzogs chen theory, the successful accomplishment of its esoteric practices can also bring about the reverse, resulting at death in the complete disappearance of the physical body of flesh and blood. One who realizes this state is said to have attained the rainbow body (*'ja lus*), which signifies the complete reversal of the process of materialization; the dissolution of all reifications. In the words of the fourteenth-century rDzogs chen master kLong chen Rab 'jams pa (quoted in Kapstein 2004: 145):

> As when a pot breaks, so that the space within and the space without become so intermingled that one cannot tell them apart, here one is awakened in buddhahood, not distinguishing the body that has been reduced to its atomic constituents from the awareness within.

In the rDzogs chen tradition, the universe of sense experiences and separate existents is a function of the dynamic nature or presence (*lhun grub*) of an ineffable ground of being (*gzhi*), which is imbued with primordial awareness (*ye shes*), and which spontaneously actualizes itself out of a state of 'interiorized potentiality', manifesting initially as light (Cuevas 2003: 59–60). According to Dudjom Lingpa's *sNang sbyang* text (2002: 173), when awareness does not recognize itself in the display of its own qualities, then the natural energy of that ignorance manifests as the conceptualizing mind, which mistakenly appropriates self and other as separate substantial entities, thereby investing its own formless, limitless qualities with the boundaries of space, time, and materiality that it does not inherently possess. That which appears to possess separate existence is said to be like the reflection of stars in the ocean. In reality, there is nothing but water, regardless of the number of stars reflected in it (2002: 103). This metaphor, of course, breaks down if we consider the stars to have some separate reality, even if the reflection does not. The point of the example, however, is to show that nothing exists above or beyond the disparate reflections, which are nothing but the ground of being manifesting its own qualities of emptiness and awareness, inseparable from the appearances themselves.

Such a view would seem to undermine utterly the world of separate existences. It implies that self and other are mere illusions and that relationship of any kind is ultimately deception. Yet, on closer examination, from the rDzogs chen perspective, the ground of existence is not any kind of ground as such, from which all things arise and into which all things resolve. 'Ground of existence' is better understood as signifying the dynamic relations between certain fundamental qualities or capacities that exist primordially: emptiness or spaciousness (*stong pa nyid*) – the limitless potential for all phenomena to arise; timeless intelligence or awareness (*ye shes*); and pervasive compassion (*thugs rje*). Here, compassion has the sense of responsiveness, resonance or pervasive energy. At the same time it indicates that in rDzogs-chen theory, the ultimate nature of all existence is invested with the ethic of compassion – not as belonging to the dichotomy of good and evil, but as a natural function of interrelatedness actualized by those who attain Buddhahood. These qualities do not inhere in any more basic state; they do not exist apart from the separate entities of the phenomenal world that alternately appear and disappear, manifesting the dynamic energy of the interplay between emptiness and awareness. To attain the rainbow body is to attain the complete dissolution of the person experienced as a material entity, but at the same time, it heralds the arising of a buddha person in which personhood is not limited either by the individuation and separateness characteristic of material entities, or by the non-differentiation and non-action characteristic of sheer immateriality or nothingness.

## Conclusion

Soul discourse in shamanism deals with the recognition of the quality of personhood and intentionality inherent in all things. Shamanic soul theories are, therefore, the conceptual means by which every aspect of human experience, all 'others', can be personalized, both in the sense of apprehending the other as person, capable of direct communication and interaction, and in the sense of making the relationship personal, that is, concerned with me as an individual or with us as a group. In contrast, for Vajrayāna Buddhism, notions of subtle body serve as the conceptual means by which personhood and the individual identity of things can be progressively apprehended as illusory and empty of any real existence. The illusion of difference, identity and substantial reality, however, is not to be replaced by the illusion of its opposite: non-difference, non-identity and unreality.

The widespread Mahāyāna doctrine of the three bodies of the Buddha is based on the idea that embodiment – however refined or rarified – is characteristic of Buddhahood. The reality body (*dharmakāya*), which represents enlightened mind, emptiness, limitless potential for being, is formless, but the enjoyment body (*sambhogakāya*) is the luminous subtle form of an enlightened one, perceived by those who have realized a commensurately subtle mind; and the emanation body (*nirmāṇakāya*) is the compassionate buddha form perceived by ordinary conceptual minds. Bryan Cuevas points out that in the doctrines of the rDzogs chen tradition, the three bodies are intimately related to the fundamental ground of existence, which is described in terms of its essence (*ngo bo*) that is emptiness – corresponding to the reality body; its nature (*rang bzhin*) that is luminous awareness – related to the enjoyment body; and its pervasive compassion (*thugs rje*) that is energy or responsiveness – related to the emanation body. He states: 'The cosmos in its primordial condition is thus shown to be always already harmonious with the thoroughly awakened embodiment of buddhahood' (2003: 59).

Just as Siberian shamanic culture recognizes and expresses the personhood of the humblest object – human excrement – in the humorous image of 'a ribald old man dressed in sleek brown furs, boastful but secretly afraid of being eaten by dogs' (Reid 2002: 4), so the three bodies of the Buddha express the primordial personhood of the most sublime state of liberation. By very different routes the concepts of soul and subtle body both lead to the resolution of the physical and the spiritual in the notion of 'person', not as a fixed category but as limitless dynamic potential for action, communication, and relationship – inseparable from being.

## Notes

1 In his work on the Tibetan narrative tradition relating to the *'das log*, Bryan Cuevas (2008) has translated a number of reports dating from the sixteenth to the eighteenth centuries. In all these writings, the person's 'death' is the involuntary result of a serious illness, and the various experiences are linked to that single dramatic event. The research of Françoise Pommaret in the 1980s, however, presents a different pattern. She notes: 'they do not travel to the netherworld only once, as the biographies let us suppose, but at regular intervals during "séances", which occur on auspicious days of the month. In fact, delok are akin to shamans, but shamans who have been Buddhicized in such a way and for such a long time that they have lost the memory of their shamanistic origin' (1997: 508). In Dawa Drolma's account, her death is voluntarily induced as a remedy for the illness. In that way, she may represent a position somewhere between the earlier narratives and the *'das log* studied by Pommaret, who, like shamans, enter into their journeys voluntarily and regularly in order to benefit their clients or to act as guides for the dead.

2 Very simply put, the Gelug order regards emptiness as a 'non-affirming negative', meaning that it refers only to the fact that phenomenal entities lack inherent existence, whereas the Nyingma order regards emptiness as a positive quality of the ultimate nature of existence. One might think of it a bit like the difference between the perception of an empty bucket as containing nothing versus the perception of it as full of space.

3 Whether or not the Indian Tantric subtle-body system originated indigenously or through the influence of the alchemical endeavors of the Chinese is still a matter of debate. However, Geoffrey Samuel notes: 'The elaborate internal structure of the subtle body, with the series of *cakras* along the central channel, has no real precedent in Indian material, for all that the language in which it is described is entirely Indic' (2008: 281).

4 Interesting exclusions to this ability are gold, silver, jewels, state securities, and things like a brick of Russian tea because of the state emblem on it.

5 According to Purev (2002: 91), the *lus* are said to have specific running routes through the atmosphere between earth and sky that are about 1.6 metres in width and of indefinite length.

6 Traditionally, Mongol shamans were identified as either White or Black; White shamans worshipped and called on peaceful, benevolent White spirits, Black shamans dealt with the powerful and terrifying Black spirits. Under the influence of Buddhism, those that followed the new faith were known as Yellow shamans. Although distinctions between the three are still drawn, eventually 'Black Faith' (*qara šajin*) became the general signifier of the shamanic tradition in contradistinction to Buddhism, the 'Yellow Faith' (*sira šajin*) (Banzarov 1981: 56; Yöngsiyebü 1984b; Purev 2002).

7 The bone soul exists as a kind of ghost that wanders about at night and can harm those it encounters.

8 The fourteenth-century rDzogs chen master kLong chen Rab 'jams pa identifies four types of bodily dissolution at death based on esoteric practice: passing away with no physical remains; vanishing in the midst of a mass of light and sound; vanishing in a great conflagration of light; and the dissolution of the body into space and awareness. This last is known as rainbow body (Kapstein 2004: 144–5; Thondup 2002: 82–6).

9 Private conversation with Khenpo Tsewang Gyatso, August 2005. From a Bon rDzogs chen perspective, see also Lopon Tenzin Namdak's commentary on the relationship between rainbow body and the three bodies of the Buddha in Shardza Tashi Gyaltsen (1993: 79).

10 For a concise summary of rDzogs chen cosmogony see Cuevas (2003: 59–60).

## References

Banzarov, D. (1981 [1846]) 'The Black Faith, or shamanism among the Mongols', trans. J. Nattier and J. R. Krueger, *Mongolian Studies* 7: 53–91.

Basilov, V. N. (1999) 'Cosmos as everyday reality in shamanism: an attempt to formulate a more precise definition of shamanism', in R. Mastromattei and A. Rigopoulos (eds) *Shamanic Cosmos: From India to the North Pole Star*. Venice: Venetian Academy of Indian Studies.

Bogoras, W. (1904–09) *The Chukchee*, Jesup North Pacific Expedition, vol. 7, New York.

Cuevas, B. J. (2003) *The Hidden History of the Tibetan Book of the Dead*. Oxford: Oxford University Press.

—— (2008) *Travels in the Netherworld: Buddhist Popular Narratives of Death and the Afterlife in Tibet*. Oxford: Oxford University Press.

Dorje, G. (trans) (2006) *The Tibetan Book of the Dead*. New York: Viking.

Drolma, D. D. (1995) *Delog: Journey to Realms Beyond Death*, trans. R. Barron. Junction City, CA: Padma Publishing.

Dudjom Lingpa (2002) *Buddhahood Without Meditation: A Visionary Account Known as Refining One's Perception (Nang-jang)*, trans. R. Barron. Junction City, CA: Padma Publishing.

Eberhardt, N. (2006) *Imagining the Course of Life: Self-Transformation in a Shan Buddhist Community*. Honolulu: University of Hawai'i Press.

Hoppál, M. (1998) 'Shamanism: an archaic and/or recent system of beliefs', in M. Hoppál and A.-L. Siikala (eds) *Studies on Shamanism*. Budapest: Akadémiai Kiadó.

Humphrey, C. (1999) 'Rituals of death in Mongolia: their implications for understanding the mutual constitution of persons and objects and certain concepts of property', *Inner Asia* 1: 59–86.

Humphrey, C. and Onon, U. (1996) *Shamans and Elders: Experience, Knowledge, and Power Among the Daur Mongols*. Oxford: Clarendon Press.

Kapstein, M. T. (2004) 'The strange death of Pema the demon tamer', in M. T. Kapstein (ed.) *The Presence of Light: Divine Radiance and Religious Experience*. Chicago: University of Chicago Press.

Karmay, S. G. (1998) 'The soul and the turquoise: a ritual for recalling the bla', in S. G. Karmay (ed.) *The Arrow and the Spindle: Studies in History, Myths, Rituals and Beliefs in Tibet*. Kathmandu: Mandala Book Point.

Lewis, I. M. (1971) *Ecstatic Religion: A Study of Shamanism and Spirit Possession*. London: Routledge.

Pommaret, F. (1997) 'Returning from hell', in D. S. Lopez Jr (ed.) *Religions of Tibet in Practice*. Princeton: Princeton University Press.

Purev, O. (2002) *The Religion of Mongolian Shamanism*, trans. G. Purvee, N. Pureviin and E. Cheng, 2nd edn, vol. 1. Ulaanbaatar: 'Genco' University College.

Reid, A. (2002) *The Shaman's Coat: A Native History of Siberia*. London: Phoenix.

Samuel, G. (1993) *Civilized Shamans: Buddhism in Tibetan Societies*. Washington DC: Smithsonian Institution Press.

—— (2008) *The Origins of Yoga and Tantra: Indic Religions to the Thirteenth Century*. Cambridge: Cambridge University Press.

Shardza, T. G. (2002) *Heart Drops of Dharmakaya*, trans. Lopon Tenzin Namdak, 2nd edn. Ithaca, NY: Snow Lion Publications.

Thondup, T. (trans.) (2002) *The Practice of Dzogchen by Longchen Rabjam*, 3rd edn. Ithaca, NY: Snow Lion Publications.

Varela, F. J. (ed.) (1997) *Sleeping, Dreaming, and Dying: An Exploration of Consciousness with the Dalai Lama*. Boston, MA: Wisdom Publications.

Walshe, M. (trans.) (1987) *Thus Have I Heard: The Long Discourses of the Buddha Digha Nikaya*. London: Wisdom Publications.

Wierzbicka, A. (1989) 'Soul and mind: linguistic evidence for ethnopsychology and cultural history', *American Anthropologist*, 41–58.

Yöngsiyebü, R. (1984a) 'Everlasting bodies of the ancestral spirits in Mongolian shamanism', *Journal of the Anglo-Mongolian Society* 9: 25–6.

—— (1984b) 'White, Black and Yellow shamans among the Mongols', *Journal of the Anglo-Mongolian Society* 9: 19–24.

# 5 On the 'subtle body' and 'circulation' in Tibetan medicine

*Barbara Gerke*

## Subtleties or 'subtle body'?

In recent years, the term 'subtle body' has appeared in the discussion of Tibetan medicine in both academic and popular literature by Tibetan and Western authors, myself included (e.g. Asshauer 2005: 52; Clifford 1994: 71; Drungtso 2008: 171; Gerke 2007: 193; Millard 2007: 265; Parfionovitch *et al.* 1992: 39). These authors talk about the 'subtle body' in relation to mind-body connections, in particular the channels of the body (*rtsa*), the movement of wind (*rlung*), and the subtle life essence (*bla*). Although discussed in medical contexts, the term 'subtle body' remains medically largely undefined, and its understanding is mostly linked to Tibetan Buddhist tantric body concepts.

Without discrediting the contributions of these individual authors and their scholarship, in this chapter[1] I want to reflect critically on two issues arising from an uncritical use of the term 'subtle body' in a Tibetan medical context. First, I want to analyse in more detail what is 'subtle' about this 'subtle body' and what links the *rtsa* to a notion of a 'subtle body' in classical Tibetan medicine. Second, again without doubting the valuable work of these authors, I want to question the use of terms involving ideas of circulation when talking about *rtsa*, for example 'circulatory channel' (Garrett and Adams 2008: 92; Garrett 2008: 9) or 'circulatory system' (Clark 1995: 56; Garrett 2008: 64).

This chapter sets out two arguments. My argument in relation to the first issue is that while there are subtle aspects in Tibetan medical concepts of the body, we need to be careful in talking about a separate entity of a 'subtle body' as such. My second argument is more preliminary in nature and suggests that Tibetan medical 'circulatory systems' or 'circulatory channels' do not necessarily move in circulation in the Western sense of the term, and therefore such terms, both in themselves or as translations of Tibetan medical terms, should be used more cautiously.

*Rtsa* in Tibetan medical usage are complex pathways; the term has been translated as 'channel', 'vein', 'artery', 'nerve' or 'pulse',[2] depending on the context (Millard 2007: 265). *Rtsa* mainly transport blood (*khrag*), wind/respiration (*rlung*), and water (*chu; chu'i rtsa* are often translated as 'nerves'), but also the mind (*sems*), nutrients and waste products. In the eighth to tenth century Tibetan medical texts from Dunhuang – the first documented mention of *rtsa* in a medical context – *rtsa* relate mainly to the practice of blood-letting (Yan 2007: 302). Around the twelfth century, the Rgyud bzhi[3] mentions four main types of channels with sub-channels and a wide variety of functions. They can only be briefly summarized here:[4]

1   The 'channels of formation' (*chags pa'i rtsa*) are three channels that extend up, down and outwards from the navel during embryonic formation and generate (a) the brain and its white channels (*rtsa dkar*), (b) the black channel (*rtsa nag*) and its vessel, and (c) the genitals. The second of these three channels – the black channel – is the disputed life-channel (*srog rtsa*), further discussed below.

2   The 'channels of existence' (*srid pa'i rtsa*) are situated in the brain, heart, navel and genitals and are responsible for sensory experience, memory and clarity of mind, body growth, and the continuation of the family lineage respectively.

3   The 'channels of connections' (*'brel ba'i rtsa*) are black (blood) and white (water) channels that each diffuse from the right and left main channel.

4   The 'vitality channels' (*tshe'i rtsa*), also called 'channels where life abides' (*tshe gnas pa'i rtsa*), 'form the basis of life as such' (Parfionovitch *et al.* 1992: 39–40). They are discussed in the last section of this chapter.

All of these four main types of channels have been the cause for debate for centuries in terms of their functions and categories, their link to Buddhist tantric body concepts, as well as the hundreds of auxiliary channels surrounding them (Gyatso 2004: 87–90).

In Tibetan medical contexts, the first group of the above listed four main types of channels – the three 'channels of formation' – are linked to the three *nyes pa* in the sense that each of the channels reaches the upper, middle and lower areas of the body respectively, each of which is the predominant seat of one of the three *nyes pa*.[5] The three *nyes pa* – the term has often erroneously been translated as 'humour' – are the basic principles of Tibetan medical physiology that are embedded within the larger cosmology of the five elements: water, fire, earth, wind and space. The three principles are *rlung* (in which the wind element dominates), *mkhris pa* (in which the fire element dominates), and *bad kan* (in which the elements of earth and water dominate).[6] Each *nyes pa* has five subdivisions, is connected to a specific location in the body, and has its own functions. Very briefly, the five types of *rlung* organize all functions related to movement, e.g. of blood, muscles, breath, food, thoughts; the five types of *mkhris pa* are mainly responsible for the digestive process and for regulating body temperature; the five types of *bad kan* lubricate the joints, make the tissues soft, and give stability to the whole body.

Channels were not only linked to the three *nyes pa* but also to tantric Buddhist views of the body. Here are two examples of how Tibetan physicians – who were also trained in Buddhism – consolidated tantric Buddhist views with the medical views of the channels in the body. Zurkar Lodo Gyalpo (*zur mkhar blo gros rgyal po*; 1509–79), Desi Sangye Gyatso (*sde srid sangs rgyas rgya mtsho*; 1653–1705), and the twentieth-century scholar Tsultrim Gyaltsen (*tshul khrims rgyal mtshan*; d. 2001)[7] have linked the three 'channels of formation' to the three tantric channels, explained below (Garrett and Adams 2008: 89).[8] In particular, the life-channel (*srog rtsa*) has been seen by some Tibetan doctors as equivalent to the central channel (Skt. *suṣumnā*, Tib. *dbu ma*) of the Buddhist tantric system (Garrett and Adams 2008: 92). Tsultrim Gyaltsen also correlates the four 'channels of existence' to the four *cakras* of the Buddhist tantric tradition even though this is not mentioned in the Rgyud bzhi (Garrett and Adams 2008: 89).

Such associated interpretations of Tibetan medical and Buddhist body concepts are not unusual. The corpus of Tibetan medical textual knowledge developed from the eighth century onwards, drawing from Indian and Chinese as well as other neighbouring and indigenous medical, religious and tantric knowledge systems. Increasingly after the fourteenth century, medicine in Tibet was deeply interlinked with Buddhism,[9] and also state control (Schaeffer 2003). Therefore, we often find medical texts referring to advanced Buddhist practices, and boundaries between what is considered medicine and what belongs to religious realms become blurred.

The ideas of the Indian tantric body channels came to Tibet along with tantric Buddhist knowledge, particularly through the Kālacakra Tantra in the eleventh century. In the Indian Tantric traditions, the channels are called *nāḍīs* and in their subtle form are understood as inner pathways for the motile wind. The Kālacakra Tantra mentions 72,000 *nāḍīs* – some of which are presided over by deities in the form of consonants. This alludes to a view of the body 'as a tantric text, consisting of mantras and letters that provide a blueprint of the mind-body complex' (Wallace 2008: 179, 184). *Cakras* (lit. 'wheel') are the nexus centres in the body where many *nāḍīs* come together. There are many different traditions, but the main *cakras* are generally shown vertically aligned along the spine and linked to the three tantric channels – the 'central', 'flavour' and 'solitary' channel (Skt. *suṣumnā, piṅgalā, iḍā*); in Tibetan they are known as *dbu ma, ro ma* and *rkyang ma*; *cakras* are known as *'khor lo*.

Among the Tibetan tantric body concepts of the Kālacakra Tantra, the 'vajra body' (*sku rdo rje* or *rdo rje lus*) comes probably closest to an idea of a 'subtle body', and it is usually this 'vajra body' that Tibetan doctors refer to when asked about a 'subtle body'. Some Tibetan physicians apologize, saying that the 'subtle body' is not really part of their medical domain, but then refer to this tantric 'vajra body' (Asshauer 2005: 52–3). Medically, the 'vajra body' plays a role in the *rtsa rlung* practices (*rtsa rlung 'khrul 'khor gyi bcos thabs*; Skt. *yantra yoga*), advanced yogic Vajrayāna practices that influence the flow of *rlung* inside the *rtsa* (Chaoul 2007; Loseries-Leick 1997; Norbu 1998). These practices are not part of regular institutional Tibetan medical education and require special initiations, visualization training, and retreat conditions.

The channel debate in Tibetan medicine has mainly centred on the three tantric channels, their formation and visibility, as well as the movement of the 'subtle life essence' (*bla*). In the following, first I want to analyse various 'subtle' forms of the body as described in Tibetan medical texts, specifically the Rgyud bzhi (Gonpo 1992) and its famous commentary, the Baiḍūrya sngon po by Desi Sangye Gyatso (Gyatso 1982). I limit myself here to those medical ideas that are literally labelled 'subtle' in these two medical texts. In a preliminary attempt to trace the movement in the channels, I then look at visual presentations of the channels in medical paintings (*sman thang* or *thang ka*), which were prepared in the seventeenth century on the basis of the Baiḍūrya sngon po (Parfionovitch *et al.* 1992).

The Tibetan terms for 'subtle' are *'phra ba, 'phra' ba, phra ba,* or *phra mo,*[10] which all indicate the concept of something subtle, fine or slender that is small in size and hard to see with one's eyes, such as in *gzugs phra mo* ('a small body'), in *yul phra ba* ('little things'), or *skye ldan phra rab* ('micro-organism'). We find a distinction between 'subtle' (*'phra ba*) and 'extremely subtle' (*shin tu phra ba*), as well as 'subtle' in opposition to 'coarse' (*rags pa*).

That for Tibetans 'subtle' (*phra ba*) is primarily associated with something 'small in size' became clear to me when I asked Dr Tsering Wangdue, lecturer at the Men-Tsee-Khang College in Dharamsala, India, about the 'subtle body' in Tibetan medicine. He first said that it was something monks would sometimes debate about when discussing tantric texts, but he had not heard of it in medicine. He thought that if there is anything like a 'subtle body' at all it would appear in the embryology section and describe the early union of the sperm and the egg, when the human body is still very small in size.[11] He did not think that a 'subtle body' would have much connection to the channels, perhaps more to the *bla* and *thig le.*[12] I mentioned to him Western esoteric concepts of a 'subtle body' in terms of 'energy bodies' or 'auras' that appeared transparent but were about the size of the adult body or even larger. He had heard about the aura, but thought that nothing similar existed in Tibetan medicine, especially not that size. When we discussed suitable Tibetan terms for 'subtle body' he suggested *gzugs phra ba* (lit. 'subtle form').[13] He said not to use *lus phra ba*, since Tibetans would immediately associate this with the poetic term *lus phra mo*: a beautiful woman with a slender body.[14]

*Gzugs phra ba* or *phra ba'i gzugs* as possible translations for 'subtle body' do not appear in the Rgyud bzhi. The tantric 'vajra body' (*sku rdo rje* or *rdo rje lus*) and the 'illusory body' (*sgyu lus*), which also consists of *cakras* and *nāḍīs* (Samuel 1993: 237), also do not feature in the Rgyud bzhi. I also cannot find any Tibetan medical technical term for 'subtle body' in the Tibetan medical dictionaries at hand (Drungtso and Drungtso 2005; Wangdue 1982).[15] What we find in the medical texts are certain subtle aspects of the body that are explained in relation to the mind (*sems*), the three *nyes pa*, embryology (*chags pa'i tshul*), and the 'anatomy' (*gnas lugs*)[16] of the channels. Some of these topics have strong links to Buddhism, and Garrett argues that embryology, anatomy and physiology, 'may be most fruitfully classed less as medical topics, than as Buddhist religio-philosophical ones' (Garrett 2007: 422).

In the Rgyud bzhi (fifth chapter, second treatise) we find *'phra ba* as one of the twenty characteristics (*mtshan nyid*) that describe the qualities of the three *nyes pa*, particularly *rlung*. As a technical term *rlung* serves to denote forces in the organism that manifest themselves physically with a characteristic of the element wind. *Rlung* is used to translate both the Tantric *prāṇa* and the Ayurvedic *vāta*. 'Wind' in these various traditions can probably be seen as a very early notion that influenced ideas to imagine, experience and perceive more subtle aspects of the human body.[17] In classical Tibetan medicine, the meaning of *rlung* cannot be confined to the physical sensation of wind, such as gas in the intestines or breath in the lungs. All movements in the organism – including the flow of everything from blood to thoughts, all nerve activity, and the movement of the muscles and bowels – are governed by *rlung*.

According to the Rgyud bzhi, the six qualities of *rlung* are subtle (*'phra*), rough (*rtsub pa*), light (*yang ba*), cold (*grang ba*), hard (*sra ba*) and mobile (*gyo ba*). These six functional qualities describe the nature of *rlung* and refer to the quality of aspects of the body, mind, food, the environment and climate. 'Subtle' in this context denotes the capacity of *rlung* 'to move everywhere' (Donden and Hopkins 1986: 48), not because *rlung* is small in size but because it is subtle in nature. It is the subtle nature of *rlung* that allows it to move through the body without being held up by firm visible structures. It is also said to be the carrier of the mind (*sems*) in the sense that the mind 'rides on the currents of "wind"' (Millard 2007: 265, quoting Samuel 1989).

*'Phra ba* does not appear as one of the 'eight powers' (*nus pa brgyad*) or the 'seventeen qualities' (*yon tan hcu hdun*), which define pharmacological characteristics of medicinal ingredients. The discussion of the 'subtle' in Tibetan medicine thus centres more on physiology and 'anatomy', not pharmacology.

Since subtlety in Tibetan medicine is intrinsically linked to *rlung*, the pathways through which *rlung* travels give further insight into the subtle aspects of the body. The Rgyud bzhi (third chapter, first treatise) describes fifteen pathways for the three *nyes pa*, among which bones (*rus pa*), ears (*rna ba*), the skin as a sensory organ (*reg bya*), the heart (*snying*), the life-channel (*srog rtsa*), and the large intestine (*long*) are mentioned as the pathways of *rlung*. At first sight, they seem arbitrary and unlinked, but they follow a set framework in that each pathway of a *nyes pa* is related to at least one of the seven bodily constituents, the *lus zungs bdun*[18] (in the case of *rlung*, i.e. the bones), a waste product (i.e. ear wax), a sensory organ (i.e. the skin),[19] a vital organ (i.e. the heart and the 'life-channel') and a vessel organ (i.e. the large intestine). Exceptionally, the 'life-channel' (*srog rtsa*), which is not one of the five vital organs, is listed here 'in addition to the heart'.[20] It is one of the most important pathways for *rlung*, but does not fit neatly into the pathway categories provided for the three *nyes pa*.

The 'life-channel' has an unusual, often contested place among the channels.[21] In the Rgyud bzhi, it is mentioned in the chapter on embryology, where it is translated as 'central life channel' (Men-Tsee-Khang 2008: 51), and it is also one of the 'channels of formation'. In the 'anatomy' chapter, it is translated as 'aorta' (Men-Tsee-Khang 2008: 61). It has also been translated by various authors as 'spine', when linked to the tantric central channel, and to the two main 'connecting channels' (Garrett 2008: 69–70), thus varying in subtlety.

The subtleness of *rlung*'s mobility is evident from some of the names of the five types of *rlung* that indicate the direction of its flow in the body. The 'all-pervading *rlung*' (*khyab byed rlung*) moves throughout the body, whereas the 'downwards-moving *rlung*' (*thur sel rlung*) and 'upwards-moving *rlung*' (*gyen rgyu rlung*) move vertically either upwards (e.g. through the lungs and throat) or downwards (e.g. through the colon, urinary bladder and genitals). The 'fire-like *rlung*' (*me mnyam rlung*) fans the digestive fire in the stomach and intestines and transports the food and nutrients. The subtlest *rlung* is the 'life-sustaining *rlung*' (*srog 'dzin rlung*), which moves throughout the body. Again, some of these *rlung* movements follow solid pathways, such as the intestines, and others, such as the 'life-sustaining *rlung*', are linked to finer channels that allow for their flow throughout the body.

Within this physiology, there are so far no clear demarcations in the subtleties of *rlung* or *rtsa* that could be singled out as a 'subtle body'. Several of the five types of *rlung* influence emotional and mental processes (see Millard 2007: 270–1), which is the reason why *rlung* is linked closely to the mind as well as mental illnesses. In this context, the 'life-sustaining *rlung*' is described as having gross, subtle and very subtle aspects; of these, the very subtle *rlung* supports the very subtle mind in the transmigration between lives (2007: 266). This mind-body link, however, is not articulated in terms of a 'subtle body'.

## The 'root' nature of Rtsa

To better situate the issues surrounding *rtsa* in the Tibetan channel debate, I want to analyse further the Tibetan medical understanding of *rtsa*. The Sanskrit term *nāḍī* means 'river' or 'stream'; this meaning is not found in the Tibetan translation of *nāḍī* as *rtsa*, which literally means 'root'. The 'root' nature of *rtsa* can be interpreted in at least two ways. First, the image of a root resembles a well-branched system of organized, harmonious pathways, which are well connected but not necessarily circular in nature. 'The healthy channels should be like the nerves of the leaves,[22] well branched and not disconnected,' says the Tibetan doctor Dr Passang Yontan Arya (Beguin 2009). Second, the 'root' nature of the channels refers to the function of a root – to draw water and nutrition from the soil and sustain the plant. The 'channels where life abides' (*tshe'i rtsa*), discussed in the last section, are called *rtsa*, 'since they are the roots of life' (Gonpo 1992: 68). Dr Passang Yontan Arya similarly maintains that the channels function 'like roots that sustain the life of the person' (Beguin 2009). These interpretations, as well as some of the medical paintings (see Parfionovitch *et al.* 1992: *thang ka* nos. 9–15, pp. 33–46, and nos. 47–8, pp. 109–12),[23] at least on a visual level, seem to give us some indication that the channels in Tibetan medicine are largely perceived as open-ended ducts or fine networks, but not necessarily as closed circular systems, as is the case with the blood circulation in biomedicine. I analyse the circularity of *rtsa* later in this chapter.

## Consolidating disparate body concepts in Tibet

When analysing subtle aspects in Tibetan 'anatomy', we need to take into account that ideas surrounding Tibetan medical channels developed at different times in history, drawing from different, unrelated medical and philosophical systems. While *bla* is a non-Buddhist idea of vitality prevalent in many Himalayan and Asian communities (see Gerke 2007), the three tantric channels and *cakras* clearly derive from Indian tantric material (see Samuel, this volume) that came to Tibet along with Buddhism and was incorporated in religious and medical thought. All the channels and *cakras* were expressed in Buddhist terms. It comes as no surprise then to find Indic, Tibetan Buddhist and popular Tibetan vitality concepts, such as the *bla*,[24] in one and the same medical painting (e.g. *thang ka* no. 12, p. 40), or to have Tibetan physicians correlate the medical channels with tantric Buddhist channels, debating their visibility and 'reality' in the body. Medicine in Tibet struggled with classical Buddhist doctrine throughout its history, and some of these struggles are based simply on a discrepancy between different systems that Tibetan authors tried to reconcile (Gyatso 2004: 87).

We know that contemporary Tibetan doctors in Lhasa, who have been exposed to biomedical ideas, interpret the nature of the *rtsa* in varying ways. Some try to link the three tantric channels directly to the 'anatomically visible nervous system, the arterial flow of the blood, and the venous flow of blood which, respectively, stand for the white, red, and black channels in the Tibetan system' (Adams 2002: 550). Others argue that the invisible channels 'are the location of the body's subtle wind' and are integral to scientific Tibetan medical theory (2002: 546). Remarkably, both sides have labelled their investigation 'scientific'. This exemplifies how Tibetan physicians today deal with the subtleties of their own traditions that do not always fit neatly into their changing medical views.

Already in the earlier days of Tibetan medicine, the channels, their subtlety and invisibility caused confusion among Tibetan doctors. Janet Gyatso summarizes the medieval parts of this debate well, illustrating where Buddhist and medical perceptions collided in the fifteenth century in Tibet (Gyatso 2004). How did Tibetan physicians deal with the subtleties of the tantric channels that could not be seen in 'real bodies' of dissected human corpses?[25] Gyatso argues that it was through a method of dividing bodies into 'inner' invisible (but considered 'real' and 'correct' according to the Buddhist doctrine) and 'outer' visible bodies (following the medical empiricism of the time) that the obvious discrepancies could be reconciled without having to criticize the authoritative 'word of the Buddha' (2004: 88). A similar distinction is found in the common triad of 'outer', 'inner' and 'secret' levels, for example, applied to the classification of illnesses (Tsultrim Gyaltsen, in Garrett and Adams 2008: 98), or the classification of 'tantric medicine', which belongs to the 'inner level' (Clifford 1994: 66).

With the help of various theories, authors tried to establish tantric ideologies in physical realities. In the process, Indian tantric ideas were reworked into a workable Tibetan medical body. For example, as already mentioned, the three main channels of the Indian tantric system were seen by some authors as equivalent to the three 'channels of formation' (Garrett 2008: 68). Others moved the tantric channels into the realm of visualization, so that they only possessed valid 'reality' in a meditative state (Gyatso 2004: 89). This has been disputed by, among others, the late Tsultrim Gyaltsen, who according to medical historian and former director of the Lhasa *Mentsikhang* Jampa Thinley, 'solved' the tantric channel debate in an essay in the late 1990s. This essay was recently translated into English (Garrett and Adams 2008).

Gyaltsen follows the sixteenth-century physician and author Zurkar Lodo Gyalpo in many points (Gyalpo 1991); he argues that there are invisible things in the body that prove their existence through their effect on the body. This means that the three tantric channels must exist since otherwise meditation could not have the effect it has (Garrett and Adams 2008: 94), even though in terms of visibility, the channels might be so subtle that only spiritual advanced meditators can actually see them (2008: 112). They also *must* exist, since otherwise there 'would be a contradictory relationship within the Tibetan scholastic tradition', and 'a thesis that invalidates the scriptures would be established' (2008: 100, 110), something unthinkable for most Tibetan scholars, where – in Tsultrim Gyaltsen's words – invalidating the scriptures is indicative of 'personal arrogance', and the best choice is considered to 'follow the experts' (Gyaltsen in Garrett and Adams 2008: 110). Limited by such scholarly constraints, Gyaltsen does not 'solve' the debate, but shows what is at stake.

In the remaining section, I want to analyse the notion of circularity with respect to various channels and their subtleties.

## On the circularity of Tibetan channels

*Rtsa* are often talked about in terms of a 'circulatory system', which is either used as a general umbrella term for the *rtsa* system or as a loose translation of *'brel pa'i rtsa* (lit. 'connecting channels'). The 'circulatory system' is a Western notion that can be linked to William Harvey, who is now primarily known as the co-creator of the 'circulation concept' rather than the 'discoverer of blood circulation' (Duden 1991: 27). The 'circulation concept' established itself in European thought around 1750, emerging simultaneously in medicine, economics, natural sciences and journalism, even though it took until the late eighteenth and early nineteenth centuries for it to become firmly established in popular thought (Duden 1991: 3–4, 27).

'Circulation' involves a movement in a circle or circuit and is an idea that, in medicine, developed with the 'discovery' of blood circulating through the entire body's vessels as a result of the heart's pumping action. Since Galen and before Harvey, it was believed that blood was created in the liver and flowed one way, away from the liver, giving the body nutrition, but not back to the liver (Gregory 2001: 4).

Duden points to the difficulties we confront when historicizing the body; how we are pinned down by our own Western body perceptions that take 'the body for granted as an unchanging biological reality' (Duden 1991: 3). Acknowledging a

Foucauldian awareness of a 'medical gaze', it is now possible to admit that bodies are not self-evident but fabricated.[26] With this in mind, we might be better able to appreciate when classical Tibetan medical 'circulatory systems' do not necessarily move in circulation.

With regard to the movement of channels, White makes a crucial observation: in tenth-century Indian yoga texts the three main channels resemble three river systems in the north Indian plains near the sacred city of Benares. As mentioned above, *nāḍī* means 'river' or 'stream'. Their seasonal tides and reversed monsoon flows are synonymous of the upward flow of semen, life force, breath and mind in the *suṣumnā* channel (White 1996: 227). This adds an interesting perspective to the discussion on culture-specific constructions of body perception, since it reveals how what is perceived as natural movement in a particular environment is projected into similar movements within the body by people influenced by this environment.

In the analysis of subtle aspects of the body in Tibetan medicine, I want to follow Duden's advice that 'if we start from the assumption that the imaginations and perceptions of a given period have the power to generate reality, we can approach phenomena that are usually rendered invisible because of some a priori axiom of what is natural' (1991: 6).

If we look at the different types of 'circulation' of subtle substances in the Tibetan medical body, we might understand why Westerners tend to talk about them in terms of a 'subtle body'. We seem to have difficulties conceiving of a solid body with subtle substances, such as 'winds' or 'life essences' that move beyond the boundaries of visible pathways. The four major types of channels mentioned in the Rgyud bzhi and described above do not directly or implicitly reveal a medical perception of 'circulation'; they were classified according to their function.

While the seventeenth-century medical paintings do not give 'proof' of the actual medical perception at the time, they might provide a visual representation of certain patterns in medical thought. In the Tibetan medical paintings under discussion, most channels appear to be open-ended, not circular. Some run straight from top to bottom as open-ended ducts, or just branch out like a tree; some of them correspond to visible 'realities', such as blood vessels (e.g. *thang ka* nos. 9–11, pp. 33–8); others depict invisible subtle channels (e.g. *thang ka* no. 12, p. 40). The second 'vitality-channel' accompanying the breath even begins outside the body, namely sixteen fingers away from the tip of the nose (*thang ka* no. 12, p. 40).

For some *rtsa* the images of roots or leaf veins seem appropriate, since they are branching off harmoniously, such as the channels that connect hollow and solid viscera at the spinal column (*thang ka* no. 47, lower side-drawing, p. 110). The only *rtsa* that give the impression of a kind of 'blood circulation' are those *rtsa* that hold blood and converge at certain *cakras*, but not in capillaries (e.g. *thang ka* no. 47, central drawing, p. 110).

In terms of their nature and function, some channels 'pulsate' (*'phar rtsa*, often translated as 'arteries') or 'stay' (*sdod rtsa*, often translated as 'veins'); other channels 'pervade' (*khyab pa*), 'spread out' (*gyes pa*), 'connect' (*'brel pa*), or 'roam/wonder around' (*rgyu ba*) (Rgyud bzhi, fourth chapter, second treatise; see Men-Tsee-Khang 2008: 59–66). The Tibetan verb *'khor ba* (to circulate) is not used in the section on *rtsa*; *'khor* indicates the wheels of circulation in themselves – the *cakras*.

The three main tantric channels move from top to bottom and are connected at the nexus of each *cakra*, from which several channels branch off like flower petals (*thang ka* no. 12, p. 40). The central channel itself appears like an open-ended empty tube, opening above the crown *cakra* into the sky and below the root *cakra* towards the ground. The so-called 'seven hundred minor channels' (*rtsa phran bdun brgya*) cover the body like a net. On the *thang ka*, they have been painted in the form of fine waves that exit from various vertebrae of the spine, and then take their own course across the entire body, finely meshed, reaching out to the extremities where they end in the tips of fingers and toes (*thang ka* no. 12, p. 40).

This topographic net of the subtle channels does not have circular features. Moreover, the very subtle channels on the right body side are painted in red, while the ones on the left body side are painted in blue, showing a clear partition between the left and right side of the body. This partition seems to link up with the waxing and waning moon cycle and the movement of the *bla*. The *bla* moves in 30 days around the body in a set fashion, following the moon cycle through 30 places (*bla gnas*), which are mostly located in joints, but also in other tissues (Gerke 2007: 195; 2012: 137–54; Parfionovitch *et al.* 1992: 39–40). But in medical commentaries, *bla* is also said to 'wander around' the body (*bla 'khyams pa*) and to 'permeate the entire body' (*lus kun du khyab pa*; Gyatso 1982: 109).[27]

To conclude, the subtle channel network in Tibetan medical paintings and my initial reading of the Rgyud bzhi seems to be variable in terms of direction and flow; it allows for linear, circular and permeating movements of vital forces in all directions. It might well be that a concept of 'circulation' in the biomedical sense is not an established notion in classical Tibetan medicine. A very careful and detailed reading of the relevant chapters in the Rgyud bzhi, the Baiḍūrya sngon po, and other commentaries,[28] is necessary to further establish this argument.

Nowadays, a shift in Tibetan medical views of circulation is evident from contemporary Tibetan medical publications that have adopted the notion of circularity from biomedicine. Contemporary Men-Tsee-Khang commentaries on the 'anatomy' chapter of the Rgyud bzhi now include biomedical sketches of the Harvey-type blood circulation and neuro-anatomy with new Tibetan technical terms (Men-Tsee-Khang n.d.: 167–96).

The next section looks at channel movements in more detail, taking the example of the 'channels where life abides'.

## The channels where life abides

One section in the 'anatomy' chapter of the Rgyud bzhi deals with the vitality channels, called 'the channels where life abides' (*tshe gnas pa'i rtsa*). How do these channels relate to the issues of circularity discussed above, and what is 'subtle' about them? The section in the Rgyud bzhi itself is brief:

> The human [body] has three types of vitality channels. [The first] one pervades the head and the entire body. [The second] one flows along with the breath. [The third] one is like the life essence (*bla*) and roams around [the body].[29]

Pervading the head and the entire body, flowing along with the breath, and roaming around, are all movements that do not directly indicate an idea of 'circulation'. Sangye Gyatso in his commentary mentions three traditions with varied explanations on the functions of these vitality channels (Garrett and Adams 2008: 91; Gyatso 1982: 109; Parfionovitch *et al.* 1992: 39). They differ mainly in levels of subtlety and link up with the debate described above in that they reflect an attempt by Tibetan medical authors to integrate subtle-body concepts into their medical textbooks without having to give up their own sense of medical empiricism. One expression of this debate is visible in Sangye Gyatso's commentary Baiḍūrya sngon po and the relevant *thang ka* (no. 12, p. 40). The captions of the medical paintings describe the 'vitality channels' referring explicitly to the meaning given to these channels in accordance with either the 'medical tradition', the 'tantric tradition' or both (Parfionovitch *et al.* 1992: 195, 5–9).[30] In the 'anatomy' chapter of the Baiḍūrya sngon po, Sangye Gyatso also makes a point of stating the different views of each tradition and clarifies which tradition he is talking about (1982: 89–115).

Tsultrim Gyaltsen argues (following Lodo Gyalpo) that the 'vitality channels' are not real (*dngos*) but 'they refer to forces within the body that maintain life' (Garrett and Adams 2008: 90). What becomes clear from these initial observations is that the reality of the channels seems particularly contested in terms of the movement of vital forces, which appear to have the most varying traditions.

Sangye Gyatso concludes the section on the channels as follows:

> All the winds, the blood, the nutrients, the waste products, all move through the subtle and coarse pathways, connecting the entire outer and inner body. Due to this fact, such a body will grow well and will last for a long time; the channels of the body are like this. Especially, because they are like roots where the life-force resides, they were given the name *rtsa*.[31]

Following the Rgyud bzhi, Sangye Gyatso emphasizes the interconnectedness of substances that flow through the coarse and subtle channels that *together* maintain the body and provide health and longevity. The clue for good health actually seems to lie in the variety of these channels and substances and their interconnectivities. As did others, he had to somehow accommodate the ('inner' or 'hidden') 'reality' of the tantric channels, since contradictory positions between science and religion were not an option in seventeenth-century Tibet; but articulating a separate entity of a 'subtle body' in medicine was not an issue in the channel debate. The extent to which he might have assumed a concept of circulation in the channels needs further investigation.

## Summary and conclusions

Recently, subtle aspects of the body in classical Tibetan medicine have frequently been translated into notions of a 'subtle body'. This chapter has focused on two aspects of these discussions: first, the link between the notion of a 'subtle body' and the channels (*rtsa*) and second, the importance of channel movements for the understanding of subtleties in the body. In the first part, I analysed the subtleties of the five types of wind (*rlung*) and their direction of movement in the seminal classical Tibetan medical text Rgyud bzhi and the characteristics of the coarse and subtle channels (*rtsa*; lit. 'root'), showing the 'root' nature in the topography and function of *rtsa*.

I think one reason why the debate on Tibetan channels has been so vigorous in the past is that there was no existing concept in medical knowledge to accommodate a subtle 'vajra body', which was clearly part of Indic tantric Buddhist knowledge and influenced Tibetan medical practice only indirectly. At certain times in history, however, subtle body concepts *had* to be debated theoretically because of issues of authority and the Buddhist state control of institutionalized (mostly monastic) medical practice (Gyatso 2004). We can therefore understand the Tibetan channel debate as a reworking of Indian tantric ideas into Tibetan medical texts in the context of Buddhist hegemony in Tibet. Moreover, authors of medical works in Tibet also had to account for popular ideas of vitality, such as the *bla*, which was in some ways linked to the 'anatomy' of the channels.

In the second part of the chapter I suggested that Tibetan channels are not necessarily circulatory in nature. *Rtsa* are often talked about in terms of a 'circulatory system', probably because of our Eurocentric internalization that bodily channels follow a circulatory fashion, but – even though Tibetans might have had an idea of blood circulating in the body – the classical Tibetan medical presentations of *rtsa* are much more 'root-like', open-ended, or diffuse in nature. I suggest that the terms 'circulatory system' and 'circulatory channel' both in general and as a translation of *'brel ba'i rtsa* (lit. 'connecting channels') should be used with caution, since they give the impression that the Tibetan channel system consists of closed circulatory pathways. This is far from certain, and as stated above, the visual presentations of the channels show otherwise. The question of the circularity of the flow in Tibetan channels certainly warrants further research. The classical texts might reveal a very different image from that found in modern Tibetan medical textbooks that include sketches of biomedical blood circulation (e.g. Men-Tsee-Khang n.d.: 167, 173, 178, 180–1).

Tibetan medical ideas of *rtsa* incorporate both subtle and coarse pathways for various visible and invisible substances that flow in numerous ways in and out of the body. Some of them even start outside the body, such as one of the vitality channels. From analysing the ways in which bodily subtleties are described in some of the key Tibetan medical texts and are depicted in medical paintings,

I argue that we cannot talk about a unified Tibetan medical concept of a 'subtle body', but only of various subtle aspects of the body.

The variety of subtle-body concepts and practices might get confusing in terms of medical practice. On a theoretical and textual level, Buddhist and medical epistemologies were easier to conflate. Due to the variety of coarse and subtle bodily pathways, disparate body concepts could be integrated into a workable 'natural condition of the body' that emphasizes their interconnectedness in the promotion of good health and long life.

## Notes

1  I want to thank Janet Gyatso, Stephan Kloos, Dr Pema Dorje, and Florian Ploberger for their valuable comments on this chapter.

2  In this context *rtsa* indicates the pulsating vessels (*'phar rtsa*) that are linked to pulse diagnosis (*rtsa lta ba*), which I do not cover here.

3  Most probably compiled in the twelfth century, the Rgyud bzhi, consisting of four main treatises with 156 chapters and 5,900 verses, has – with regional variations – remained the most influential medical text among Tibetans today.

4  A detailed English description of these four types of channels can be found, for example, in Clark 1995: 56–8; Garrett 2008: 64–70; Garrett and Adams 2008: 88–92; Men-Tsee-Khang 2008: 61–4; Millard 2007: 266–7; Parfionovitch *et al.* 1992: 33–42.

5  The 'white channel' reaches the brain, i.e. the seat of *bad kan*; the 'black channel' extends vertically into the middle part of the body, i.e. the seat of *mkhris pa*; and the third channel is associated with desire and extends into the pelvis, i.e. the seat of *rlung*.

6  Debatably, the three *nyes pa* have often been rendered as 'wind', 'bile' and 'phlegm' respectively. Their physiological functions have been explained in numerous publications (e.g. Clark 1995; Donden and Hopkins 1986; Drungtso 2007, 2008; Men-Tsee-Khang 2001).

7  Tsultrim Gyaltsen was an eminent Sakya scholar of Buddhism and Tibetan medicine and a well-known Tibetan physician at the *Mentsikhang* in Lhasa.

8  For a more detailed discussion of these three tantric channels see Garrett 2008: 64–70; Garrett and Adams 2008: 92–4.

9  Garrett, for example, argues that the 'resurgence in interest in theorizing about the human body in Tibetan medicine by the fourteenth to fifteenth centuries is a sign of the "Buddhification" of Tibetan medicine' (Garrett 2007: 422).

10  All translations refer to the THL online Tibetan dictionary: www.thlib.org/reference/dictionaries/tibetan-dictionary/translate.php

11  Similarly, Dr Pema Dorje, at the Men-Tsee-Khang in Dharamsala, commented in February 2012 that a draft version of this paper had sparked a discussion during a conference among Tibetan doctors with a few Geshes on whether there was a subtle body in Tibetan medicine or not. He remarked that in the intermediate *bar do* state between death and rebirth there was a subtle body that consisted of the very subtle forms of the five elements (*shin tu 'phra ba'i 'byung ba lnga*). This would also be relevant in a medical context, especially in embryology. Without the very subtle five elements, he said, consciousness (*rnam shes*) would not have a basis to take form and build the foetus. He concluded, 'If the very subtle five elements exist, the very subtle body exists' (*shin tu phra ba'i 'byung ba yod na shin tu phra ba'i lus yod*). Thus for this group of doctors and Geshes, the 'subtle body' was a phenomenon associated with the process of death and rebirth, rather than with the functioning of the normal body.

12  *Thig le* (lit. 'dot') is a polysemous tantric term that indicates, among other things, the vital essence of the body (white and red seminal fluids) or the nucleus of the enlightened mind, often linked to the 'vajra body'.

13  Tsultrim Gyaltsen lists *phra ba'i gzugs* as one of the synonyms for the tantric central channel (Garrett and Adams 2008: 105).

14  Personal communication, Dr Tsering Wangdue, Dharamsala, 5 August 2010.

15  Drungtso and Drungtso mention the 'illusory body', but without any medical explanations (2005: 102).

16  'Anatomy' is a loose translation of the Tibetan *lus kyi gnas lugs* (lit. 'the natural condition of the body'). The term 'anatomy' derives from the Greek *anatomē* (lit. 'dissection'); the Tibetan view of the 'natural conditions of the body' also involves subtle and invisible aspects that have not been detected through dissection (see also Garrett and Adams 2008: 98, n.17).

17  For an example of notions of 'wind' in the Chinese tradition see Kuriyama 1994; and in early Indian Ayurveda see Zysk 1993, 2008.

18  These seven bodily constituents are distilled in a continuous process from food nutrients through the stages of nutritional essence (*dvangs ma*), blood (*khrag*), flesh (*sha*), fat (*tshil*), bone (*rus*), bone marrow (*rkang*), and regenerative fluids (*khu ba*), eventually creating the body's vital radiance (Tib. *mdangs*; Skt. *ojas*).

19  Some texts list the secretion of skin pores as waste product and the ears as sensory organ (Men-Tsee-Khang n.d.: 41; Drungtso 2007: 71).

20  *snying dang zhar byung du srog rtsa* (Men-Tsee-Khang, n.d.: 41).

21  For historical debates about this life-channel see Garrett and Adams (2008: 92).

22  This simile is also mentioned in the section on channels in Vāgbhaṭa's ayurvedic treatise *Aṣṭāṅgahṛidayasaṃhitā* (Hilgenberg and Kirfel 1941: 182). This work was translated into Tibetan in the eleventh century and was one of the sources of the Rgyud bzhi.

23  All *thang ka* mentioned here refer to Parfionovitch *et al.* 1992.

24  This does not mean that the popular *bla* is equivalent to the *bla* we find in Tibetan medical texts.

25  Since sky burials are common in Tibet, physicians had the opportunity to study the anatomy of corpses (Gyatso 2004: 83).

26  In this regard, Kuriyama 1999 offers a good example on the Greek and Chinese construction of the body.

27  I analysed the significance of this 'wandering around' of the *bla* and its movement in terms of temporalization in my doctoral thesis and monograph (Gerke 2008: 146ff., 2012: 140–1).

28  I am thinking here, among others, of Zurkar Lodo Gyalpo's Mes po'i zhal lung, which in many parts reappears verbatim in the later Baiḍūrya sngon po.

29  *mi la tshe yi rtsa ni gsum yod de/ gcig ni mgo lus thams cad khyab par gnas/ gcig ni dbugs dang 'grogs nas rgyu ba ste/ gcig ni bla dang 'dra ste 'khyam pa yin/* (Gonpo 1992: 68); my translation.

30  For example, captions 5 and 8 of *thang ka* no. 12 mention *rgyud sde dang mthun pa* ('according to the tantras'), captions 6 and 9 refer to *gso ba rig pa'i ... tshul* ('according to medical science'), caption 7 reads *rgyud sde dang tshe rig gnyis ka mthun pa* ('according to both tantras and medical science'); note that here *tshe rig* (lit. 'science of life'), the literal translation of the term Ayurveda, is used (Parfionovitch *et al.* 1992: 195).

31  *rlung rnams dang khrag dang dangs ma/ rnams dang snyigs ma thams cad rgyu ba'i bu ga/ phra rags rnams kyis lus kyi phyi nang kun du 'brel bar byas pas lus 'di ni legs par bskyed cing yun ring du gnas par byed pa'i don gyis na lus kyi rtsa ba lta bu dang/*

*lhag par srog gnas pa'i rtsa ba lta bu yin pa'i phyir/ rtsa zhes bya bar ming gis btags pa yin no/* (Gyatso 1982: 109); my translation.

## References

Adams, V. (2002) 'The sacred in the scientific: ambiguous practices of science in Tibetan medicine', *Cultural Anthropology* 16: 542–75.

Asshauer, E. (2005) *Tantrisches Heilen und Tibetische Medizin: Die Zusammenhänge von Geist und Körper aus tibetischer Sicht.* Grafing: Aquamarin Verlag.

Beguin, S. (2009) 'The vajra body: interview with Dr Pasang Y. Arya', *TME Newsletter* 7, January 2009. Online at: www.tibetanmedicine-edu.org/index.php/n-articles/vajra-body (accessed 10 June 2010).

Chaoul, A. M. (2007) 'Magical movements (*'phrul 'khor*) in the Bon tradition and possible applications as a CIM therapy', in M. Schrempf (ed.) *Soundings in Tibetan Medicine: Anthropological and Historical Perspectives.* Proceedings of the 10th Seminar of the International Association for Tibetan Studies (IATS), Oxford 2003. Leiden: Brill.

Clark, B. (1995) *The Quintessence Tantras of Tibetan Medicine.* Ithaca, NY: Snow Lion Publications.

Clifford, T. (1994) *Tibetan Buddhist Medicine and Psychiatry: The Diamond Healing.* Delhi: Motilal Banarsidass.

Donden, Y. and Hopkins, J. (1986) *Health Through Balance: An Introduction to Tibetan Medicine.* Ithaca, NY: Snow Lion Publications.

Drungtso, T. T. (2007) *Basic Concepts of Tibetan Medicine: A Guide to Understanding Tibetan Medical Science.* Dharamsala: Drungtso Publications.

—— (2008) *Tibetan Medicine: The Healing Science of Tibet,* 2nd revised edn. Dharamsala: Drungtso Publications.

Drungtso, T. T. and Drungtso, T. D. (2005) *Tibetan–English Dictionary of Tibetan Medicine and Astrology.* Dharamsala: Drungtso Publications.

Duden, B. (1991) *The Woman Beneath the Skin: A Doctor's Patients in Eighteenth-Century Germany.* Cambridge, MA and London: Harvard University Press.

Garrett, F. (2007) 'Embryology and embodiment in Tibetan literature: narrative epistemology and the rhetoric of identity', in M. Schrempf (ed.) *Soundings in Tibetan Medicine: Anthropological and Historical Perspectives.* Proceedings of the 10th Seminar of the International Association for Tibetan Studies (IATS), Oxford 2003. Leiden: Brill.

—— (2008) *Religion, Medicine and the Human Embryo in Tibet,* Routledge Critical Studies in Buddhism. London and New York: Routledge.

Garrett, F. and Adams, V. (2008) 'The three channels in Tibetan medicine', *Traditional South Asian Medicine* 8: 86–114.

Gerke, B. (2007) 'Engaging the subtle body: re-approaching bla rituals among Himalayan Tibetan societies', in M. Schrempf (ed.) *Soundings in Tibetan Medicine: Anthropological and Historical Perspectives.* Proceedings of the 10th Seminar of the International Association for Tibetan Studies (IATS), Oxford 2003. Leiden: Brill.

—— (2008) 'Time and longevity: concepts of the life-span among Tibetans in the Darjeeling Hills, India', unpublished thesis, University of Oxford.

—— (2012) *Long Lives and Untimely Deaths: Life-span Concepts and Longevity Practices among Tibetans in the Darjeeling Hills, India.* Leiden: Brill.

Gonpo, Yuthog Yonten (g.yu thog yon tan mgon po, 1112–1203) (1992) *Bdud rtsi snying po yan lag brgyad pa gsang ba man ngag gi rgyud.* Darjeeling: Chagpori Tibetan Medical Institute.

Gregory, A. (2001) *Harvey's Heart: The Discovery of Blood Circulation.* Cambridge: Icon Books.

Gyalpo, Lodo (zur mkhar blo gros rgyal po, 1509–79) (1991) *Rgyud bzhi'i 'grel pa mes po'i zhal lung,* Vol. 1. Dharamsala: Men-Tsee-Khang.

Gyatso, Desi Sangye (sde srid sangs rgyas rgya mtsho, 1653–1705) (1982) *Gso ba rig pa'i bstan bcos sman bla'i dgongs rgyan rgyud bzhi'i gsal byed bai ḍūr sngon po'i ma lli ka.* Lhasa: Bod ljongs mi dmangs dpe skrun khang.

Gyatso, J. (2004) 'The authority of empiricism and the empiricism of authority: medicine and Buddhism in Tibet on the eve of modernity', *Comparative Studies of South Asia, Africa and the Middle East* 24: 83–96.

Hilgenberg, L. and Kirfel, W. (1941) *Vāgbhaṭa's Aṣṭāṅgahṛdayasaṃhitā: Ein altindisches Lehrbuch der Heilkunde.* Leiden: Brill.

Kuriyama, S. (1994) 'The imagination of winds and the development of the Chinese conception of the body', in A. Zito and T. Barlow (eds) *Body, Subject and Power in China.* Chicago: University of Chicago Press.

—— (1999) *The Expressiveness of the Body and the Divergence of Greek and Chinese Medicine.* New York: Zone Books.

Loseries-Leick, A. (1997) 'Psychic sports – a living tradition in contemporary Tibet?', in H. Krasser, M. T. Much, E. Steinkeller and H. Tauscher (eds) *Tibetan Studies.* Proceedings of the 7th Seminar of the International Association for Tibetan Studies, Graz 1995, vol. II. Wien: Verlag der Österreichischen Akademie der Wissenschaften.

Men-Tsee-Khang (2001) *Fundamentals of Tibetan Medicine.* Dharamsala: Men-Tsee-Khang.

—— (2008) *The Basic Tantra and the Explanatory Tantra from the Secret Quintessential Instructions on the Eight Branches of the Ambrosia Essence Tantra.* Dharamsala: Men-Tsee-Khang.

—— (n.d.) *Bod kyi gso rig slob deb,* 2 vols. Dharamsala: Bod gzhung sman rtsis khang.

Millard, C. (2007) 'Tibetan medicine and the classification and treatment of mental illness', in M. Schrempf (ed.) *Soundings in Tibetan Medicine: Anthropological and Historical Perspectives.* Proceedings of the 10th Seminar of the International Association for Tibetan Studies (IATS), Oxford 2003. Leiden: Brill.

Norbu, N. C. (1998) *Yantra Yoga: The Tibetan Yoga of Movement.* Ithaca, NY: Snow Lion Publications.

Parfionovitch, Y., Meyer, F. and Dorje, G. (1992) *Tibetan Medical Paintings: Illustrations to the Blue Beryl Treatise of Sangye Gyatso (1653–1705).* London: Serindia.

Samuel, G. (1989) 'The body in Buddhist and Hindu tantra: some notes', *Religion* 19: 197–210.

—— (1993) *Civilized Shamans: Buddhism in Tibetan Societies.* Washington, DC: Smithsonian Institution Press.

Schaeffer, K. R. (2003) 'Textual scholarship, medical tradition, and Mahayana Buddhist ideals in Tibet', *Journal of Indian Philosophy* 31: 621–41.

Wallace, V. A. (2008) 'The body as a text and the text as the body: a view from the Kālacakratantra's perspective', in E. A. Arnold (ed.) *As Long as Space Endures: Essays on the Kālacakra Tantra in Honor of H. H. The Dalai Lama.* Ithaca, NY: Snow Lion Publications.

Wangdue (1982) *G.yu thog gso ba rig pa'i tshig mdzod g.yu thog dgongs rgyan.* Lhasa: Mi rigs dpe skrun khang.

White, D. G. (1996) *The Alchemical Body: Siddha Traditions in Medieval India.* Chicago and London: University of Chicago Press.

Yan, Z. (2007) 'rTsa in the Tibetan manuscripts from Dunhuang', *Asian Medicine* 3: 296–307.

Zysk, K. G. (1993) 'The science of respiration and the doctrine of the bodily winds in ancient India', *Journal of the American Oriental Society* 113: 198–213.

—— (2008) 'The bodily winds in ancient India revisited', in E. Hsu and C. Low (eds) *Wind, Life, Health: Anthropological and Historical Perspectives*. Oxford: Blackwell.

# 6 Open channels, healing breath[1]

## Research on ancient Tibetan yogic practices for people with cancer

*Alejandro Chaoul*

Ten years ago, I found myself in a locus where the application of meditative practices meets the treatment of people with cancer. After a year of facilitating meditation at The Place of Wellness (now Integrative Medicine Center) in the University of Texas MD Anderson Cancer Center (MD Anderson), Dr Lorenzo Cohen, a behavioural researcher there, asked me to propose a research 'intervention' based on Tibetan mind-body practices that could be applied for people with cancer. After asking approval and support from my Tibetan teachers, Yongdzin Tenzin Namdak and Tenzin Wangyal Rinpoche, I joined a research team, led by Dr Cohen, with the aim of investigating the possible effects of a Tibetan mind-body intervention for people with cancer.

In this setting, 'mind-body' refers to the experience of our existence as a whole, to not having our mind experience isolated from that of our body. In the Tibetan traditions they add what I like to call the 'missing link' between 'mind' and 'body' and that is 'energy' (*rtsal*), which is mostly expressed as speech and breath. 'Intervention' refers to a particular programme design, in this case Tibetan yoga, with a particular population, in this case cancer patients, where this programme may help improve an aspect of health in these people with cancer.

Tibetan medical texts, from both the Bönpo *Four [Medical] Collections* (*'Bum bzhi*; Sangpo 1999) and the Buddhist *Four Tantras* (*rGyud bzhi*),[2] explain the 'science of healing' (*gso ba rig pa*) in terms of balance of one's internal constitution defined by the three *nyes pa* (sometimes translated in English as 'humours')[3] and the five cosmo-physical elements (*'byung*). Health in this context is not solely the concern with the body's illness or disease, but, most importantly, the harmony of body, energy and mind.

Among the three *nyes pa*, *rlung* – the 'wind' humour – is described as having five distinctive kinds. Interestingly, the Bönpo *Mother Tantra* (*Ma rgyud*; Samlek 1985) describes a set of five *rtsa rlung* or channel-breaths yogic movements, where each movement is explained in terms of those same five *rlung* as in the Tibetan medical system (also equivalent to those in the Indian medical system of Ayurveda), and that have correlations with the five cosmo-physical elements. In this chapter, I present an intervention for women with breast cancer undergoing chemotherapy which uses these *rtsa rlung* yogic movements from the Bönpo *Mother Tantra*. In this present research study we made more explicit the use of subtle body: channels (*rtsa*, Skt. *nāḍī*), vital breath (*rlung*, Skt. *prāṇa* or *vāyu*, similar to Chi. *qi*) and energetic centres (*'khor lo*, Skt. *cakra*). This, we hypothesize, may help these women connect more to their spirituality, no matter what religious background they are coming from, with the aim of improving their quality of life (QOL), and their connection to themselves and to others. In other words, this intervention aims to provide a healing focused not just on the physical but also on the psycho-social-spiritual aspects of the person, which sometimes seems to be forgotten in conventional allopathic medicine (see Engel 1977, where he proposes the need of a biopsychosocial model to supplement the current biomedical model).

## *rTsa rlung* and research

*rTsa rlung* or channel-breaths[4] is a distinctive Tibetan mind-body practice (sometimes also in conjunction with *'phrul 'khor*, 'magical movement') in which breath and concentration of the mind are integrated with particular body movements. *rTsa lung* has been part of spiritual training in Tibet since at least the tenth century. The globalization of the twentieth century has not only allowed many of the Asian mind-body practices to take root in the West, but some practitioners have also adopted what anthropologist Joseph Alter (2005) calls the 'medicalization' of modern yoga – in other words, emphasizing the healing properties of yoga, sometimes even more than the original texts would. These concepts, I believe, stem from the intimate relationship that these yogic practices have with their medical counterparts (*haṭha yoga* with *ayurveda*, *rtsa rlung 'phrul 'khor* with Tibetan medicine).

Mind-body practices such as meditation and yoga have become extremely popular in Europe and the US in the last decade as a way to reduce stress and enhance spiritual growth. This is especially true for medical populations.[5] Many people with cancer believe that stress plays a role in the aetiology and progression of their disease.

In that fertile environment, since 2000 the research team at MD Anderson in conjunction with the Ligmincha Institute, an international centre for Bön study and practice in Charlottesville, Virginia and Houston, Texas, has conducted two pilot randomized controlled trials (RCT). These pilot programmes were among the few RCT studies of yoga in a cancer patient population and the only scientific study to date of Tibetan yoga in any patient population.

As I mention elsewhere (Chaoul 2007), in those two earlier pilot studies, one for people with lymphoma and the other for women with breast cancer, we used a Tibetan Yoga (TY) intervention that included not only the *rtsa rlung* practices from the Bön *Mother Tantra* but also the *'phrul 'khor* ('magical movement') practices from the *Oral Transmission of Zhang Zhung* (*Zhang zhung snyan rgyud*). These pilot studies suggested that these ancient Tibetan Bön yogic practices may be beneficial adjuncts to conventional medicine and contribute importantly to the well-being and quality of life of people with cancer (Cohen *et al.* 2004; Chaoul 2007, 2011; Chandwani *et al.* 2008).

With that precedent and findings (see Cohen *et al.* 2004), in 2006 the US National Institutes of Health (NIH) awarded a large National Cancer Institute grant to this team to support a five-year randomized trial to examine a TY programme for women with breast cancer undergoing chemotherapy. Based on previous participant and instructor's feedback, the intervention was adjusted to focus more exclusively on the *rtsa rlung* Tibetan yogic practices from the Bön *Mother Tantra*. This work has not only put Western scientific ideas on medical research in dialogue with Tibetan *dharmic* practice; it has also allowed for changes in both sides towards finding a sound methodological research, and more importantly, bringing some benefit to people with cancer and their families.

The present intervention, also chosen in consultation with Tenzin Wangyal Rinpoche, consists of three main components: (1) breathing exercises; (2) meditative concentration; (3) *rtsa rlung* sitting yogic postures. These components have been used in the Bön tradition for centuries, and were chosen as an intervention specific for cancer patients undergoing chemotherapy or having completed treatment in the last twelve months, with the intention of helping in their recovery and buffering side effects of the treatment. Participants were taught this programme as a progressive didactic and experiential set of classes with the aim of helping the patient incorporate these techniques into their everyday lives. From the Tibetan tradition perspective, these practices clear away obstacles (*gegs sel*)[6] and enhance one's meditative state of mind (*bog don*) in order to incorporate that cultivated meditative state of mind into everyday behaviour (*spyod pa*). The breathing exercises help participants not only to regulate their breath, but also to calm their mind, and help in clearing physical, emotional and mental obstacles. The meditative concentration techniques help to harness the calmness of mind towards self-observation and use the breathing exercises to clear away obstacles.

Commenting on these yogic practices, the great Tibetan Bönpo scholar and meditator Shardza Tashi Gyaltsen (1859–1934) instructs the practitioner that in order to enter well into the path of this method of *rtsa rlung* practices, one must first train in the concentration of the mind and avoid falling after deluded thoughts (Shardza 1974b: 28). Thus, not only the breathing is emphasized but the concentration of the mind with it. In fact, in the patient's manual this is named after the *Mother Tantra*'s metaphor of the 'rider and that horse', where the horse refers to the breath and the rider to the mind guiding it. Therefore the participants begin their training with this meditative technique to help them calm and focus their mind, utilizing their breath as a means to train in focus and concentration.

The *rtsa rlung* movements work by applying the meditative concentration techniques and the breathing exercises to different areas of the physical body. Once the participants have learned and practised these movements they are introduced to the subtle body as an inner structure with its energetic centres or *cakras*. This deeper engagement with the practice helps participants to relax and feel invigorated, as well as to 'cleanse' different areas of the body (and subtle body) through the integration of the movement with the meditative and breathing techniques.

All classes are taught by instructors authorized by the Ligmincha Institute, and run in one-and-a-half-hour sessions, once a week (or every three weeks for those in that chemotherapy regimen) for four classes, and then three booster sessions once a month thereafter. This gives participants the opportunity to learn the techniques and practise them with the instructor, so that they could then continue to practise them on their own. At the end of each class, the participants receive printed material and a DVD of what was learned to take home and use as support to their home practice. The language in which the techniques are explained is simple, and the manual is illustrated with photographs. Patients are also asked to log in the times they practise in the last pages of their manual. At the end of the course, the participants are given a DVD and a CD with guided practices of all the techniques, and they return their practice log to the research team. Participants are advised to continue daily practice at home in addition to the class at the clinic and also to continue their practice after the course is over.

The study is measuring the possible stress relief, improvement of Quality of Life (QOL), and immune system level (through blood analysis), as well as reduction in anxiety and sleep disturbances that the TY intervention can provide to women with breast cancer undergoing chemotherapy, in comparison to two control groups: those doing a series of stretching exercises[7] and those receiving what is called the 'standard of care', which in this case does not include any particular intervention. The two control groups are wait-list control groups following the same measures and assessment times, and thus, the participants in the two control groups will have the opportunity to receive the TY programme after the twelve-month follow-up assessment – hence the name 'wait-list'. In addition, the study will measure outcomes in terms of psychosocial models of benefit finding and spirituality.

## Emphasizing the subtle body

An important change in the TY intervention group was the possibility of going deeper into the *rtsa rlung* practices and its subtle-body components of *rtsa* explained as subtle channels, *cakras* or *'khor lo* as energetic centres and *rlung* as vital breaths. Responding to patients' comments on the TY group that there were too many movements to be learned and practised, the MD Anderson-Ligmincha team decided to focus only on the *rtsa rlung* movements and not include the *'phrul 'khor* component. This gave us the opportunity to focus more on the *rtsa rlung*, including the more inner or subtler aspects.

Thus, participants first learn breathing with awareness ('the rider and the horse') and a 'classic' set of nine breathings of purification (*dgu rlung sang*). Then, they are introduced to the external *rtsa rlung* movements from the Bön *Mother Tantra*. And after that, when they are more familiar with the breath, awareness and movements, patients learn about the subtle body (having heard briefly about it in previous sessions) by using the channels and the vital breaths circulating though them as they perform the nine breathings and the *rtsa rlung* movements. Through these, participants may also strengthen the power of the concentration of the mind and utilize the power of the breath to cleanse obstacles and nurture themselves at the physical, emotional, mental and spiritual levels. As they continue practising the breathings and the *rtsa rlung* movements, participants may also strengthen the experiential understanding of mind-body practices and the understanding of their own subtle body and how it can be of benefit to use it.

The ancient Tibetan texts and oral teachings make it clear that the combination of the physical posture, the mind's focus, and the guidance of the vital breath currents have the power to release external, internal and secret obstacles.[8] Furthermore, as mentioned earlier, these practices help to enhance one's meditative state of mind, which can then be incorporated into everyday behaviour. Thus, by utilizing the subtle body in their practice patients can sharpen the focus of their mind as they guide it through their channels and connect more deeply to the power of their breath circulating through their channels, the pathways through which the mind as rider guides the breath as the horse. We hypothesize that through this TY intervention, participants would be able to alleviate their mental and physical stress caused by the severe side effects of the cancer treatment, such as chemotherapy. The breathing exercises help participants not only to regulate their breath, but also, as they guide it through the channels, to focus and calm their mind; and to use the power of their breath to help them clear their physical, emotional and mental obstacles. Pain, anger and intrusive thoughts are just some examples of the physical, emotional and mental obstacles, respectively, that these patients report. The meditative concentration techniques help the patients to use the calmness of the mind towards self-observation and guide their breath in a way that helps them to clear away obstacles. The *rtsa rlung* movements from the Bön *Mother Tantra* work by applying the meditative concentration techniques and the breathing exercises learned before with different areas of the physical and subtle body, to help participants relax and feel invigorated. In other words, as they practise, participants can achieve a sense of release from obstacles, maintain a calmer and clearer state of mind, and have the opportunity to apply these abilities in their everyday life. Furthermore, as they connect more deeply through the subtle body as 'mediator' they can connect more deeply to their own spirituality or what in the class we also call one's 'inner home'.

A nurse from another hospital, who is also a *dharma* practitioner, was happily surprised that our intervention included subtle-body practices and supported 'pushing the envelope' in this way. In other words, he was supportive of a framework that explained and utilized the subtle body in a lay or secular context for patients. Tenzin Wangyal Rinpoche's description of how one can connect to one's subtle or vital breath may prove useful here:

We can sense prana [vital breath, rlung] directly at the grosser levels in the air we breathe. We can also sense its flow in our bodies. It is at this level, in which prana can be felt both in its movement and in its effects, that we work in Tantra. We become sensitive to and develop the flow of prana using mind, imagination, breathing, posture, and movement. By guiding the grosser manifestations of prana, we can affect the subtle levels. As our sensitivity increases, we can directly experience prana in subtler dimensions.

(Wangyal 2002: 77)

This suggests that everyone who practises these sorts of exercises, not just Tibetans or *dharma* practitioners, can become more sensitive to the subtle aspects of breath, body and mind. *rTsa rlung* practices are crucial in the training and harmonizing, or balancing (*mnyam*), of the channels and the vital breath currents of the practitioner, within a *dharma* context and also within a medical environment. Put simply, in these practices the practitioner becomes familiar with the channels first through visualization and then by using the mind to direct the vital breath currents along those channels. In this way, one allows the vital breath currents to circulate through one's channels more evenly in terms of the rhythm of the inhalation and exhalation, and seeks a greater balance in terms of the amount and strength of the breath through the different channels. The mind is said to 'ride' on the vital breath currents, like a rider on a horse, and the two travel together through the pathways of the channels. By familiarizing themselves with the channels in this way, patients can do these practices more deeply, working through the current issues in their lives, whether related to the cancer itself or to other aspects. This is a way to open the door to better quality of life, a term that has become more and more important in bio-behavioural research under the acronym QOL.

## Subtle body as a bridge?

As Samuel rightly asserts, '"subtle body" concepts ... represent aspects of these traditions that are problematic for biomedical science' (2006: 79). Mainstream Western medicine supposes a far more ironclad division between physical illness and energetic or mental obstacles, and thus it becomes difficult for most Western physicians to accept the connection that Tibetan medicine sees between the health and meditative benefits, including those of yogic practices. Part of this difference may arise from the dichotomy between mind and body that Western biomedicine inherited and absorbed from Cartesian dualism. In contrast, in Eastern thought, a subtle or energetic body or dimension mediates between mind and body.[9]

Furthermore, Tibetans involved in this dialogue may also find the subtle-body concepts unsettling or tricky. The tradition is not univocal with respect of the description and usage of the channels,[10] and those engaged in the dialogues of these traditions and the sciences, through forums such as the Mind-Life Institute, express some concern regarding the concept of subtle channels in medical settings, and whether they belong as part of the religious concepts of these traditions and thus in possible conflict with a secular setting.[11]

As Garrett (2008: 70) argues, Tibetan medical texts such as the *Four Tantras* did not necessarily describe the channels in exactly the same way as *dharma* texts, and therefore, 'it is clear that many Tibetan medical scholars over the centuries have been concerned with reconciling the two systems, and that the discrepancies bothered them'. This dialogue in Tibet between *dharma* and medicine, from the twelfth century onwards, may even be understood as a 'medicalization' of those practices and viewpoints that have their roots in religious or spiritual traditions. And the other side was there too. The twelfth-century Sakya master Drakpa Gyaltsen asserted that an understanding of subtle physiology was of vital importance for the religious contemplative. 'Attempting contemplative practices without a clear understanding of the body, is like trying to milk an animal by tugging his horns,' he illustrated (Garrett 2008: 70).

Therefore, the difficulty of applying these Tibetan concepts does not lie merely in their marginalization by the Western biomedical communities; we also need to acknowledge the complications that arise from within the Tibetan traditions and its contemporary practitioners themselves, although their reasons for doing so may be quite different.

In clinical research we should provide an intervention that we believe is the most suitable and effective for our patients, as we draw from the wisdom of these ancient traditions. In medical research institutions such as MD Anderson, and in particular within the area of complementary and integrative medicine (CIM), these Tibetan Yoga studies may provide the right context to turn this into an opportunity to bridge both sides and create an easier way for patients to incorporate conceptually and experientially the use of the subtle body in their contemplative *rtsa rlung* practice (i.e. TY intervention).

As mentioned earlier, women with breast cancer in the current TY study learn the nine breathings of purification, which is a common foundational set of breathing among Bönpo practitioners, both lay and monastic, and also similar to the nine-breathings sets in other Tibetan Buddhist traditions. Once becoming familiar with the mechanics of this set of breathings, they learn the subtle body inner structure and physiology. Tibetan texts explain how when the mind is distracted by one of the afflictions, such as anger (*zhe sdang*), attachment (*'dod chags*) and unawareness or 'foggy mind' (*gti mugs*), the vital breath currents cannot flow in the proper way, together with the mind, through the channels. Thus, with the help of the nine breathings of purifications, the patients can get rid of whatever discomforts exist.

Tenzin Wangyal Rinpoche emphasizes that it is important that the discomforts with which the patients work should be 'fresh, personal and recent'.[12] In other words, it is not as powerful to work on something that they think they might feel or something old that they are trying to remember from childhood. Instead, working on something that at the moment of practice arises as a personal obstacle to them will have a greater effect. People with cancer tend to focus on physical pain and anecdotally report how after the practices the pain diminishes and even disappears. Others have mentioned how their anxiety is reduced after just one session. In other words, some of their obstacles are reduced or dissolved. Tenzin Wangyal Rinpoche emphasizes the importance of the 'transformation' that occurs when practising these powerful methods. Therefore, utilizing these ancient practices in this way can be seen as constituting a way of breaking open the space of biomedicine to include these benefits in its repertoire. Or, simply expressed, perhaps we can think about such dialogues as possible bridges to communicate the wisdom of these ancient practices, including the subtle body, to scientists, patients and practitioners.

## The landscapes of the subtle body

Acknowledging the challenges in bringing the mind-body concepts and practices into Western scientific fields, Samuel also adds that the introduction and acceptance of medicine from Asia, biofeedback and measurable experiments of inner heat 'demonstrate the mind-body linkage in a form accessible to Western science, [and thus] the subtle body is beginning to make more sense' (2006: 237).[13]

As mentioned earlier, Asian medicine and spiritual practices consider the subtle body as a vessel through which transformation may occur. It is the internal dimension that allows the practitioner to travel on the path to healing (and enlightenment). Tibetologist Elizabeth Stutchbury posits an 'epistemic status' for these practices that can prove very useful (1998: 103ff.).[14] She contends that although it is difficult to find correspondences of the subtle-body elements (channels and vital breath currents) with biomedicine, 'different systems of advanced "inner yoga meditation" [i.e. her translation of *rtsa rlung*] manufacture and employ different structures, suggesting that the potentiality for creating these pathways exists' (1998: 115). Stutchbury rightly proposes that these elements arise or are perceived by the practitioner through specific methods of practice, including those discussed here, which she terms 'technologies of consciousness' (1998: 115). Intrigued by the mechanisms of these technologies of consciousness, for centuries Tibetans also investigated this kind of correspondence between the tantric vista and medical knowledge of the subtle body, as Garrett's work (cited earlier) shows.

There are different kinds of subtle-body presentations not only among Tibetans but also among Indian and Chinese presentations.[15] Samuel asserts that Tibetans 'are aware that there are significant discrepancies between the descriptions in different traditions ... the coexistence of apparently irreconcilable descriptions in and of itself is not seen as a problem. Each description is valid in its own context' (1989: 201). Thus, these technologies of consciousness, such as meditative techniques, and channels-breaths practice, are means or methods that allow the practitioner and patient to connect with one's inner home, or natural state of mind, with the support of the landscape of his/her subtle body.

## The subtle body described in the Bön *Mother Tantra*

> I offer my whole body containing the *three channels* with its *five energetic centers*, the *five vital breaths* and the light coming forth from them, together with the sixteen mind-essences – or essential spheres.
>
> (Shardza 1974b: 102)[16]

Although all traditions do not necessarily agree on all the details of the subtle dimension(s), they are composed of a subtle channels structure through which subtle breaths travel together with subtle aspects and attention of the mind.

### The three channels

The channels are the architectural support of the subtle body and act as pathways through which fluids and energies travel. Some, like the veins and arteries, are the pathways for blood to circulate around our body. Subtler channels are the roads through which vital breath currents travel, nurturing the subtler dimensions of the body.

There is a consistent description of the principal three channels of the subtle body in the Indian and Tibetan tantric literature,[17] and the *Mother Tantra* follows along the same lines in defining those three channels. For patients, the description is simple. Rather than calling them by the Sanskrit or Tibetan names, we use Central, Right and Left channels, supported by the visualization of their respective blue, white and red colours. The importance of the central channel and of bringing the mind's attention and breath into the central channel is discussed with patients in simple terms. In fact, the central channel is introduced first, and in a later session the side channels are 'added'. Patients are encouraged first to imagine, then visualize and then feel those channels as made of light and being flexible, so that when vital breath travels through them one can feel they inflate like a balloon.[18]

### The five energetic centres

Along this supporting structure of the channels lie the energetic centres or *cakras*. Their numbers and locations vary according to the tradition describing them or even according to the specific practice in which they are engaged, but in general the most important ones are located along the central channel. The *Mother Tantra* mentions five of them that are engaged through the *rtsa rlung* practice: Crown, Throat, Heart, Navel and Secret energetic centres. Patients are introduced to them not only conceptually, but also experientially by bringing the breath supported with the mind's attention to each energetic centre, and then apply the prescribed *rtsa rlung* movement.

### The five vital breaths

The *rtsa rlung* movements described in the *Mother Tantra* correlate with five kinds of vital breath currents. Shardza, basing his description on the *Mother Tantra*, describes the five vital breath currents as follows (1974b: 28):[19]

> Upward moving (*gyen du rgyu*) vital breath at throat centre,
> Life upholding or life force (*srog 'dzin pa*) vital breath at the heart centre,
> Fire-like (*memnyam pa*) vital breath at the navel centre,

Downward (*thur du*) clearing (*sel ba*) vital breath at the secret centre,
Pervasive (*khyab*) vital breath at the central channel and all the channel
petals – or connections with all smaller channels.

Shardza writes that in *rtsa rlung* practices one brings the air with one-pointed
concentration (*sems gtad*) to each centre (1974b: 28). By engaging in these yogic
practices, practitioners and patients can produce that shift or transformation, even
possibly as an experience of light coming forth, as illustrated in the above prayer.
Allowing the air to move along and around (*gyi gyi kor kor*) each of the centres, as
one performs the *rtsa rlung* practices, one helps the clearing of those areas and the
mind to focus better and rest more comfortably. From the practitioner's perspective, these yogic practices provide the methods to transform from the state of an
ordinary sentient being into that of a Buddha. For patients, the goal is to have these
methods help them be relieved of obstacles, such as pain, emotional distress, intrusive thoughts, and be able to have an improved/better quality of life. Patients notice
when these occur that they also feel more connected to themselves and others,
which is encouraged in the instructions by the connecting to one's inner home and
sharing the benefits with others. Patients often comment that they feel empowered
by these practices and the experience of sharing the benefits with others.

## Keeping the channels and the dialogue open for more healing opportunities

The yogic RCT studies mentioned above are among those that highlight the
possible efficacy of meditative and yogic techniques that exist in some of these
centuries-old Asian traditions, and reinforce the idea that there can be health
benefits by applying them in Western medical settings. In that context, the subtle
body can be maintained as a ground where the participant can find that inner
mind-body dialogue taking place, and where their experiences may facilitate the
understanding of the ancient Tibetan practices and their application to contemporary settings. In the model we are using here, the movements can function as a
tool that makes the integration with the contemplative aspect easier than if it was
just merely a still-seated meditation. Therefore, with the help of the movements,
patients learn to guide their mind and vital breath currents through the channels
into different areas, opening themselves up to the possibility of healing or harmonizing body, energy and mind, or the body-energy-mind system. This is a goal
shared by yogic practices, and it is also a model of good health that is in line with
the concept of health or well-being in Tibetan medicine (Dhonden 1986). Tibetan
texts do not explicitly mention concepts of stress reduction, the elimination of
intrusive thoughts, or improvement of sleep as benefits. However, as the head
teacher of Menri monastery in India, Lopon Thinley Nyima, states, these
and other related outcomes may be included as secondary benefits related to the
clearing away of obscurations.[20] In other words, as the channels open up,
the breath travelling through them, guided by one's mind's attention, brings
experiences of mind-energy-body healing.

Many Tibetan doctors have also expressed support for and interest in our studies over the years (see Chaoul 2011). Dr Yangbum Gyal stated:

> Overall, working with the five *lung* with *tsalung*, it revitalizes the body and mind by balancing and promoting the free flow of prana or *lung*-energy. Regular practice of *tsalung* exercises relieves muscular tension and nervous stress, improves respiration and digestion, benefits the cardiovascular system and leads to deep relaxation and well-being.[21]

This is also in line with the emerging fields of CIM and behavioural science, which include yogic practices as part of their 'mind-body' and 'energy medicine' categories.[22] These fields use some measurements that are objective and others subjective, such as the ones mentioned in our studies. Interestingly, although the concept of measurement may seem counter-intuitive to contemplative practices, it is found in Tibetan yogic texts and oral instructions. However, the measurements are not done by drawing out blood or saliva for analysis or by filling in charts to determine stress level, mood or anxiety, or if you slept well. The texts not only mention the idea of releasing obstacles, as mentioned earlier, but discuss measuring the heat that related practices (i.e. *gtum mo* or 'inner heat') may create by the number of breaths needed to dry an almost frozen towel on their bare back or wet it with their perspiration, or methods of counting how long one can hold one's breath during a particular exercise. Clearly such measurements are not the same as those utilized in Western biomedical sciences or CIM, but these examples can provide a glimpse into the idea that qualitative and quantitative measurement is not totally absent in the Tibetan yogic traditions. Furthermore, many contemporary Tibetan lamas have shown interest and support in this kind of scientific research of contemplative practices. In our research, the constant support of Tenzin Wangyal Rinpoche has been vital to the integrity of our studies.

As these studies continue, all of us who participate in them are constantly being reshaped, which in turn reshapes the field in which we work. I hope that these Tibetan Yoga research studies contribute in a small way to the bigger picture of the exploration of a new medicine that includes science and spirituality, and where concepts that seem foreign or unseen, like the subtle body, may prove of use, not only for the ultimate truth of healing (i.e. enlightenment) but also towards the conventional truth of healing. In that way, we can see why these are not only mentioned in Tibetan *dharma* texts but also in medical ones.

## Notes

1 Thanks to Laura Shekerjian for helping me brainstorm to come up with this title.
2 Bön is the native religious tradition of Tibet, that claims its origins in Buddha Tönpa Shenrab 18,000 years ago; their texts, including the *'Bum bzh*i, claim its origins from Tönpa Shenrab, and therefore considered earlier than the *rGyud bzhi*. However, there are quite some polemics of its origins and the relation of Bön with the tradition that we call now Buddhism.

3  See Barbara Gerke's discussion of the appropriation of the word 'humour' for *nyes pa* (2011: especially 128–30).

4  Borrowing from David Germano's translation 'channel-winds practices' (Germano 1994: 662), I use the term 'channel-breaths' practices. I feel this translates it accurately from the Tibetan and brings a better sense of the subject matter: a specific practice that utilizes the channels and different aspects of breath.

5  Jon Kabat-Zinn's Mindfulness Based Stress Reduction (MBSR) programme at the University of Massachussetts Medical School pioneered this area. Through clinical applications and research it has opened the doors to the acceptance of meditative programmes in the medical arena. It is a still small, yet significant, openness in the Western medical system at large.

6  Although many times written as *bgegs*, this type of 'obstacle' or 'hindrance' is spelled *gegs* in Shardza 1974a, and in Chandra and Namdak 1968 as *gags*. Thus far I have not been able to find if there are any significant differences in meanings among them.

7  The stretching movements came from breast cancer exercise manuals (Davis 2002; Halverstadt and Leonard 2000) and were chosen to match, in the best way possible, the physical component of the channel breaths movements.

8  Chandra and Namdak 1968: 632.2–632.3; Shardza 1974a: 322.2–322.3.

9  Numerous Tibetan, Indian and Chinese texts describe the subtle body (see also the pioneering work by Scheper-Hughes and Lock 1987, contextualizing these in a Western medical setting). Anne Harrington (2008) portrays some of the most recent works contextualizing this thought in the West.

10  See Garrett 2008; Gyatso 2004; Gerke 2011. As Janet Gyatso has noted in recent articles, especially in Gyatso 2004, and which Barbara Gerke discusses in her chapter in this volume.

11  See my comments on this issue in Chaoul 2011: especially 308–9.

12  Tenzin Wangyal Rinpoche, personal conversation with the instructors of the TY programme for people with cancer, Houston, February 2008.

13  As for the inner heat experiment, Samuel refers to Benson and Hopkins 1982.

14  Her study focused on the Six Yogas of Naropa, from her field research on how they were practised in Apo Rinpoche Gonpa (*A pho rin po che dgon pa*) in Manali, India, during 1986 and 1992.

15  David White asserts that there are Indian Tantric texts and Taoist sources as early as the fourth century, describing subtle-body practices (1996: 250). Eliade also mentions early Indian and Chinese sources, although the latter are more related to alchemy (1958: 284–92).

16  Shardza Tashi Gyaltsen, 'Channels-breaths supplication prayer' (*Rtsa rlung gsol 'debs*), in *Mass of Fire*, p. 102, lines 1–2 *mandala* offering (*mandal 'bul ba*) section (from my unpublished translation – italics added for emphasis).

17  The general agreement in Hindu and Buddhist subtle-body descriptions is that there are three channels of utmost importance: a 'central channel' (*dbu ma, suṣumnā*), or 'all-encompassing' channel (*kun 'dar ma, avadhūtī*), sometimes known as the 'Royal Road' (Avalon 1958); flanked on the right by the white-coloured 'solitary' channel (*rkyang ma, piṅgalā*), and on the left by the red-coloured 'flavour' channel (*ro ma, iḍā*).

18  H. H. Lungtok Tenpa'i Nyima mentioned how Tibetans would traditionally use the metaphor of intestines (*rgyu ma*) as channels, but felt that the balloon metaphor may seem more appropriate for a Western audience (Menri monastery, oral communication, 2002).

19 Shardza 1974b: 28. Also *Mother Tantra*, pp. 603ff.
20 Ponlob Thinley Nyima, 'Mind-body practices of the ancient Tibetan Bön tradition', talk at Rice University, Houston, Texas, April 2005.
21 Personal communication, 2007.
22 See the National Center of Complementary and Alternative Medicine (NCCAM) (2004) Online at: www.nccam.nih.gov (accessed June 2009). Besides 'mind-body medicine' and 'energy medicine', the two main categories among CAM modalities are 'ingestives' (including vitamins, herbs) and 'body manipulation' (such as massage, chiropractic and so forth). The report also mentions whole systems (such as Traditional Chinese Medicine, Indian Ayurveda and Homeopathy) as another category altogether in complementary and alternative medicine – one that I believe should be paid more attention in how they are integrated with the predominant Western allopathic system. In some medical institutions, such as MD Anderson's Integrative Medicine Program and the McGovern Center for Ethics and Humanities in UT Health, Engel's 1977 biopsychosocial model mentioned earlier is used as an example to follow.

# References

Alter, J. S. (2005) 'Modern medical yoga: struggling with a history of magic, alchemy and sex', *Asian Medicine: Tradition and Modernity* 1: 119–46.

Avalon, A. (Sir John Woodroffe) (1958) *The Serpent Power*. Madras: Ganesh.

Benson, H. and Hopkins, J. (1982) 'Body temperature changes during the practice of gTum-mo yoga', *Nature* 295: 234–6.

Chandra, L. and Namdak, T. (eds) (1968) *The Great Perfection Oral Transmission of Zhang Zhung (Rdzogs pa chen po Zhang zhung snyan rgyud): History and Doctrines of Bonpo Nispanna Yoga*. New Delhi: International Academy of Indian Culture.

Chandwani, K. D., Chaoul, M. A. and Cohen, L. (2008) 'Mind-body research in cancer', in L. Cohen and M. Markman (eds) *Integrative Oncology: Incorporating Complementary Medicine into Conventional Cancer Care*. Totowa, NJ: Humana Press.

Chaoul, M. A. (2007) 'Magical movements (*'phrul 'khor*) in the Bon tradition and possible applications as a CIM (Complementary and Integrative Medicine) therapy', in M. Schrempf (ed.) *Soundings in Tibetan Medicine: Anthropological and Historical Perspectives*. Proceedings of the International Association of Tibetan Studies (IATS), Oxford 2003. Leiden: Brill.

—— (2011) 'Re-integrating the Dharmic perspective in bio-behavioural research of a "Tibetan Yoga" (*tsalung trülkhor*) intervention for people with cancer', in V. Adams, M. Schrempf and S. Craig (eds) *Medicine Between Science and Religion*. Oxford: Berghahn.

Cohen, L., Warneke, C., Fouladi, R. T. *et al.* (2004) 'Psychological adjustment and sleep quality in a randomized trial of the effects of a Tibetan Yoga intervention in patients with lymphoma', *Cancer: Interdisciplinary Journal of the American Cancer Society* 100(10): 2253–60.

Davis, S. L. (2002) *Thriving After Breast Cancer: Essential Exercises for Body and Mind*. New York: Broadway Books.

Dhonden, Y. (2000) *Healing from the Source*. Ithaca, NY: Snow Lion Publications.

Eliade, M. (1958) *Yoga: Immortality and Freedom* (reprinted 1990). Princeton, NJ: Princeton University Press.

Engel, G. L. (1977) 'The need for a new medical model: a challenge for biomedicine', *Science*, New Series, 196(4286): 129–36.

Garrett, F. (2008) *Religion, Medicine and the Human Embryo in Tibet*. London: Routledge.

Germano, D. (1994) 'Mini-encyclopedia of great perfection terminology', unpublished manuscript. Charlottesville: University of Virginia.

Gerke, B. (2011) 'Correlating biomedical and Tibetan terms in Amchi medical practice', in V. Adams, M. Schrempf and S. Craig (eds) *Medicine Between Science and Religion: Explorations on Tibetan Grounds*. New York and Oxford: Berghahn Books.

Gyatso, J. (2004) 'The authority of empiricism and the empiricism of authority: medicine and Buddhism in Tibet on the eve of modernity', *Comparative Studies of South Asia, Africa and the Middle East* 24: 83–96.

Halverstadt, A. and Leonard, A. (2000) *Essential Exercises for Breast Cancer Survivors*, Boston, MA: Harvard Common Press.

Harrington, A. (2008) *The Cure Within: A History of Mind-Body Medicine*. New York: Norton.

Samlek, M. (Rgyal gshen Mi lus bsam legs) (1985) *Ma rgyud thugs rje nyi ma'i rgyud skor* (ed. T. Tashi), *gter ma* rediscovered by Guru Nontse (Gu ru rnon rtse) in the eleventh century. Reproduced from original manuscript belonging to the Samling Monastery (bSam gling), in Dolpo, northwest Nepal. Dolanji, India: Tibetan Bonpo Monastic Community.

Samuel, G. (1989) 'The body in Buddhist and Hindu Tantra', *Religion* 19: 197–210.

—— (2006) 'Tibetan medicine and biomedicine: epistemological conflicts, practical solutions', *Asian Medicine: Tradition and Modernity* 2: 72–85.

Sangpo, J. (ed.) (1999) *The Four Collections of Nectar Treasures of Medicine Science (Gso rig bdud rtsi'i bang mdzod 'bum bzhi)*. New Delhi: Paljor Publications.

Scheper-Hughes, N. and Lock, M. M. (1987) 'The mindful body: a prolegomenon to future work in medical anthropology', *Medical Anthropology Quarterly* 1: 6–41.

Shardza, T. G. (Shar rdza bkhra shis rgyal mtshan) (1974a) 'Channels-breaths magical movements of oral tradition [of Zhang Zhung]', in N. Sonam, S. T. Gyaltsen and K. Gyatso (eds) *The Great Treasury of the Ultra Profound Sky (Yang zab nam mkha' mdzod chen las Snyan brgyud rtsa rlung 'khrul 'khor bzhugs so)*, Vols I–III. New Thobgyal, India: Tibetan Bonpo Monastic Centre.

—— (1974b) 'Mass of fire primordial wisdom: bringing into experience the common inner heat' (*Thun mong gtum mo'i nyams len ye shes me dpung*), in Khedup Gyatso (ed.) *The Self-Arising of the Three Buddha Bodies (Rdzogs pa chen po sku gsum rang shar)*. Delhi: Tibetan Bonpo Monastic Centre.

Stutchbury, E. A. (1998) 'Tibetan meditation, yoga and healing practices: mind-body interconnections', in M. M. Del Monte and Y. Haruki (eds) *The Embodiment of Mind: Eastern and Western Perspectives*. Delft: Eburon Publishers.

Wangyal, T. (2002) *Healing with Form, Energy, and Light*. Ithaca, NY and Boulder, CO: Snow Lion Publications.

White, D. G. (1996) *The Alchemical Body: Siddha Traditions in Medieval India*. Chicago: University of Chicago Press.

# Part Three

# Subtle bodies in Europe and Islam

# Introduction to Part Three

*Jay Johnston*

The boundaries that demarcate (indeed construct) 'Asia' and the 'West' are of course far from solid: as amply demonstrated in postcolonial studies and critical, comparative religious studies. The permeability of the categories – temporal and geographical – used to order the contents of this volume are similarly not hermetically sealed but porous. Moving from a focus on Asian traditions in the last two sections, the next three chapters provide case studies not only of specific European and Muslim traditions but also of the exchange of ideas across social, cultural and geographic boundaries. Ideas travel: concepts of subtle anatomy and agency seem well suited to moving across boundaries and in the process being adapted to new contexts. Indeed, these chapters also open out considerations of comparative scholarship on subtle bodies which are more fully embraced by the contributions in Part Four, 'Subtle Bodies and Modernity'. In this introduction, a brief contextualization for each of the chapters is provided by way of a necessarily reductive overview of subtle-body traditions from Antiquity to the Enlightenment. This overview touches upon numerous rich, fascinating and complex areas of study. To this, each of the following case studies will speak with a unique particularity of analysis: providing targeted and specialist contributions to the scholarship of the broader area plotted below.

Opening this section, Joseph S. Alter takes us into a comparative exploration across the 'east–west' binary in his analysis of the embodied physicality of ascetic and athletic practices in South Asia and Ancient Greek philosophy (and the understanding and positioning of sex within such). The influence of South Asian traditions on philosophy of the Mediterranean region has generated a rich vein of academic research, and in the context of subtle-body models, the influence and exchange with Alexandrian Neoplatonists is of special note (see Harris 1982) as one such site of conceptual exchange. It is here that Egyptian, Greek and Indic traditions met with a particular resonance for the figuring of the Hermetic Arts: what we would now term astrology, divination and magic. Crystal Addey provides a detailed analysis of the figuring of subtle bodies in Neoplatonic thought. Highlighting the astral nature of the conceptualization of the 'soul vehicles' found in this tradition, Addey artfully demonstrates their centrality in ritual (including theurgic) practice (a role that can even today be found in ritual practices of contemporary occult groups). Here in Neoplatonic thought, Addey identifies concepts of 'body' and 'mind' that undermine the sharp Cartesian dualism so characteristic of post-Enlightenment dominant discourse.

This Neoplatonic tradition was to enjoy a renewed flourishing among the elite in the Renaissance, especially with the translation of Platonic philosophy and the *Corpus Hermeticum* by Marsilio Ficino (1433–99) in Florence (Allen 2006: 360). Ficino's own work of Neoplatonic/Hermetic philosophy developed the Galenic belief that an individual was primarily dominated by one of four humours, while also being constructed of celestial substance. For example, an overtly Melancholic person (associated with scholars in particular) was viewed by Ficino to be overtly influenced by Mercury and Saturn (1996: 6). In his thought Ficino intertwined the celestial, spiritual and physical with the individual being placed in a relation of *correspondences* via an existing invisible sympathy with all phenomena. This sympathy was built on relations of celestial affinity and was apprehended by a specific type of imagination. Therefore a skilled doctor could manipulate these invisible agencies via the use of phenomena that bore their 'signature'. For example, Jupiter's invisible signature was found in items as diverse as a type of thought ('religious and law-abiding'), specific animals (lamb, peacock, eagle, calf), food items (honey and white sugar), and rocks and minerals (amethyst and silver) (1996: 90–1).

Conceptualizations of the subtle body (such as Ficino's), from the Renaissance to the early Modern period are among those most well represented in scholarship. This has been especially buoyed by the increasing profile and disciplinary developments of the study of Western esoteric traditions (see Faivre 1994; Stuckrad 2005). Such studies, for example, have considered the 'sidereal' body of Paracelsus (*c.*1493–1541), Jacob Boehme's ontological desire or spirit 'forces', and the various constructions of magical agency and efficacy that are linked to the presence of a mediating subtle matter. This subtle material fluctuates from being a characteristic of all divine and worldly phenomena to being considered the substance of spirits. As Christine Göttler and Wolfgang Neuber recount, this is also a feature of subtle bodies in early Modern Europe:

> In medieval and early modern culture 'spirit' (*spiritus*) or 'subtle bodies' (*corpora subtilia*) were frequently pictured as vapours or gaseous substances as indeed the words 'spirits' and 'vapours' (*vapors*) were used interchangeably in physiological and medical language.
>
> (2008: xv)

European traditions include the Jewish mystical traditions of the Kabbalah, which have also significantly influenced Western esoteric traditions (including Ficino). The *Sefer Yetzirah*, composed in the late seventh century, incorporated Neoplatonic elements into Jewish mystical traditions, including 'the esoteric doctrine of correspondences between the microcosm and the macrocosm' (Stuckrad 2005: 34). Key to corollaries with subtle matter (and which feature very strongly in the Kabbalah of contemporary self-directed spiritual practices) were the Sefirot ('number' or 'counting'), which over time were developed in Jewish mysticism to be considered as 'emanations of divine power' that ranged (in the form of a tree) between the world and the divine (*Ein Sôf*) (Stuckrad 2005: 35–9). In micro–macrocosmic relations they were also ascribed associations with physical anatomy (figuring of Adam Kadmon) and have been creatively interpreted in popular cultural texts on the subtle body as corollaries to the *cakra* system (see Dale 2009).

An 'esoteric' or subtle anatomy also features in Islamic mystical traditions. In the third and final chapter in this section, Milad Milani presents the subtle body as found in Sufi traditions from the middle ages into the contemporary period. As with both Alter's and Addey's chapters, Milani focuses not only on the conceptualization of subtle bodies but also on their articulation into a spiritual practice. The similarity of the system of *lata 'if* to the Tantric *cakra* systems is noticeable, particularly in versions deriving from South Asian Sufi traditions such as the Mujaddedi Naqshbandi version discussed by Milani, and both has been noted by Sufi teachers (e.g. Lizzio 1998: 204 n.16) and picked up in the wider contemporary New Age context.

While by no means an exhaustive overview of the numerous European and Islamic subtle-body traditions, this section presents three focus points that mark significant constellations in the rendering of subtle bodies. These constellations illuminate either the conceptual relations between Asia and the West and the development of dominant traditions within a broadly Western and Islamic context.

# References

Allen, M. J. B. (2006) 'Ficino, Marsilio', in W. J. Hanegraaff (ed.) *Dictionary of Gnosis and Western Esotericism*. Leiden and Boston, MA: Brill.

Dale, C. (2009) *The Subtle Body: An Encyclopaedia of Your Energetic Anatomy*. Boulder, CO: Sounds True.

Faivre, A. (1994) *Access to Western Esotericism*. Albany: State University of New York Press.

Ficino, M. (1996 [1489]) *The Book of Life*, trans. C. Boer, 2nd edn. Woodstock, CT: Spring Publications.

Göttler, C. and Neuber, W. (2008) 'Preface: Vapours and veils: the edge of the unseen', in C. Göttler and W. Neuber (eds) *Spirits Unseen: The Representation of Subtle Bodies in Early Modern European Culture*. Leiden and Boston, MA: Brill.

Harris, R. B. (1982) *Neoplatonism and Indian Thought*, International Society for Neoplatonic Studies. Albany: State University of New York Press.

Lizzio, K. P. (1998) 'Saving Grace: Naqshbandi Spiritual Transmission in the Indian Sub-Continent, 1928-1997', PhD dissertation, Department of Near Eastern Studies, University of Arizona.

Stuckrad, K. von (2005) *Western Esotericism: A Brief History of Sacred Knowledge*, trans. N. Goodrick-Clarke. London and Oakville, CT: Equinox.

# 7 Sex, *askesis* and the athletic perfection of the soul

## Physical philosophy in the ancient mediterranean and South Asia

*Joseph S. Alter*

> Borrowed from the vocabulary of athletics, the concept of 'discipline' (*askesis*) was not used by the Cynics only in a metaphorical sense. Like the athlete's, the philosopher's 'discipline' (*askesis*) was wholly concrete: while the athlete trained his body with a view to victory in the stadium, the Cynic trained it in order to strengthen his will and to ensure his capacity for endurance.
>
> (Branham and Goulet-Cazé 1996: 26)

> In tantrism, the human body acquires an importance it had never before attained in the spiritual history of India: the Upanisadic and post-Upanisadic pessimism and asceticism are swept away. The body is no longer the source of pain, but the most reliable and effective instrument at man's disposal for 'conquering death'. Since liberation can be gained even in this life, the body must be preserved as long as possible, and in perfect condition, precisely as an aid to meditation.
>
> (Eliade 1990: 227)

This chapter provides a broad, comparative perspective on subtle-body development in southern Asia and the classical world of ancient Greece. Although exercise and self-discipline in both contexts has focused on the problem of self-development and the perfection of the physiological self in relation to the soul, a critical difference is found concerning the question of sex, sexuality and self-perfection. In terms of how the subtle body takes shape, this chapter traces out the relationship among asceticism, sexual physiology and athleticism in early Greece and the articulation of comparable issues in the development of yoga in ancient India.

### Subtle athleticism

> Among the Indians there is a class of the gymnosophists who, in addition to natural philosophy, likewise take great pains in the study of moral science and thus make their whole existence a sort of lesson in virtue.
>
> (Philo of Alexandria, *Every Good Man is Free*)

It is safe to assume that most people regard sport as an institution linked to fitness, entertainment and business – and perhaps to the extra-curricular development of character –but as decidedly anti-intellectual. Athleticism finds expression in the brawny heroics of *arête,* victory and championship, not in the embodied articulation of great insights on the nature of the soul. To be sure, there is a sub-field of sport philosophy (Davis and Weaving 2010; Hyland 1990; Kretchmar 2005; McNamee 2008), where sport is the subject of intellectual analysis. But one does not think of sport itself as a way of understanding things apart from sport. Few people – especially very few philosophers (for exceptions see Mihalich 1982; Weiss 1971) – find it odd that philosophy and physical fitness have little, if anything, in common.

Yet this is very odd, in terms of the 'long' history of philosophy, the clearly demarcated history of ancient sport (Gardiner 1930; Golden 1998, 2008; Kyle 1987; Newby 2006; Sansone 1988; Robinson 1955) that is congruent with the history of philosophy (see Dombrowski 2009; Miller 1991), as well as the very 'short' and curious history of modern sport which for a brief period of time around the turn of the past century was intimately linked to morals, ethics and values (Guttmann *et al.* 1990; Hall 1994; MacAloon 1981; Semple 2008). Consequently, the purpose of this chapter is to think against odd elisions in the history of the relationship between mind and body; to think against the gross disambiguation of physical fitness, athletic perfection and metaphysics, by way of a subtle analysis of sex and embodied self-discipline in the practice of philosophy.

Following an enlightened intellectual trajectory that draws directly and explicitly on the world of the classical Greek gymnasium, Euro-American philosophy is noticeably and ironically – but decidedly unself-consciously – disembodied. Conversely, modern sport, as an institution rooted in turn-of-the-century classicism, is distinctly anti-intellectual. In conjunction with this, questions about the bio-moral value of sex, that were integral to the practice of philosophy and classical athleticism, have been parsed according to, and in accordance with, the disciplinary structure of modern knowledge and the articulation of 'sexuality' as a discrete entity. In the post-Enlightenment, where reductive intellectualism devolves from the powerful logic of empiricism, it is difficult to think against this normative delineation: the rather unnatural and strange disarticulation of sex, physical fitness and philosophy in the history of ideas that structure the body in European thought.

Whereas several decades of scholarship on the history of sexuality (Foucault 1986; Laqueur 1990, 2003; Phillips and Reay 2002; Rousselle 1988) has provided a framework for a revisionist appraisal of embodied philosophy, the curious history of modern sport –anchored in turn-of-the-century muscular Christian public school moralism and masculinity (Bundgaard 2005; Hall 1994; Putney 2001) – has produced a skewed and fragmented understanding of athleticism in relation to physical fitness on the one hand and the development of character on the other. It is curious that in the history of modern sport, personal character is the product of ethically gendered sportsmanship rather than embodied practice. Scholarship on the history of sexuality has highlighted the subtle features of athleticism as an exercise in self-perfection, but physical fitness – almost by definition –succumbs to the logic of gross Cartesian dualism. At the other end of the spectrum, sportive athleticism (Guttmann 1994, 1996) and body-building in particular (Dix 1972; Fussell 1994; Guttmann 1996: 75–8; Klein 1993; Miles 1994) are charged with intense eroticism, a factor that significantly complicates the subtle nexus of sex, athletics and physical philosophy.

Coloured by the problematic principle of *arête*, athleticism is, arguably, the most misunderstood, and least appreciated, component of a holistic history of classical philosophy. As Stephen Miller puts it:

> the word arête has imbued ancient athletics with an aura of the quest of man for perfection, a quest which – at least in the eyes of moderns – was isolated from more practical matters such as politics and economics. Arête – incompletely understood – has hereby dimmed our picture of the realities of antiquity and has robbed us of many of the real lessons to be learned from ancient athletics.
>
> (1991: vii)

Since the terms of misunderstanding athleticism are, in large part, a function of the disciplinary structure of modern intellectual history, it is useful to engage in critical cross-cultural comparative analysis in order to reformulate an understanding of how the body is engaged in exercises of self-perfection. It may seem odd – if not outright perverse – to use South Asian embodied philosophy as a comparative point of reference, since the Sanskrit literature has much to say about asceticism, but virtually nothing to say about athleticism. But critical comparison cuts both ways, shedding as much light on the athletic nature of yoga as on the 'yogic' structure of classical athleticism.

South Asia provides an important point of comparison, given the centrality of the self and the body to many articulations of thought over the past several millennia, and the conceptualization of subjectivity as a particularly knotty problematic with reference to questions of transcendence and the nature of the embodied self. Until very recently *Samkhya* philosophy, and its various permutations, was interpreted, within the Orientalist logic of Enlightenment reasoning (see Garbe 1896, Keith 1918; see also Larson 1969; Larson and Bhattacharya 1987), as having a negative, if not also nihilistic, attitude towards the body and embodied reality. But even now that it is recognized that the body is directly and intimately implicated in transcendence (see Samuel 2008; Sarbacker 2005; Staal 1993; Whicher 1998, White 1996, 2000, 2009; see also Agehananda Bharati 1993), and not something to be renounced *tout court*, the albatross of the flesh still hangs heavy around the neck of South Asian scholarship (so to speak) making it very difficult to think past the hegemonic logic of mind–body duality in its various contorted permutations, especially as concerns sex-in-renunciation and ascetic self-discipline.

Terminology is problematic when developing a synthetic comparative analysis, especially when ontological differences extend beyond vocabulary to the formal range of language. On this point, therefore, use of the modern term 'athletic' in this chapter is strategic, and draws explicitly on the standard

OED definition: 'pertaining to an athlete or to contests in which physical strength is vigorously exercised'. Although public games – ancient and modern – measure strength in terms of muscles, physique and victory, athletic self-discipline involves subtle dynamics, especially when perfection structures exercise and training, and when perfection relates to, but is not restricted by, the terms of competitive victory. In other words, athleticism is a concept that does not simply resolve into *arête* or directly anticipate the physical fitness of sport, and it is in this more generic, encompassing and somewhat unstable sense that the term is used here. As it is used here, athleticism is vigorously exercised philosophy.

## Athletic cynicism: *askesis*, fitness and self-control

After the conquest of Cyrus (who died *c.*530 BCE), the Persian Empire stretched from Ionia to the Indus. From that time on, if not before, it was clearly possible for oriental doctrines to travel to the West. How exactly they reached Pythagoras we cannot even guess. But we can at least see that the later legend of Pythagoras' journey to India in search of the wisdom of the East may very well contain a grain of allegorical truth (Kahn 2001: 19).

Side-stepping the vexingly seductive, and endlessly disappointing, question of direct contact and communication between the lovers of wisdom in the ancient Mediterranean and gymnosophists of South Asia (see Kingsley 1995; Rawlinson 1971; Velissaropoulos 1991; West 1971) – and history-of-idea inferences of hybrid wisdom so produced – there are two starting points for a productive synthetic comparison. One is with Cynicism and several closely intermeshed principles: *askesis* as a form of physical fitness, and a naturalistic, 'animalistic' conception of human nature as it relates to the process of self-discipline. The other is the thoroughly grounded cosmic philosophy of life manifest in a Pythagorean theory of the immortal soul and its transmigration (Luchte 2009; Riedweg 2005). To start with Diogenes the Cynic and Pythagoras is to define the embodied soul – as very distinct from the metaphysical soul vested with idealized virtue – as having pre-eminent importance. And this importance is defined in terms of the self as an embodied subject. A key issue here is the inclusive holistic subjectivity of the body.

*Askesis,* in its most archaic sense, meaning 'disciplined practice', provides an important perspective on the body in early Greek philosophy. While characteristically revisionist and important, Foucault's extensive discussion of *askesis* in relation to the moral problematization of pleasure is ambiguous (McGushin 2007). It is ambiguous because *askesis* is said to be an end in itself, and yet also put into practice so as to serve various other ends, each directly linked to, but at various degrees of logical remove from, the self of the citizen subject. After indicating that Plato conceptualized spiritual exercise as a means by which to insulate the soul from desire, Foucault points out that

> apart from these Pythagorean practices, one finds few instances – whether in Xenophon, Plato, Diogenes, or Aristotle – where *askesis* is specified as an

exercise in self-control. There are two likely reasons for this: first, exercise was regarded as the *actual practice of what one needed to train for*; it was not something distinct from the goal to be reached. Through training one became accustomed to the behavior that one would eventually have to manifest.

(1990: 74, my emphasis)

Read literally, this is a contradictory statement: how can *askesis* be the goal itself, when its practice is meant to produce some future effect, even if that effect is almost identical to the form of ever-present practice that anticipates it? As soon as the self is defined as a subject apart from the body – and time is added to the equation – *askesis* must become a means rather than an end. The tension manifest in this contradiction runs throughout Foucault's work, given that his focus is on pleasure, desire and sexuality and not on the body as such.

An objection may be raised here on the grounds that *askesis* is not restricted to the body or limited to physical fitness, but includes meditation, ethical practices, intellectual exercise and other things that are not 'strictly speaking' physiological. The point, however, is that if *askesis* is understood as an end in itself, its end is very much the lived body of experience, regardless of the extent to which the form of training might seem to involve a link between the self and abstracted morals, ethics and values. It is the nature of the training itself – rather than any sense of a natural priority of body over mind – that substantiates the soul as such. To quote Foucault once again:

> In a word, we can say that the theme of an *askesis*, as a practical training that was indispensable in order for an individual to form himself as a moral subject, was important – emphasized even – in classical Greek thought, especially in the tradition of Socrates. And yet this 'ascetics' was not organized or conceived as a corpus of separate practices that would constitute a kind of specific art of the soul, with its techniques, procedures, and prescriptions. It was not distinct from the practice of virtue itself; it was the rehearsal that anticipated that practice.

(1990: 76)

Apart from reflecting the same contradiction noted above – a rehearsal that is also not distinct from the practice of virtue itself – this clearly indicates the extent to which *askesis* was the practice of virtue itself as embodied exercise. Moreover, it was the training itself which gave embodied form to the individual as a moral subject.

It would seem, therefore, that the question of pleasure or desire must be somewhat epiphenomenal, and already one or two steps removed from the problem of self-subjectification. Desire and pleasure are concerned with the virtue of embodiment rather than the embodiment of virtue, and the virtue of embodiment is, in essence, a question of fitness. The regulation of sex, and a discourse of sexuality, was in service of this more basic principle.

If *askesis* was an end in itself, its practice was endless: not in any pejorative sense, but in producing a short circuit in the way in which the relationship between body and soul involved virtue. Here it is useful to go beyond the Socratic notion of *enkrateia* as such – which involved 'self mastery, where self includes both body and mind' (Long 1996: 32) – and focus on the Cynics.

If the body was important in the context of Socratic training, it was of central importance in the so-called 'short cut' to virtue afforded by the physical philosophy expounded by, and embodied by, Diogenes (see Downing 1992; Dudley 1967; Navia 1998):

> the emphasis on bodily hardiness is distinctively Cynic ... A good physical condition helps to promote a steady flow of 'mental impressions that provide easy access to virtuous deeds'. Cynicism presumably gets you to virtue quickly because, if you can actually live the Cynic life – if you can master your passions, restrict your needs and interests solely to what your rational nature requires, treat no contingencies as capable of disturbing your strength of mind – you have acquired or come close to acquiring a virtuous character, as the Stoics conceived of this. And you have done so without spending years of study in logic, physics and ethics. Accordingly, if by 'virtuous deeds' Diogenes meant actions that stem from a character fortified in the ways just mentioned, it would not be absurd to suppose that a hardy physical condition is conducive to the formation of such a character. The Cynic has trained himself to be utterly indifferent to what he eats or drinks, where he sleeps, how he satisfies his sexual desires, and so forth; and thanks to his frugality he probably enjoys excellent health. Consequently, it is reasonable to think that his bodily condition frees him from many of the fears and desires that disturb people of less robust condition and from many of the characteristic motives for unethical behavior. It would be absurd, of course, to suppose that a robust physique entails a virtuous character, but Diogenes is not said to have made this claim. His doctrine is that good physical condition promotes states of mind that facilitate virtuous deeds – *mens sana in corpore sano.*
>
> (Long 1996: 38–9)

The reason for quoting this passage at some length is to emphasize the importance of the body to training and 'deliberate practice', but also to show how any characterization of the Cynic lifestyle as other than an end in itself is to articulate a contradiction. Long's analysis of the Cynic's *askesis*, for example, both entails a body/mind distinction and makes that distinction untenable with reference to the question of self-mastery. It is, therefore, problematic. One can, it seems to me, have a robust body through which there is a steady flow of mental impressions, and even experience mental impressions as robustly physiological. Given the nature of the Cynic lifestyle there is no need to suggest that one promotes or facilitates the other, or to suggest that the logical entailment of one in the other is 'absurd'.

Beyond this, Cynicism provides an important perspective on the question of *askesis* as both means and end. As Branham and Goulet-Cazé point out, doubt about Cynicism's status as philosophy can be raised in terms of an absence of *dogmata* (a principled set of beliefs) and *telos* (goal) and the rejection of *paideia* (intellectualism) (1996: 21–3). With respect to *telos* in particular, the 'goal' was to 'live in accordance with virtue', as Diogenes Laertus put it (in Branham and Goulet-Cazé 1996: 22), so long as virtue is taken to be cognate with nature. This brings us to a consideration of the seemingly paradoxical concatenation of self-control and the apparent disregard for self-control manifest in the literal meaning of Cynic – dog-like – as this meaning came to characterize the 'shameless indifference' of the Cynics to social and cultural ideals of behaviour. As Branham and Goulet-Cazé write, their

> deliberate rejection of shame, the cornerstone of traditional Greek morality, authorized them to engage in modes of life that scandalized their society but that they regarded as 'natural'. Their radical idea of freedom – 'to use any place for any purpose' (Diogenes Laertius 6.22) – made the insulting canine epithet so appropriate to our philosophers that they defiantly claimed it as a metaphor for their novel philosophers stance. Or so the story goes.
>
> (1996: 5)

To train oneself to live as a dog was to be human in accordance with nature. This involved mimesis, to be sure. But it also involved a kind of *askesis* that conformed to principles that were not defined by culture. To achieve the perfect indifference of a dog was to experience what the Cynics regarded as true human nature.

In many respects, therefore, Cynicism can be understood as a lifestyle. But it is a disciplined lifestyle with profound philosophical implications (Cutler 2005; Desmond 2006; Navia 1996). This fits well with the argument that Cynicism is best known through the lives of its key proponents – Antisthenes, Diogenes, Crates, Hipparchia, Menippus, and Bion of Borysthenes, for example – who, in important ways, can be said to have taught by example. The key lesson was that civilization was a pretence and that a philosophy of virtue based on that pretence was meaningless. A lifestyle of detached, unaffiliated self-discipline designed to experience nature as truth, and to embody the experience of truth as a human animal – on a par with other animals but capable of reason – was probably the single most radical and important contribution of the early Cynics. While it might be easy to dismiss Cynicism on purely intellectual grounds, it is best understood as a grounded, natural physical philosophy of the human animal.

## Pythagoras: harmonics, the body and the immortal soul

Pythagoras and the Pythagoreans developed and practised *askesis*, although somewhat differently than did the Cynics. The primary Pythagorean principle was harmony, and this is reflected in the regimen of the community, which involved dietary prescriptions, exercise – more walking than wrestling, it is said (but perhaps the first use of meat in the training regimen of athletes) – study, contemplation and silence, among many other things (Guthrie 1987: 73, 81). The idea was to establish a community based on equipoise, and it was upon the harmony of the psyche, the emotions and the body that this equipoise was established and maintained. In this the relationship between the body and the soul is of crucial importance with regard to both the metempsychosis and the ultimate experience of harmonizing one's own being with the cosmos. As Kahn puts it, 'the highest reward was for the soul to join in the life of the gods, in a partial or permanent escape from the cycle of rebirths' (2001: 53). The goal of the Pythagoreans was to become godlike in their being through *homoiôsis theôi*, the imitation of god (Hermann 2004).[1] Whereas becoming dog-like lionized the value of nature, as against the artifice of civilization, becoming god-like and immortal involved purification. Intimations of divinity extended the body into a supernatural arena that mimicked the purity of nature.

What is called 'becoming like god' in the *Theaetetus* was described in the *Phaedo* as the purification of the soul from bodily pleasures, pains, fears, by the practice of the virtues under the guidance of wisdom (69b–c). As a discourse on immortality in the shadow of Socrates' impending death, the *Phaedo* is the most otherworldly and in this sense the most explicitly Pythagorean of all the dialogues (Kahn 2001: 53). According to Guthrie, Pythagorean philosophy was inspired by the lifestyle associated with Orphism.

According to Orphism, the soul, a divine spark of Dionysus, is bound to the body (*soma*) as to a tomb (*sema*). Mankind is in a state of forgetfulness of its true, spiritual nature. The soul is immortal, but descends into the realm of generation, being bound to the 'hard and deeply-grievous circle' of incarnations, until it is released through a series of purifications and rites, regaining its true nature as a divine being (Guthrie 1987: 31).

As Guthrie points out, the transformation of Orphism into philosophy involved the literalization of god-like being and a kind of physiological naturalism that demystified cultish mysticism. It was in the context of applied, social Pythagoreanism that wisdom superseded ritual by taking form as embodied praxis. Beyond this, both the principle of harmony – involving mathematics and music most explicitly – and the principle of immortality were linked to the inherent symmetry of the microcosmic/macrocosmic relationship manifest in human kind and the universe.

This relationship was, quite clearly, a relationship of duality. But it was understood as a duality that had emerged from a primordial monad reflected in the principle of '1'. One is not so much a number as the 'principle of Number'. Thus the number one reflects perfect unity, and, as Theon of Smyrna puts it (quoted in Guthrie 1987: 21):

> Unity is the principle of all things and the most dominant of all that is: all things emanate from it and it emanates from nothing. It is indivisible and it is everything in power. It is immutable and never departs from its own nature through multiplication.

Significantly, dyadic relationships – such as that involving the microcosm and the macrocosm – involve multiplication and the generation of all things, most primarily the relationship between 'subject and object, knower and the known' (Guthrie 1987: 22). Harmony may, in some respects, be thought of as a sensory response to discordant multiplication in so far as it shares the exact same nuanced meaning as the term *yoga*: 'joining together'.

As we shall see, there is a certain harmony (or meta-harmonic relationship) between the ideas developed by Pythagoras and those of Patanjali, as expressed in the *Yoga Sutra*. There is an even greater correspondence between Pythagorean *askesis* and *hatha yoga*. Harmony in general, but the specific attempt to embody god-like harmony and effect a harmonic relationship between the embodied soul and the cosmos in particular, resonates clearly with the central goal of yoga: union and the realization of the atmic self as identical to the universal, singular monadic principle of the cosmic, *paramatmic* Self. A discrete concept of the culture-bound self falls away in light of embodied supra-human unity, just as the Cynics saw it fall away in the natural dispassion of dog-like indifference.

Although the Cynics and the Pythagoreans embodied philosophy as a way of life that involved athletic regimens of inclusive fitness, it is noteworthy that sex was of no more, and perhaps less, significance than many other things – speaking and eating, for example. Sex was, of course, morally problematic, but only as one specific issue in the larger question of the relationship among the body, nature and the soul. In relation to these concerns, the world of the gymnasium has a direct bearing on the soul, and is the nexus of philosophical learning writ large, but clearly problematizes sex in relation to the body in a particular way. This, as we shall see, leads to the objectification of the heroic athlete, and the iconicity of muscular perfection, in a way that is comparable to the objectification of anti-social asceticism in South Asia, and the iconic importance of semen as a gross substance with subtle significance in the practice of yoga athleticism.

## *Palaestrita*: exercise, erotics and the embodiment of fitness

The Scythian [Anacharsis] observes that each of the Greek cities has a designated place in which they go mad every day – the gymnasium (Martin 1996: 138).

Most broadly, the point of the discussion so far has been to show how *askesis* as physical fitness encompasses sexuality and 'asceticism' – or proto-asceticism – as a technique of the self, and how this was conceptualized as a moral problem with regard to the soul. The reason for engaging in this analysis is to question some of the assumptions about the relationship between sexuality and athleticism in the gymnasium, since it was in this classical institution that both sex and physical fitness flourished, and where they were regarded as intimately connected.

Recently there has been some interest in the study of the relationship between sport and sexuality in ancient Greece (Cohen 1992; Golden and Toohey 2003; Guttmann 1996: 15–37; Hoffman 1980; Loraux 1990). Guttmann and most others (Halperin *et al.* 1990; Rousselle 1999; Scanlon 2005; Sutton 1992) who have studied the topic point out that the gymnasium was an erotic environment. The 'young but fully grown body, molded by gymnastics to the peak of its power' was most certainly the object of desire. The body was, as Guttmann points out, 'erotically charged when in motion', and clearly the gymnasium was a place where bodies were set in motion (1996: 18).

Beyond this, the athletic body was thought to be charged with sexual power, and here, as Loraux points out (1990), Heracles is paradigmatic of athleticism, albeit with gendered twists (see also Griffiths 2002; Simons 2008). In the logic of interpretation, the 'sexually powerful body' was measured in terms of what might be called kinetic sexuality and the calculus of sexual exploits. This was – and continues to be – a very common motif, almost to the point that the enumeration of sexual exploits has become paradigmatic of heroic masculinity. In conjunction with this, scholars have noted that in the classical gymnasium the naked body was on display. And although there is nothing intrinsically sexual about the naked body, nakedness allowed for the body to become the object of desire even when it was not erotically engaged. There is no sense in which the ancient gymnasium was purely and simply hedonistic. But the logic of most interpretations of sexuality in the gymnasium is that exercise increased both eroticism and sexual power, and that the intimate reciprocality of this relationship produced an escalating scale of desire.

To a large extent this interpretation is legitimate. But it draws attention away from an alternative interpretation that is more directly focused on the body as a whole. Sexuality – in the kinetic, erotic and ultimately moral and ethical sense – may in some ways be regarded as derivative of exercise, which, unto itself, was primarily engaged in to produce physical strength. Sex is directly relevant to strength and exercise, but not simply in terms of erotics. In this regard it is important to make a distinction between wrestlers and boxers as well as other athletes whose training regimens were extreme and produced 'heavy muscularity' on the one hand, and on the other the fit, healthy and balanced – as well as beautiful – body of the *palaestrita*. Quoting Margaret Walters (1978: 14), Guttmann points out that *palaestrita* were 'boys, youths or young men who were adept at the exercises of the gymnasium and whose bodily beauty and grace of movement marked them … as shining examples of the physical ideal at which the gymnasium … aimed' (1996: 18). The body of the wrestler and the body of the *palaestrita* were not different in kind; they were different in degree, and the question of degree was calibrated, at least to a large extent – if not exclusively – with reference to what might be called the physiology of sexual fitness.

In an important way the physiology of sex – arousal, coitus, orgasm and ejaculation – was directly linked to questions of health and fitness, and it is noteworthy that in his study of sexuality in classical Greece Foucault is far less concerned with erotics than he is with the way in which sexuality was regulated and how this regulation was linked to dietetics, health and physical fitness, although he does not use the term 'physical fitness' as such. With this in mind it becomes clear that eroticism is only one aspect of sex, and not one that is especially problematic unto itself. The gymnasium was less an environment for the expression of erotic desire – as more or less separate from sport and athleticism as such – and more a place where the problem of fitness and health engaged directly with the problem of desire.

As Foucault points out, the key problem with regard to sex in classical Greece was not whether it was good or bad, but what effect it had on one's own health and on the health of the children so conceived. Most certainly in medical texts (see Manos 1983) but also, it seems, in more general works, the basic principle was that one should abstain from sex as much as possible in order to promote health and strength. Diogenes Laertius along with Pythagoras claimed that sex dissipated strength. In the Aristotelian framework sex was recommended only in the case of 'pressing need', since the act itself was like doing to the body what is done to a plant when it is uprooted from the soil (Foucault 1990: 118). It is noteworthy that the violent pathology of ejaculation is explained in detail with regard to the body as a whole. Aristotle theorized that the ejaculation of semen over-cooled the brain by drawing away the body's natural heat. Others, working with an understanding of the way in which the body produced semen from marrow, identified the spinal cord as vulnerable. Perhaps the most comprehensive treatment of the subject is in a Hippocratic text, *The Seed*. As Foucault states, in this text:

> The sexual act is analyzed, from start to finish, as a violent mechanical action that is directed toward the emission of sperm. First, the rubbing of the genitals and the movement given to the whole body produce a general warming effect; the latter, combined with agitation, gives the humor, diffused into the whole body, a greater fluidity, so that it begins to 'foam' (*aphrein*), 'in the same way as all other fluids produce foam when they are agitated'. At this stage a phenomenon of 'separation' (*apokrisis*) occurs; the most vigorous part of this foaming fluid, 'the most potent and the richest' (*to ischyrota to kai piotaton*) is carried to the brain and the spinal marrow, descending its length to the loins. Then the warm foam passes to the kidneys and from there through the testicles to the penis, from which it is expelled by means of a violent spasm (*tarach*).
>
> (1990: 127)

Ejaculation was a whole-body process, just as semen was understood to be the potent extract of all the body's fluids.

Plato, Aristotle and Hippocrates offer different explanations for how and from what semen is produced within the body, but there is general consensus that it is precious, and that ejaculation is a kind of fluid drain on the body as a whole. Foucault paraphrases Aristotle as follows:

> it is understandable that the discharge of ... semen constitutes an important event for the body: it withdraws a substance that is precious, being the end result of a lengthy distillation by the organism and concentrating elements which, in accordance with nature, might have gone 'to all parts of the body', and hence might have made it grow if they had not been removed from the body.
>
> (1990: 132)

Ejaculation thus not only causes weakness but stunts growth and development. And yet, as is quite obvious, the act of sex is necessary: it is the basis of life that extends beyond the bounded body of a single person. The tension between life and death manifest in the act of sex itself points to the cycle of life and death and to ideas about immortality, albeit somewhat different ideas than those articulated in the Pythagorean tradition. As Foucault puts it:

> For Aristotle and Plato alike, the sexual act was at the point of junction of an individual life that was bound to perish – and from which, moreover, it drew off a portion of its most precious resources – and an immortality that assumed the concrete form of a survival of the species. Between these two lives, the sexual relation constituted, as Plato says, an 'artifice' (*mēchanē*) that was designed to join them together so that the first might, in its own way, participate in the second; this *mēchanē* provided the individual with an 'offspring' of himself (*apoblastēma*).
>
> (1990: 134)

To define the physical act of sex as an artifice is significant on a number of different levels. Quite apart from the fetishism of Freudian interpretation, it anticipates the artifactual relationship between life, death and immortality in yoga, and the subtle physiology of sexual power that is at the heart of yoga.

Before turning to an analysis of yoga as a kind of metaphysical fitness training, it is relevant to consider the training of Greek athletes, as this training involved a very specific and regulated form of what Foucault refers to more broadly as the 'exercise of existence' and the management of pleasure as a technique of the self. In many respects, the male Greek athlete seems to most clearly embody the principles of Galanic medicine, at least to the extent that his physical fitness reflects a theory of sexual physiology. Insofar as medicine was very much akin to philosophy in the classical period, it is possible to appreciate the intersection of philosophy, medicine and sport at this time. But it is also possible to see how the later development of sport and the refinement of medical knowledge combined to extract the body from philosophy by reifying it as a thing unto itself, reflecting physical strength and beauty on the one hand and physical health on the other.[2]

Plato, among many others, makes reference to the way in which some athletes practised sexual abstinence while involved in training, and that this abstinence could be extreme. Of note in this regard is not just the practice of abstinence, but the way in which the loss of semen through nocturnal emission was regarded as pathological on account of being involuntary; beyond the reach of the self, one might say. As Foucault points out, however, the pathologizing of sex in medical terms involved 'the involuntary violence of tension and an indefinite, exhausting expenditure' (1988: 113, see also 105–16). This pathologizing of sex was profoundly physiological and linked to substance rather than to the question of moral or immoral behaviour (see Manos 1983). Philostratus explains that athletes must gradually rebuild their strength – particularly their endurance and breath – after losing their semen, and must get rid of the excess perspiration that seems to result from this as well. As Scanlon points out, Galen advocated the use of 'flattened leaden plates' placed over the groin to prevent nocturnal discharge: although how this was supposed to work is not clear. Another technology known as the 'dog's leash' (*kunodesem*) was used to tie up the foreskin, apparently to prevent erections and, by extension – or, in fact, the lack thereof – ejaculation. Thus, the extreme form of the athlete's training reflected the particular pathology of sex:

> For as soon as the act takes place, it is, in its unfolding, regarded as intrinsi-
> cally dangerous. Dangerous because it is a wasting of the precious substance
> whose accumulation nevertheless incites one to commit it – it allows all the
> life force that the semen has concentrated to escape.
>
> (Foucault 1988: 112–13)

Extreme abstinence is a solution; although it can also be regarded as exacerbating the pathology of sex by enhancing desire through extreme accumulation. It is, therefore, a contingent and rather problematic solution.

What is most interesting about this is that it produces two levels of apparent contradiction. First, how does one reconcile the fact that gymnasiums were places for sexual liaison – *eros* as such (see Scanlon 2002) – with the ideal of athletic chastity? Second, and perhaps more significantly, how does one make sense of the fact that Plato and Aristotle, among others, applauded the practice of strict sexual abstinence among athletes while they criticized athletic excess in general – for abstinence is, in fact, precisely a form of negative excess. The locus of the problem seems to have been in the way in which excessive training offset the balance between body and soul, involved an exaggerated concern for oneself, and, correspondingly, a shirking of civic responsibility. In this there was a definite parallel between athletic and valetudinarian excess. Both were

> characteristic of those who, in order to keep from losing their hold on life,
> tried their utmost to delay the term that had been appointed by nature. The
> practice carried the danger – moral but political as well – of exaggerating
> one's care of the body (*peritté epimeleia tou sēmatos*).
>
> (Foucault 1990: 104–5)

In other words, an excess of physical training was seen as a kind of embodied self-absorption; a doomed attempt to become immortal. Whereas the act of sex was conceptualized as an artifice of immortality, athletic excess – including absolute chastity – was unnatural and contrived: artificial rather than an artifice. As we shall see, in the case of athletic *hatha yoga* the artifice of sexual immortality is more subtly embodied.

There is, needless to say, a degree of contradiction and ambivalence in the Greek understanding of sportive athleticism and sex. Abstinence is good since one's ability to retain semen – and to embody the power thereby derived – would seem to have no limit, but too much abstinence is bad if combined with other kinds of excess. In this instance, citing Plato's praise for the chaste Olympian Iccus of Tarentum, Foucault makes the remark, consistent with the inconsistency of the Greeks, that 'men could – in certain cases at least – retain all their semen; far from causing them harm, strict abstinence on their part would preserve their force in its entirety, accumulate it, concentrate it, and carry it finally to a higher level' (1990: 120).

As Foucault's work makes clear, for the early Greeks sexual behaviour was problematized in terms of 'its quantitative gradations' (1990: 45), and in many ways the gymnasium marks a locus point of two possible extremes. From the perspective of a history of sexuality that is concerned with the development of ideas about propriety and impropriety, as well as the whole apparatus of Christian morals, the purely 'eros' end of spectrum is most interesting and telling. It is this that most scholars seek to explain, even when they rightly focus on the broader techniques of the self and the physiology of sex. After all, is not the 'problem of pederasty' – and more broadly 'homosexuality' – the infuriatingly disorienting subtext of this entire history?

Clearly it is important to focus on the kinetics of sex in order to understand the development of moral and spiritual injunctions against acts and behaviour. But to focus on kinetics alone – or chastity alone, for that matter – is to forget that the gymnasium brought two opposing principles into a single gambit. The athlete embodied two extremes, and a key problem for the Greeks was how to make sense of sex as a physiological act linked to the problem of fitness.

Ironically, the concept of athleticism and the category of sport as such – particularly as it is so central to early Greek public life – gets in the way of understanding the significance of 'physical education' and sexual fitness to self-development in general. That is, the problem of fitness can all too easily be displaced onto the figure of the athlete, making it seem like it is only he or she who must be concerned with the problem of excess. The association between athletic prowess and chastity on the one hand and gymnastic movement and eroticism on the other has made it possible for the gymnasium to be seen as a 'world apart', and for the athlete to be seen as categorically different from other kinds of men, rather than a model citizen or a lover of wisdom. Recall, for example, that Heracles embodied iconic athletic strength (*alkē*), *and* the power to 'deflower fifty virgins in one night'. One is tempted to find in the figure of the athlete the precursor of a whole panoply of sexual identities that became similarly defined as categorically different and, ultimately, abnormal and immoral.[3]

If Foucault is right about the history of sexuality, it should be acknowledged that the celebration of the athletic hero in Greek writing probably anticipates the emergence of the perverted sinner in Christendom, more so than do various discrete acts of sex or sexual behaviour as such. Sex came to be an act unto itself that could be engaged in, in any number of ways, thus enabling the classification and sub-classification of types of people based on 'sexual preference' – paedophiles, homosexuals, and even, for that matter, fornicators. But, in the Christian formulation, this scheme of elaborate classification was contained within a more simple, binary typology of sinful indulgence and celibate salvation. With regard to fitness, the question of the relationship between soul and soma came to be an either/or distinction of mutual exclusion, ultimately rendering moot the question of the body's relationship to moral self-development.

Whereas sex – in the sense that it was 'invented' as sexuality in the context of modern Christendom – has, needless to say, remained a key problem on many different philosophical, moral and psychological levels, the Greek 'invention' of sport and athleticism signalled the ultimate demise of physical fitness – *askesis*, let us say – as a serious philosophical question and moral problem. While clearly other factors are involved, the objectification of the athlete may be seen as one of the first steps in the objectification of sex as a distinct thing, and of the categorization of sport and physical fitness as somehow different from self-development as a moral, spiritual and ultimately intellectual exercise. This process has made modern philosophy what it is: 'the love and pursuit of wisdom by *intellectual* means and moral self-discipline', as the *American Heritage Dictionary* puts it (emphasis added). Not counting Merleau-Ponty – whose phenomenology remains largely intellectual – only Nietzsche among Western philosophers seriously struggled with the physiological nature of moral self-discipline (see Blondel 1990; Moore 2002; Morrison 1997: 96–113). In any event, it does not take a Cynic, much less a late nineteenth-century pre-Socratic neo-Cynic to recognize the inherently intellectual bias of modern Western philosophy. Using Pythagorean terminology this bias reflects the discord of a dyadic unit masquerading as Unity itself.

## Yoga: physical philosophy

In his analysis of the care of the self and the 'work of the soul' as implicated in the body, Foucault makes an important point about Greek philosophy that can be used to set the stage – both evocatively and with reference to the specific components of structure – for a more systematic discussion of Yoga philosophy in South Asia.

The reasonable soul thus has a dual role to play: it needs to assign a regimen for the body that is actually determined by the latter's nature, its tensions, the condition of circumstances in which it finds itself. But it will be able to assign this regimen correctly only provided it has done a good deal of work on itself: eliminated the errors, reduced the imaginings, mastered the desires that cause it to misconstrue the sober law of the body (Foucault 1988: 133).

Yoga is, fundamentally, a materialist philosophy of the embodied soul, which reflects the Greek concern with physical self-discipline, but even more so Foucault's analysis of the relationship between the self and the body. Unfortunately, however, on account of Orientalism and New Age neo-Orientalism – beginning with Vivekananda at the end of the nineteenth century (see de Michelis 2004) and finding expression, most recently, in modern aerobic studios, health spas and school gymnasiums – Yoga has been exoticized, farcically banalized and fetishistically classified and sub-classified to the point that there is a radical disconnection between contemporary practice (see Singleton 2010; Smith 2007; Hoyez 2007) and the representation of historical forms of practice in the classical and medieval literature of South Asia (see Alter 2004; Singleton and Byrne 2008).

Of concern here, obviously, is not the form of contemporary practice, or the modern history of this practice, but rather the formulation of physical philosophy in the standard canon of yoga: the *Yoga Sutra* of Patanjali on the one hand, and the three primary *hatha yoga* treatises on the other, the *Hathayogapradipika*, the *Gherandasamhita* and the *Sivasamhita*. The argument is not that these texts define what is authentic yoga, as against all other interpretations and representations; rather it is that an analysis of these texts provides an interesting and illuminating comparative framework for understanding what modern philosophy might be if the Greeks had not fetishized the hero athlete, and Christians not turned this into the fetishization of the flesh as such.

The argument is not, by any means, that the Natha Siddhas of medieval India, who composed the medieval *hatha yoga* literature, define the exclusive 'origin point' for this alternative modern philosophy; their embodied practice simply allows for a critical triangulation of aspects – involving sex, fitness and the soul – that can help to deconstruct the idea that philosophy as a way of life is circumscribed by the history of a discipline (philosophy) that has been rooted in modern, Western interpretations of Greek antiquity.

The argument is that it is possible and important to compare *askesis* and yoga so as to put sex in its place – as a biomoral entity linked to fitness – as well as open up the history of philosophy so as to better understand how philosophy as such does not just entail intellectual exercise but also a physiological process of fitness and moral self-development. To put sex in its place within an expanded history of philosophy means that Christianity and its modern politico-disciplinarily entailments – including Orientalism and the neo-Orientalism manifest in Area Studies, both marked and unmarked as such – must be subverted. This is painting with rather broad strokes, to be sure, and inevitably there will be questions and objections. But a focus on 'dislocated' subtle physiology can provide a way to think against the reification of the body and the mind in relation to sport, philosophy and sex.

Although it is hopefully clear, it is worth being explicit about why the point of comparison between South Asia and Greece should not involve sport: sport fetishizes the body and makes sex into a means to an end. It prevents sex and the body from being understood as parts of a more holistic enterprise that is an end unto itself. Although there could be interesting ways in which epic wrestling in both traditions might be analysed through comparison – Hanuman and Heracles virtually beg to be sized up, for instance (although neither one is really an athlete, and Lakulisha and Heracles probably have a greater affinity – see Ingalls 1962) – the example of yoga helps to break down and disarticulate the contrived and ambiguous relationship among sex, *askesis* and fitness in the gymnasium.

There are many interesting and important parallels between the practice of *hatha yoga* and *askesis* as it is framed by various philosophical traditions, especially those of the Cynics and the Pythagoreans. But it is necessary to be clear on the differences, both on the level of practice as well as in terms of the frames.

First of all, Cynicism is a much broader and more encompassing framework, being 'a practical ascetic morality for the have-nots ... a universal ethical model of freedom and autonomy, [and] a cultural practice devoted to "defacing" the false values of the dominant culture' (Branham and Gouylet-Cazé 1996: 21). While counter-cultural to the core, *hatha yoga* is more narrowly construed as a form of embodied training, but it developed in an environment that included a similarly broad range of concerns, including tantric 'defacement' and *pashupata* 'bestiality' (see Ingalls 1962), as well as other less direct routes to immortality and freedom. *Tantrism* – provided it is taken to encompass *hatha yoga* (see White 1996) – is more directly comparable to Cynicism. But even so, as a form of practice *hatha yoga* is much more elaborate, codified and formally structured than *askesis*. Most significantly, where the Cynics trained the body to pervert and subvert culture and the pretence of civilization, the Natha Siddhas who 'invented' *hatha yoga* did so to transubstantiate the body as a whole, to 'up-end' reality itself. This only contingently involved the subversion of culture, and that too by progressive control and structured training rather than through defacement and the kind of counter-cultural antics practised by Aghoris, Kapalikas (Lorenzen 1972) and Pashupatas (Bisschop and Griffiths 2003; Ingalls 1962). In other words, what was more or less discrete and delineated in the South Asian context was part and parcel of a less discrete and more encompassing Cynic lifestyle in Greece around the fifth century BCE. And it is, in part for this reason, that comparison is useful and interesting.

Second, medieval *hatha yoga* is heavily influenced by *siddha* alchemy. At base it is concerned with the embodiment of magical power. As intimated above, there are ways in which *askesis* invokes certain principles of immortality with regard to the retention of semen. And there are ways in which the Pythagorean concern for the regimentation and care of the body – including sexual austerity – was designed to magically harmonize soul and cosmos, and render this harmonic pure and transcendent. But the link between sex, body and power among the early Greeks was, beyond what is articulated in mythology and ritual, primarily ethical, moral and medical. Although magic was very much an important part of Greek life – particularly in the area of astrology, divination and alchemy (see Dickie 2001; Kingsley 1995; Lindsay 1970; Ogden 2009) – the body itself was not particularly magical in the ancient Peloponnesus, or the object of magical transformation on the level of physiology.[4]

Therefore, it is in the magical aspect of *hatha yoga*, which involves both fitness and sex, that one can identify an analogous but quite different understanding of how the body is integral to moral self-development, and how the exercise of 'moral' self-development is an end in itself that is both virtuous and transcends virtue: a subtle regimen that is not at all a technique of the self, but is – with apologies to Foucault – a use of the embodied self to transcend pleasure, among other things.

The magical and mystical nature of yoga as studied by early Orientalists led to a long-standing misunderstanding of the relationship among the body, the self of direct experience, and the cosmic, universal Self of transcendence.[5] In essence the body was understood as a problem to be overcome; as one particular manifestation of the grand illusion that inhibited a realization of absolute Truth. Mircea Eliade's classic 1969 study *Yoga: Immortality and Freedom* did much to correct this misunderstanding, although only recently has scholarship begun to fully come to grips with the way in which yoga works through and with rather than against the body and nature (Samuel 2008; Whicher 1998; White 1996). Understanding yoga in this way draws attention away from austerity, abnegation and asceticism *per se* – as well as nihilism as such – to the more proactive and concrete domain of alchemy and supernatural power in particular and mimesis in general. Thus the contrast between the Greek and the Southern Asian world-view as concerns the body is not one of radical, categorical opposition but of subtle distinction as concerns the relationship among body and soul, sex and physiology, magic and musculature, fitness and immortality.

## Yoga: subtle physiology

> By practising to draw in the *bindu* [semen], discharged during cohabitation, whether one be a man or a woman, one obtains success in the practice of *Vajroli*. By means of a pipe, one should blow air slowly into the passage in the male organ. By practice, the discharged *bindu* is drawn out. One can draw back and preserve one's own discharged *bindu*. The Yogi who can protect his *bindu* thus, overcomes death; because death comes by discharging *bindu*, and life is prolonged by its preservation.
>
> (*Hathayogapradipika* 3: 83–7)

As clearly explained by Mircea Eliade (1990), David G. White (1996, 2003), Geoffrey Samuel (2008: 271–90) and others (Feuerstein 1989, 1992; Snellgrove 1987), *hatha yoga,* both when it directly involves sex – as in the case of *vajroli* – and when it does not, is structured around the way in which the material nature of the body, both subtle and gross, is linked to inner alchemy and the transubstantiation and flow of sexual fluid.

There can be great disagreement on what counts as yoga, and how the practice of yoga is classified and sub-classified. The position taken here is that yoga in general, but most certain the practice of *hatha yoga,* meaning 'forceful union [of *atma* and *parmatma*]', involves the body, both directly in practice but also more 'abstractly' with regard to the way in which consciousness as such – which manifests the individual self – is understood to be an evolute of *prakriti,* or matter (Whicher 1996). As a technique for realizing transcendent consciousness, yoga works through the structure of *prakritik* manifestation: the world as experienced by the senses.

The clearest way to appreciate this – keeping the principle of *askesis* in mind, as well as the strategic extension of the term athleticism – is with reference to yoga physiology. This physiology is based on the movement of *prana* (vital air) through the body. This movement requires exercise, training and discipline known as *pranayama* (see Green 2008; Zysk 2007).[6] In essence, *hatha yoga* postulates a theory of the body that is structured in terms of layered sheaths, each one more or less subtle than the next. Significantly even the most subtle sheath is constituted of matter. *Prana* is understood to flow through myriad *nadi* conduits, and this flow animates the sentient body; *prana* is the agency of everything, including consciousness, and it cross-cuts, or permeates, all of the sheaths, from the most gross to the most subtle. There are three primary *nadi*: the axial *susumna* and the *ida* and *pingla*. Starting at a common base point, the *ida* and *pingla nadi* are, respectively, on the left and right of the *susumna*, intersecting it at seven points along the gross axis of the spinal column, thus defining the *cakras* as the subtle 'back bone' of yoga physiology. *Pranayama* exercises are designed to clear and purify all of the *nadi*, draw the *prana* to the base point of the *susumna* and then channel it upwards along the *susumna* and through the subtle roundabouts or *cakras*.

This channelled flow of *prana* ends in enlightenment, the dissolution of the self in the Self, but it produces what might be called an embodied state of perfection, or absolute union, called *samadhi*. In a state of *samadhi*, the body no longer flows with *prana*, is not sentient, and is both immobile and immortal. As Eliade first pointed out and as David G. White has most recently made clear (1996), *samadhi*, achieved through the practice of *hatha yoga* in general and *pranayama* in particular, is a condition in which the body is rendered pure, all-powerful and impenetrable, just as base metal is turned into gold through the agency of mercurial transubstantiation in the technology of alchemy. In this scheme *asanas* (seats) – the iconic posture exercises of the yoga tradition – are conceptualized as training the body to withstand the force of enlightenment. Together, therefore, *asana* and *pranayama* primarily but also the preliminary moral and ethical restraints and modes of self-purification known as *yama* and *niyama* – involving physiologically based methods for cleaning the eyes, ears, sinuses, digestive tract, brain and alimentary canal – should be understood as modes of physical fitness training oriented towards transcending consciousness and embodying a perfected soul.

Most significantly (both in general but specifically for the purposes of the argument being developed here), the channelling of *prana* through the *susumna* is understood very clearly as the internalization of orgasmic ejaculation (Samuel 2008: 274; Silburn 1988; Snellgrove 1987; White 2003). Mercury is to alchemy what semen is to the body, and in the physiology of yoga, *prana* is cognate with semen. Referring to the broader tantric tradition, of which medieval *hatha yoga* was a specific manifestation, David G. White elaborates on the embodiment of sexuality in practice:

> Here, all humans were viewed as essentially androgynous with sexual intercourse an affair between a female serpentine nexus of energy, generally

called *kuṅdalini,* and a male principle, identified with Siva, both of which were located in the subtle body. An intricate metaphysics of the subtle body – its relationship to the brute matter of the gross body as well as the universal divine life force within, the bipolar dynamics of its male and female constituents, etc. – was developed in every tantric school ... For the Natha Siddhas, the *siddhis* and *jivanmukti* were the direct results of the internal combination and transformation of sexual fluids into *amrta,* the divine nectar of immortality.

(1996: 5)

Most significantly, the 'intricate metaphysics of the subtle body' are not abstractions or esoteric metaphoric entailments, but realized in fact through the physical act of exercise, noting that even meditation involves a kind of athletic physical exercise since consciousness is a manifestation of matter.

> Through heroic efforts of mental concentration and physical exertion, the yogin now initiates a controlled rising of his seed, the heat of his solar fires, and his breath along the medial channel ... This heat, concentrated within the infinitesimal space of the medial channel, effects the gradual transformation of 'raw' semen into 'cooked' and even perfected nectar, *amrta*; it is this nectar that gradually fills out the moon in the cranial vault such that, at the conclusion of this process, the lunar orb, now brimming with nectar, is possessed of its full complement of sixteen digits ... This transformation of semen into nectar wholly transforms the body, rendering it immortal.
>
> (1996: 40–1)

*Hatha yoga* did not, of course, emerge *sui generis* in the ninth century, but developed as a dynamic response to a long series of philosophical and spiritual questions dating back to at least the eighth or ninth century BCE (see Samuel 2008). There are also intriguing links to comparable forms of practice discussed in the Daoist literature as well as Tibetan traditions (see Samuel 2008: 278–82; Schipper 1994; Alter 2009). In most general terms, one of the key issues in the structure of this series of questions was the relationship between what might be called a sacrificial mode of apprehending reality by ritual means and a mystical mode of apprehending reality by means of integrated self-discipline (see Alter 2012). The mystical mode, articulated first in the Upanisads (800–500 BCE) (see Olivelle 1992, 1998), involves the internalization of the sacrifice (see Bentor 2000); that is, the embodiment of Vedic ritual so as to use the self to experience the Self. As Ian Whicher puts it:

> Once it is understood that life perpetuates itself through its transformative or changing nature, that is, the creation, maintenance, and dissolution of separate life-forms, the only appropriate and spiritually mature response is to relate to existence as a continual sacrifice of the sense of separate selfhood or individuality. While the external rituals of orthodox Brahmanism were

acknowledged as having a proper place in the social order, the Upanisadic adepts denied outright their soteriological efficacy.

(1998: 13)

The internalization of sacrifice, as a revolutionary, paradigm-shifting idea, was predicated on the fact that 'the essential core of one's own existence' was identical to transcendental reality, and that egoic identity – the self as commonly experienced – was based on, and produced by, an illusion. Stated this way, one is better able to understand the significance of both the similarities and the difference between some key aspects of Classical Greek philosophy and the post-Upanisadic philosophy of South Asia.

What was problematic for Socrates among others was a moral principle worked out with reference to pleasure, and that self-perfection involved the discriminate use of pleasure. What was problematic for Yajnavalkya and his compatriots was the self itself in relation to the Self. As a 'technique of the self' that involved self-into-Self transcendence, yoga was a comprehensive and holistic form of athletic self-discipline rather than one that was derivatively and discriminately calculated. As texts outlining the practice make clear, over time physiological yoga came to involve precise rules, detailed instructions and the careful elaboration of regimens and instructions.

Without question, the *Yoga Sutra* is about the mind, and the technique of yoga expounded by Patanjali is concerned with *cittavrttinirodha*, the 'cessation of the misidentification with the modifications of the mind' (Whicher 1998: 2). Not so much a guidebook or manual of instruction on how to achieve this goal, the *Yoga Sutra* is a collection of terse aphorisms that outline key concepts and a sequence of development based on both theory and practice. The text does not have much to say about the body as a whole, although it cryptically mentions *pranayama* and emphasizes the need for both mental and physical self-purification. Even so, in an important way the *Yoga Sutra* anticipates a more direct and comprehensive integration of the body into philosophical practice, since the mind itself is understood to be a material evolute of *prakrti*, and the process of controlling the mind produces supernatural effects that are clearly physiological in nature.

The development of yogic ideas from the period of the Upanisads on is linked to, but not identical with, the development of ideas concerning renunciation manifest in the ascetic institution of *sannyas*. Chastity is central to the practice of ascetic renunciation (see Samuel 2008: 173–90). From it the *sannyasi* derives the inner heat of *tapas*, the brilliance and power of *tejas*, as well as radiance, strength and vitality (Olivelle 1992). The principle of *tapas* is linked to the power of fire both in the cosmic form of solar energy and in the specific ritual technology of fire sacrifice. Thus, *tapas* involves the internalization of the sacrificial fire and the embodiment of cosmic radiance. On this level there are obvious parallels between asceticism and yoga, and the *Yoga Sutra* clearly stipulates the value of chastity and the observance of *tapas* as self-discipline.

Incorporating *tapas*, which is asceticism broadly defined – and an ancient concept found in the earliest Vedas – the formalized institution of *sannyas*, which emerged in the post-Vedic period, is philosophically closely akin to yoga insofar as the *sannyasi* is seeking to experience reality as transcendental truth beyond the illusion of consciousness. The means to this end, however, are significantly different. Among other things, what distinguishes the institution of *sannyas* from the practice of yoga is the fact that the *sannyasi* renounces the world *and* his body as a manifestation of worldly attachment. Although there are many different formulations in the literature about the relationship between the body and asceticism within the framework of *sannyas,* it is clear that the body presents a radical problem with regard to the ideal of absolute renunciation. In the *Maitrayaniya Upanisad* the most radical position is put this way:

> In this ill-smelling, pithless body, which is a conglomerate of bone, skin, muscle, marrow, flesh, semen, blood, mucus, tears, rheum, feces, urine, wind, bile, and phlegm – what good is the enjoyment of desire? In this body, which is afflicted with lust, anger, greed, delusion, fear, despondency, jealousy, separation from what is loved, union with what is unloved, hunger, thirst, senility, death, illness, grief, and the like – what good is the enjoyment of desires.
>
> (1.2ff., quoted in Feuerstein 2001: 69)

Clearly this signals the need for a radically relativist understanding of desire and pleasure.

Beyond the problem of the body in relation to desire in particular, and worldly attachment in general, *sannyas* is a lifestyle rather than a set of techniques. As Georg Feuerstein writes:

> Although renunciation can be identified as a lifestyle, it cannot be performed as one might perform austerities or meditation. It is primarily a fundamental *attitude* toward life. Hence the tradition of renunciation can be said to be counter-technological: It aims at leaving everything behind including, if it is pursued rigorously enough, all methods of seeking.
>
> (2001: 68)

Where the *sannyasi* struggles with his body and the world to which he is attached by affecting an attitude towards life, the yogi uses his body and the embodied techniques of meditation to transcend the world of experience. *Hatha yoga* is, in this sense, often referred to as a technology of the self.

Set against a backdrop of institutionalized asceticism – as the binary opposite of institutionalized sport in ancient Greece – it is possible to see how yoga developed as a mode of metaphysical fitness training. Chastity, dietary control, structured isolation and various other aspects of austere self-discipline were incorporated as a comprehensive set of techniques. Although in many ways radical and revolutionary – and therefore disparaged by late classical and Puranic redactors of the *Yoga Sutra* – *hatha yoga* reflects the logical outcome of classical yoga's break with Brahmanical ritualism on the one hand and pre-classical and epic-age asceticism on the other.

## Comparative conclusion

Arguably, a history of sexuality for this period would reveal a progressive convergence of sex and physical fitness, rather than their divergence, and the disarticulation of the self from one exclusively into the other. One is tempted, for example, to speculate on the physical fitness reflected in the dynamic postures and positions depicted in Khajaraho and Konarak (Danielou 2001; Elisofon and Watts 1971; Fouchet 1959; Lal 1965), which are, so to speak, at the far end of the athletic spectrum from the subtle physiology of internalized ejaculation! Most certainly a history of sensual sexuality in ancient India (see Comfort 1965; Zysk 2002) – as distinct from ritualized and internalized forms – would reflect a different dynamic between pleasure and self-discipline than was institutionalized in the early Greek *polis*. And, as argued here, a clearer understanding of how sexual power is athletically developed and channelled in yoga provides a philosophical point of reference for such a history (see also Alter 2011).

Within the framework of metaphysical fitness, a key difference between *askesis* and *hatha yoga* is that yoga's understanding of the egoistic self as illusory served to locate the morality of sex firmly in the body of the adept rather than in the domain of public life, as public life was manifest most clearly in the gymnasium. This could well mean that the convergence of sexuality and fitness in the practice of *hatha yoga* did not so much make *hatha yoga* a form of proto-physical education, as modern reformers have argued, as generate a powerful counterpoint to the expression of sexuality in courtly life as described and delineated by Vatsyayan in the *Kamasutra* (Doniger 2003). In any case, *hatha yoga* renders purely sportive physical education – as a manifestation of military training and martial arts – rather meaningless as a distinct disciplinary category in ancient India. And it may well help to explain why, within the pantheon of epic heroes and erotic ascetics in the classical literature of South Asia, there are champions – who compete with one another and come out on top based on skill, guile, and, much more often, games of chance (Doniger 2009) – but no athletes, celibate or non-celibate.

If one takes the *Yoga Sutra* as a pivotal text in a history of the self in South Asia that led, over time, to the development of various tantric traditions wherein the body was affirmed and used as 'an immensely valuable instrument for reaching liberation' (Feuerstein 1990: 365), then it is possible to compare this history of the self in South Asia – as it is deeply vested in the problem of sexuality – with the history of Greek 'sexuality' developed by Foucault. As the problem of the self became more and more a question of socio-moral self-discipline, *askesis*, both in and out of the gymnasium, ultimately led to the disarticulation of sex and fitness. Then, within the purview of Christian theology and priestly power, it became a matter of asceticism. The disarticulation of sex and fitness allowed for sex itself to become a problem of and for the self in relation to original sin. In many ways philosophy as a discipline is the corollary of asceticism, the latter having fetishized the flesh and the former the intellect, logic and reason among other forms of knowledge. What seems to have happened in South Asia, most clearly between the fifth and the tenth centuries, is that sex became ever more important to an understanding of the self in relation to bio-moral transcendence. But this happened through an integration of sex into the domain of fitness, as fitness was experienced as a more clearly embodied set of metaphysical practices than sex as a thing unto itself.

## Notes

1 Quite apart from Pythagoras hearing voices from another life in the yelping of a beaten dog, this produces an anagramically interesting parallel to Cynical mimesis, albeit only sophomoriphically so; but, then again, it was the wise *sophos* who anticipated philosophy as a lifestyle – the precise coinage attributed to Pythagoras – devoted to the 'love of wisdom'.

2 In this regard it is important to keep in mind the relationship between yoga and Ayurveda in the history of South Asian philosophy. Although this is a question that would entail a much more comprehensive analysis, I would argue that Ayurveda, like yoga, is intrinsically and ontologically sexual, and this most clearly distinguishes it from Greek medicine, even though both are, on the level of epistemology and practice, much more concerned with dietetics (Foucault 1988: 140–1). The sexual physiology that is common to yoga and Ayurveda has produced a very different dynamic in the relationship between medicine and philosophy in South Asia.

3 In this regard it is important to note, following Scanlon, that although he was an iconic figure in the gymnasium, Heracles himself was not an athlete in the sportive sense of the term. He performed 'labours' which were not contests as such. Thus Heracles's *alkē*, his monumental physical strength, is of a more encompassing, heroic type than the athletes.

4 It should be noted, however, that Empedocles embodied magical power and there are interesting parallels between his understanding of medicine as a solution to the problem of old age – which entails the magic of immortality (Kingsley 1995: 222–7) – and comparable ideas in Ayurvedic medicine with regard to the consumption of *soma*, the elixir of immortality.

5 When discussing yoga it is possible to translate the term *brahman* as either universal soul or universal self. This flexibility is significant. But, although there are obvious parallels, it is important not to think of *brahman* as the same thing as the soul as such in Greek philosophy. The term Self is used here to designate the principle of *brahman* so as to avoid any tendency towards simplistic comparison and inadvertent philological confusion.

6 Yoga physiology is based on significantly different principles from those of Ayurvedic medicine, although they are both based on the same *Samkhyan* ontology.

## References

Agehananda Bharati, S. (1993) *Tantric Traditions*, rev. and enl. edn. Delhi: Hindustan Publishing.

Alesse, F. (2008) *Philo of Alexandria and Post-Aristotelian Philosophy: Studies in Philo of Alexandria*. Leiden and Boston, MA: Brill.

Alter, J. S. (2004) *Yoga in Modern India: The Body Between Science and Philosophy*. Princeton, NJ: Princeton University Press.

—— (2009) 'Yoga in Asia – mimetic history: problems in the location of secret knowledge', *Comparative Studies of South Asia, Africa and the Middle East* 29: 213–29.

—— (2011) *Moral Materialism: Sex and Masculinity in Modern India*. New Delhi: Penguin.

—— (2012) 'Sacrifice, the body, and yoga: entailments of embodiment in Hathayoga', *South Asia* 35(2): 408–33.

Bentor, Y. (2000) 'Interiorized fire rituals in India and in Tibet', *Journal of the American Oriental Society* 120: 594–613.

Bisschop, P. and Griffiths, A. (2003) 'The Pashupata observance (Atharvavedaparisista 40)', *Indo-Iranian Journal* 46: 315–48.

Blondel, E. (1991) *Nietzsche: The Body and Culture: Philosophy as a Philological Genealogy*, trans. S. Hand. San Francisco: Stanford University Press.

Branham, R. B. and Goulet-Cazé, M. O. (1996) *The Cynics: The Cynic Movement in Antiquity and its Legacy*. Berkeley: University of California Press.

Bundgaard, A. (2005) *Muscle and Manliness: The Rise of Sport in American Boarding Schools*. Syracuse, NY: Syracuse University Press.

Cohen, D. (1992) 'Sex, gender and sexuality in Ancient Greece', *Classical Philology* 87: 145–60.

Comfort, A. (1965) 'Introduction', in A. Comfort (ed.) *The Koka Shastra*. New York: Stein and Day.

Cutler, I. (2005) *Cynicism from Diogenes to Dilbert*. Jefferson, NC: McFarland & Company.

Daniélou, A. (2001) *The Hindu Temple: Deification of Eroticism*. Rochester, VT: Inner Traditions.

Davis, P. and Weaving, C. (2010) *Philosophical Perspectives on Gender in Sport and Physical Activity*. London and New York: Routledge.

De Michelis, E. (2004) *A History of Modern Yoga: Patañjali and Western Esotericism*. London and New York: Continuum.

Desmond, W. D. (2006) *The Greek Praise of Poverty: Origins of Ancient Cynicism*. Notre Dame, IN: University of Notre Dame Press.

Dickie, M. (2001) *Magic and Magicians in the Greco-Roman World*. London and New York: Routledge.

Dix, U. (1972) *Sport und Sexualität*. Frankfurt: März-Verl.

Dombrowski, D. A. (2009) *Contemporary Athletics and Ancient Greek Ideals*. Chicago: University of Chicago Press.

Doniger, W. (2003) *Kamasutra*. Philadelphia, PA: Miniature Editions.

—— (2009) *The Hindus: An Alternative History*. New York: Penguin.

Downing, F. G. (1992) *Cynics and Christian Origins*. Edinburgh: T & T Clark.

Dudley, D. R. (1967 [1937]) *A History of Cynicism: From Diogenes to the 6th Century AD*, Reprografischer Nachdruck der Ausg. London: Hildesheim: G. Olms.

Eliade, M. (1990 [1969]) *Yoga: Immortality and Freedom*, 2nd edn. Princeton, NJ: Princeton University Press for Bollingen Foundation.

Elisofon, E. and Watts, A. (1971) *The Temple of Konarak: Erotic Spirituality*. Delhi: Vikas.

Feuerstein, G. (1989) *Yoga: The Technology of Ecstasy*. Los Angeles: J. P. Tarcher.

—— (1990) *Encyclopedic Dictionary of Yoga*. New York: Paragon House.

—— (1992) *Sacred Sexuality: Living the Vision of the Erotic Spirit*. Los Angeles and New York: J. P. Tarcher.

—— (2001) *The Yoga Tradition: Its History, Literature, Philosophy, and Practice*. Prescott, AZ: Hohm Press.

Foucault, M. (1986) *Foucault: A Critical Reader*, ed. D. C. Hoy. Oxford and New York: Blackwell.

—— (1988) *The Care of the Self: The History of Sexuality*, Vol. 3. New York: Vintage Books.

—— (1990) *The Uses of Pleasure: The History of Sexuality*, Vol. 2. New York: Vintage Books.

Fouchet, M. P. (1959) *The Erotic Sculpture of India*. London: Allen and Unwin.

Fussell, S. (1994) 'Bodybuilder Americanus', in L. Goldstein (ed.) *The Male Body*. Ann Arbor: University of Michigan Press.

Garbe, R. (1896) *Samkhya und Yoga: Grundriss der Indo-Arischen Philologie und Altertumskunde*. Strasbourg: K. J. Trübner.

Gardiner, E. N. (1930) *Athletics of the Ancient World*. Oxford: Clarendon Press.

Golden, M. (1998) *Sport and Society in Ancient Greece: Key Themes in Ancient History*. Cambridge and New York: Cambridge University Press.

—— (2008) *Greek Sport and Social Status*. Austin: University of Texas Press.

Golden, M. and Toohey, P. (2003) *Sex and Difference in Ancient Greece and Rome*. Edinburgh: Edinburgh University Press.

Green, N. (2008) 'Breathing in India, c.1890', *Modern Asian Studies* 42: 283–315.

Griffiths, E. M. (2002) 'Euripides' "Herakles" and the Pursuit of Immortality', *Mnemosyne* 55: 641–56.

Guthrie, K. S. (1987) *The Pythagorean Sourcebook and Library: An Anthology of Ancient Writings Which Relate to Pythagoras and Pythagorean Philosophy*. Grand Rapids, MI: Phanes Press.

Guttmann, A. (1994) *Games and Empires: Modern Sports and Cultural Imperialism*. New York: Columbia University Press.

—— (1996) *The Erotic in Sports*. New York: Columbia University Press.

Guttmann, A., Kyle, D. G. and Stark, G. D. (1990) *Essays on Sport History and Sport Mythology*. College Station: Texas A & M Press.

Hall, D. E. (1994) *Muscular Christianity: Embodying the Victorian Age*. Cambridge and New York: Cambridge University Press.

Halperin, D. M., Winkler, J. J. and Zeitlin, F. I. (1990) *Before Sexuality: The Construction of Erotic Experience in the Ancient Greek World*. Princeton, NJ: Princeton University Press.

Hermann, A. (2004) *To Think Like God: Pythagoras and Parmenides, the Origins of Philosophy*. Las Vegas: Parmenides Publishing.

Hoffman, R. J. (1980) 'Some cultural aspects of Greek male homosexuality', *Journal of Homosexuality* 5: 217–26.

Hoyez, A. C. (2007) 'The "World of Yoga": the production and reproduction of therapeutic landscapes', *Social Science and Medicine* 65: 112–24.

Hyland, D. A. (1990) *Philosophy of Sport*. New York: Paragon House.

Ingalls, D. H. H. (1962) 'Cynics and Pashupatas: the seeking of dishonor', *Harvard Theological Review* 55: 281–98.

Kahn, C. H. (2001) *Pythagoras and the Pythagoreans: A Brief History*. Indianapolis: Hackett Publishing.

Keith, A. B. (1918) *The Samkhya System: A History of the Samkhya Philosophy. The Heritage of India*. Calcutta, London and New York: Association Press and Oxford University Press.

Kingsley, P. (1995) *Ancient Philosophy, Mystery, and Magic: Empedocles and Pythagorean Tradition*. Oxford and New York: Clarendon Press and Oxford University Press.

Klein, A. M. (1993) *Little Big Men: Bodybuilding Subculture and Gender Construction*. Albany: State University of New York Press.

Kretchmar, R. S. (2005) *Practical Philosophy of Sport and Physical Activity*, 2nd edn. Champaign, IL: Human Kinetics.

Kyle, D. G. (1987) *Athletics in Ancient Athens: Mnemosyne*, Bibliotheca Classica Batava Supplementum. Leiden: Brill.

Lal, K. (1965) *Immortal Khajuraho*. Delhi: Asia Press.

Laqueur, T. W. (1990) *Making Sex: Body and Gender From the Greeks to Freud*. Cambridge, MA: Harvard University Press.

—— (2003) *Solitary Sex: A Cultural History of Masturbation*. New York: Zone Books.

Larson, G. J. (1969) *Classical Samkhya; An Interpretation of its History and Meaning*. Delhi: Motilal Banarsidass.

Larson, G. J. and Bhattacharya, R. S. (1987) *Samkhya: A Dualist Tradition in Indian Philosophy. Encyclopedia of Indian Philosophies*. Princeton, NJ: Princeton University Press.

Lindsay, J. (1970) *The Origins of Alchemy in Graeco-Roman Egypt*. London: Muller.

Long, A. A. (1996) 'The Socratic tradition: Diogenes, Crates, and Hellenistic ethics', in R. B. Branham and M.-O. Goulet-Caze (eds) *The Cynics*. Berkeley: University of California Press.

Loraux, N. (1990) 'Herakles: the super-male and the feminine', in D. M. Halperin, J. J. Winkler and F. I. Zeitlin (eds) *Before Sexuality: The Construction of Erotic Experience in the Ancient Greek World*. Princeton, NJ: Princeton University Press.

Lorenzen, D. N. (1972) *The Kapalikas and Kalamukhas: Two Lost Saivite Sects*. Berkeley: University of California Press.

Luchte, J. (2009) *Pythagoras and the Doctrine of Transmigration: Wandering Souls*. London and New York: Continuum.

MacAloon, J. J. (1981) *This Great Symbol: Pierre de Coubertin and the Origins of the Modern Olympic Games*. Chicago: University of Chicago Press.

Manos, N. (1983) 'Sexual life, problems and attitudes of the prospective Greek physician', *Archives of Sexual Behavior* 12: 435–43.

Martin, T. (1996) *Ancient Greece: From Prehistoric to Hellenistic Times*. New Haven: Yale University Press.

McGushin, E. F. (2007) *Foucault's Askesis: An Introduction to the Philosophical Life*. Evanston, IL: Northwestern University Press.

McNamee, M. J. (2008) *Sports, Virtues and Vices: Morality Plays*. London and New York: Routledge.

Mihalich, J. C. (1982) *Sports and Athletics: Philosophy in Action*. Totowa, NJ: Littlefield, Adams.

Miller, S. G. (1991) *Arete: Greek Sports From Ancient Sources*. 2nd edn. Berkeley: University of California Press.

Moore, G. (2002) *Nietzsche, Biology, and Metaphor*. Cambridge and New York: Cambridge University Press.

Morrison, R. G. (1997) *Nietzsche and Buddhism: A Study in Nihilism and Ironic Affinities*. Oxford and New York: Oxford University Press.

Navia, L. E. (1996) *Classical Cynicism: A Critical Study*. Westport, CT: Greenwood Press.

—— (1998) *Diogenes of Sinope: The Man in the Tub*. Westport, CT: Greenwood Press.

Newby, Z. (2005) *Greek Athletics in the Roman World: Victory and Virtue*. Oxford and New York: Oxford University Press.

—— (2006) *Athletics in the Ancient World*. Bristol: Bristol Classical.

Ogden, D. (2009) *Magic, Witchcraft, and Ghosts in the Greek and Roman Worlds: A Sourcebook*, 2nd edn. Oxford and New York: Oxford University Press.

Olivelle, P. (1992) *Samnyasa Upanisads: Hindu Scriptures on Asceticism and Renunciation.* New York: Oxford University Press.

—— (1998) *The Early Upanisads: Annotated Text and Translation.* New York: Oxford University Press.

Phillips, K. M. and Reay, B. (2002) *Sexualities in History: A Reader.* New York: Routledge.

Putney, C. (2001) *Muscular Christianity: Manhood and Sports in Protestant America, 1880–1920.* Cambridge, MA: Harvard University Press.

Rawlinson, H. G. (1971) *Intercourse Between India and the Western World; From the Earliest Times to the Fall of Rome,* 2nd edn. New York: Octagon Books.

Riedweg, C. (2005) *Pythagoras: His Life, Teaching, and Influence.* Ithaca, NY: Cornell University Press.

Robinson, R. S. (1955) *Sources for the History of Greek Athletics in English Translation, with Introductions, Notes, Bibliography, and Indices.* Chicago: Ares Publishers.

Rousselle, A. (1988) *Porneia: On Desire and the Body in Antiquity.* Oxford and New York: Blackwell.

Rousselle, R. (1999) 'Pederasty and pedagogy in archaic Greece', *Journal of Psychohistory* 26: 810–18.

Samuel, G. (2008) *The Origins of Yoga and Tantra: Indic Religions to the Thirteenth Century.* Cambridge and New York: Cambridge University Press.

Sansone, D. (1988) *Greek Athletics and the Genesis of Sport.* Berkeley: University of California Press.

Sarbacker, S. R. (2005) *Samadhi: The Numinous and Cessative in Indo-Tibetan Yoga.* Albany: State University of New York Press.

Scanlon, T. F. (2002) *Eros and Greek Athletics.* New York: Oxford University Press.

—— (2005) 'The dispersion of pederasty and the athletic revolution in sixth-century bc Greece', *Journal of Homosexuality* 49: 63–85.

Schipper, K. (1994) *The Taoist Body.* Taipei: SMC Publishing.

Semple, R. A. (2008) 'Missionary manhood: professionalism, belief and masculinity in the nineteenth-century British imperial field', *Journal of Imperial and Commonwealth History* 36: 397–415.

Silburn, L. (1988) *Kundalini: The Energy of the Depths.* Albany: State University of New York Press.

Simons, P. (2008) 'Hercules in Italian Renaissance art: muscular labour and masculine libido, *Art History* 31(5): 632–48.

Singleton, M. (2010) *Yoga Body: The Origins of Modern Posture Yoga.* Oxford: Oxford University Press.

Singleton, M. and Byrne, J. (2008) *Yoga in the Modern World: Contemporary Perspectives.* London; New York: Routledge.

Smith, B. R. (2007) 'Body, mind and spirit? Towards an analysis of the practice of yoga', *Body & Society* 13: 25–46.

Snellgrove, D. L. (1987) *Indo-Tibetan Buddhism: Indian Buddhists and Their Tibetan Successors.* Boston, MA and New York: Shambhala.

Staal, F. (1993) 'Indian bodies', in T. P. Kasulis, R. T. Ames and W. Dissanayake (eds) *Self as Body in Asian Theory and Practice.* Albany: State University of New York Press.

Sutton, R. F. (1992) 'Pornography and persuasion on attic pottery', in A. Richlin (ed.) *Pornography and Representation in Greece and Rome.* New York: Oxford University Press.

Velissaropoulos, D. C. (1991) 'The Ancient Greek knowledge of Indian philosophy', in U. P. Arora (ed.) *Graeco-Indica: India's Cultural Contacts with the Greek World:*

*In Memory of Demetrius Galanos (1760–1833) A Greek Sanskritist of Benares.* New Delhi: Ramanand Vidya Bhavan.

Walters, M. (1978) *The Nude Male: A New Perspective.* New York: Paddington Press.

Weiss, P. (1971) *Sport: A Philosophic Inquiry,* Arcturus Books. Carbondale: Southern Illinois University Press.

West, M. L. (1971) *Early Greek Philosophy and the Orient.* Oxford: Clarendon Press.

Whicher, I. (1998) *The Integrity of the Yoga Darsana: A Reconsideration of Classical Yoga.* Albany: State University of New York Press.

White, D. G. (1996) *The Alchemical Body: Siddha Traditions in Medieval India.* Chicago: University of Chicago Press.

—— (2000) *Tantra in Practice.* Princeton, NJ: Princeton University Press.

—— (2003) *Kiss of the Yogini: 'Tantric sex' in its South Asian Contexts.* Chicago and London: University of Chicago Press.

—— (2009) *Sinister Yogis.* Chicago and London: University of Chicago Press.

Zysk, K. G. (2002) *Conjugal Love in India: Ratisastra and Ratiramana.* Leiden and Boston, MA: Brill.

—— (2007) 'The bodily winds in Ancient India revisited', *Journal of the Royal Anthropological Institute* 13: S105–S115.

# 8 In the light of the sphere

## The 'vehicle of the soul' and subtle-body practices in Neoplatonism

*Crystal Addey*

The concept of the 'subtle body' is familiar to many through encounters with Indian, Indo-Tibetan and East Asian religious and spiritual traditions, and the ritual and physical practices derived from or associated with them. However, as evidenced herein, philosophers from European antiquity have produced their own well-developed ideas and concepts of the 'subtle body' and developed or reiterated practices that are considered to utilize, affect and influence it. The idea of the 'vehicle of the soul' (*ochêma pneuma*), the subtle or astral body, which acts as a bridge between the soul and body, was discussed and developed by various Neoplatonist philosophers between the second and sixth centuries CE. In terms of its central role as a bridge between the soul and body, the 'Vehicle of the Soul' was considered to have a mediating and median nature, since it was considered to be less material than the physical body but more material than the soul.

Neoplatonism refers to a philosophical school or movement which arose during the second century C.E. This movement developed and functioned, broadly speaking, within the polytheistic context of traditional Graeco-Roman religious tradition, although some Neoplatonist philosophers were more ostensibly concerned with ritual and religious practices than others. The philosopher Plotinus (*c*.204–70) is often seen as the 'founder' of Neoplatonism; however, it is important to note that 'Neoplatonism' is a modern term coined by scholars (Gregory 1999: vii; Smith 2004: 3; O'Meara 2003: 3, n.1): Neoplatonist philosophers claimed to be following the philosophy of Plato (rather than being innovators and creating their own philosophy) and considered themselves to be 'Platonists'.

The theory of the soul vehicle finds its first developed expression in the work of two Neoplatonist philosophers of the third and early fourth centuries, Porphyry (*c*.234–*c*.305) and Iamblichus (*c*.240–*c*.325). It was further developed and discussed by later Neoplatonist philosophers, such as Proclus and Hierocles (fifth century). Neoplatonist philosophers derived their ideas about the soul vehicle from Plato's *Timaeus*, which relates how the Demiurge (creator god) mounted the souls each upon a star 'as upon a vehicle' (*Timaeus* [Bury 1929], 41e), and from the myth of Plato's *Phaedrus*, where the soul is likened to a winged chariot travelling through the heavens (*Phaedrus* [Fowler 1982], 246a). These Platonic allusions were combined with Aristotle's concept of *pneuma*, the warm airy substance which serves as the locus of the sensitive and imaginative soul, which

Aristotle had compared with the element of which the stars are made (*ether*) (*Generation of Animals*, 736b.35–9). We do not know who first combined Plato's *ochêma* (vehicle) with Aristotle's idea of *pneuma*, but by the late third century the *ochêma pneuma* was an established philosophical doctrine (Dodds 1963: 316–17; Schibli 2002: 98). Drawing on these Platonic and Aristotelian allusions, Neoplatonists claimed that the vehicle of the soul was made of ether, the substance of the stars. The soul vehicle was variously described by these philosophers as 'ethereal' (*aitheriôdes/aithérion*), 'astral' (*astroeidés*), 'luminous' (*augoeidés*), congenital (*symphués*) or 'pneumatic' (*pneumatikon*) (see Kissling 1922: 320; Schibli 2002: 99).

As well as being considered as the seat of *phantasia* (the imagination or image-making faculty of the soul) and sense perception (Kissling 1922: 321), the vehicle of the soul, the subtle or astral body, was offered as a practical explanation of how the human soul travels between lives and chooses its future lives (since many of these philosophers subscribed to the idea of reincarnation), how the human soul receives rewards and punishments for its past behaviour in Hades (the Greek underworld) and how the human soul originally descended into a physical body before its first incarnation and ascends to the gods. Many Neoplatonist philosophers maintained that when the soul became completely purified and ascended to higher ontological grades of reality, including the divine realm, it became a perfect sphere and rotates in harmony with both the World Soul (a notion arising from the idea that the world or cosmos also has a soul) and with the gods and their 'bodies' or 'vehicles', the planets. Therefore, as well as having important eschatological roles, the soul vehicle had important soteriological and spiritual functions which were very closely linked with its role in ritual practices.

The soul vehicle was considered by some of these philosophers to have an important role to play in ritual practices, particularly divination and theurgy, a type of ritual discussed and endorsed by Iamblichus and other later Neoplatonist philosophers (Iamblichus, *On the Mysteries* [Clarke, Dillon and Hershbell 2003], 1.1 (4.5–5.6); 1.2 (6.6–7); 2.11 (96.11–97.15); 3.1–31 (divination); 10.1–8; Marinus, *Life of Proclus*, 28 (trs. Edwards 2000); Proclus, *Theol. Plat.* 4.9 p.31, 12–16; 1.25 p.113, 6–8 (Saffrey and Westerink 1968–78); Hierocles, *Commentary on the Golden Verses*, 25.18; 26.22; 26.25–27; cf. Rosán 1949: 209–13; Shaw 1985, 1995, 1999; Uzdavinys 2010). Iamblichus discusses the role of the soul vehicle in oracular ritual: Oracles were one of the most ubiquitous and widespread types of divination in the ancient world.[1] Oracle centres were specific temples of deities which both individuals and state delegations frequently visited to ask for guidance. The oracle was obtained through a prophet or prophetess who was considered to be 'inspired' or 'possessed' by a god or goddess or by a *daimon*, a type of semi-divine spirit. Specific Oracles were dedicated to a specific god or goddess who was thought to give oracular responses through the prophet or prophetess: as the god of oracles and divination, Apollo was especially popular but other Oracles were dedicated to other deities (Halliday 1913; Fontenrose 1978; Parke and Wormell 1956; Parke 1967: 72–89; Burkert 1985: 114–18; Lane Fox 1986: 102–261; Bowden 2005; Johnston 2008).

Theurgy, which literally means 'divine work', was a type of ritual whose central goal was the ascent of the human soul to the divine realm and the divinization of the human being: the idea was that those who become like a god use their full range of powers and activate their complete essence or nature, both of which are considered to bring complete happiness (Iamblichus, *On the Mysteries*, 10.4 289.3–5; 10.5). Within these ritual practices (as they are discussed by these philosophers) the purification of the soul vehicle was a vital element which enabled the ritual practitioner to receive oracles and other types of divinatory knowledge and wisdom. It also played a central role in theurgic ritual, whose ultimate aim was to enable the ritual practitioner to ascend to the gods and live a 'divine life'. Herein, the role of the vehicle of the soul in ancient divination and theurgic rituals is examined. This chapter also considers the ways in which the philosophical idea of the soul vehicle, and its role in ancient ritual practices, can assist us in extending or moving beyond the Cartesian mind–body dualism, a feature of dominant modern Western thought and discourse.

## The vehicle of the soul (*ochêma pneuma*) in Neoplatonism

According to both Porphyry and Iamblichus, the soul vehicle is made of ether, the substance of the stars. However, this seems to be where their agreement about the nature of the soul vehicle ends. According to John Finamore (1985: 5, 11), who has written the seminal study on the theory of the soul vehicle in Iamblichus' works, Porphyry and Iamblichus disagreed about the composition, nature and ultimate fate of the soul vehicle. It remains difficult to reconstruct Porphyry's philosophical position on the soul vehicle in its entirety due to the fact that many of his works are no longer extant. However, we do know that Porphyry claimed that the soul vehicle was composed of a series of mixtures collected from the planets, the celestial spheres, during its descent into the physical cosmos, and when the human soul developed its full potential and ascended to the realm of *Nous* (or Divine Mind) it discarded its vehicle, which at this point is dissolved back into the heavenly spheres of the cosmos (Proclus, *In Tim*, V: 234.18–24 (311A) Diehl; Kissling 1922: 318; Finamore 1985: 11, 16–18). While much of Porphyry's theory remains difficult to reconstruct due to lack of evidence, his notion that the soul vehicle was composed of a series of mixtures collected from the celestial spheres surely has astrological connotations, since the central crux of ancient astrological theory and praxis was the notion that each human being is made up of a portion of each of the planets; the *horoskopos*, the map of the native's birth, depicts the position of the planets and the fixed stars at the native's birth, which were considered to reflect his essential character and attributes (Pingree 1986; Barton 1994: 92–102).

We know that Porphyry was thoroughly familiar with and knowledgeable about astrology: in a treatise he refers to astrological theory (Porphyry, *On the Cave of the Nymphs*, 21–24; 28 in Nauck 1886) and he had addressed a series of questions about astrology to Iamblichus in his *Letter to Anebo* (Iamblichus, *On the Mysteries*, 1.17 (50.12–13); 1.18 (52.14–53.1); 1.19 (57.3–4); 9.3; 9.5). It is also reported that he wrote an introduction to Ptolemy's *Tetrabiblos*, an extant handbook of astrology in four books, although it should be noted that Porphyry's authorship of this work is disputed and therefore somewhat uncertain (Smith 1993: 490).[2] In his now fragmentary treatise *On What is Up to Us*, Porphyry details the seven spheres (or planets) which souls pass through in their descent into a mortal body, each sphere inciting the soul with different desires (Smith 1993: Fragment 271: 68–71). This fragment helps to clarify Porphyry's position on the soul vehicle: if the soul was considered to be incited by desires through its contact with the planets during its descent, Porphyry presumably thought that these desires had to be shed, together with the soul vehicle, in the soul's return to *Nous*, which he often describes as necessarily involving a purification from human passions and desires.

The possible implications of Porphyry's theory of the soul vehicle for the use of divinatory rituals using astrology have largely been unobserved by scholars, remain unexplored and would be difficult to reconstruct from his fragmentary works. However, it is likely that Porphyry did discuss the role of the soul vehicle in ritual which also uses astrology as a form of divination, given the obvious connotations of his theory. That this is the case is further supported by his discussion of the use of astrology in polytheistic ritual practices in the *Philosophy from Oracles*, a work which is only extant in fragments (Porphyry, *Philosophy from Oracles*, Fragments 330, 330a, 342, 333, 336, in Smith 1993).

Iamblichus, on the other hand, asserted that the soul vehicle is immortal; it is created as a whole from ether itself by the Demiurge (Iamblichus, *In Tim*, Fragment 84 Dillon). Furthermore, since it is created whole it will continue to live on as a whole after its separation from the soul (Finamore 1985: 17). The later Neoplatonist philosopher Proclus seems to combine the views of Porphyry and Iamblichus (Dodds 1963: 320), since he maintains that there are two soul vehicles: first, a higher, ethereal vehicle which is immortal and is implanted around the human soul by the Demiurge (Proclus, *In Tim*, III. 236. 31ff (213A) Diehl; *Elements of Theology*, Propositions 196, 207–8, in Dodds 1963: 171, 181–3). Proclus argues that there must be an immortal (or, at least, perpetual) vehicle so that the human soul can receive rewards and punishments after death in Hades (*In Tim*, V. 279: 11–26 (324F–325A) Diehl; Finamore 1985: 19). Second, he postulates a pneumatic vehicle which is a temporary vehicle, surviving death along with the irrational soul but ultimately mortal rather than immortal (Kissling 1922: 323–4; Dodds 1963: 320). Proclus asserts that this second, pneumatic vehicle is woven to the first, ethereal vehicle by the young gods (the encosmic gods, or gods of the cosmos) (*In Tim*, III. 237: 2–6 (213A) Diehl; Finamore 1985: 86). Proclus' notion of an immortal vehicle seems to be equivalent to Iamblichus' idea of the soul vehicle, while his notion of a second, pneumatic vehicle which only has a temporary existence seems to correlate with Porphyry's notions about the nature of the soul vehicle.

Iamblichus also claims that the vehicle of the soul is ultimately, when using its full powers, spherical in shape, reflecting the shape of the World Soul and the circuits of the gods (portrayed in Plato's myth in the *Phaedrus*) which it must both imitate and align itself with, in order to achieve its full potential and effect its immortalization (*On the Mysteries*, 10.6. (292.4–9); Finamore 1985: 49; Shaw 1995: 51). The World Soul was considered to be the soul of the universe or cosmos: just as human beings are considered to have a soul, so the universe was also considered to; this cosmology is based on the microcosm–macrocosm notion and the idea that all things are connected to each other and to the gods. Since Iamblichus endorsed the Neoplatonic principle of 'like approaches like', the only way for the embodied soul to reach the universality of the World Soul and the gods was to become like them – that is, spherical (Shaw 1995: 52). In Iamblichus' view, the task of the human being who wishes to attain knowledge of his or her true nature is to fully realize the sphere of the soul through self-intellection, insight and wisdom:

> Since, then, the cosmos must be rendered similar to the universal Soul that presides over it, it must be made to resemble the lifegiving pattern of the Soul. Therefore, according as the Demiurge has established it in terms of two circles, so he constructed the Universe in the form of a sphere, to be an image of the Soul's self-motion. For which reason also our vehicle is made spherical, and is moved in a circle, whenever the soul is especially assimilated to Mind; for the intellection of the soul and the circular motion of bodies imitates the activity of Mind, even as the ascents and descents of souls motion in a straight line, for these are motions of bodies which are not in their proper places.
>
> (Iamblichus, *In Tim* [Dillon 2009], Fragment 49)

Iamblichus emphasizes that the vehicle is made more spherical whenever the human soul is assimilated to the Divine Mind or *Nous* (see Finamore 1985: 50). The spherical image deliberately evokes the nature of contemplation and self-intellection, which was conceptualized by these philosophers as a 'turning inwards' to oneself which reflects the activities of the World Soul and the gods, who are circular and spherical in shape because they contain all things within them and know the beginning and end of all things: 'with knowledge of the gods follows a turning towards ourselves and knowledge of ourselves' (Iamblichus, *On the Mysteries*, 10.1 (286.9–10); Hierocles, *Commentary on the Golden Verses* [Koehler 1974], 25.5–6). Since Iamblichus saw divination as the attainment of divine knowledge and the transmission of this knowledge in human language, it is unsurprising that he, and other philosophers such as Proclus and Hierocles, attributed an important role to the soul vehicle in divination and in theurgy (which was also considered to use divination).

## The role of the 'Vehicle of the Soul' in divination and theurgic ritual

According to later Neoplatonist philosophers, beginning with Porphyry and Iamblichus, various ritual practices are considered to purify the soul vehicle.

According to Iamblichus, this purification consequently enables the ritual practitioner to receive the illumination of the gods in a full and balanced way, so that oracles and divine messages do not get distorted or disturbed in their transmission to the human initiate, who is consequently able to receive divine insight and wisdom through his purification and appropriate receptivity (*On the Mysteries*, 1.8 (29.1–3); 1.18 (55.3–56.4); 3.11 (125.11–126.3, 127.10–13); 3.12 (129.9–11); George 2005: 287–303). It is important to note that Iamblichus envisages divine inspiration (which is considered to underlie divination practices in the ancient world) in terms of illumination, the emanation of an incorporeal light from the divine realm with no detraction or diminution to the gods themselves; the 'divine light remains whole and incorporeal' (Finamore 1993: 59) and the human recipient participates in it. John Finamore (1993: 59) describes this process as 'the interpenetration of the immaterial with the material, with no contamination of the immaterial element'.

In order to understand the role of the vehicle of the soul in ritual, it is important to understand that it was seen as the literal seat of images and was connected very closely with the image-making faculty or imagination (*phantasia*) (Sheppard 1997: 206; Finamore 1999: 89; Hadot 2006: 58–66). However, the word 'imagination' may be misleading to modern readers as a translation for the Greek term *phantasia*, since it implies a faculty for receiving images that may or may not be real (whereas, for modern Westerners, the word 'imagination' is often taken to imply something that is not real); for Iamblichus and many other Neoplatonist philosophers, this faculty not only receives images that are purely human (and derived from sense perception) but also has the potential to receive images from the gods, which have a reality and 'being' far exceeding that attributed to humans. During oracular and other types of divination rituals, the *phantasia* is said to be emptied of all of the ritual practitioner's images and human images, and thus is receptive to and able to receive the images sent from the gods (Sheppard 1997: 208).

Iamblichus discusses the role of the vehicle of the soul in two types of divination, oracles and a divinatory practice which he refers to as 'evoking the light' (*On the Mysteries*, 3.11 (123.9–128.3); 3.14 (132.3–134.7)). In both of these types of divination, examined in turn below, the vehicle has an important role to play in ensuring that the human can receive the images and illumination of the gods fully. Iamblichus discusses the ritual operation and practices associated with the Oracle at Claros, which he refers to by its alternative name, Colophon:

> It is agreed by everyone that the oracle at Colophon prophesies by means of water. There is a spring in the subterranean chamber, and from it the prophet drinks on certain appointed nights, after performing many preliminary ceremonies, and after drinking, he delivers his oracles, no longer seen by the spectators present. That this water has oracular power is immediately obvious … For it seems that some prophetic spirit passes through the water; but this is not correct, for the divine does not permeate what partakes in a fragmented

and divided manner, but it is by exercising its power from without, and illuminating the spring, that it fills it with its own prophetic power. Still, not every inspiration that the water gives is from the god, but this only bestows the receptivity and purification of the luminous spirit in us [a reference to the soul vehicle], through which we are able to receive the god. But the presence of the god is different from and prior to this, and flashes like lightning from above. This holds aloof from no one who, through a kindred nature, is in union with it; but it is immediately present and uses the prophet as an instrument ...

(Iamblichus, *On the Mysteries*, 3.11 (124.8–12; 124.13–125.9))

Iamblichus' discussion of the ritual preparations undertaken by the prophet at the Oracle of Claros clearly shows the important role of the vehicle in allowing human beings to obtain oracles from the gods. The ritual procedure discussed in the above passage is the drinking of water from the sacred spring within the oracular temple, but Iamblichus goes on to reiterate the other preparations undertaken by the prophet, which includes fasting for a full day and night prior to the oracular ritual and 'withdrawal to sacred, inaccessible places', a clear reference to contemplation or meditation on the part of the prophet (*On the Mysteries*, 3.11 (125.11–126.3)). Iamblichus maintains that drinking the water from the sacred spring and other ritual preparations purify the soul vehicle and make it receptive, thus allowing it to fully receive the divine illumination and inspiration which causes oracles to be pronounced. Divine illumination emanates from the god's ethereal vehicle to the human's ethereal vehicle, which is wholly taken over by the gods, and the oracular message (such as future events or the hidden truth comprising the oracle) is pictured in the soul's imagination: these 'pictures' or images come from the gods; thus, divine illumination irradiates the vehicle, causing divinely inspired images in it (Finamore 1999: 89–93).

Iamblichus also discusses the role of the soul vehicle in another type of divination, which he terms 'evoking the light' (*phôtos agôge* or *phôtagôgia*), which involved shining light on water in bowls or cups, or on a wall, in order to invoke the appearance of gods, goddesses or other divine beings (Iamblichus, *On the Mysteries*, 3.14 (132.7–9, 133.13–134.7); Clarke *et al.* 2003: 155, n.208).[3] When he explains how this type of divination works, it is clear that he envisages the role of the soul vehicle to be very similar to that involved in the oracle ritual: 'This somehow illuminates the aether-like and luminous vehicle surrounding the soul with divine light, from which vehicle the divine appearances, set in motion by the gods' will, take possession of the imaginative power in us' (Iamblichus, *On the Mysteries*, 3.14 (132.9–12)).

Again, the central section of the divination ritual is considered to involve the gods shining their divine illumination into the soul vehicle, which enables the divine images to take possession of the human imagination, allowing the human to 'imagine' or 'perceive' divine images and thus attain and utter divine oracles (Sheppard 1997: 207). Iamblichus elaborates on what this process involves:

And this happens in one of two ways: either from the presence of the gods in the soul, or from their shining on it some advanced light. In either case, both the divine presence and its illumination are separate from the soul. The soul's attention and intellect thus closely follow what is happening, since the divine light does not touch upon these. But the imagination is inspired because it is not roused by itself, but by the gods, to modes of imagination when normal human behaviour has been completely displaced.

(*On the Mysteries*, 3.14 (133.1–7))

Iamblichus explains that the process can be caused in two ways: first, from the innate presence of the divine in the soul, an idea that he discusses elsewhere (*On the Mysteries*, 1.8 (29.1–3); 1.15 (46.9, 47.3–9); 7.4 (255.13–256.2); 8.7 (269.11–13, 270.6–14); *In Phaedrum*, Fragment 6 Dillon). Second, by the gods shining some 'advanced light' on the soul. In both cases, Iamblichus stresses that the divine presence and illumination are separate from the soul; by which he means that they are ultimately caused by an agency separate from the human soul (i.e. the gods). The human being is conscious of the divine inspiration and follows the unfolding events of the ritual, since their intellect and concentration (focus) are unaffected; rather, the gods illuminate the imagination through the illumination of the soul vehicle, causing the human being to 'imagine' or perceive divine visions (which Iamblichus refers to as 'modes of imagination when normal human behaviour has been completely displaced'). In both types of ritual the vehicle of the soul plays a vital role. When he describes the oracular ritual (as practised at the Oracle of Claros), Iamblichus emphasizes the importance of the prophet drinking the water from the sacred spring; it is important because it is one of the ritual measures used to purify the soul vehicle so that it can fully receive the divine illumination in an unimpeded and undistorted manner. In the ritual of 'evoking the light' the gods shine their illumination onto the soul vehicle, which acts as the channel through which it reaches the *phantasia* (imagination), which can then become inspired by the divine images and visions received from the gods.

## The role of the 'vehicle of the soul' (*ochêma pneuma*) in ritual: beyond Cartesian dualism

As we have seen, Neoplatonist philosophers held that the vehicle of the soul had a mediating function between the wholly immaterial soul and the material, physical body. Many of these philosophers also maintained that the soul vehicle played a vital role in ritual practices. Given these important functions of the soul vehicle and the ascription of a mediating nature to it, it seems worthwhile to question whether the idea of the soul vehicle can assist us in extending or moving beyond the Cartesian mind–body dualism so prevalent in modern Western thought and discourse. In particular, assumptions based upon a dichotomous opposition between thought and action have deeply influenced modern scholarship on ritual and, in particular, its relationship to philosophy.

Historians of philosophy have generally conceived of the relationship between philosophical rationality and religious ritual according to a rigid Cartesian dichotomy between thought and action. Thus, rational philosophical cognition is imagined to be the absolute antithesis of religious ritual (Mazur 2004: 42–3). Scholars of religion and anthropologists also typically rely on a conceptually impoverished definition of ritual, limited to the repeated performance of physical actions involving material objects and bodies. Since ritual is still typically understood according to the conventional dichotomy between thought and action (or according to the duality of mind and body); it is seen as the physical complement of a corresponding cognitive system (i.e. a belief or a myth) but not as a cognitive process itself (Bell 1992: 19, 47–8; Mazur 2004: 43). This is particularly problematic for scholarship on theurgy, which is described by Iamblichus as involving contemplation (discussed below).[4] In a broader sense, it is also problematic for modern scholarship on Neoplatonism, which has claimed a sharp division between the 'rational' contemplation advocated by Plotinus and the theurgic ritual endorsed by Iamblichus, Proclus and others.[5]

Recently, however, scholars of religion, anthropologists and postcolonial theorists have challenged this conventional characterization of ritual. The postcolonial theorist Talal Asad has offered a compelling critique of the modern scholarly understanding of ritual as based on post-Enlightenment constructions of agency and subjectivity: he argues that rituals are seen as outward representations that are viewed either as guises or as symptoms of human needs, but that such views are based on a Western, individualized model of subjectivity that locates religiosity in the mind (an individual's beliefs or thoughts) rather than understanding rituals as practices that are part of a lifelong endeavour of moral development and constituting activity in the world (Asad 1993: 79; see also Keller 2002: 56–9; Rangos 2000: 78–9). This critique seems particularly relevant to theurgy as it is delineated by Iamblichus, Proclus and Hierocles, who describe the theurgic path as a continual, lifelong endeavour that is dependent upon a combination of ritual, ethical and intellectual praxis (Hierocles, *Commentary on the Golden Verses*, 26.3–28 Koehler).[6]

Catherine Bell (1992: 47–8) has also found the category of 'ritual', as currently formulated by scholars, to be problematic: she argues that it is dependent upon thought–action/mind–body dichotomies and further that such dichotomies tend to reinforce and elevate the status of scholar as thinking subject and devalue the status of the ritual participants as possessing less agency (moulded, controlled, doing-without-reflecting): 'there is a logic of sorts to most theoretical discourse on ritual and this discourse is fundamentally organized by an underlying opposition between thought and action' (see also Keller 2002: 65–6). As Mazur (2004: 43–4) notes, the arbitrary nature of this division (between thought and action, or mind and body) becomes clear from even a brief examination of religious examples from other traditional contexts, such as Kabbalah, Sufism and Tantra, in which ritual actions or utterances are progressively interiorized until they are iterated through thought or imagination alone.

## Mind and body, thought and action in Neoplatonism: philosophical cognition versus theurgic ritual?

Until very recently, scholars have often contrasted *theôria*, the 'philosophical contemplation' endorsed by Plotinus and Porphyry, with the theurgy of Iamblichus and Proclus.[7] Although Plotinus' mysticism is commonly recognized by scholars, it is sharply distinguished from and contrasted with theurgic ritual practices.[8] While Iamblichus is recognized as a philosopher, scholars argue that he prioritized theurgy over philosophy and explicitly disassociated himself from the more 'theoretical' views of Plotinus and Porphyry. As Mazur (2004: 30–1) has noted on Plotinus:

> With a few notable exceptions, the tendency has been … to disavow any relationship between his [i.e. Plotinus'] transcendental mysticism and ritual practices. Thus it is frequently asserted that Plotinus was able to obtain union with the One solely through 'rational' methods of pure contemplation, methods which are then contrasted with those of his ostensibly less philosophically-sophisticated successors, who were (according to this scheme) obliged to resort to the supposedly 'irrational' ritualism of theurgy in order to attain this goal.

Plotinus' views on union with the One (the supreme deity who presided over the other gods) are seen as being obtained through 'rational' methods of pure contemplation, which are sharply contrasted by scholars with the theurgical practices of Iamblichus, which they have consequently characterized as irrational'. However, this view of the relationship between 'rational contemplation' and philosophy on the one hand and theurgic ritual on the other does not seem to correlate to the evidence provided by these ancient philosophers or to provide an accurate or even useful representation of their practices of contemplation *or* ritual. For example, in *On the Mysteries*, Iamblichus includes many positive references to the role of contemplation within theurgic praxis (1.12 (41.10); 1.19 (59.10); 2.4 (77.3); 2.9 (88.1); 3.1 (102.2); 3.2 (104.8–10); 3.3 (106.11–12); 3.6 (112.11); 3.28 (167.10–11); 5.18; 10.5 (290.8–11; 291.2–3)),[9] of which one instance is particularly revealing. The philosopher discusses visions of the gods and maintains that contemplation is vital for attaining such visions: the gods and divine beings 'reveal at the outset their own being to those who contemplate them; hence, they show in particular performers of the sacramental rites the fire in a direct vision of divinity' (*On the Mysteries*, 2.10 (92.14–93.2)).

Elsewhere, Iamblichus (*On the Mysteries*, 10.2 (287.3–4)) declares that truth coexists with the gods and that truth, knowledge and goodness become fully established only in those who have been possessed by the gods:

> it is only with us and those who are similarly possessed by the greatest kinds [i.e. the gods] and have genuinely gained union with them that the beginning and end of all good is seriously practised. It is there, then, *that there occurs*

> *the vision of truth and intellectual understanding, and with knowledge of the*
> *gods follows a turning towards ourselves and knowledge of ourselves.*
>
> *(On the Mysteries*, 10.1(286.4–10), my emphasis)

This suggests that, at least in Iamblichus' view, the relationship between rationality, intellectual understanding, contemplation and ritual is subtle, complex and inter-linked. However, despite statements such as these, scholars have established a sharp opposition and dichotomy between the contemplation advocated by Plotinus and the theurgic ritual endorsed by Iamblichus and Proclus. This scholarly consensus seems to have arisen from the manner in which historians of philosophy and religion have typically sought to evaluate ritual. Mazur (2004: 43) argues that this sharp division is particularly misleading when attempting to understand Plotinus' contemplation, the final phase of which is a prescribed technique of meditation or visualization referred to by Mazur as 'inner ritual': 'our categorical division between thought and action has made this mode of ritual praxis very difficult to imagine in a philosophical context'. This sharp opposition between thought and action, and between mind and body, also seems to be unhelpful when attempting to understand theurgy as a ritual practice that involved contemplation and depended on the practitioner practising philosophy as a way of life. Moreover, the central role attributed to the vehicle of the soul in theurgy and divination, and its key function as providing a mediating link between the physical and non-physical elements of the human being, are suggestive of the inadequacy of interpretative models of ritual involving rigid dichotomies between thought and action, and mind and body.

## The role of the 'vehicle of the soul' (*ochêma pneuma*) in theurgy and ritual praxis

As the locus of mediation between the immaterial soul and the material, physical body, the idea of the soul vehicle may offer a way of moving beyond Cartesian mind–body dualism and sharp dichotomies between thought and action when attempting to analyse theurgic ritual. For example, we have examined the views of Neoplatonist philosophers regarding the role of ritual in purifying the soul vehicle, a necessary prerequisite for attaining oracles and visions from the gods in divinatory and theurgic ritual. Indeed, for philosophers such as Iamblichus, Proclus and Hierocles, a simultaneous 'purification' via ethical, intellectual and ritual means was necessary in order to increase one's receptivity so that one could fully receive visions of the gods, ascend to the divine realm and, ultimately, to become divinized (Schibli 2002: 115). All these purifications must be effected by the adept simultaneously if he wishes to ascend to the gods:

> For he who pays attention to his soul alone, but neglects the body, does not
> purify the whole man. Conversely, he who thinks he must care for the body
> apart from the soul or that the treatments of the body will accomplish anything
> for the soul, if the soul is in no wise being purified in itself, makes entirely

the same mistake. But he who continues properly with both becomes wholly perfected. Accordingly, philosophy has been joined to the art of sacred rites, on the grounds that this art engages in the purification of the luminous body. If you should separate it from the philosophical intellect, you will find that it no longer has the same power.

(Hierocles, *Commentary on the Golden Verses* [Koehler 1974], 26.24–5)

Since late Neoplatonic cosmology and metaphysics was based upon the notion that everything in the cosmos was connected to each other and to the gods and higher ontological realms through cosmic sympathy (*sympatheia*) and divine love (*theia philia*), the ritual adept had to purify and perfect the whole of their being: their soul, body and soul vehicle (referred to as the 'luminous body' by Hierocles in the above passage):

Surely then it is necessary that telestic [ritual] purifications go along with the mathematical purifications and that hieratic elevation [theurgic ascent to the divine realm] accompany the deliverance wrought by dialectics [reason and discursive philosophy]. These practices in a special way purify and perfect the pneumatic vehicle of the rational soul: they separate it from the lifelessness of matter, and they also render it to be in a capable state for the fellowship with pure spirits. For it is not lawful for the impure to lay hold of the pure.

(Hierocles, *Commentary on the Golden Verses* [Koehler 1974], 26.22.1–6)

Hierocles emphasizes that ritual purifications must accompany philosophical purification, which he refers to as 'dialectics' and 'mathematical purifications'. In this he follows the Platonic programme which sees mathematics as a crucial part of philosophy, and recommends both as a means of elevating the soul from the sensible realm to the realm of Ideas or Forms, immaterial entities that inhabit the realm of *Nous* or divine Mind (Schibli 2002: 115). Both sets of practices are said to purify the soul vehicle and render it capable of receiving visions of and messages from the gods (here referred to as 'pure spirits'). What is the purpose of the purification of the soul vehicle in ritual? It might help to remember that these Neoplatonist philosophers thought that the soul vehicle became weighed down with material stains and pollution through its over-identification with matter: 'a mortal body has attached itself to the luminous body, from which the luminous body, too, must be purified and delivered of its sympathy for it' (Hierocles, *Commentary on the Golden Verses* [Koehler 1974], 26.8.3–5).

The soul vehicle, through its close association and subsequent over-identification with matter, has a sympathy for the physical body which has to be purified if the individual is to receive the messages of the gods whole and intact (Finamore 1985: 53). Such material stains and pollution could interfere with or distort (for the human recipient) the transmissions of the gods. If the human imagination (*phantasia*) had been polluted by its identification with matter, then it might be distracted during the divination ritual by purely human impressions and imaginings and therefore not be able to fully receive the divine visions intact; this is because the vehicle of the soul, the astral or luminous body, was seen as the seat of imagination and sense perception and therefore it was thought to receive all sorts of impressions and imaginations that come to us from the sensations experienced through the earthly body (Schibli 2002: 100). The ritual practitioner might misinterpret or misconstrue the true meaning of the divine images if they are too attached to matter as an end in itself rather than as a receptacle for the manifestation of the gods. Just as one of the first stages of philosophy was seen as a purification from false ideas and opinions, so ritual purification involved the ritual removal or conversion of pollution which had been gathered by the human soul falsely identifying itself *solely* with its physical body (which is what Hierocles says about separating the soul vehicle from the 'lifelessness of matter').

As Shaw points out (1995: 54), however, the mistake of an embodied soul was not in having a body, nor in being fully aware of physical existence; the error lay rather in the weighing of the soul's attention: its consciousness needed to be anchored in the whole, the harmonic unity of the World Soul and the gods, with only minimal attention given to one's localized self. When Iamblichus discusses the purposes of purification, he emphasizes the perfection and fulfilment of the soul and restoration of one's own essence over deliverance from matter and the processes of generation:

> Let us consider the following as the most useful of all the ends of purification: removal of foreign elements, restoration of one's own essence, perfection, fulfilment, self-sufficiency, ascent to the engendering cause, conjoining of parts to wholes, and the gift of power, life and activity from wholes to individuals. Others, however, are not persuaded by the ancients when they emphasize the real benefits of purification, but they give prior place to deliverance from the body, release from bonds, freedom from decay, escape from generation and such minor ends of purification, as though they were superior to the universal ones.
>
> (*De Anima* [Dillon and Finamore 2002], 43)

Iamblichus maintains that through purification the human being is enabled to participate in the whole, the World Soul and the gods, thus restoring and perfecting their own essence, becoming immortal and universal (Shaw 1995: 54). These philosophers considered the gods to be completely good and to possess all knowledge in the purest sense, so they advocated ethical, intellectual and ritual practices and encouraged the simultaneous undertaking of such practices in order to render the adept god-like through a sympathetic alignment with knowledge, virtue and ritual purity:

> Just as it is fitting to adorn the soul with knowledge and virtue, that it may be with those beings who are always like that, so, too, one must render the luminous [body] pure and immaterial to stand the company of ethereal bodies.
>
> (Hierocles, *Commentary on the Golden Verses* [Koehler 1974], 26.22.6–10)

Since these philosophers argued that the gods had bodies or vehicles made of ether, they also encouraged the perfection of the soul vehicle (also made of ether) through a kind of sympathetic alignment so that it would become spherical and imitate the celestial orbits and the circuits of the gods. Iamblichus maintains that the spherical bodies of the World Soul and the gods were purely for adornment and revelation and did not entail a consequent distraction by and contamination from passions (*On the Mysteries*, 5.2 (200.7–8); 5.4 (202.14–203.9)); thus, through purification, the human being must make their soul vehicle spherical by reorientating their approach towards embodiment and matter, seeing these phenomena as a means for manifesting divinity rather than as an end in themselves. Here, we return to the idea of 'turning towards oneself', seen as the necessary approach towards not only self-knowledge, but also knowledge of (and a consequent approach towards) the gods:

> For although the soul is one, none the less, with its vision, so to speak, it beholds the plain of truth, and with a force that is like that of a grip it holds the congenital body [the soul vehicle] and turns it towards itself, so that in its entirety it may look to the divine and acquire a divine likeness.
>
> (Hierocles, *Commentary on the Golden Verses*
> [Koehler 1974], 26.17.13–17)

Thus theurgy involved practices that combined ethical behaviour, conduct and preparations with contemplative and meditative practices designed to purify the adept and thus allow him or her to attain 'a divine likeness' through making the soul vehicle spherical, in imitation of the gods.

Plotinus, who does not discuss or endorse theurgy but who constantly urges the philosopher towards contemplation and philosophical exercises and meditations, lays out an exercise for contemplation that is extremely interesting in relation to the issue of ritual praxis involving the vehicle of the soul:

> Let us then apprehend in our thought this visible universe, with each of its parts remaining what it is without confusion, gathering all of them together into one as far as we can, so that when any one part appears first, for instance the outside heavenly sphere, the imagination of the sun and, with it, the other heavenly bodies follows immediately, and the earth and sea and all the living creatures are seen, as they could in fact all be seen inside a transparent sphere. Let there be, then, in the soul a shining imagination of a sphere, having every-thing within it, either moving or standing still, or some things moving and others standing still. Keep this, and apprehend in your mind another, taking away the mass: take away also the places, and the mental picture of matter in yourself, and do not try to apprehend another sphere smaller in mass than the original one, but calling on the god who made that of which you have the mental picture, pray him to come.
>
> (*Enneads* [Armstrong 1984], 5.8.9)

Although ostensibly describing the cosmos and the World Soul, Plotinus' words evoke the idea of the vehicle of the soul in its spherical state, perhaps because later philosophers describe the soul vehicle as a reflection of the vehicle of the World Soul. However, Plotinus also ascribed a microcosmic nature to the human being. Since this passage comprises a spiritual, contemplative exercise designed to reveal to the philosopher important insights, it might be tentatively suggested that this passage represents an 'inner ritual' designed to work not only on the soul of the philosopher but also on his soul vehicle.

## Conclusion

Within Neoplatonism, the vehicle of the soul (*ochêma pneuma*) had various important functions: it functioned as the centre and seat of sense perception and imagination (*phantasia*). It had important eschatological functions: housing the soul in its journey after death into Hades (the Greek Underworld) in order to receive its rewards and punishments and acting as the vehicle that enabled the soul to choose its future lives and carried the soul between its human lives and incarnations, for those philosophers who subscribed to the idea of reincarnation. The soul vehicle also had soteriological functions central to the ultimate destiny of the human soul: it carried the soul into a physical body in its original descent into incarnation. Even more importantly, the soul vehicle was thought to become spherical in shape as the adept actualized and perfected themselves through philosophical, ritual and ethical means, allowing the human being to ascend to the gods and to rotate in harmony with the World Soul and with the circuits of the gods through its circular and spherical nature. This process was conceptualized as the divinization of the human being, enabling him or her to become godlike. For this reason, many Neoplatonists discuss the central role of the soul vehicle in ritual practices such as divination and theurgy, which were considered to effect communication between humans and gods through the purification of the soul vehicle and, consequently, the purification of the human powers of perception and imagination. In this sense, the soul vehicle was considered to act as an intermediary not only between the immaterial soul and the physical, material body but also between divine illumination and imagination (*phantasia*).

## Notes

1 Throughout this chapter, I use the term 'Oracle' (with capitalization) to refer to an oracular temple or sanctuary where oracular practices were located and I use the term 'oracle' (without capitalization) to refer to the oracular response given by a prophet or prophetess to an enquirer.

2 Porphyry's authorship of this work is disputed, chiefly by Franz Boll 1894: 112–18. However, most scholars accept the work as genuine, expect for the last chapters 46–55, which have been shown to be late additions to the text. Stefan Weinstock and Emilie Boer, who edited the original *CCAG* version of the text, accept it as genuine (*CCAG* V/4, p. 187), as does Bidez 1964: 72, no. 70; Pingree 2001: 7–8; Greenbaum 2009: 26, n.112–15. Smith (1993: liii) includes it as a genuine work of the 'Scientifica et Miscellanea' and numbers it P.64, 490.

3 A fragment from the *Philosophical History*, a work by the later Neoplatonist philosopher Damascius, also refers to the practice of 'evoking the light': 'The mass of light on the

wall seemed to condense and take on the shape of a face that was truly divine and supernatural and which gloried in a grace that was not sweet but severe; a face that was nevertheless very beautiful to behold and which for all its severity displayed no less of gentleness' (Damascius, *Philosophical History*, Fragment 75F, trans. Polymnia Athanassiadi 1999).

4  Cf. Bussanich 2005: 483: 'It seems to me doubtful that the social and collective function of ritual, as it is generally understood by historians and anthropologists, really fits Iamblichus or any of the later Neoplaonists.' For an example of such a view of ritual in Greek religion cf. Burkert 1985: 54–5.

5  Cf. n.6 below. It should be noted that the division imposed by scholars between Plotinus' 'rational' mysticism and the theurgy of the later Neoplatonists is a complicated and nuanced issue which (given space limitations) can only be briefly discussed here, in relation to the wider questions of analyses of ritual in modern scholarship (and particularly dichotomies between thought and action based on Cartesian mind–body dualism), and of the role of the vehicle of the soul in ritual, which might offer ideas and suggestions for modes of analysing ritual that move beyond such Cartesian dichotomies. For a fuller discussion see Addey 2009: 175–213 (Chapter 4) and the following studies: Mazur 2004: 29–56; Shaw 1985: 1–28; 1999: 121–43. It should also be noted that scholars have typically cited a famous passage from the later philosopher Damascius in order to support their categorical division between the rational contemplation of Plotinus and the theurgy of the later Neoplatonists: 'To some philosophy is primary, as to Porphyry and Plotinus and a great many other philosophers; to others, hieratic practice, as to Iamblichus, Syrianus, Proclus and the hieratic school generally' (Damascius, *Commentaries on Plato's Phaedo* II.I.172; Westerink 1977). However, the interpretation of this quotation is debatable given the context of the passage in which it occurs: Damascius does not write as if 'philosophy' and 'hieratic practices' are in any way mutually exclusive but rather points to a difference of emphasis between the two sets of philosophers whom he discusses. Athanassiadi (1993: 129) has also called into question the opposition possibly implied by Damascius' comment and its exploitation by modern scholars: 'Yet the pattern that emerges from these men's writings is different. Whereas for Plotinus and Iamblichus, the highest qualities in the spiritual and the moral spheres respectively are intuition and virtue, and their teaching manner is rather careless, concentrating as it does on the essential, often to the detriment of clarity and detail, Porphyry and Proclus keep good company with the rest of the philosophers mentioned by Damascius as thinkers attached to the letter of the Platonic texts under discussion or of cult.' Schibli (2002: 108): 'But though Damascius' contrast is apt enough as a general characterization, it is oversimplified.'

6  Iamblichus' view of theurgy as a continual, lifelong endeavour that is dependent upon a simultaneous combination of ritual, philosophical and ethical praxis, is implicit in his criticisms of magicians, those who 'stand on characters' in rituals (a typical characterization of those who undertake magical practices in Antiquity): 'For there are some who overlook the whole procedure of effective contemplation, both in regard to the one who makes the invocation and the one who enjoys the vision; and they disdain the order of the sacred observance, its holiness and long-protracted endurance of toils, and, rejecting the customs, prayers and other rituals, they believe the simple standing on the characters to be sufficient, and when they have done this for a mere hour, they believe that they have caused some spirit to enter. And yet how could anything noble or perfect result from this? Or how can the eternal and truly existing essence of the gods be united with ephemeral acts in sacred procedures? Hence, because of these things, such rash men go wholly astray, and are not worthy

to be counted among diviners' (*On the Mysteries* [Clarke, Dillon and Hershbell 2003], 3.13 (131.1–132.2)). From the context of this statement, it is clear that Iamblichus is deliberately contrasting the hasty and ephemeral practices of the magicians with the practices of theurgy, which include 'the procedure of effective contemplation' and the 'long-protracted endurance of toils', practices that involve lifelong preparation, devotion and continual observance. Thus, these practices are characterized as a lifelong activity of ethical and philosophical development and a 'constituting activity' in the world that is considered to affect the ritual practitioner's ability to communicate with and to receive the gods.

7 The classic statement of this position is that of Dodds (1951: 286): 'Plotinus is a man who ... raised himself by a strong intellectual and moral effort above the fog-ridden atmosphere which surrounded him. While he lived, he lifted his pupils with him. But with his death the fog began to close in again, and later Neoplatonism is in many respects a retrogression to the spineless syncretism from which he had tried to escape.' Dodds characterized Iamblichus and his endorsement of theurgy as a retrogression into irrationalism: 'The *de mysteriis* is a manifesto of irrationalism, an assertion that the road to salvation is found not in reason but in ritual' (1951: 187): the dichotomy imposed by Dodds between thought (reason/rationality) and action (ritual) is obvious here. Dodds also disparaged theurgy: 'As vulgar magic is commonly the last resort of the personally desperate, of those whom man and God have alike failed, so theurgy became the refuge of a despairing intelligentsia which already felt *la fascination de l'abîme*' (1951: 288). Majercik states: 'The later Neoplatonists recognized the difficulties in Plotinus' strictly intellectual ascent and thus turned towards more popular forms of religiosity as a way of universalizing Plotinus' system' (1995: 55). And Sheppard: 'It is still a common view that with [Iamblichus'] advocacy of theurgy a decline sets in and the rational basis of Plotinian mysticism is abandoned [in the Neoplatonic school]' (1982: 212).

8 For a tiny but representative sample of scholarly views on this matter: Dodds: 'And as to the Plotinian *unio mystica*, it must surely be clear to any careful reader of passages like *Enn* 1.6.9 or 6.7.34, that it is attained, not by any ritual of evocation or performance of prescribed acts, but by an inward discipline of the mind which involves no compulsive element and has nothing whatsoever to do with magic' (1951: 287). Boyancé: 'Parmi les néoplatoniciens la théurgie ... est ignore par Plotin, qui est bien au-dessus de cette forme inférieure de mysticisme' (1955: 189–209). Dodds: 'The substitution of theurgy for the personal mysticism of Plotinus ...' (1963: 319); '[Plotinus'] approach is severely intel-lectual, not physiological as in some oriental sects or sacramental as with some Christian mystics. He prescribes no breathing exercises, no navel-brooding, no hypnotic repetition of sacred syllables; and *no ritual is needed to provoke the experience*' (1965: 86, my emphasis). Armstrong: 'There can be no place, or at least no important place, for rites or sacraments in the religion of Plotinus' (1967: 260). Smith: 'Plotinus was not denying the existence or the importance of the gods but rather placing a priority on the inner spiritual life and a philosophical rather than ritual encounter with the divine' (2004: 77).

9 It is important to note that Iamblichus' references to the role of contemplation in theurgy (particularly his comments at *On the Mysteries* 5.18) has encouraged some scholars to divide theurgy into two forms: higher theurgy (based on contemplation and immaterial worship) and lower theurgy (based on material rituals). See Sheppard 1982: 212–24; Smith 1997: 32–99. For a convincing critique of this division see Shaw 1985: 8–10, especially n.39; 1995: 190–1. Such a division seems merely to relocate the dichotomy between thought and action into theurgy itself rather than attempting to re-examine or reconsider the applicability of this dichotomy.

## References

Addey, C. J. (2009) 'Oracles of the gods: the role of divination and theurgy in the philosophy of Porphyry and Iamblichus', dissertation, University of Bristol.

Armstrong, A. H. (1967) *Cambridge History of Later Greek and Early Medieval Philosophy*. Cambridge: Cambridge University Press.

Armstrong, A. H. (1984) *Plotinus: Ennead V*, Loeb Classical Library. Cambridge, MA and London: Heinemann and Harvard University Press.

Asad, T. (1993) *Genealogies of Religion*. Baltimore: Johns Hopkins University Press.

Athanassiadi, P. (1993) 'Dreams, theurgy and freelance divination: the testimony of Iamblichus', *Journal of Roman Studies* 83: 115–30.

——— (1999) *Damascius: Philosophical History*. Athens: Apamea Cultural Association.

Barton, T. (1994) *Ancient Astrology*. London: Routledge.

Bell, C. (1992) *Ritual Theory, Ritual Practice*. Oxford: Oxford University Press.

Bidez, J. ([1913], 1964) *Vie de Porphyre, le philosophe neo-platonicien*. Ghent: E. van Goethem.

Boll, F. (1894) *Studien über Claudius Ptolemäus: ein Beitrag zur Geschichte der griechischen Philosophie und Astrologie*. Leipzig.

Bowden, H. (2005) *Classical Athens and the Delphic Oracle: Divination and Democracy*. Cambridge: Cambridge University Press.

Boyancé, P. (1955) 'Théurgie et télestique néoplatoniciennes', *Revue de L'Histoire des Religions* 147: 189–209.

Burkert, W. (1985) *Greek Religion: Archaic and Classical*. Oxford: Blackwell.

Bury, R. G. (1929) *Plato: Timaeus*. London and Cambridge, MA: Heinemann and Harvard University Press.

Bussanich, J. (2005) Review article: 'Iamblichus: *De Mysteriis*, translated with an Introduction and Notes by Emma C. Clarke, John M. Dillon and Jackson P. Hershbell, Iamblichus: *De Anima*. Text, Translation, Commentary by John F. Finamore and John M. Dillon', *Ancient Philosophy* 25.2: 478–94.

Clarke, E. C., Dillon, J. M and Hershbell, J. P. (2003) *Iamblichus: On the Mysteries*. Atlanta: Society of Biblical Literature.

Diehl, E. (1903–6) *Proclus' Commentary on Plato's Timaeus (In Platonis Timaeum Commentaria)*, 3 vols. Leipzig: Teubner.

Dillon, J. M. ([1973], 2009) *Iamblichi Chalcidensis In Platonis Dialogos Commentariorum Fragmenta*. Westbury: Prometheus Trust.

Dillon, J. M. and Finamore, J. F. (2002) *Iamblichus: De Anima*. Leiden: Brill.

Dodds, E. R. (1951) *The Greeks and the Irrational*. Berkeley and Los Angeles: University of California Press.

——— (1963 [1933]) *Proclus: Elements of Theology*, 2nd edn. Oxford: Clarendon Press.

——— (1965) *Pagan and Christian in an Age of Anxiety*. New York: Norton.

Edwards, M. (2000) *Neoplatonic Saints: The Lives of Plotinus and Proclus by their Students*. Liverpool: Liverpool University Press.

Finamore, J. F. (1985) *Iamblichus and the Theory of the Vehicle of the Soul*. Chico, CA: Scholars Press.

——— (1993) 'Iamblichus on light and the transparent', in H. J. Blumenthal and E. G. Clark (eds) *The Divine Iamblichus: Philosopher and Man of Gods*. Bristol: Bristol Classical Press.

——— (1999) 'Plotinus and Iamblichus on magic and theurgy', *Dionysius* 17: 83–94.

Fontenrose, J. E. (1978) *The Delphic Oracle: Its Responses and Operations with a Catalogue of Responses*. Berkeley and Los Angeles: University of California Press.

Fowler, H. N. ([1914] 1982) *Plato: Euthyphro, Apology, Crito, Phaedo, Phaedrus*. London and Cambridge, MA: Heinemann and Harvard University Press.

George, L. (2005) 'Listening to the Voice of Fire: Theurgical Fitness and Esoteric Sensitivity', in R. M. Berchman and J. Finamore (eds), *History of Platonism: Plato Redivivus*. New Orleans: University Press of the South.

Greenbaum, D. G. (2009) 'The Daimon in Hellenistic astrology: origins and influences', dissertation, Warburg Institute.

Gregory, J. ([1991] 1999) *The Neoplatonists: A Reader*, 2nd edn. London and New York: Routledge.

Hadot, P. (2006) *The Veil of Isis: An Essay on the History of the Idea of Nature*. Cambridge, MA: Harvard University Press.

Halliday, W. R. (1913) *Greek Divination: A Study of Methods and Principles*. London: Macmillan.

Johnston, S. I. (2008) *Ancient Greek Divination*. Oxford: Wiley-Blackwell.

Keller, M. (2002) *The Hammer and the Flute: Women, Power and Spirit Possession*. Baltimore: Johns Hopkins University Press.

Kissling, R. C. (1922) 'The Oxhma-Pneuma of the Neo-Platonists and the *De Insomniis* of Synesius of Cyrene', *American Journal of Philology* 43(4): 318–30.

Koehler, F. G. (1974) *Hierocles: In Aureum Pythagoreorum Carmen Commentarius*. Stuttgart: Teubner.

Lane Fox, R. (1986) *Pagans and Christians in the Mediterranean World from the Second Century AD to the Conversion of Constantine*. London: Penguin.

Majercik, R. (1995) 'Plotinus and Greek mysticism', in D. H. Bishop (ed.) *Mysticism and the Mystical Experience East and West*. London: Associated University Press.

Mazur, Z. (2004) '*Unio Magica*: Part II: Plotinus, theurgy, and the question of ritual', *Dionysius* 22: 29–56.

Nauck, A. (1886) *Porphyrii Platonici: Opuscula Selecta*. Leipzig: Teubner.

O'Meara, D. (2003) *Platonopolis: Platonic Political Philosophy in Late Antiquity*. Oxford: Clarendon Press.

Parke, H. W. (1967) *Greek Oracles*. London: Hutchinson.

Parke, H. W. and Wormell, D. E. W. (1956) *The Delphic Oracle*. I: *The History*; II: *The Oracular Responses*, 2 vols. Oxford: Blackwell.

Pingree, D. (1986) *Vettii Valentis Antiocheni Anthologiarum Libri Novem*. Leipzig: Teubner

—— (2001) 'From Alexandria to Baghdād to Byzantium: the transmission of astrology', *International Journal of the Classical Tradition* 8: 3–37.

Rangos, S. (2000) 'Proclus and Artemis: on the relevance of Neoplatonism to the modern study of ancient religion', *Kernos* 13: 47–84.

Rosan, L. J. (1949) *The Philosophy of Proclus: The Final Phase of Ancient Thought*. New York: Cosmos.

Saffrey, H. D. and Westerink, L. G. (1968–78) *Platonic Theology* (*Théologie Platonicienne*), 3 vols. Paris: Les Belles Lettres.

Schibli, H. S. (2002) *Hierocles of Alexandria*. Oxford: Oxford University Press.

Shaw, G. (1985) 'Theurgy: rituals of unification in the Neoplatonism of Iamblichus', *Traditio* 41: 1–28.

—— (1995) *Theurgy and the Soul: The Neoplatonism of Iamblichus*. University Park: Pennsylvania State University Press.

—— (1999) 'Eros and Arithmos: Pythagorean theurgy in Iamblichus and Plotinus', *Ancient Philosophy* 19: 121–43.

Sheppard, A. (1982) 'Proclus' attitude to theurgy', *Classical Quarterly* 32(1): 212–24.

—— (1997) '*Phantasia* and inspiration in Neoplatonism', in M. Joyal (ed.) *Studies on Plato and the Platonic Tradition: Essays Presented to John Whittaker*. Aldershot: Ashgate.

Smith, A. (1993) *Porphyrii Philosophi Fragmenta*. Leipzig: Teubner.

—— (1997) 'Porphyry and Pagan Religious Practice', in J. J. O'Cleary (ed.) *The Perennial Tradition in Neoplatonism*. Leuven, Belgium: Leuven University Press.

—— (2004) *Philosophy in Late Antiquity*. London: Routledge.

Uzdavinys, A. (2010) *Philosophy and Theurgy in Late Antiquity*. San Rafael, CA: Sophia Perennis.

Westerink, L. G. (1977) *The Greek Commentaries on Plato's Phaedo*, Vol. II. Amsterdam, Oxford and New York: North Holland Publishing.

# 9 The subtle body in Sufism

*Milad Milani*

I know God by God, and I know that which is not God by the light of God.

(Imam Ali, in Hujwiri 1976: 269)

It is God that opens and seals the heart of men.

(Koran, 39:23)

This chapter is taking up the subtle body in the Islamic/Sufi traditions. It clarifies the place of subtle bodies in Islamic understanding through the lens of key Sufi thinkers from the ninth century to the modern time. Important to this work are the early chroniclers of Sufi doctrine and praxis (who are also compilers of major works of Sufism) such as Hujwiri, Attar and Rumi. This chapter aims to highlight important themes that are connected to the theory and practice of Sufism overall, but more importantly, to offer some degree of clarity on the fascinating subject of the subtle body in Sufism. The present brief examination also pays close attention to the synthesizing efforts and reformist impulse of the Sufis in the development of working theories of the subtle body.[1]

Early Islamic materials, on their own, tell us little in terms of an explicit reference to the 'subtle body'. What is known, however, can be gleaned from the Koran and hadith by way of the experiences of the Prophet Mohammed. Such an exercise no doubt required the mystical eye of certain early Muslim thinkers of Basra and Baghdad, such as Rabia the female mystic, Tustari and Junayd and his contemporaries. These Muslims sought to understand the inner meaning of their faith. The 'Sufis', as these pious men and women came to be called, developed systems of spiritual hierarchies made possible through contact with earlier systems (of Greek, Persian, Hermetic and Indian philosophies).

From the time of the early Middle Ages the Sufis had the explicit idea that the 'subtle centres' were actually a series of coexisting psycho-spiritual 'bodies' that mediate between the material and transcendent realms (Buehler 1998: 106). There is probably an important link between this notion and that of the spiritual 'double', which can be found in Plato's theory of the 'astral plane' (Plato 2003) and the 'astral body' incorporated by Theosophists and Rosicrucians. This idea of a 'divine likeness', or 'twin' (popular among the Gnostics), is nevertheless timeless, since earlier instances of it can be found in the ancient Persian notion of *fravashi*, the divine 'guardian spirits' (Corbin 1978: 32f.). In connection, in later

Islamic thought there developed the interesting notion that 'Mohammed', meaning 'worthy of praise' (Declais 2010: 501) was an allusion to the Paraclete. Even so, it is not difficult to interpret the 'mystical prophetology' of the Light of Mohammed as the connection with, and a continuum of, the divine essence (Schimmel 1985: 125–6). In the same way, the Sufi master is seen as the worldly intercessor whose presence is deemed necessary for the activation of these centres.

Sufism is the mystical school of Islam whose tradition records the language and experience of those Muslims seeking intimacy and union with God. The past century has seen the popular growth of Sufism in the West, catering to the needs of Westerners in search of alternative means of religion (Westerlund 2004: 138). This movement has given rise to renewed (and broad) interpretations of Sufism that have set it apart from its traditional Islamic setting (Sedgwick 2005: 846). As such, modern Sufism possesses its own unique view of the subtle body, which is discussed below.

## The subtle-body concept in the Koran and beyond

The use of the subtle body or spiritual centres (*latâ'if*) in Sufism can be understood primarily as a theory of personhood and self-transformation (Hermansen 1988: 1). The Sufi term *latîfa* (plural *latâ'if*) is derived from the Arabic word *latîf* meaning 'gentle', 'sensitive' or 'subtle', and in Sufi terminology describes the non-material component of the person capable of being influenced or 'awakened' through spiritual practices (1988: 1). However, a coherent vision of the subtle body in Sufism is often difficult to ascertain. From what can be deduced, there are two ways we can understand the subtle body in Sufism – the perfection and ascent of the soul, and the psychological 'mapping' of the human consciousness – and both are suggested in the Koran. The Koran talks about the soul or *nafs* and describes three stages of the soul's transformation (12:53; 75:2; 89:27); the hadith literature presents a quasi-notion of an astral body (most likely the soul) that leaves the body in its ascent of the heavens. This recounts the Prophet's night ascension (*isra* and *mi'raj*), also alluded to in the Koran (17:1; 81:19–25; 53:12–18). The psychological aspect, explained by Qushayri (d. 1072) in a four-dimensional structure of human consciousness (Qushayri 1959), is drawn from the Koranic reference to *akhfa*, which seems to suggest secret or hidden aspects of human consciousness (Kamada 2010).

The idea, or reality, of the subtle body was elaborated in Sufi works as early as the tenth century. Prior to this, it can be said that all Sufis were aware of the magnificence of the subtle body, which was limited only to their imagination and their expression of it in lyrical verse or ecstatic utterances later recorded by Sufi chroniclers (Mojaddedi 2001). For instance, it can be deduced that the early Sufi female mystic of Basra, Rabia al-Adawiyya (d. 801), knew of aspects of the subtle body when she says: 'It is the Lord of the house I need, what have I to do with the house?' When asked to come outside to witness the works of God, she replies: 'Come you inside that you may behold their Maker. Contemplation of the Maker has turned me aside from what He has made' (Smith 1978: 219). The allusion made to the 'house' and to 'outside' and 'inside' can be read as implying the degrees of the subtle body – in short, saying that the ultimate expression of the divine is within.

That God is found at the centre of being was never a great mystery to the mystic, but the idea was quite clearly forwarded in the twentieth century by Meher Baba by way of his theory of 'involution' (1973). In other words, for Meher Baba the 'soul' evolves from a state of mineral to its final physical form as human (the height of the soul's physical expression), from which it is then possible to go 'within' (as a kind of inward ascension) through to God. How appropriate, then, to locate the source of Sufi mystical understanding in the hadith qudsi: 'I [God] was a hidden treasure and I longed to be known, so I created the creation that I may be known.' Indeed, how controversial. According to Ibn Taymiyya, this particular citation is disputed as it is authenticated through [Sufi] *kashf* (insight), and not a recognized chain of transmission.

The concept of the subtle body is certainly not original to Sufism (or Islam for that matter), as it belongs to a wider, more ancient scope of spiritual philosophy. Yet Sufis by the ninth and tenth centuries had become adept in formulating their own theories on the subject. The Sufis drew predominantly on the Koran and hadith to validate their spiritual world-view, but it would seem that the Sufi notion of the subtle body was mainly inspired through extra-canonical material, since it is not Koranic in origin. The influence of Neoplatonism is the most recognized factor, influencing the early Islamic philosophers and interpreters of Koran, such as Avicinna and Averoes. For instance, Proclus' three-tiered system, echoed in Hujwiri – Spirit (*ruh*), Lower Soul (*nafs*), and Physical Body (*jasad*) – was the basic model most Sufis worked off (Hermansen 1988: 7; Hujwiri 1976: 196–200). Another prominent model, originating with Abu Hafs Haddad (d. 879), is the idea of the heart as mediator between *nafs* and *ruh* (Hujwiri 1976: 276–7).

Explicit formulations regarding the subtle body within Sufism can be traced to ninth-century Iraq, where several early Sufis first cultivated the notion of *latífas* in the human body. Junayd (d. 910), the grand sheikh of Baghdad, is perhaps the most recognized figure of early Sufism to have formulated important ideas to do with subtle centres, but his contemporaries were equally important to its development in Sufism. Basra was host to a small group of remarkable Sufis consisting of Sahl al-Tustari (d. 896), Amr ibn Uthman al-Makki (d. 909) and Hussein Ibn Mansour al-Hallaj (d. 922). According to Al-Tustari there are two forms of 'subtle substance' associated with the individual. The first gives life to the natural self and the second is linked to the spiritual self. The latter is acquired by Sufi meditation (*dhikr*) (Böwering 1980: 244–5, cited in Buehler 1998: 106, n.31). Amr al-Makki imagined *latífas* as though veils encased in one another, for example, the *nafs* in *qalb*, *qalb* in *ruh*, and *ruh* in *sirr*, which were successively removed, as one got closer to God (Massignon 1982: 3, 17). Al-Hallaj, in like fashion, portrays Mohammed in the night ascension (*mi'raj*) shedding one subtle covering (*latífa*) of his soul for each heaven he passed through (1982: 1, 14, n.78).

All the above figures conceived of the *latífas* as 'subtle bodies' or coverings which the self or soul progressed through by way of prescribed spiritual practices.

Later in the eleventh, twelfth and thirteenth centuries, a more specific notion of the subtle body as spiritual 'organs' connected to the human body is expressed by Abu Abdurrahman al-Sulami (d. 1021), Abu Hamid al-Ghazali (d. 1111), and Shihabuddin Abu Hafs Umar al-Suhrawardi (d. 1234). Najmuddin Kubra (d. 1221) examined the finer workings of the subtle body that was grounded in a tripartite system of the heart, spirit and mystery, perceived as an internal human phenomenon (Buehler 1988: 107). His pupil Najmuddin Razi (d. 1256) further elaborated the philosophy of subtle bodies into a pentad (Buehler 1988: 108). A transmitter of the Kubrawi tradition, Ala-uddawla Simnani (d. 1336) produced a seven-tiered model of the subtle body and presented the correlation between the seven *latîfas* and seven colours, seven prophets, seven spiritual types and seven levels of the cosmos (Corbin 1971: 3, 275–355, cited in Buehler 1998: 108). However, it isn't until the nineteenth century that we have a discernible colour association with the notion of a seven-fold nature of the human being (Buehler 1998: 109f.).

An understanding of the concept of the *latîfas* in Sufism is very much dependent on the functional context that is examined. Nevertheless, a common factor that remains consistent is the Sufi use of *latîfa* as a heuristic device for the disciple to advance through spiritual realms (Buehler 1998: 112). In this way, the Sufi system of the subtle body is rather analogous to other South Asian systems, such as the Buddhist tantric concepts discussed elsewhere in this volume (cf. Buehler 1998: 112).

## The subtle body (*Jismi Latif*) in the work of Abu Bakr Wasiti, Sumnun and Amr al-Makki

The previous section offered important thematic links and chronological detail for understanding the basic philosophy of the subtle body in Sufism. In short, the Sufis devised a mystical system to elaborate their unique cosmogony of 'inward transcendence'. In this and the following sections, the historical development of this design will be traced in more detail through an examination of a number of particular figures. I commence with Abu Bakr Wasiti (d. 932), nicknamed 'soaring minaret', who earned his fame due to his contribution to Islamic mysticism and metaphysics; he was the first to bring the Baghdad Sufi tradition to Khurasan (Silvers 2010). Hujwiri notes him as an authority on one of the aspects of the subtle body, the 'spirit' (1976: 265). Wasiti explains that there are ten stations (*maqâmât*) of spirits, at the head of which is the spirit of dervishes. These depict Wasiti's vision of spiritual maturity and nearness to God, which is worth exploring in full, but for the sake of brevity a sample is offered here, followed by a summary:

> (1) the spirits of the sincere (*mukhlisân*), which are imprisoned in a darkness and know not what will befall them; (2) the spirits of pious men (*parsâ mardân*), which in the heaven of this world rejoice in the fruits of their actions and take pleasure in devotions, and walk by the strength thereof; (3) the spirits of disciples (*muridân*), which are in the fourth heaven and dwell with the angels in the delights of veracity, and in the shadow of their good works ...
>
> (Hujwiri 1976: 265)

Wasiti goes on to record that next come 'the spirits of the beneficent' (*ahl-i minan*), who are hung in lamps of light on the throne of God, defined by mercy, favour and proximity. Next, the 'the spirits of the faithful' (*ahl-i wafâ*) who are the pure and elect; and 'the spirits of martyrs' (*shahîdân*) who are free to roam paradise. The last four stations take us through the final sequence of the psycho-spiritual stations and towards annihilation of the ego. Thereby 'the spirits of those who yearn' (*mushtâqân*) are clothed in light and divine attributes, while the spirits of gnostics ('*ârifân*) hear only the word of God. Then comes 'the spirits of lovers' (*dustân*) who perceive nothing but God in all that they do, and lastly 'the spirits of dervishes' who having become annihilated are utterly transformed in both 'quality' and 'state' (Hujwiri 1976: 265).

Another mystic of Baghdad, Sumnun al-Muhibb ('the lover') ibn Hamza al-Basri (d. 900), held love to be the 'foundation and principle of the way to God'. A peculiar doctrine among Baghdadi Sufis, since Sumnun asserted that every 'state' and 'station' experienced by the Sufi is actually the 'stages of love', and that every stage and abode of the Sufi is destructible except the abode of love, which is indestructible so long as God wills the way to him to exist (Hujwiri 1976: 309). Sumnun's controversial placing of love as the superior method to God revealed one of the treasured secrets of the Sufis, which the other sheikhs preferred to remain hidden. Although they agreed with him about the importance of love, they replaced the term 'love' with terms like 'purity' and 'poverty' (Hujwiri 1976: 309).

Amr al-Makki (d. 909), an 'austere mystic' primarily concerned with the 'strict observance of ritual practices', was true to the Baghdadi Sufi tradition of 'sobriety' over intoxication (*sukr*) (Massignon 1982: 37). In his *Kitab al-Mahabbat* ('The Book of Love') he gives us a wonderful allegory of the 'fall' using the example of the subtle bodies. Al-Makki's model consists of the three-tiered system of heart, spirit and soul, but adding the body as the final layer in which all three are contained. It seems he wants his readers to know that spirituality is, in and of itself, inevitably flawed with pride. It is adherence to ordained customs that promote healthy mysticism – all but promoting the Baghdadian agenda of maintaining a Sufi orthodoxy. Al-Makki's intriguing arrangement of the *latîfas* is certainly worth closer examination; here just a brief overview of his vision is given.

In his book al-Makki mentions that the hearts (*sirrhâ*) were the first to be created, followed by the spirits (*janhâ*) and souls (*dilhâ*) – each 7,000 years apart (Hujwiri 1976: 309). Note the Apostolic tradition, 'God created the spirits two thousand years before the bodies', also offered by Hujwiri elsewhere in his book (1976: 263). Each of these is then specified a degree of proximity in relation to God. The hearts were kept in the degree of union (*wasl*); the spirits were kept in the degree of intimacy (*uns*); and the souls were kept in the degree of proximity (*qurb*) (1976: 309). Now when God bestowed upon them the esteem of his attention, they 'were filled with vanity and pride' in knowing of their exclusivity. Al-Makki says God revealed the 'epiphany of His beauty to the heart three hundred and sixty times every day' and again 'bestowed on it three hundred and sixty looks of grace'; then, he caused the spirits to 'hear the word of love' and finally 'manifested three hundred and sixty exquisite favours of intimacy to the soul'. Next, al-Makki explains the purpose behind the subtle centres within the human body. They are intermingled as part of a probatory period, being encased in one another and then confined to physical form, for God 'imprisoned the heart in the spirit and the spirit in the soul and the soul in the body' (1976: 309). Following this, God mixed reason (*aql*) with them, and sent prophets and gave commands, until each of them were awakened to their flaw and began to seek their 'original station', and lastly, prayer was made incumbent (1976: 309). Here one cannot help but notice the parallel with the Prophet's ascension, since God also gives Mohammed the command to pray. So it is that al-Makki tells us, 'the body betook itself to prayer, the soul attained to love, the spirit arrived at proximity to God, and the heart found rest in union with Him' (1976: 309).

## The theme of lover and beloved in Ahmad Ghazali and Rumi

At this stage it would be rewarding to have a glimpse at just one of the many notable figures of the Khurasani Sufi tradition, the brother of the renowned Imam Ghazali (d. 1111), Ahmad Ghazali (d. 1126). He spoke of three worlds or stages (singular, *manzil*) – *dil* (heart), *ruh* (spirit), and *sirr* (mystery) – through which the Sufi passed (Purjavadi 1979: 208, cited in Buehler 1998: 107, n.32). In true antinomian Sufi style, it is perhaps enough to view his analogy of the moth as presented in his *Sawanih al-'ushshaq* ('The Intuitions of Lovers'), summarized by Henry Corbin who notes: 'When love really exists, the lover becomes the nourishment of the Beloved; it is not the Beloved who is the nourishment of the lover ...'. So when 'the moth which has become the lover of the flame' is nourished, yet at a distance by the light, the moth must, nevertheless, 'go on flying until it reaches it [the flame]'. Once there, the moth 'can no longer advance *towards* the flame'. At this moment the very essence of Ghazali's verse is revealed: for he tells us that it is 'the flame which advances *within*' the moth. Now to explain the opening lines: the 'flame is not nourishing the moth; the moth is nourishing the flame'. Still, the last lines yield the true mystery of Ghazali's insight when he explains that 'for a fleeting instant' the moth 'becomes its own Beloved (since it *is* the flame). And in this it is made perfect' (Corbin 1993: 201).

Apropos, the above is the first treatise on the Sufi doctrine of love written in the Persian language. Ahmad Ghazali extends the bounds of traditional Sufism by touching on comparative themes (as invoked through the language) from Persia's religious past, which, incidentally, by the eleventh and twelfth centuries had been a more consistent feature of Persian Sufism (Milani forthcoming). This is important when noting the sudden further development of the concept of the subtle body in Sufism during this period.

However, it is the mystic and poet Rumi (d. 1273) who by far is the standard bearer of the 'Sufism of love' as well as being the only Sufi to achieve international fame by transcending the classical period and having his philosophy revitalized in the modern era. His renowned book of spiritual poems, the *Mathnawi*, contains many colourful examples of the subtle body. In one story Rumi explains the relationship between the subtle bodies through a love story between a king (*ruh*) and a handmaiden (*nafs*). This story is both pertinent, since Rumi acts as a departure point to Sufism in the modern time and also because the story itself underlines the significant role of the spiritual guide in the awakening of the subtle bodies in the novice Sufi. A summary of the tale is given below:

The story opens with a king who is out hunting and has a chance encounter with a beautiful maiden. He falls helplessly in love with her and takes her back to his palace. Before long she falls ill and the king is distraught at the court physicians' inability to cure her. The king, by this time, willing to forgo his stature and wealth for the sake of the girl, desperately searches for a cure. Unsuccessful, the king falls before God and pleads with God to cure his beloved; that night he is told through a dream that a certain sage will be sent to help him. The next day the sage arrives and immediately identifies the girl's ailment. It turns out that the girl is love-sick, wanting to be with a certain goldsmith in another village. The king had promised to place his trust in the sage and on his advice sends for the goldsmith and arranges for the two to be married. The goldsmith, however, did not come for the girl but for the promise of riches. He leaves his wife and children in pursuit of worldly gain. Sure enough, the girl begins to recover but the sage had also instructed that the goldsmith be slowly poisoned. As the goldsmith's good looks fade, so does the maiden's superficial attachment to him. When the goldsmith eventually dies the maiden begins to see the prospect of true love with the king (Nicholson 1994: 6–17).

The meaning of the story lies in the hidden symbolism that is carefully threaded by Rumi.[2] The girl represents the soul (*nafs*), while the king is the spirit (*ruh*). The courtly physicians are made to represent the rational intellect. The goldsmith symbolizes worldly attachment. The sage, however, is 'the perfect man' (*insane al-kamil*) or Sufi saint who is capable of guiding the soul to its higher purpose. Rumi places special emphasis on the mediation of the sage in the story. The helplessness of the king (despite his stature and power) 'is another insightful analogy demonstrating the love of God for Man, but also Man's distraction with worldly prospects' (Milani forthcoming).

## Understanding the subtle body: self-transformation in Sufi doctrine

The Koran makes mention of three stages of the soul's transformation that feature in three separate *surahs*. The Sufis, on the other hand, have made good use of these passages by linking them into a coherent system of purification: the commanding soul (*nafs ammara*), the blaming soul (*nafs lawwama*), and the soul at peace (*nafs mutma'inna*). The first stage indicates the urge of the lower soul to have its way. In Sufism, the 'lower soul' is usually associated with the 'ego' or 'carnal' self, suggesting the lowest point of human awareness. The second stage represents the soul's acknowledgement and reproach of its base nature, signified by the gradual growth of awareness. The third and final stage denotes the level at which the soul is in compliance with divine will and sees the signs of God reflected within, a level signified by the height of awareness.

The Sufis quickly refined these early ideas into a sophisticated ontology – to be dissolved in the Godhead (*fana fi'llah*) and to subsist through his attributes (*baqa bi'llah*) (Rahman 2010). The doctrine of *fana o baqa*, or 'annihilation and subsistence', which is central to Sufism, is built on the earlier Sufi refinements of the stages of the *nafs* in the Koran. The idea was first cultivated by the Khurasanian Sufi Bayazid al-Bistam (d. 874), and since then it was gradually made the principal tenet of the Sufi tradition (Nicholson 1994: 77). Hand in hand with this principle went the doctrine of altruism, also an early development in Sufism that appropriated the chivalric ideal (*javanmardi*) and cultural etiquette (*adab*) (Ridgeon 2010: 3ff.).

Accordingly, in Sufism the idea of the subtle body is essentially about the transformation of the self (*nafs*), the Sufis explaining this by a basic three-tiered system of soul (*nafs*), heart (*qalb*) and spirit (*ruh*). Such is the classical view found in the expressions of the ninth to the thirteenth centuries. An example of this is seen in the poetry of Rumi:

> He doesn't have a palace, he was told
> Except his soul, illumined like pure gold ...

Rumi then wittingly uses the example that the vision of the 'heart's eye' (the subtle organ capable of beholding 'such a palace') can be barred by 'one stray hair'. His advice is to remove the hair, that you may have a chance, then revealing what is possible, indeed that which is the aim of the spiritual quest (Mojaddedi 2001: 88):

> Mohammad, purged of fire and smoke's last trace
> Whichever way he turned saw just God's face

Rumi was not only a keen mystic but an astute theologian; note the last verse (above), which is a clever hint to the Koranic verse, 'Whichever way you turn there is the face of God' (Koran, 2:115). Rumi's allusion to the subtle body here, which fits in with the model of Abu Hafs (see above), carries the classical Sufi view of the subtle body as a concept that primarily concerns itself with self-transformation. Moreover, transforming the *nafs* is based on freedom from lust (one of the aspects of the lower self), an idea that comprises the basic early Sufi attitude of disciplining the soul in order to gain a measure of proximity with God. Rumi, who was sharply aware of his Sufi forebears, reflects the attitude of

Suhrawardi maqtul (d. 1191), who said: 'Once the soul is purified, it will be illuminated by divine light' (Suhrawardi 1945: 184).

## Pinpointing the subtle body in Sufi works

The idea of *latīfa* originates in the ninth century where it began as a generic 'subtle substance' before it was defined functionally as a 'subtle body' (Buehler 1998: 107). It wasn't until the eleventh century that the idea of *latīfa* became a localized 'subtle entity' or 'organ' within the human body (Buehler 1998: 107). Still, it remains difficult for one to procure a coherent image of the subtle body in Sufi thought, even though copious amounts of Sufi works are on hand. Yet there is good reason for why it is complex. Sufism by nature has always maintained a certain degree of elusiveness when it comes to its doctrinal and practical methods, truly living up to its label of mysticism. The Sufi works, therefore, mostly 'hint' or 'allude' to deeper matters, never revealing too much on any subject, allowing the reader to apprehend certain truths in their own good time. Even Hujwiri's grand corpus entitled *kashf al-mahjoub* ('Revelation of Secrets'), which sets out literally to reveal all manner of Sufi secrets (and of course to settle accounts with pretenders to the Sufi name), would be of little value to the adherent who knew naught by way of having spiritually 'tasted' truth to some degree.

The message is that Sufis see no point in revealing more than the seeker can digest, and this is nowhere better illustrated than the saying of Hasan-i Basri in reply to his audience who demanded he deliver his speech in the absence of Rabia: 'That wine which we've made for the capacity of elephants cannot be poured into the chest of ants' (Nurbakhsh 1980: 9). A candid report comes from the Naqshbandi sheikh, Faqirullah Shikarpuri, who admits the complexity of the subtle body but says reassuringly, 'their appearance depends on the differing capacities of those travelling on the path (*salikin*)'. Therefore to make it easy for wayfarers some sheikhs established points in the body where the subtle centres can be located (see Table 9.1) (Buehler 1998: 111; Shikarpuri 1978: 565).

## The example of the Prophet's ascension

Next is the question of the meaning of the term *latâ'if* as either 'stages' within a quasi-physical body or 'realms' of ascension, which may, of course, affect a reading

*Table 9.1* An example taken from Mujaddedi positions for *latīfas* (Buehler 1998: 111)

| Latîfa | Colour | Location |
|---|---|---|
| super-arcanum (*akhfa*) | green | sternum |
| arcanum (*khafi*) | black | above right breast |
| mystery (*sirr*) | white | above left breast |
| spirit (*ruh*) | red | below right breast |
| heart (*qalb*) | yellow | below left breast |
| soul (*nafs*) | – | middle of forehead |

of the Prophet's *mi'raj* (heavenly ascent). Several passages in the Koran hint at the Prophet's transportation to the 'furthest mosque' and his ascent to the seventh heaven (17:1; 81:19–25; 53:12–18). What is later made clear in Muslim sources is that there are seven layers and associated with each are the prophets of the Old Testament. The orthodox view is that this was a bodily experience in which Mohammed was awake (Tabari, *Tafsir* xv, 13; Schrieke 2010: 97). In contrast, mystics and philosophers have favoured the allegorical interpretation (Schrieke 2010: 97). For the Sufis the ascension of the Prophet is 'the rise of the soul from the bonds of sensuality to the heights of mystic knowledge' (2010: 97). The Sufi view tends to imply an internal experience with regard to the ascension. In this light, a reading of the account of the ascension becomes a ready description of the subtle body as 'stages' within the quasi-phsyical body in Islamic Mysticism. On the other hand, it is very easy to read the account as though it were of the soul's travelling through subtle 'realms' beyond the material plane. The hadith give a more coherent account, making sense of the earlier Koranic allusions; but they are again made sense through the mystical imagination of Sufis.

The event of the Prophet's ascension begins in Mecca (in the neighbourhood of the Ka'ba), where Gabriel awakens Mohammed from sleep and directs him to the winged creature, *burâq*. Together they journey to Jerusalem, from whence the ascent takes place. Accompanied by Gabriel, at each level Mohammed meets a certain prophet. Narrated by Anas Ibn Malik, tradition mentions in order of appearance, from the first to the seventh heaven, the prophets appearing and conversing with Mohammed: Adam, John the Baptist and Jesus, Joseph, Enoch, Aaron, Moses and Abraham – beyond which not even Gabriel ventures, for Mohammed alone is made to converse with God (Colby 2006, 2008). The story is suggestive of the necessary role of divine assistance during the Prophet's ascension. First we have the assistance of *burâq* and then Gabriel, until arriving at the vicinity of God's domain (beyond the heavens) where only Mohammed is permitted to enter.

Buehler also raises the question as to whether a *latîfa* is a 'place' or a 'subtle body' (1998: 112). He notes that some Sufis (the Mujaddidis) 'mention travelling in a certain *latîfa*'. He cites one Sufi (Simnani) in particular who 'postulated ten *latîfas* emanating from the Essence while discussing the subtle, acquired body moving through these *latîfas*' (1998: 112). Buehler presents the notion, and I agree with him, that 'the body or sheath a human being occupies at a given moment determines the corresponding ontological reality' (1998: 113). In other words, as we develop these subtle bodies, or learn to move between them at will, we can experience different realities, but ultimately access to each of these 'various levels of the cosmos are inside each human being'; the person has to go 'inside' from 'subtle body to subtle body' (1998: 113). In another way, Shikarpuri mentions, 'as the disciple eliminates veils to receive more light, he or she enters an enlightened existence (*wujud-i nurani*), presumably closer to God' (Buehler 1998: 112, n.51; Shikarpuri n.d.: 236). This last example resembles that of Fariduddin Attar's Seven Valleys in his *Mantiq al-Tayr* ('Conference of the Birds').

## Qushayri and Attar on the subtle body

Attar's narrative poem *Mantiq al-Tayr*, which dates from the twelfth century presented the didactic tale of a large congregation of birds who, inspired by their leader, the hoopoe, set out to meet the king of birds, the *Simurgh*. The birds are compelled to journey through seven valleys, which represent the stations a Sufi novice must traverse in order to realize the true nature of God. The valleys are set out as follows: Quest (*talab*), Love (*eshq*), Gnosis (*ma'rifat*), Detachment (*istighnah*), Unity (*tawhid*), Bewilderment (*Hayrat*) and Poverty (*faqr*). In the end only 30 birds or *si-murgh* remain, since others have become victim to their own vice and perished along the way. The 30 birds discover their king through reflection of their own self in the lake (hence, *si-murgh* [*Simurgh*], a witty play on words), thus affirming the intrinsic Sufi view of the God within (Attar 1984).

Prior to Attar, in the eleventh century, Qushayri's four-dimensional structure of human consciousness is probably the most popular among the different schemes of *latâ'if* used by the Sufis. His model works off the three-tiered system of soul, heart and spirit, but brings into play the fourth component of the 'inmost consciousness/secret' (*sirr*). This last level is properly understood as the 'deepest dimension of human consciousness' and a place of contemplation and unification where one is able to realize 'enlightenment with a divine encounter' (Kamada 2010). Here interpreting *latâ'if* as 'inner subtleties', Kamada suggests a psychological reading that draws on the Koranic mention of the words *sirr* and *khafi* (*akhfa*). Once again, the theme that is presented in all the models previewed indicates a movement 'within', which then admits to the probability of travelling inwards to transcend.

## The subtle body in modern Sufism

Modern Sufis have placed particular emphasis on the immanence of divine presence and the availability of spiritual nourishment, so much so that the doctrine of *fana o baqa* openly presented the experience of God-consciousness. In the social domain, Sufism stressed the importance of 'balance' between the mundane and the transcendent, highlighting the fact that the Sufis were from the very beginning involved in the world and in making it better (Ridgeon 2010: 2). The Sufis were never recluse monks, since most of them had professions of some kind (physicians, merchants and so on). For the late master of the Nimatullahiyya, Javad Nurbakhsh (d. 2008), the modern Sufi is a person of this world, who lives in the world and is not detectable by the ordinary eye. This means that most modern Sufis have abandoned the strict adherence to traditional dress and ritual practices (at least in public spaces), where the verse from Sa'di's *Bustan* ('The Orchard') is recalled: 'Religion consists alone in the service of the people; it finds no place in the prayer-beads, or prayer-rug or tattered garment.' In short, modern Sufism displays adaptability to changing conditions of modernity, presenting an ethical spirituality and oftentimes reinventing itself as other than Islamic. To that purpose, the aim of Sufism is made very clear in the modern period: to 'die to self' and to 'live in God', which is to be achieved through the practice of selfless (worldly) service (*khidmat*).

There are several recent collections addressing modern Sufism and its relationship with traditional Islam. For example, the work of Howell and van Bruinessen, *Sufism and the 'Modern' in Islam* (2007), is significant in showing how Western Sufi movements have pushed the boundaries of traditional Islam through their extraordinary ability to adapt their teachings and accommodate for a Western audience. This puts into question the congruency of modern Sufism and Islam, but we can rest assured that the attitude of modern Sufis is far from inconsistent. Recent research, including Raudvere and Stenberg's collection *Sufism Today* (2009), highlights the ingenuity of Sufi orders and movements in finding their feet in modern contemporary society. Many examples are drawn from around the globe to illustrate the development of contemporary Sufism such as found in Turkey, Iran, Indonesia, North Africa and India. As can be imagined, the material on the subject is vast, covering the intricacies of Sufism in the above-mentioned societies, and remaining beyond the immediate concern of this chapter. It would be useful, however, to highlight the views of just four major figures of the twentieth and early twenty-first centuries – Inayat Khan, Meher Baba, Javad Nurbakhsh, and Robert Frager.

One of the chief figures of modern Sufism is Hazrat Inayat Khan (d. 1927), who introduced Sufism to the West during his travels in the early twentieth century. Along with his wife Ameena Begum, he founded a new Sufi order, Universal Sufism, which promoted spirituality as the basis for the unity of religions. Inayat Khan translated the Sufi notion of *baqa* as 'perfection'; he says in his book *A Sufi Message of Spiritual Liberty* that it is the highest condition available which was taught to the world by ancient sages (Inayat Khan 1914: 27–8). He defines *baqa* as the original state of God, a state achievable through practices of concentration. Using traditional language, these practices would in turn allow the seeker to pass through three stages of development: *fana fi'l-shaikh* (annihilation in the astral plane), *fana fi'l-rasul* (annihilation in the spiritual plane) and *fana fi'llah* (annihilation in the abstract), the final stage being the state of *baqa bi'llah* (annihilation in the eternal consciousness). Colour association was recognized by Inayat Khan but not central to his model of subtle bodies. Music, instead, was to play the central role in Inayat Khan's system of morphology. As a master musician he was aware of the mystery of tone and rhythm and its influence on the human soul. For Inayat Khan, sacred music was able to touch the heart and illuminate the soul. The power of music was to awaken the memory of the soul to its origin – God. Music was 'food for the soul'.

Another important contributor to the development of modern Sufism was Meher Baba (d. 1969), who founded in 1952 the American Sufi order Sufism Reoriented. Meher Baba's metaphysics uniquely incorporated Vedanta, Sufism and Christianity (Meher Baba 1973). His system of the subtle body paralleled that of his view on reincarnation and God-realization; that is, Meher Baba talks about the soul's pursuit of liberation as the evolution of the immanent divine consciousness. He mentions seven 'kingdoms' – stone/metal, vegetable, worm, fish, bird, animal and human – through which the soul experiences what is required for the next level of awakening. However, only the final stage, in human form, allows access to the soul's own divinity (Purdom 1964). This is possible through the process of what Meher Baba calls 'involution', or what he describes as journeying within (1973: 40).

Other developments in Sufism in the modern era are worth mentioning here, such as the transplantation of several traditional Sufi orders to the West. These include variations of the Naqshbandis, Chishtis, Qadiris, Mevlevis, Alawis, Shadhilis and Tijanis (Geaves 2006: 142). The Nimatullahis, on the other hand, have proven an interesting case study, since they more than any other group have dislocated themselves from the main body of Islam (Lewisohn 2006). Both in their use of terms and expressions of Sufi concepts, the Nimatullahis discretely reinvented themselves by envisioning the roots of Sufism in the Persian (pre-Islamic) past (Milani, forthcoming). Formerly a psychologist, Javad Nurbakhsh, the late master or *pir* of the order, formulated the classical Sufi concept of the subtle body that reflected a Zoroastrian model. He mentions the world as the battleground between the two forces, the *nafs* and spirit, who are both aiming to apprehend the heart (Nurbakhsh 1996: 42). He offers a five-tiered model of the subtle body, presented in order of ascension or introspection (that is, going within onself): *nafs*, heart, spirit, inner consciousness, and innermost consciousness (Nurbakhsh 1993: 3).

Also in the domain of Sufism and psychology, Robert Frager deserves mention, since he wrote extensively on Sufi psychology, especially with regard to the relationship between the subtle bodies and the self (1999). An American-born trained psychologist, Frager converted to Islam through his contact with the Helveti Jerrahi Sufi order. He edited and wrote the introduction to *Love is the Wine: Talks of a Sufi Master in America* by Sheikh Muzaffer Ozak (d. 1985), under his converted name and title, Sheikh Ragip Frager.

## Conclusion

In retrospect, Sufi representations of the subtle body gradually developed in the ninth century and have been formulated into elaborate systems in the modern age. Prior to this, and very much due to the mystical nature of Sufism, the subtle centres remained a hidden and integrated aspect of Sufi theosophy. Given that the idea does not originate in the Koran, it was only with gradual freedom of expression that the Sufis were able to delineate a codified system of subtle bodies. Interestingly, however, the concept of a subtle body had always been discernible in early Sufism, going back to the early ninth century among the Sufis of Basra. But an interest in subtle bodies as a colour-coded system associated with levels of prophetic avatars was definitely a later nineteenth-century development, probably due to 'generations of mystical activity over centuries of experimentation' (Buehler 1998: 111). It is likely that there have been borrowings from Tantric Yoga (Whitcomb 1993: 113), but the fact that the *latifas* do not correlate with the human body in the way that *cakras* do (Dale 2009: 240) is perhaps proof of independent development.

From the earliest allusions to the subtle bodies it is clear that the Sufis were concerned with the refinement of Islamic cosmology. In their literature, the Sufis are especially concerned with divine union, which subsequently leads them to discussions on the 'method' of ascent, and oftentimes the reasons for descent. For example, let us observe a verse from Rumi (2003):

> I am a bird of the heavenly garden
> I belong not to the earthly sphere.
> They have made for two or three days
> A cage of my body.

For the Sufis, there is a persistent preoccupation with the 'return' of the soul to its divine source. The Sufis, always carefully instructed under the guidance of a master of the path, were more or less left to their own devices, albeit in a controlled environment – that is, the *Khaniqah* or Sufi House. This means that in the end there are too many variations of the subtle-body system in Sufism to chart in a brief study, and even then, variations exist both between and within different orders. At most, it might be possible to speak of a generic model within Sufism and this would typically be the three-tiered system of soul, heart and spirit combination; then again, perhaps even this would be too bold.

## Notes

1 The present author recognizes, and is grateful to, the scholarly efforts of Marcia K. Hermansen and Arthur F. Buehler on the subject of the subtle body (see text).
2 The interpretation of the story is thoroughly documented in two essays: see Safavi 2005; Nurbakhsh 1991.

## References

Attar, F. (1984) *The Conference of the Birds*. Harmondsworth: Penguin.

Böwering, G. (1980) *The Mystical Vision of Existence in Classical Islam: The Qur'ainc Hermeneutics of the Sufi Sahl at-Tustari*. New York: Walter De Gruyter.

Buehler, A. F. (1998) *Sufi Heirs of the Prophet: The Indian Naqshbandiyya and the Rise of the Sufi shaykh*. Columbia: University of South Carolina Press.

Colby, F. S. (2006) *The Subtleties of Ascension*. Louisville, KY: Fons Vitae.

—— (2008) *Narrating Muhammad's Night Journey: Tracing the Development of the Ibn Abbas Ascension Discourse*. Albany: State University of New York Press.

Corbin, H. (1971) *En Islam Iranien*, 4 vols. Paris: Editions Gallimard.

—— (1978) *The Man of Light in Iranian Sufism*. London: Shambhala.

—— (1993) *History of Islamic Philosophy*. London: Kegan Paul.

Dale, C. (2009) *The Subtle Body: An Encyclopedia of Your Energetic Anatomy*, Boulder, CO: Sounds True.

Déclais, J.-L. (2010) 'Names of the Prophet', *Encyclopaedia of the Qur'an*, 3 s.v.

Frager, R. (1999) *Heart, Self and Soul: The Sufi Psychology of Growth, Balance, and Harmony*. Wheaton, IL: Quest Books.

Geaves R. (2006) 'Learning the lessons from the neo-revivalist and Wahhabi movements: the counterattack of the new Sufi movements', in J. Malik and J. Hinnells (eds) *Sufism in the West*. London: Routledge.

Hermansen, M. K. (1988) 'Shah Wali Allah's theory of the subtle spiritual centers (Lataif): a Sufi model of personhood and self-transformation', *Journal of Near Eastern Studies*, 47: 1–25.

Howell, J. D. and M. van Bruinessen (2007) *Sufism and the 'Modern' in Islam*. London: I.B. Taurus.

Hujwiri (1976) *Kashf al-Mahjub (The Revelation of the Veiled)*. London: Luzac.

Inayat Khan (1914) *Sufi Message of Spiritual Liberty*. London: Theosophical Publishing Society.

Kamada, S. (2010) 'Secrets', *Encyclopaedia of the Qur'an*, 4 s.v.

Lewisohn, L. (2006) 'Persian Sufism in the contemporary West: reflections on the Ni'matu'llahi diaspora', in J. Malik and J. Hinnells (eds) *Sufism in the West*. London: Routledge.

Malik, J. and Hinnells, J. (eds) (2006) *Sufism in the West*. London: Routledge.

Massignon, L. (1982) *The Passion of Hallaj: Mystic and Martyr of Islam*, trans. H. Mason, 4 vols. Princeton: Princeton University Press.

Milani, M. (forthcoming, 2013) *Sufism in the Secret History of Persia*, Gnostica series. London: Equinox-Acumen.

Meher Baba (1973) *God Speaks: The Theme of Creation and Its Purpose*. New York: Dodd, Mead.

Mojaddedi, J. (2001) *The Biographical Tradition in Sufism: The Tabaqat Genre from al-Sulami to Jami*. London: Curzon Press.

Nicholson, R. A. (1994 [1921]) *Studies in Islamic Mysticism*. Cambridge: Cambridge University Press.

Nurbakhsh, J. (1980) *Masters of the Path*. New York: Khaniqahi-Nimatullahi Publications.

—— (1993) *The Psychology of Sufism*. London: Khaniqahi-Nimatullahi Publications.

—— (1996) *Discourses*. London: Khaniqahi-Nimatullahi Publications.

—— (1991) *'irfan va ravaan-shenaasi mawlana: dar daasstaneh paadeshah va kanizak'*, *Sufi* 8: 7–10, Autumn 1369.

Plato (2003) *The Republic*. London: Penguin.

Purdom, C. B. (1964) *The God-Man: The Life, Journeys and Work of Meher Baba with an Interpretation of His Silence and Spiritual Teaching*. London: Allen & Unwin.

Purjavadi, N. (1979) *Sultan-i tariqat: sawanih zindagi wa-sharh-i athar-i Khwaja Ahmad Ghazzali*. Tehran: Intisharat-i Agah.

Qushayri (1959) *al-Risâla al-qushayriya*. Cairo.

Rahman, F. (2010) 'Baka wa-Fana', *Encyclopaedia of Islam* (new edition), 1 s.v.

Raudvere, C. and Stenberg, L. (eds) (2009) *Sufism Today: Heritage and Tradition in the Global Community*. London: I.B. Tauris.

Ridgeon, L. (2010) *Morals and Mysticism in Persian Sufism*. New York: Routledge.

Rumi (1982) *The Mathnawi of Jalaluddin Rumi: Translations of Books III and IV*, ed. and trans. R. A. Nicholson. Cambridge: Cambridge University Press.

Rumi (2003) *The Masnavi: Book One*, trans. J. Mojaddedi. Oxford: Oxford University Press.

Safavi, S. G. (2005) 'Synoptic approach to story of the King and the Handmaiden of Book One of the *Mathnawi* of Rumi', *Transcendental Philosophy: An International Journal for Comparative Philosophy and Mysticism* 61 a2: 37–50.

Schimmel, A. (1985) *And Muhammad is His Messenger*. Chapel Hill: University of North Carolina Press.

Schrieke, B. (2010) *Encyclopaedia of Islam*, 7, s.v.

Sedgwick, M. (2005) 'Neo-Sufism', in W. J. Hanegraaff (ed.) *Dictionary of Western Esotericism and Gnosis*, vol 2. Leiden: Brill.

Shikarpuri, F. (1978) *Qutb al-irshad*. Quetta: Maktaba-yi Islamiyya.

—— (n.d.) *Maktubat-i Faqirullah* (ed.) Maulwi Karam Bakhsh. Lahore: Islamiyya Steam Press.

Silvers, L. (2010) *A Soaring Minaret: Abu Bakr al-wasiti and the Rise of Baghdadi Sufism*. Albany, NY: State University of New York Press.

Smith, M. (1978) *The Way of the Mystics*. New York: Oxford University Press.

Suhrawardi (1945) *Opera Metaphysica et Mystica 3*. Istanbul.

Westerlund, D. (2004) *Sufism in Europe and North America*. Oxfordshire: Routledge.

Whitcomb, B. (1993) *The Magician's Companion: A Practical and Encyclopedic Guide to Magical and Religious Symbolism*. St Paul, MN: Llewellyn Publications.

# Part Four
# Subtle bodies and modernity

# Introduction to Part Four

*Jay Johnston*

Ephemeral bodies of a subtle substance may seem a galaxy away from the fleshy material bodies of the empirical-based reason that has come to signify the dominant discourse of modernity (yet, of course, such a dualism is far too reductive and general). However, subtle-body models have remained – and are increasingly – a feature of the Western cultural landscape, from self-directed spiritual practices and avant-garde art to Complementary and Alternative Medicine (CAM). Part Four illustrates and investigates this vast array of subtle-body practices and cultural formations that feature in Modernity, and also considers the appeal of this model of the body for the contemporary citizen and for comparative cross-cultural academic analysis. The following chapters demonstrate how concepts of the subtle body are assisting scholars to rethink categorical dualisms and divisions, the concept of the 'self', varieties of epistemology and indeed the very ontological and ethical agency of contemporary subjectivity.

The Hermetic Arts that flourished so markedly in Late Antiquity and the Renaissance continued their journey across conceptual and geographic borders in the Early Modern period and on into the eighteenth and nineteenth centuries.[1] In the West the late nineteenth and early twentieth centuries marked a more lively and public debate about such traditions, especially with the advent of Spiritualism and the founding of the Theosophical Society by Madame Helena Blavatsky and Colonel Henry Olcott in 1875. This association and its public debates exemplified the influence of growing scholarship in Asian and Indigenous religious traditions in middle-class culture. They also reflected and intersected with the suffragette movement and science's emerging new discourses (parapsychology is also a feature of this period). Indeed, Blavatsky's text in her multi-volumed tomes *Isis Unveiled* and *The Secret Doctrine* draw together scientific aspirations (and nomenclature), Eastern religious ideas (adapted and changed), and Hermetic ideas of magic and astrology. Core to the complex cosmology of 'planes of existence' and 'root races' (like much science of the times, the Theosophical discourse was heavily influenced by Social Darwinism) was the subtle body. As it is this form of the body that has furnished many contemporary subtle-body schemas, a very brief overview is given below.

In Theosophical narratives, the subtle body comprises seven layers or sheaths, each interpenetrating and exceeding the other. These sheaths are given names from both European and Asian traditions, including the *cakra* system. Each separate subtle body is considered to be formed of matter-consciousness that also comprises the 'plane of perception' from which it is understood (ontologically) to be drawn. For example, the Mental subtle body (*manas*) is described as being made of the material that makes up the Mental Plane of Perception. The subtle matter of each 'body' is distinguished by its 'density' and energetic texture; the physical body was understood as subtle-matter consciousness in its densest form. Importantly, no ontological distinction was made between 'gross' physical matter and 'refined' spirit. They were understood to be fundamentally the same ontological 'stuff' vibrating at different degrees of intensity and 'purity' (Blavatsky 1971, 1995; Bailey 1953).

These subtle bodies underpinned many of the Theosophists' epistemological and metaphysical systems that have continued to be developed and adapted over time. Charles W. Leadbeater and Annie Besant went on to propose the theory of 'Thought Forms' (which, as is noted below, was strongly influential in Modernist art practices and contemporary energetic healing techniques). Alice Bailey (founder of the Arcane School) published a whole series of books, known as the 'Blue Books', that outlined complex beliefs and practices built upon this seven-layered subtle body. She claimed that these were not her own words but were dictated to her by an Ascended Master, the Tibetan Djhwal Khul. These texts included explication of magical efficacy and practices in *A Treatise on White Magic* (published 1934), energetic healing in *Esoteric Healing* (1953), and a complex astrological system (popularized within New Age circles by Alan Oken) in *Esoteric Astrology* (published 1951). These works have left a long conceptual heritage. For example, Barbara Brennan's mega-seller on energy medicine, *Hands of Light: A Guide to Healing Through the Human Energy Field* (1988), employs Besant and Leadbeater's 'thought-forms' to develop a psychology of thought, emotion and subtle matter; while this same idea and the subtle ontology that supports it informed Kandinsky's understanding of colour agency (Johnston 2012).

Indeed, numerous esoteric theories of matter informed the development of avant-garde art, aesthetic and literature throughout the twentieth century. Visual artists have been discussed in a number of publications, with Tuchman's magisterial exhibition and catalogue on non-objective art (1986) as a stellar example; while Marc C. Taylor took up the influence of Blavatsky, Besant and Leadbeater's energetic ontology in aesthetics (1992). In the final section of our volume, John Bramble looks at the take-up of a specifically 'Western' Tantra in early Modernism, highlighting its occult foundations and clearly making the case for the centrality of concepts of the subtle body in the development of Modernism. His analysis features occult groups – like the Hermetic Order of the Golden Dawn – that also position the subtle body as a key aspect of their esoteric, especially ritual, practices. Bramble also teases out the conceptual transference of the erotic relation as a characteristic of this modern Tantra. It, too, has a central role to play in the development of contemporary esoteric practices (see also Urban 2006).

Occult or esoteric groups, like the Golden Dawn, inherited a conceptual legacy from Hermetic traditions and often employed concepts of subtle material to explain the efficacy of magic and ritual. Giordano Bruno (1548–1600) proposed a theory of divine and magical power that relied on an ontological substance that could be used as a binding agent to effect magic (indeed, he identified *eros* as a potent form of binding agent). Imagination (as a particular creative faculty) and images were prime techniques for magical efficacy and ritual. Susan Greenwood steps into a phenomenological account of a popular ritual activity of contemporary shamanism. In understanding her own visceral experience of shamanic journeying (of the type advocated by Michael Harner (1980)) she proposes a significantly innovative way of understanding 'magical consciousness' and its role in perceiving subtle matter. In exploring how to integrate – at an epistemological level – personal, phenomenological and physiological experiences of subtle selves into academic analysis, Greenwood highlights the role of emotion, intuition and imagination. While there have been valid critiques of the appropriation of 'shamanic' spiritual traditions within Western consumer culture and the politics of difference this practice often so clearly disregards (for example, see Donaldson 1999), Greenwood's chapter draws attention to the valency of lived experience for those who participate, and the reconceptualization of self and agency that such experiences can potentially engender.

The animal–human relation is also core to Greenwood's discussion, and the role of the subtle body is garnering yet another facet in its application in contemporary Otherkin (especially Therian and Faery) communities. For those who understand their concept of self as comprising (at an ontological level) an animal (Therian) or Faery, the attributes of the 'other self' are often rendered in subtle anatomy: claws, wings, tails (Lupa 2007). The role that subtle bodies are understood to play in 'slipping' across species boundaries is ethically complex but of increasingly noted interest in human–animal relations.

The contemporary popularity of subtle bodies, especially in alternative health practices and what has come to be known as New Age Religion, is the focus of Ruth Barcan's chapter. In particular she examines the social imaginary that supports the subtle body's appeal, considering how it 'fits' with current cultural ideologies, communication and technological paradigms. Barcan explores the tension inherent in the concept of the subtle body and its take-up in the contemporary West; between imagining the body/self as fragmented and imagining it as whole. The expansive and nebulous subtle body can be considered to furnish both images of the body, and Barcan skilfully unpacks the operation of the subtle body in the contemporary cultural imagination.

Chapter 13 canvasses post-structural and feminist conceptualizations of 'de-centred' subjectivity and some of the conceptual influences and corollaries to subtle-body models. The affective and disembodied body has been a feature of especially Continental philosophical inquiry and is core to the agenda of the 'new materialists'. In addition, this chapter considers how contemporary Buddhist scholars are using such expansive concepts of the self to interpret (academically and personally) Tantric belief and practice. Some of what is considered to be very radical reinterpretations of the self in philosophical discourse can be seem to be quite closely analogous to subtle bodies: as this volume attests, a concept of embodiment that has been around for some time!

Taking the volume full circle, Geoffrey Samuel returns to a consideration of Tantra, but this time to consider how subtle-body forms of subjectivity or experiences of such may be understood. In particular, he proposes a new scientific model that is able to encompass modes for the understanding of subtle bodies and related phenomena, especially as they are utilized and experienced in Complementary and Alternative health practices.

Subtle bodies are part of the landscape of contemporary culture; they are found in the arts, in health services, in stress management courses, in popular entertainment and in religious practices of a startling diversity. Although they have 'slipped' considerably from their articulation in early Yogic, Tantra and Daoist traditions, their contemporary popularity is a salient marker that, for many, the experience of self is lived between mind and body.

## Note

1  For a tracing of such history see McIntosh 1972.

## References

—— (1953) *Esoteric Healing*. New York: Lucis Publishing.
—— (1974 [1934]) *A Treatise on White Magic*. New York: Lucis Publishing.
Bailey, A. A. (1989 [1951]) *Esoteric Astrology*. New York: Lucis Publishing.
Besant, A. and Leadbeater, C. W. (1969 [1901]) *Thought-Forms*. Wheaton, Madras and London: Theosophical Publishing House.
Blavatsky, H. P. (1971 [1877]) *Isis Unveiled, Vol. 1 Science; Vol. 2 Theology*. London, Adyar and Wheaton: Theosophical Publishing House.
Blavatsky, H. P. (1995 [1888]) *The Secret Doctrine*, electronic book edn. Quezon City: Theosophical Publishing House.
—— (1988) *Hands of Light: A Guide to Healing Through the Human Energy Field*. New York: Bantam.
Donaldson, L. E. (1999) 'On medicine women and white dhame-ans: New Age native Americanism and commodity fetishism as pop cultural feminism', *Journal of Women in Culture and Society* 24(3): 677–96.
Harner, M. (1980) *The Way of the Shaman*. New York: Harper and Row.
Johnston, J. (2008) *Angels of Desire: Esoteric Bodies, Aesthetics and Ethics*. London and Oakville, CT: Equinox.
—— (2012) 'Theosophical bodies: colour, shape and emotion from modern aesthetics to healing therapies', in C. Cusack and A. Norman (eds) *Handbook of New Religions and Cultural Production*. Leiden and Boston, MA: Brill.
Lupa (2007) *A Field Guide to Otherkin*. Stafford: Megalithica Books.
McIntosh, C. (1972) *Eliphas Lévi and the French Occult Revival*. London: Rider.

Taylor, M. C. (1992) *Disfiguring: Art, Architecture and Religion*. Chicago and London: University of Chicago Press.

Tuchman, M. (1986) *The Spiritual in Art: Abstract Painting 1890–1985*, ed. E. Weisberger. New York: Abbeville Press.

Urban, H. (2006) *Magia Sexualis: Sex, Magic, and Liberation in Modern Western Esotericism*. Berkeley: University of California Press.

# 10 Sinister Modernists
## Subtle energies and yogic-tantric echoes in early Modernist culture and art

*John Bramble*

The early Modernist period, 1880–1930, is marked by many new, 'non-respectable' interests: occult and pagan revival (including witchcraft and the Mother Goddess, both reminiscent of the Tantric cult of yoginis and 'mothers'), resurgent pan-sexualist views of religious origins, elaborate Indo-Tibetan cosmo-conceptions, extraordinary epistemologies, and the darker, vernacular side of the oriental religions. Where the arts availed themselves of these often surprising materials – of strange Eastern cosmologies, of yogic lore and Theosophical doctrines about 'man invisible' with their accompanying fluidic, 'electro-magnetic', photic, energetic and sonic theologies – the results might be said to amount to a home-grown form of 'tantra' (lower case): or at least to converge with the later elite, 'aestheticized' Tantric tradition. As defined by White, this form of Tantra is characterized by its 'progressive refinement of antinomian practice into a gnoseological system grounded in the aesthetics of vision and audition', and transformation of 'particles of love' into 'particles of speech' (White 2003: 242).

To fully argue such a proposition here is impossible. Metaphysical Orientalism is a hall of mirrors, reflecting the assumptions and preconceptions of Western occultists from Greco-Roman antiquity on: a no man's land of neither East nor West. Nevertheless, the following intellectual historical sketch of the aesthetics and meta-politics of the subtle body and subtle realm, as elaborated by early Modernists, can hopefully be read as a preliminary to a more ambitious venture which restores the 'yogic-tantric' dimension to Modernist practice and goals. To acknowledge an important debt: in writing, *inter alia*, of the Tantrika's cosmocratic capacity to 'bless' or 'blast' – key terms in Wyndham Lewis's Vorticist manifesto (1914) – David Gordon White's Tantric triptych (1996, 2003, 2009) has midwifed some ideas about Modernist entanglement with Oriental Gothic as a left-handed source of power which had been gestating for some time.

### Passage to more than India: Modernist pranasophy in its meta-political and aesthetic guise

In an area dense with quaint neologisms, ingenious syncretism, and creative reinterpretations of the yogic East, Whitman's 'body electric' grew out of an 'electro-magnetic' nexus of ideas relating to nineteenth-century mesmero-spiritualism's 'second self' and 'secondary consciousness' (Crabtree 1998). The Gothic psychology that accompanied Mesmerism's rise explored extraordinary cognition and 'phenomena', while Theosophists identified the 'body electric' with the soul's pranic vehicle, with its apparatus of *nadis* and *cakras*. Rama Prasad's *Nature's Finer Forces: The Science of Breath* (1890) was a 'Tantrik' milestone here, influential with Theosophists and the Hermetic Order of the Golden Dawn.

W. B. Yeats' friend George Russell claimed a 'glowing' *kundalini* experience (Summerfield 1975: 4); 'oriental' Lawrence (D. H. not T. E.) packed his metaphysical writings, and later novels, with pranasophical and sexo-yogic lore (Doherty 2001); in 1931, Mircea Eliade experienced 'tantric sex' in an Indian ashram with one Jenny Isaac. And if strangely frigid in their sexual esotericism (Dixon 2001) – and prone to inspire turn-of-the-century art (Tuchman 1986) – the Theosophists multiplied subtle body on subtle body, correlating them with a hierarchy of pre-material planes. All this might seem familiar enough; nevertheless, the period 1880–1930 saw a genuine crisis of subjectivity (Owen 2004) as well as communitarian, *volkisch*/anarchist attempts to create a 'new mandala', or sacred, utopian space, for modern times. From Gnosticism to Cabala to Swedenborg and Blake, the West had its own sexual mysticism (Schuchard 2006). With the help of mid-Victorian bad boys like Richard Burton and Edward Sellon (both advance warning of the Edwardian returning repressed), newly arrived erotica and Orientalia could be grafted onto this (Urban 2006).

But 'tantric sex' aside, a dynamic meta-politics of 'force' and 'power' is involved in early Modernism's cosmic-erotic constructions of subtle energy lore. Examples might be Valentine de Saint-Point's 'lust excites energy and releases strength' in her 1913 *Futurist Manifesto of Lust*[1] (Orientalist undercurrents are implied by this Modernist yogini's interest in Blavatsky and conversion to Sufism in 1918); Lawrence's yogic 'power mode' – the Holy Ghost ruled antitype of the 'reign of love' or *Bhakti*; and the 1925 *L'Uomo come Potenza*, 'man as power', a study of Tantrism by the Sicilian esotericist and one-time Dadaist, Julius Evola. In such byways of Modernist spirit wars with bourgeois Victorianism, with their echoes of earlier erotic occultism (mesmero-spiritualism, Cabala), notions of energy, power and the metaphysics of sex were emphatic.

Much as in Tantra, a distinctive 'cosmocratic' or magical 'power-broking aesthetics' is intertwined with these 'as above, so below' spirit wars against stolid Victorian moralism and realism. The elaborate symbolism and micro–macrocosmic equivalences of the Tantric universe are regularly noticed, as are the photic and sonic effects (light rays and rainbow colours, vibrating mantra chains and seed syllables) displayed by its interfacing, subtle energy-cum-visionary imagery realm. But granted avant-garde enthusiasms for Theosophy and yogic-tantric lore during the 1910s, and the quasi-tantric tendency of that decade's aesthetic to a vibratory and correspondential economy; to special photic and sonic effects; to elementary forms and art's 'primary pigment' (so Wyndham Lewis), the analogies between the two ways of depicting the energies and imageries of the 'intermediate state', the Modernist and the Tantric, look worth pursuing. Modernist habits relating to imagination and vision are anarchic and free-form; the Tantric controlled and precise. But at the cosmocratic, power-broking level (also of shared attraction to photemes, phonemes and graphemes) the Modernist and the Tantric could be said to overlap.

To refine my meta-political and aesthetic points so far: by the earlier 1920s the subtle self had become an actor in a new 'politics of myth and the unconscious' (Thomas Mann's expression). During the 'degenerate' Fin-de-Siècle, subjects and their cognitive capacities had allegedly been disappearing into the maelstrom of modern flux; hence this new, super-conscious self – what Brancusi called his 'very old new I' and Lawrence a 'consciousness underneath' – came as welcome compensation for tottering subjectivity and cognitive disarray (Asendorf 1993; Crary 1999). Not only that, the push towards 'revitalized consciousness' led to obsessions with the unconscious, myth and the sacred, to an about-turn on the limited and limiting bourgeois ego. Equally, spirits or 'alters' could inspire Modernist work, another point that subordinated gross to subtle, and ostensible I's to 'second selves' (Treitel 2004: 119).

Whether mystical left or sacred right, the new post-liberal meta-politics, with its debts to Theosophy, Nietzsche and Bergson, was inseparable from the new Modernist art. Futurism, Expressionism, Cubo-Futurism, Dada: all pretended to (post-degenerate) 'expanded consciousness', to expertise in subtle reality, in vibrations, synaesthesia and cosmic equivalences, in the primal energetic forces and building blocks of cosmogony (Ringbom 1970; Hahl-Koch 1984; Tuchman 1986; Gordon 1992; Watkins 1994). They also proffered visions of a future, utopian polity (Timms and Collier 1988) where, like the Kapalika in White's account of Tantric politics, the artist-adept would be a bridge-builder between the supernatural and earthly worlds. In the sphere of 'force' and 'energy' the artist-adept was a broker of divinely sanctioned power. A cosmocratic role of this kind was literally hawked around the USSR and USA by the Theosophist-painter Nicholai Roerich, latterly of the Ballets Russes (Roerich designed the sets for *The Rite of Spring*). By the 1920s the Shambhala Chakravartin's 'Plan' for humanity had become his visiting card (Meyer and Brysac 2001: 450ff.).

Aurobindo Ghose, bicultural terrorist-then-guru, helped to reinstate this royal road, whereby the earthly utopia became dependent on a cosmic mandala (a concentration of 'the power and the glory') known only to the esoteric few. With its Saktist resort to imprecations of Kali, the separatist Swadeshi movement of Bengal (1903–08), led by Aurobindo among others, had invoked a version of this principle (Heehs 1994). Equally, as forerunners of the cosmocratic aesthetic of the 1910s, the esoteric elites of the turn of the century had their lexicon expanded by terms like *rajas* and *tamas*, the first corresponding to 'strenuosity' or *élan vital*, the second to 'inertia' or 'degeneration'. Thanks to Swami Vivekananda, a rationalist who introduced mystic America to Raja Yoga, not to mention second-generation Theosophists like Annie Besant and Charles Leadbeater, authors of tracts on the subtle realm, degeneration – but lately considered the era's plague (Pick 1989) – found its remedy in the yogic East. Active, not cessationist, the embodied mind of India (and 'Thibet') was now a support for the West, as it shook off 'neurasthenia' and related civilizational ills

(Lears 1981). Like the 'Yogi books' read by Ezra Pound – and the 'sounding', mystico-aesthetic-cosmic nostrums of Kandinsky and Schoenberg during the 1910s – Edward Carpenter's primitivizing *Civilization: Its Cause and Cure* (1906) belongs to this post-Decadent, world-renewing shift.

With his profession to 'contain multitudes', Walt Whitman – undergirded by his habit of cosmic merging and, in Hermann Bahr's words, of 'philosophizing with his phallus', Whitman's 'I, me, monomania' – had set the stage for suchlike regenerative utopian schemes. (For a 'tantric key' to Indian Walt, see Allen and Folsom 1995: 396; for the 'yogi as cosmos', White 2009: 168.) The bestselling 1901 study of 'cosmic consciousness' by Whitman's pupil R. M. Bucke assisted this soon international fashion for 'cosmified' auto-apotheosis; so did William James's 1902 book on religious experience: both literally upwardly mobile primers for all aspirants to a post-egoic (or monomanic) 'new I'. Whitman duly influenced Carpenter, a theorist of the *cakras*, who influenced Lawrence in turn (Delaveny 1971).

In sum: the post-degenerate Modernist self had become an aperture for revivificatory cosmic influx, if not the actual deity at the centre of a new mandala. The multiplicitous influences of archaic-oriental renaissance and occultism on the avant-garde need to be considered afresh. The most I can do here is rough out the nature of, and possible causes for, Modernism's rupture with gross reality, and its 'step up' into the radiant and vibrating subtle dimensions of the intermediate plane. Corresponding to the sequence 'spirit-soul-ostensible self', and akin to the Buddhist *trikaya*, a tripartite (internally sub-divisible) scheme is at work here: indeed, even if Kandinsky arrived at his 'inner sound' and vibrational, soul-string aesthetic without its aid, Traditionalist 'triple cosmos' theory was known to some Modernists through A. K. Coomaraswamy, anarchist art critic and one-time member of Sir John Woodroffe's Calcutta circle (Sedgwick 2004; high empire needs restoring to the picture of Modernist origins too).

In addition to occult revival and the new Orientalism – the last, in the spirit of Frazer, something of a sensuous 'horizontal' reaction against the pious 'vertical' spirituality of Max Muller (Waghorne 1994) – vitalist life-philosophy, especially that proposed by Henri Bergson (developing Schelling) and Nietzsche ('transvaluing' Schopenhauer) was instrumental in this post-realist change of focus from the objective to the fluidic, from the gross to the vital and subtle, from the world-to-hand to the intermediate realm. Like Mann's 'politics of myth and the unconscious' in the meta-political sphere, and serving as another augury of universal regeneration in Kandinsky's epoch of 'the great spiritual' non-objective art (Kandinsky's term, sometimes wrongly identified with 'abstraction') was the virtuoso expression of this cognitive and cosmo-conceptual shift, or jumping of tracks, in the arts.

Both easily identified with Theosophy's 'evolving' cosmos and yogic lore, Bergson's latently animistic-erotic *élan vital* and 'creative evolution' placed subtle meta-substance at the disposal of the avant-garde (Grogin 1988), who proclaimed that the next, post-materialist stage of world history would overcome the squalor of the urban-industrial nineteenth century, and re-equip humanity with its originary magical powers (Antliff 2001). Likewise, for the antinomian, Orientalizing Nietzsche, friend of the Indologist Paul Deussen (Parkes 1991), fallen modern man was 'something to be overcome', in a sphere 'beyond good and evil' which like his 'Dionysus' and 'will-to-power' cried out for assimilation to Tantrism once, thanks to Woodroffe's publications (Taylor 2001), its doctrines became better known. Like Lawrence, who could equate Dionysus, Pan, will-to-power, beyond good and evil, sexual antinomianism, the new yogic 'power mode' and the Joachimite Third Kingdom of the Holy Ghost with the aplomb of a seasoned heretic, Evola excelled at creative assimilations of this kind.

To sum up on 'sources': from around 1880, together with a new Orientalism just then beginning to delve into yogic-tantric lore, an occult revival which included the legacy of Mesmerism (another question of fluida) joined forces with vitalist philosophy (*Lebensphilosophie*) to put *prana*, subtle energies and vital fluids on the post-materialist and post-realist map. Though Tantric gnosis is explicitly sexual from the start, by Woodroffe's heyday there was sufficient fluido-energetic, cosmic-erotic and electro-magnetic subtle substance doing the rounds of occultist-vitalist circles for a more overtly sexological, yogic-tantric Modernism to become a distinct possibility within the post-realist arts. For example, Yogi Ramacharaka had been strong on electrical analogies for *prana*; German occultist groups like the Munich Cosmic Circle on 'cosmogonic *eros*'; the Asconan counter-culture on a 'sacred feminism' derived from Nietzsche's mentor J. J. Bachofen (Webb 1981; Green 1986). Lawrence's erotology derives from this *mélange*; so does its German counterparts, not to mention the Surrealist unconscious, an eroticized extension of Gothic psychology, with its interest in spirit-mediums and the 'strange fluids and forces' of pre-material life.

Without some understanding of such fluidic, energetic and mesocosmic currents of thought, the Modernist (counter-)revolution against 'bourgeois materialism' – against mid-Victorian doubt and disenchantment – cannot be understood. Nor can the alliances between occultism, *volkisch* thought, vitalism, utopian socialism and anarchism (Sonn 1989; Weir 1997) which brought the Modernist counter-culture to birth (spiritualism apart, occultist continuities had been weakened by the mid-Victorian 'bourgeois interlude', hence talk of occult *revival*). To see Modernism as 'the shock of the new' might be superficially valid at the level of its formal experiments – which would anyway be necessary (or desirable) for representations of the meta-real dimensions under discussion here – but looked at from the archaic-oriental spirit wars perspective outlined above Modernism becomes more a matter of the 'shock of the old'. Albeit twinned with a forward utopian evolutionism, itself endemic to the meta-politics of subtle energy and vital force that supervened on mid-Victorian liberalism, this inclination to the oriental and archaic, together with the occult and folkloric, is found across the whole spectrum of the Modernist arts – drama, music, dance, painting, literature – a wholesale 'magic socialist' (not bourgeois individualist) restoration of humanity to the 'magic theatre' of its extensible and imaginative, subtle self being the prime, cosmocratic objective of the early avant-garde.

To resolve the surface antithesis between shock of the old and shock of the new, 'progress-through-primitivism' could be a useful term. But enough has perhaps been said to suggest that textbook accounts of Modernism must be tempered by some very unusal period evidence, if we are truly to understand the hopefully now less baffling topic in hand. What was the broader context of the shift from gross to subtle reality, from the world of 'his majesty the I' to that of the multiplicitous and often unruly, 'middle-world' soul? And what were the stages and sources of the thought and practice involved in this very signal, magico-reanimating transition? These are the questions I set out to answer now.

## 'Unknown forces': from animal magnetism to 'Tantra' by way of Whitman, Vivekananda, Theosophy, neo-paganism, Yogi Ramacharaka and Woodroffe

There is a striking coincidence between the new, energetic and anticlassical cosmo-conception of the turn of the century, the achievement of occultists and *demi-monde* as much as 'new physicists', and the post-realist drive towards what, by 1910, is generally recognized as Modernism in the arts. Partly in a context of degenerationist thought – preoccupations with sensory overload and the imploding modern subject (Crary 1999) – matter, it was feared, was disintegrating, to be replaced by (initially spooky) 'energies' and 'unknown forces'. The last, according to art historian Christoph Asendorf (1993), was '*the* phantasm of the 1880s'; and subsequent to the 1900 'death of matter' he finds an art world haunted by the idea of 'streams and radiations' ('scientific' rewritings, arguably, of the ghosts of the older Gothic).

Electricity, X-rays, life-force, the recently imported idea of *prana*, the older fluids of animal magnetism – all were involved in the formulation of this, to its observers, epochal change. Gabriele Buffet-Picabia, wife of the Dadaist Francis Picabia, spoke of art world obsession, during the Teens, with 'non-perceptible forces' (modernized ghosts and spirits again); and Theosophical speculation about 'non-Euclidean geometry and the fourth dimension' (Henderson 1983) supplied another avenue for art world embroilment with what Schoenberg called 'occult puzzles beyond'. Just as at the turn of the century the cult of Pan super-vened on that of the Christian god, so reinforcing the new trend towards hypnoid (sub-)liminality, and ensuring a well-stocked *mundus medius*, gross matter went out and subtle energy came in.

Another aspect of this shift from gross to subtle – and from high Mullerite spirit to borderline Frazerian soul – was the Decadent movement's preoccupation with 'intermediate states' (Pynsent 1989: 196ff.). On a 'triple view' of the cosmos as consisting of material, subtle energetic and spiritual planes, such in-between states, often equated with Symbolist reverie (but also crucial for ghost stories, colonial romance, science fiction, trance-mediumship, children's tales and comic strips), were synonymous with the 'imaginal world' of seership, imagination and soul (Harpur 2002). Amid much erudite syncretism – Theosophists, for instance, raided the Gnostics and Neoplatonists, conflating their cosmologies and subtle-body lore with those of the East – a new/old, participatory-polymorphic model of the self and universe emerged from such psycho-cosmosophical schemes. In this, occult revival merged into the 'new Orientalism' which Kathleen Taylor (2001) dates from around 1880, a time of anti-domestic and anti-high Victorian reaction, when the initially disquieting yogic-tantric East (anathema to the liberal Muller but welcome to occultist communitarians) was making its first significant inroads into the West.

New Orientalism and occult revival were central to the Decadent and Symbolist movements of 1880–1910 and in turn seminal for the post-1910 Modernism where the correspondential/cosmocratic, modern mandala-devising initiatives of my introductory comments came to birth. The 'imperceptible forces', 'streams and radiations' of the new anti-classical cosmo-conception could now be imaged, not just in neo-mesmeric terms but also in the sometimes sinister, sometimes regenerationist idiom of the 'Eastern occult'. This last consorted freely with life-philosophy: Schopenhauer's Sakti-like Will, Bergson's *élan vital*, Nietzsche's Dionysus and Somerset Maugham's Pan, all being cousins of *prana* and life-force, as identified with electricity, an animistic-pantheistic force since its discovery (Asendorf 1993: 153ff.). With loose equivalences between *prana*, electricity, vital fluids, Pan and Dionysus (or Siva) to draw on, we could say in development of Asendorf that the lexicon of such 'batteries of life' entered the Modernist repertoire as a way of retrieving and revitalizing an otherwise fragmented and de-souled existence in a rapidly changing world.

On its turn-of-the-century debut, all-uniting, *anomie*-cancelling *prana* was an idea whose time had come. The common-sense bourgeois universe was breaking up; amid art-world talk of 'decomposition' – and later 'destruction–creation' – new post-liberal individualist subjectivities and arcane sexualities were being canvassed (Dixon 2001; Owen 2004); and the 'phantasm' of subtle fluids and energies seemed to hold the key, not only to the new decentred modern subject – where ostensible identity's loss was the second self's gain – but also to the recent 'pulverization' of matter (so Nicholai Berdyaev of the distressed canvasses of the Symbolist Mikhail Vrubel) and the subsequent etherialization of life. Amid a crisis of bourgeois legitimacy, too, new sources of power were apparently on offer from pranasophical 'life-science', an added incentive for the parricidal, Modernist sons of the Victorian fathers, as they plotted to turn the old, already reeling, Newtonian-Cartesian world upside down.

Lawrence was a major mouthpiece of the occult revival-fostered turn in the direction of yogic lore, as a key to what for Nietzsche was a new 'weightlessness' of life as lived in a post-solid universe, that had seen the demise of the four-square world of the no-nonsense Victorian bourgeoisie. Following Lewis, who detested Bergsonism and the new energy cosmos, a sceptical interpretation of this turn would be to suggest that the age's high Bohemian neo-aristocrats – and now 'irrationalist' bourgeoisie – were afraid of mass grass-roots socialism; hence, in a mood of self-protection by mimicry, they devised a top-down 'magic socialist' politics of energy, as a camouflaged way of maintaining claims to privilege and power (Vondung 1979, Edwards 2000: 300ff.). For Lewis, primitive communism, feminism, infantilism, 'wanting to be an artist', and an 'over-heated sex philosophy' (*participation mystique* more than fascism) were integral to the subterfuges of 'the revolutionary rich'. And Lawrence, a constant reference point for the discussions of Tantra by English Modernists (recalled by Mulk Raj Anand in his *Conversations in Bloomsbury*, 1981), was Lewis's *bête noire*.

With Whitman as forefather – a 'teacher of energy' for the French Symbolist Maurice Barres – many other Modernists of the 1910s and 1920s knew a surprisingly large amount of yogic and tantric lore. This, as in Symbolist-Modernist Russia, they could fuse with theurgy and collectivist 'god-building': after the fashion of the Golden Dawn or Neoplatonism (not simply Tantra), to 'arise' as a deity or the *siddha*-like New Man in a 'second creation' (Rosenthal 1997). They could also bring Theosophy's 'man invisible', channels, *cakras* and all, into a vibrational soul-string aesthetic – the aesthetic of Kandinsky's 'sounding cosmos', with its elemental lights, sounds and colours, the aim being to initiate the *chela*-observer into the cosmic attunements of the virtuoso artist-guru (Ringbom 1970; Behr *et al*. 1993). As shared by Scriabin and other synaesthetic 'sonic-phonemic-photic' artists of the Russian Teens (Gordon 1992) – the type existed in America too (Tuchman 1986: 297ff) – such 'cosmic hocus pocus' (Taruskin 1997: 359) is best related to the 'new model of the universe', namely the new/old yogic-tantric cosmos, as known through Theosophy, that depository for respectable Indology's rejects.

Another cosmocratic possibility, adopted by Scriabin in *Mysterium* and Schoenberg in *Jakobsleiter*, both unfinished 'eschatological torsos' (Taruskin 1997) of Theosophical inspiration, was 'total artwork': a multi-media form whose transformational point lay in manipulating what Gurdjieff called the 'centres'. According to Nietzsche, this was Wagner's aim, with his 'mastery of hypnotic tricks' and 'persuasion by means of the nerves'. As Max Nordau might have asked (he hated Wagner and Whitman), a quest for illegitimate power on the part of the egomaniacal, late romantic artist? Or a refreshing change from family values and the well-behaved social novel? Stockhausen, late Modernist pupil of the synaesthetic syncretist Olivier Messiaen, and reader of Aurobindo like him, had no doubts. He wrote in 1973 (cited in Godwin 1986):

> We are spirits, and [...] should be connected with the superhuman, with the Cosmos, with God
>
> with different things I can bring each center into vibration. I can set my sexual center in vibration with a certain sort of music, but with another music [...] my supranatural center [...] And I will add [...] have you gone far enough [...] to discover which parts of a type of music, or which pieces of music, set which of your centers [...] in vibration?

As is clear from his 'and how I start a body vibrating is extremely mysterious', Stockhausen is a *grand magnétiseur*, with transformational designs on a fallen humanity–like the 'Buddhist' Wagner and the Steinerite Joseph Beuys (Godwin 1986: 289; Moffitt 1988).

Whatever our moral evaluation of such a Svengali-esque aesthetics of persuasion, four reasonably distinct historical stages, two of them late romantic (or Decadent-Symbolist) and two Modernist, mark the career of otherworldly vibrations, subtle reality and occult *fluida* as governing factors in the arts. The first of these, distinguished by a mesmeric trance rationale for transmission to and bewitchment of his audience by the heroic romantic virtuoso (Winter 1998; Pick 2000: 112ff.) antedates the new Orientalism. Paganini, Liszt, Wagner, and the 'Swedish nightingale' Jenny Lind became paradigmatic for all the Symbolist arts: these are the figures who set the tone for the forthcoming 'vibrational aesthetic' (where the Dadaist Hugo Ball hazarded that 'everyone has become mediumistic'). Bridging our first two phases, Henry Steele Olcott, the Theosophical co-founder, further declared that animal magnetism was the key to Indian philosophy.

In extension of Mesmerism's already semi-erotic 'fluidic revelation', the second, proto-cosmocratic phase, 1880–1910, saw increased acquaintance with yogic lore, also tacit agreement that intermediate states and wild, yogini-like women (Dijkstra 1986) are the proper, post-realist sphere of the arts. With Bergsonian and Nietzschean vitalism eventually backing them up – and sometimes eyeing the American physician George Miller Beard's 'electrical' cure for nerves – Whitman, the Theosophists, Vivekananda and Yogi Ramacharaka (half, or whole, of the American New Thinker, William Atkinson, whose 'Yogi books' from 1903 entranced Pound) gradually built up the art world's knowledge of yogic doctrine and *prana*–the last an Indianized equivalent of occultism's universal medium, ether or astral light. Identifying subtle centres and channels with 'ganglia' and 'plexuses', utopians like Ernst Haeckel, the mystical German Darwinist, and Carpenter (who spoke of 'the ocean of sex') contributed, speculation peaking in Germany with J. H. Balzli's Theosophical periodical *Prana* (1909–19). Equally, well before Aleister Crowley – and with Swedenborg, Count Zinzendorf, Blake and Rabbi Falk as forerunners – 'sex magic' was an open secret, thanks to the resurfacing of erotic gnosis in occultists like Paschal Beverly Randolph and Theodor Reuss (Deveney 1997; Urban 2006; Schuchard 2006).

Mixed with the new, post-liberal politics, Fin-de-Siècle occult revival and 'anti-modern vitalism' (Lears 1981) certainly set the tenor for the new Orientalism of phase two. Nevertheless, the 'Buddhist' Schopenhauer, another quasi-mesmeric thinker exercised by 'energy' and the 'metaphysics of sex', still exerted great posthumous influence, particularly in the Decadent movement. Indeed, for Lewis, writing in the 1920s, Schopenhauer – who with unerring proto-Lawrentian (or post-Swedenborgian) insight had located his energetic first principle, the Brahman-Will, in the genitals – was the ultimate source of our 'characteristic semi-animistic, mystico-unconscious present-day perplexities' (Edwards 2000). Until the Teens, however, the art produced by the new 'Eastern occult' influences was patchy in quality, its tendency to 'spook style' (for example, Jan Toorop, C. R. Mackintosh) often kitsch and confused, like the late romantic 'maximalism' found in the era's music by Richard Taruskin (1997: 87ff.). The Indian Sufi musician Inayat Khan (whose esoteric music theory influenced Stockhausen) met Debussy and Scriabin. More generally, artists and poets struggled to depict the subtle planes, only to be dismissed as 'vaporous' by later critics. As Romanticism without the flab – and a more coherent middle-world mysticism – a fully developed (or reduced) Modernism had yet to arrive.

The third chapter in this occult history – within a cultural history – could fill a book in itself. During the 'expectant' 1910s, a decade marked by apocalyptic imaginings – and the Great War – matters immaterial and yogic-tantric became more scholarly and refined. I think of the breakaway Theosophist G. R. S. Mead's writings on Neoplatonism, Gnosticism and Hermeticism, culminating in his 1919 *The Doctrine of the Subtle Body in the Western Tradition*. From 1913, with some perhaps not accidental overlap (*The Serpent Power* was likewise published in 1919), Woodroffe's studies of Hindu Tantra, assisted by Sivacandra (his personal Tantric guru), had also begun to appear. Indeed, when Mead writes of 'the theurgical process of regeneration', that it is 'a bringing to birth of man's perfected subtle body', he could have been describing Tantric self-visualization as a deity. By this stage, we might even talk of a 'yogic international' – caricatured by Holbrook Jackson as Theosophy's 'yoga-stricken mugwumps' (Steele 1990: 48) – their goal post-neurasthenic renewal, after decadence and degeneration. Translation and travel contributed to this internationalism. Vivekananda, advocate of 'strenuosity' in his 1895–96 Yoga classes in New York, had been translated into Russian in 1906; and like James on religious experience, Besant and Leadbeater, experts in auras, 'occult chemistry' and all things astral (their illustrations served as sources for psychograms and cosmograms in Non-Objective art) were internationally known (Tuchman 1986).

Just as the gross universe of 'man visible' made way for the subtle world of 'man invisible' during the 1910s, so in the arts, propelled by the new/old mystical cosmologies and epistemologies, any residual dross of 'exoteric', naturalist representation was purged in favour of a Theosophically inspired reductionism, designed to penetrate to art's 'esoteric' core. The most *outré* examples of this return to art's primary, sonic, phonemic and photic constituents (Hahl Koch 1984; Watkins 1994) – a yogic-tantric, theurgical art which in the interests of initiating its audience into 'higher' planes and vibrations dispensed with what Nordau called 'art's known and standard forms' – are found in Russia and Germany.

Influenced by European *émigrés* like Oskar Fischinger and Dane Rudhyar, American experimentalism was wild as well: much concerned with eccentric 'vibratory' percussion and gamelan substitutes, most notably the West Coast group of musicians around Theosophist Henry Cowell exemplifies this trend. Their goal an 'astral' or 'non-objective' music and art, followers of Scriabin and Kandinsky, concerned as they obsessively were with capturing anterior subtle dimensions ('non-perceptible forces' again), were among the most extreme and would-be cosmocratic within this experimentalist-immaterialist camp.

In his hallucinatory *Petersburg* (1916), a shape-shifting phantasmagoria with similarities to Gustav Meyrink's occult fiction, the Russian Symbolist Andrei Bely, pupil of Rudolf Steiner (who likewise influenced Kandinsky), had written an astral non-objective novel (Carlson 1993: 198ff.). Literary non-objectivity was also found in Russian Cubo-Futurist *zaum* (Rosenthal 1997: 235ff.), a 'trans-rational' form of phonemic poetry with parallels in sectarian glossolalia, spiritualist automatism, and the invented 'Dakini speech' type languages of occult revival, like Blavatsky's 'Senzar' and St Yves d'Alveydre's 'Vattan'. Dada non-sense poetry was another such code of the soul, as were the made-up meta-languages that became fashionable after the war.

Messiaen, Edgard Varèse, the American composer Ruth Crawford, Antonin Artaud, the Chilean poet Vicente Huidobro, all dreamt up such 'second-state' meta-languages, their tenor caught by Artaud when he wrote of Balinese theatre witnessed at a Paris colonial exhibition of 1931, that its essence was 'speech anterior to words'. 'Anterior speech' (*madhyama, pasyanti*) is also a sub-department of Sanskrit linguistics, a topic studied by the Gurdjieffian Surrealist Rene Daumal (Rosenblatt 1999: 113ff.). Later still, there are the magical scripts and calligraphies of the 'mythic Forties'.

Impatient with the experimentalism of the 1910s, Lewis and T. S. Eliot eventually argued a return to 'classic', non yogic-Tantric India: the light of Asia without Hearn's shadows. Forsaking earlier 'romantic Buddhist' interests – one reviewer called *The Waste Land* a 'Theosophical tract' (Lucas 1923) – Eliot crystallized his hostilities in *After Strange Gods: A Primer of Modern Heresy* (1934). By this date, Modernism had bifurcated into two opposing currents, one orderly/ neo-classical, the other romantic/mysteriosophic: and as leading chaotic heretics (or 'sinister yogis'), it was Lawrence and Yeats, the last accused of promoting the 'wrong supernatural world' (mesocosmic fauna, drug induced reveries), who most angered Eliot here (1934: 46). Satirizing his 'trinity of the unconscious, the feminine and primitive communism', served up with 'hot sex stuff', Lewis had already lambasted Lawrence in *Paleface*, his anti-primitivist diatribe of 1929: what was forgivable in Gauguin was unpardonable among his imitators in the 'gilded rabble' (Lewis 1929: 115).

For the Brahmanical champions of 'call to order', Theosophy, Tantrism, yoga, the Gothic unconscious, 'man invisible', the astral planes – the entire occult-aesthetic history I have been outlining from Wagner on – was so much sorcery, akin to the 'witchcraft' ascribed to total art work by Brecht. If Tantrikas had been 'the Hell's Angels of medieval India' (White 1996: 306), then what Henri Massis, Traditionalist defender of the West with affinities to the post-conversion Eliot, called the '*vision catastrophique de l'univers*' of the (late) new Orientalist party of the Twenties was the work of Satan himself (Cadwallader 1981: not that it weighed with his Western followers, Tantra for Vivekananda had been 'Hindu Satanism' too).

Massis's personal bugbear (Cadwallader 1981: 1–57) was 'germano-asiatic offensive against the west' – figures like Oswald Spengler, Hesse, Tagore, also Romain Rolland with his 'un-French' attraction to Ramakrishna and Vivekananda. Like its Russian counterpart, German 'Asiaticism', prominent in the Asconan counter-culture that produced the esoteric correspondences of the modern dance guru Rudolf Laban and influenced Lawrence by way of his wife, had indeed been excessive (Green 1986; Noll 1994). Nevertheless, by the time of inter-war spirit wars, where the Surrealists as inheritors of Symbolist occultism favoured the East, the romantic-expressive cult of India (and Asia in general) had become an international, free-form phenomenon, its shape and sources much the same as those of the chaotic 'new' new Orientalism of the counter-cultural Sixties.

My fourth and final phase of specifically *Modernist* dalliance with the interface between spiritual and material reality accordingly coincides with the inter-war age of East/West quarrel, as introduced above. In fact, most of the high empire-fostered new Orientalist spadework had been done by this stage: the Forties-to-Fifties Zen vogue as an influence on Abstract Expressionism and neo-Dada raises fewer questions in the magic and mystery department ('secret scripts' and occult calligraphies excepted) and none with regard to the subtle body.

The 1920s saw the codification of much that would have been entirely unacceptable to the mid-Victorian bourgeoisie. The arrival within post-liberal politics of 'power', 'force' and 'energy' (the proto-Bergsonian terms in which the Orientalist H. H. Wilson and pornographer Sellon had explained Sakti as the active face of the sacred) was bad enough. But the new age of '*The Hidden Force*' (the title of an Indonesian-set 1900 novel about the white man's undoing by native magic and the 'Sakti of the land' by the Dutch Decadent Louis Couperus) also involved the return of what one art historian calls the 'ancient monstrosities and indecencies', complete with a 'grotesque anti-world' of their own (Kuryluk 1987). The blacker, erotically perverse and 'charnel house' aspects of Decadent and Modernist art are well served by Kuryluk's insights, about Beardsley in the first instance. With their echoes of Poe and Theosophy, Gauguin's ambiguous Tahitian mythologies fit her formula too.

Put another way, Frazer's latently indecent 'vegetation rites' had gone openly orgiastic-ecstatic and with the 'mummery' and 'hideous rites' of lived/vernacular primitive-oriental cults had reintroduced pan-sexualism into views of religion (Leech 1985). Backed up by 'unknown forces' on the home front (the electro-mesmeric-hysterical commotions described by Asendorf), occult-erotic fall-out from high empire had taken the white masters captive (a theme of Conrad and Kipling, as well as Couperus) in a two-pronged process of bewitchment and 'fascination' (*fascinare*) that extended to their plebeian charges at home. By the 1920s, the 'civilizing mission' was in tatters, and an anti-world composed of the oriental, occult and archaic – as per the 'Dravidian' Marabar Caves episode in Forster's *A Passage to India* or the final sacrificial horrors of Conrad's *Heart of Darkness* – had taken hold at popular and elite levels alike.

Black magic, the abject, the 'gnostic counter-tradition', an art of the lower chakras: the drift of the new anti-Victorian culture of the 1920s is captured by Lawrence's left-handed notion that 'god enters from below'. Georges Bataille, source for the latter-day 'transgressions' of Michel Foucault, shared Lawrence's – in origin, Frazerian (Vickery 1973) – interests in human sacrifice and *outré* sexuality. Yeats, who owned several volumes on Tantra, averred that 'fair and foul are next of kin' (Ravindran 1990: 88ff.); Brancusi, avid reader of Jacques Bacot's 1925 *Life of Milarepa*, mixed mysticism and erotology; Maria de Naglowska, yogini friend of Evola and the Surrealist Camille Bryen, abridged Randolph in her 1931 *Magia Sexualis*; Pierre Bernard, founder of the Tantrik Order of America in 1905, translated Lewis's 'hot sex stuff' into 'tantric' terms for wealthy New Yorkers; Alexandra David Neel, Theosophist traveller to Tibet, fed period appetites for *siddhis* and *prana* magic (as Yogananda's *Autobiography of a Yogi* did later); Jung thickened the subtle energetic soup with his 1932 'kundalini yoga' seminar and musings on Richard Wilhelm's version of *The Secret of the Golden Flower*, while Evans Wentz's Tibetan 'translations' (with Jungian 'psychological commentaries') brought Tantra, the after-life *bardo* and 'bewildering yogism' (Vivekananda's term) into further relief.

## Oriental Lawrence: *kundalini*, *cakras*, Holy Ghost

To wind up my comments on phase four, a last look at Lawrence and the alleged 'fascism' of his (pranasophical) 'religion of the blood. From 1918, Lawrence was obsessed by a secret yogic key to the Book of Revelation devised in 1910 by the Irish-American Theosophist James Pryse. Correlating the seven seals of the apocalypse with the seven *cakras*, Pryse influenced Lawrence's own 1931 *Apocalypse* and supplied him with the raw materials for his anti-Victorian psycho-sexual system. Mixed with some Celticism, and perhaps at its crudest a case of 'Tarzan with chakras', this side of Lawrence's archaic-oriental 'offensive against the west' is particularly noticeable in *The Plumed Serpent* (1926), a Theosophical-vitalist fiction of his American phase. Modelled to a point on the Modernist hostess Mabel Dodge (recently married to an American Indian, Dodge had 'willed' Lawrence to come to Taos as her guru), the novel's heroine, Kate Leslie, is the widow of an Irish freedom-fighter called Joachim, and now quasi-tantric consort to the Mexican-Indian avatar Don Cipriano (Cowan 1990: 178ff.).

Thereby, with shades of the cosmocratic mandala principle of the 1910s, Kate becomes a Celtic-Amerindian Sakti-figure, a millennial (that is, Joachimite) embodiment of primal cosmic-erotic power, suggestive of the Bachofenian feminism of the matriarchal left at Ascona, which Frieda Lawrence knew so well (Green 1986). The novel also evokes the German Jugendstil and Expressionist ambience, where, as in the art of Fidus and Emil Nolde, life-force and sexuality could be equated in the interests of racial renewal. As a 1924 essay, 'Pan in America', shows, the anti-world (or ante-world) of Pan, the Priapic/naturist All, is a concern of Lawrence too: supposedly still alive among the Red Indians, Mellors in *Lady Chatterley's Lover* and Don Cipriano in *The Plumed Serpent* are modelled on the god.

There is more to Lawrence's 'doctrine of the body mystical' (Cowan 1990: 115ff.) than this. *Women in Love* contains a neo-Egyptian masculinist tableau, involving life-force and the *cakras*, and *Aaron's Rod* a 'massage' scene that is as much initiatic as homoerotic. The initiation scene between the two male protagonists in *The Plumed Serpent* also suggests the transmission of life-force, along Theosophical/German vitalist lines. Finally, confirming that Lawrence was indeed a 'transvaluative' Saktist of the life-affirming Expressionist type, when the occultist Frederick Carter met him between drafts of his Mexican novel he realized that Lawrence believed that 'the dragon is the life bound in man's nervous system, the great serpent force' (Clark 1964: 136ff.).

A central feature of the 'power mode' that Lawrence opposed to the old Christian reign of love, Carter's 'serpent force' evokes Woodroffe's *Serpent Power* (known to Meyrink, who practised yoga) and both recall Wilson and Sellon's renderings of Sakti as 'power' and 'energy' (Taylor 2001). Taken with its parallels among Bengali Saktists like Aurobindo – with his wish to arouse the energies of a 'sleeping' India – the motif of awakening old Mexican energies in *The Plumed Serpent* coheres with the period interest in 'unknown forces', the revenge of the archaic on modern civilization, and occult sources of power.

Like the Lawrentian 'unconscious', itself a thoroughly yogic affair, the above suggests a dynamic proto-tantrism akin to Evola's, but invented, according to Frieda, without reading Woodroffe. Such 'metaphysic' is also related to period enthusiasm for Nietzsche's Dionysus (a transvaluation of Schopenhauer's more sinister Brahman/Will), and for the Edwardian and Jugendstil Pan. But is all this 'fascist' – or merely an idiosyncratic development of a Theosophical/vitalist energetics, which, ever since the reaction against Decadence of the early 1900s had been a faddish revitalizing focus for 'life-reform'? Like gymnastics, vegetarianism or naturism, the yogic doctrines relating to the macrocosmic-microcosmic orbits of *kundalini* (as witness the 'greater [tantric] sex' hymned in *The Plumed Serpent*) are not a monopoly of either left or right. After all, the socialist Carpenter derived 'race' and 'the gods' from the *cakras*, positing traces of the sacred past in the present (Delaveny 1971), as did many other acolytes of the 'folk-soul' (the pranic-pneumatic, 'blood'-transported *Volksgeist*), whatever their communitarian 'wing'.

Nevertheless, as with Evola's 'fascist tantrism' and its doctrine of *virya* or 'spiritual virility' – an obvious parallel, this, for Lawrence's alleged homoeroticism – the right was particularly attracted to magico-animistic arcana of this kind (Noll 1994). Thus, as in the title of Evola's early tantric work *L'Uomo come Potenza*, so in Lawrence, 'man is power', in the sense of being a receptacle of primal cosmic-erotic force. Further 'fascistoid' associations are maybe suggested by Lawrence's interest in the Thule Society member Haeckel, with his fusion of sun worship, neo-paganism and view of the life-force (or unconscious) as resident in the 'ganglionic centres', an Asconan type of formula that pervades the American fiction. Given Theosophical equations between *kundalini* and the paraclete, Lawrence's favoured theme of the 'Holy Ghost' – especially when it occurs in racial-erotic contexts – could be seen as a Joachimite relative of Baltzli's *prana*: the Ariosophical (or 'proto-Nazi') form of Nietzsche's Dionysus and Bergson's *élan vital*. But there again, Wilhelm Reich's equally pranasophical (and perhaps Ascona-indebted) concept of 'orgone' is close to Lawrentian energy doctrine: and Reich, though anti-liberal, was an anti-fascist man of the left. Finally, as another radical right point of comparison, there is the *Sexual-magie* of the 'hippie' Theosophist and later Nazi Fidus (Hermand 1975), which after the fashion of (the in fact democratic) Whitman, images the life-force as a kind of electrical, racial-erotic charge.

As in all meta-political vitalist fantasies, Lawrence's overall tendency is to oppose a degenerate West to a primordial world of healthy *Naturmenschen*, whose proximity to the life-force promises salvation – and whose cosmology coincides with that of the Theosophical Society itself. As W. Y. Tindall observed in 1939 of Pryse's influence on *The Plumed Serpent*: 'the theosophist, knowing that Hindus and Aztecs are of one primitive faith, could not but be pleased with Lawrence's discovery' (Cowan 1990: 205). During the American phase, when Lawrence played cosmocratic magus to the weak but regal Mabel Dodge (precisely the courtly king-making role ascribed by White to the pre-modern Tantrika), the 'power-broking' primitivism, yogism, paganism and utopianism – the kind of thing that Lewis hated – stand out. But whether the upshot is fascist or merely 'Taos style sinister yogi' is hard to tell.

## Modernists as occult cosmocrats: control and redefinition of Modernity through the mapping of the arts onto a yogic-tantric grid

Finally, can we situate the new energy cosmos and cosmocratic aesthetic of the above four-phase sequence of developments within any broader historical scheme? Prior to regenerationist arguments entailing backwash from empire – the ransacking of the Eastern occult for anything 'vital' that might help an urban-industrial West in distress – the supervention of Asendorf's 'unknown forces' and 'streams and radiations' on the *circa* 1900 'death of matter' could, I think, be related to the phantasmagoric sense of immateriality, of incessant energetic flux and loss of solidity, brought about by capitalist modernity. Of capitalism's impact, in conservative/Brahmanical stasis-favouring vein, Marx had written, 'all that is solid melts into air, all that is sacred is profaned': a theme about which the acolytes of dynamism like the Futurists were considerably more sanguine. The Austrian Symbolist Hugo von Hofmannsthal characterized the modern as *das Gleitende* (the slippery, the sliding). As if to order, Strindberg, another 'Buddhist', experienced 'electro-hysterical' attacks in tram-cars: the disappearing, cognitively disorientated subject again unable to cope with modern flux (Asendorf 1993, *passim*).

Asendorf amply illustrates this situation of 'nowhere to stand' – the disappearance of 'all fixed and fast frozen relations' (Marx) into a maelstrom of strange forces which, once they had ceased to unnerve, could be recast as a source of electro-pranasophical revitalization, as per Lawrence or Evola. On such a view, the commonsense (and again stasis-favouring) mid-Victorian bourgeoisie would have created its own antitype: a Modernist, yogic-tantric antitype, who like the steam-punk comic-book anarchist thrived on the dissolution of matter into energy, turning the resultant chaos to his own ends. If the bourgeoisie had brought on world-end (neurasthenia, degeneration, sensory overload, decay of cognition: Crary 1999), then out of its debris – imaged as energy – the Modernist 'occult cosmocrat' (White's term for the king-making Tantrika; 2003: 32), was in a position, particularly with the internationalization of 'the new model of the universe' during the 1910s, to institute a world-beginning. Here, new clients (repentant bourgeois irrationalist, neo-aristocratic) could shelter within his *mandala*, benefiting from his familiarity with new/old 'batteries of life' and occult sources of power.

In further explanation of 'mandala': the world's 'transcendental co-ordinates' had collapsed under mid-nineteenth-century liberalism, leaving a gap for the 'cosmically conscious' (magic socialists, occult revivalists, Modernists) to fill. Related to this, Terry Eagleton (1995) notes how the new 'esoteric elites' of our period (who liked to confound socialism, science and occultism, and play yogic *magnetiseur*) reinvented the 'symbolic order'. Borrowing some terms from White, and with the new cosmocratic – correspondential, protomorphic, synaesthetic, non-objective – aesthetic of the Teens (or Lawrence's American phase) in mind, for 'symbolic order' I would write 'reinstated a template or grid of occult, middle-world energies whereby the cosmos could be reconstituted afresh'.

In self-conception at least, the Modernist artist-adept thus becomes a figure of immense power – an occultist 'crypto-potentate' of the kind to which, in addition to White's Asian monarchs, rulers did homage in Late Antiquity and the Renaissance (Byzantine emperors, Elizabeth I of England, Rudolph II of Prague). At heart a cosmic-utopian adherent of reactionary revolution, this type of visionary artist, from Romanticism on, had sought for some equivalent of the old courtly magic, some theatre of the mind and occult energy where (like Wagner's dreams in relation to Ludwig II of Bavaria) he would arbitrate in matters of power and privilege: the 'who's in, who's out' of courtly life, revitalization of the body politic, the shape of utopia, banishment of enemies, rewards for friends.

Rasputin and Svengali aside, pretences to power of this kind were rife in the Decadent/Symbolist and early Modernist period. The central point of the break with realism and bourgeois flatland, once cultural despair had yielded to post-neurasthenic renewal, was to reinstitute the old 'power mode' (and 'great chain of being') of the magical energy cosmos of pre-modern times. (For Lawrence, Nietzsche and Evola, 'love' and democracy were out, and 'pitiless' will-to-power was in. With his interest in perverse sexuality and human sacrifice, Bataille thought along similar lines.) As in talismanic magic, the crux of the matter here, particularly during the 'cosmogrammatic' 1910s, was the mapping of the arts onto a middle-world template of (strange) forces and energies, the control and manipulation of which, after the pattern of the 'persuasion by means of the nerves' found in Wagner by Nietzsche – and in Modernism generally, by one T. H. Robsjohn-Gibbings in a 1947 attack on its sorcerers and magicians could make and unmake, bless or blast the artist-initiate's enemies and envisaged allies, so remarshalling his post-bourgeois clientele.

The blessed and 'who's in' of this magical operation ran to neo- and natural aristocrats, the 'masses' (where not too unwashed or inflamed by Marxists) and such members of the bourgeoisie as had gone irrationalist, throwing away family values and aping socialism, like Lewis's 'revolutionary rich' (Edwards 2000). The blasted and 'who's out' included anyone and anything that stood for the three C's of 'Christianity, Commerce and Civilization' in their mid-nineteenth-century form: missionaries, beaux arts, starchy dress codes, stolid burghers, sentimentalism, enemies of the exotic, liberal feminists (idols of perversity and yoginis were preferred instead). Rather as in our own day, fashion was promoted as progress, and magical glamour as power. But 'as above so below': with the assistance of conjurations at the level of the new energy cosmos, a magpie – and since reliant on sleight of hand, still unstable – post-bourgeois form of modernity was rescued from the whirling maelstrom and 'nowhere to stand' implied by Evola, Marx and Hofmannsthal. As an object of study, this essay's composite and antinomian 'tantric Modernism' (both epithets hold good of Tantra itself) might have further to go.

## Note

1 See www.unknown.nu/futurism/lust.html.

## References

Allen, G. and Folsom, E. (eds) (1995) *Walt Whitman and the World*. Iowa: Iowa University Press.
Anand, M. R. (1981) *Conversations in Bloomsbury*. Delhi: Arnold-Heinemann.
Antliff, A. (2001) *Anarchist Modernism, Art, Politics and the First American Avant-Garde*. London and Chicago: University of Chicago Press.
Asendorf, C. (1993) *Batteries of Life: On the History of Things and their Perception in Modernity*. Berkeley and Los Angeles: University of California Press.
Behr, S., Fanning, D. and Jarman, D. (1993) *Expressionism Reassessed*. Manchester and New York: Manchester University Press.
Cadwallader, B. (1981) *Crisis of the European Mind: A Study of Andre Malraux and Drieu la Rochelle*. Cardiff: University of Wales Press.
Carlson, M. (1993) *'No Religion Higher than Truth': Theosophy in Russia 1875–1922*. Princeton: Princeton University Press.
Clark, L. D. (1964) *Dark Night of the Body: D. H. Lawrence's The Plumed Serpent*. Austin: Texas University Press.
Cowan, J. C. (1990) *D. H. Lawrence and the Trembling Balance*. University Park and London: Pennsylvania State University Press.
Crabtree, A. (1998) *From Mesmer to Freud: Magnetic Sleep and the Roots of Psychological Healing*. New Haven and London: Yale University Press.
Crary, J. (1999) *Suspensions of Perception: Attention, Spectacle, and Modern Culture*. Cambridge, MA: MIT Press.
Delaveny, E. (1971) *D. H. Lawrence and Edward Carpenter*. London: Heinemann.
Deveney, J. P. (1997) *Paschal Beverly Randolph, a Nineteenth-Century Black American Spiritualist, Rosicrucian and Sex Magician*. Albany: State University of New York Press.
Dijkstra, B. (1986) *Idols of Perversity: Fantasies of Feminine Evil in Fin-de-Siècle Culture*. New York: Oxford University Press.
Dixon, J. (2001) *Divine Feminine: Theosophy and Feminism in England*. Baltimore and London: Johns Hopkins University Press.
Doherty, G. (2001) *Oriental Lawrence: The Quest for the Secrets of Sex*. New York: P. Lang.
Eagleton, T. (1995) *Heathcliff and the Great Hunger: Studies in Irish Culture*. London and New York: Verso.
Edwards, P. (2000) *Wyndham Lewis, Painter and Writer*. New Haven and London: Yale University Press.

Eliot, T. S. (1934) *After Strange Gods: A Primer of Modern Heresy. The Page-Barbour Lectures at the University of Virginia 1933*. London: Faber and Faber.

Godwin, J. (1986) *Music, Mysticism and Magic: A Sourcebook*. London: Routledge and Kegan Paul.

Gordon, M. (1992) 'Russian sound creation', in D. Kahn and G. Whitehead (eds) *Wireless Imagination: Sound, Radio and the Avant Garde*. Cambridge, MA and London: MIT Press.

Green, M. (1986) *Mountain of Truth: The Counterculture Begins, Ascona 1900–1920*. Hanover and London: New England University Press.

Grogin, R. C. (1988) *The Bergsonian Controversy in France 1900–1914*. Calgary: Calgary University Press.

Hahl-Koch, J. (1984) *Arnold Schoenberg – Wassily Kandinsky: Letters, Pictures and Documents*. London and Boston, MA: Faber and Faber.

Harpur, P. (2002) *The Philosophers' Secret Fire: A History of the Imagination*. London: Penguin.

Heehs, P. (1994) *The Bomb in Bengal: The Rise of Revolutionary Terrorism in India*. Delhi: Oxford University Press.

Henderson, L. D. (1983) *The Fourth Dimension and Non-Euclidean Geometry in Modern Art*. Princeton: Princeton University Press.

Hermand, J. (1975) *Meister Fidus: Jugendstil-Hippie to Aryan Faddist*. Pennsylvania: Penn State University Press.

Kuryluk, E. (1987) *Judas and Salome in the Cave of Sex: The Grotesque, Origins, Iconography, Techniques*. Evanston: Northwestern University Press.

Lears, T. J. (1981) *No Place of Grace: Antimodernism and the Transformation of American Culture 1880–1920*. New York: Pantheon.

Leech, E. (1985) 'Anthropology of religion: British and French schools', in N. Smart *et al.* (eds) *Nineteenth Century Religious Thought in the West*, Vol. 3. Cambridge: Cambridge University Press.

Lewis, W. (1914) 'Manifesto', *Blast* 1: 11–28.

—— (1929) *Paleface: The Philosophy of the Melting Pot*. London: Chatto and Windus.

Lucas, E. L. (1923) 'The Waste Land by T S Eliot', *The Statesman*, Nov. 23, 1923.

Meyer, K. E. and Brysac, S. B. (2001) *Tournament of Shadows: The Great Game and the Race for Empire in Asia*. London: Little, Brown.

Moffitt, J. F. (1988) *Occultism in Avant-garde Art: The Case of Joseph Beuys*. Ann Arbor: UMI Research Press.

Noll, R. (1994) *The Jung Cult*. Princeton: Princeton University Press.

Owen, A. (2004) *The Place of Enchantment: British Occultism and the Modern*. Chicago and London: University of Chicago Press.

Parkes, G. (ed.) (1991) *Nietzsche and Asian Thought*. Chicago and London: University of Chicago Press.

Pick, D. (1989) *Faces of Degeneration*. Cambridge: Cambridge University Press.

—— (2000) *Svengali's Web: The Alien Enchanter in Modern Culture*. Newhaven and London: Yale University Press.

Pynsent, J. (ed.) (1989) *Decadence and Innovation*. London: Weidenfeld and Nicolson.

Ravindran, S. (1990) *W. B. Yeats and Indian Tradition*. Delhi: Konark.

Ringbom, S. (1970) *The Sounding Cosmos: A Study in the Spiritualism of Kandinsky and the Genesis of Abstract Painting*. Helsingfors: Acta Academiae Aboensis.

Robsjohn-Gibbings, T. H. (1947) *Mona Lisa's Mustache: A Dissection of Modern Art*. New York: Alfred Knopf.

Rosenblatt, K. F. (1999) *Rene Daumal*. Albany: State University of New York Press.

Rosenthal, B. G. (ed.) (1997) *The Occult in Russian and Soviet Culture*. Ithaca, NY: Cornell University Press.

Schuchard, M. K. (2006) *Why Mrs Blake Cried: William Blake and the Erotic Imagination*. London: Century.

Sedgwick, M. (2004) *Against the Modern World: Traditionalists in the Secret History of the Twentieth Century*. New York: Oxford University Press.

Sonn, R. (1989) *Anarchism and Cultural Politics in Fin de Siècle France*. Lincoln: Nebraska University Press.

Steele, T. (1990) *Alfred Orage and the Leeds Arts Club*. Aldershot: Scholar Press.

Summerfield, H. (1975) *That Myriad-Minded Man: A Biography of George William Russell, 'AE', 1867–1935*. Gerrards Cross: Smythe.

Taruskin, R. (1997) *Defining Russia Musically*. Princeton: Princeton University Press.

Taylor, K. (2001) *Sir John Woodroffe, Tantra and Bengal*. Richmond, Surrey: Curzon Press.

Timms, E. and Collier, P. (1988) *Visions and Blueprints*. Manchester: Manchester University Press.

Treitel, C. (2004) *A Science for the Soul: Occultism and the Genesis of the German Modern*. Baltimore and London: Johns Hopkins University Press.

Tuchman, M. (ed.) (1986) *The Spiritual in Art: Abstract Painting, 1890–1985*. New York: Abbeville Press.

Urban, H. B. (2006) *Magia Sexualis: Sex, Magic and Liberation in Modern Western Esotericism*. Berkeley and Los Angeles: University of California Press.

Vickery, J. B. (1973) *The Literary Impact of the Golden Bough*. Princeton: Princeton University Press.

Vondung, K. (1979) 'Spiritual revolution and magic: speculation and political action in national socialism', *Modern Age* 23, Fall: 394–402.

Waghorne, J. P. (1994) *The Raja's Magic Clothes: Re-Visioning Kingship and Divinity in British India*. University Park: Pennsylvania State University Press.

Watkins, G. (1994) *Pyramids at the Louvre: Music, Culture, and Collage from Stravinsky to the Postmodernists*. Cambridge, MA: Harvard University Press.

Webb, J. (1981) *The Occult Establishment*. Glasgow: Richard Drew.

Weir, D. (1997) *Anarchism and Culture: The Aesthetic Politics of Modernism*. Amherst: University of Massachusetts Press.

White, D. G. (1996) *The Alchemical Body: Siddha Traditions in Medieval India*. Chicago and London: University of Chicago Press.

—— (2003) *The Kiss of the Yogini: 'Tantric Sex' in its South Asian Contexts*. Chicago: University of Chicago Press.

—— (2009) *Sinister Yogis*. Chicago: University of Chicago Press.

Winter, A. (1998) *Mesmerized: Powers of Mind in Victorian England*. Chicago and London: University of Chicago Press.

# 11  On becoming an owl
## Magical consciousness

*Susan Greenwood*

Early in my anthropological career I became an owl in my imagination during my first shamanic journey, a form of active meditation accompanied by the rhythm of a drumbeat. Afterwards, I came to understand the experience as a spiritual communication with the bird. I was engaged in participant observation research on British practitioners of magic at the time, and my experience of transformation happened during a workshop at a conference on the performing arts and shamanism in Cardiff, Wales. All the participants of the workshop were instructed to find a hole in the ground in our imaginations and to imagine our selves going down into it. The aim of the journey was to find a spirit guide. The experience had a profound effect on me: I *smelt* my warm bird smell and it took me into the experience of flight; I could *feel* the pull of the air on my wing feathers. It was surprising to me that a neo-shamanic journey at a conference could have had such a deep impact and I came to realize the power of the imagination in the mutability of subtle-body boundaries. If I, as a person untrained in such shamanic encounters, could feel that I had become an owl in spirit then some aspect of the experience must be potentially universal to human processes of mind. My experience of such communication with spirit beings would have wide implications for my research.

In this chapter I give an overview of how I have sought to remain true to the experience of my spirit communication with the owl while still seeking to maintain scientific reason and analysis. In the process of explication I delineate some obstacles to a social scientific understanding of spirit communications that stem from the historical Western exclusion of spirits and the separation of spirit from matter in dominant Western discourse. I also put forward a new approach to the anthropological study of magic through the development of what I term *magical consciousness*, a process of mind that is based on the interaction of emotion, intuition and imagination experienced within an inspirited world-view, as illustrated by my becoming an owl. Magical consciousness is characterized by the notion of *participation*, an orientation to the world based on persons and things in contact with a non-ordinary spirit reality. As a type of connective thinking, magical consciousness appears to be radically separate from, but is also ultimately linked to, more abstract, analytical or what we might call commonsense modes of thought.[1]

## Magical consciousness

When I was lying on the floor with the other participants of the shamanic workshop, my awareness shifted between my physical body (I knew that I was lying on the floor surrounded by other participants in the workshop) and what was happening in my journey. I thought about how I would find a hole to go down to the under-world, as requested by the workshop leader Dan Noel, subsequent author of *The Soul of Shamanism* (1997). I remembered a dream I had had previously in which I was climbing down a deep tunnel in the middle of the earth and it came back to me as I lay on the floor. I decided to go down this hole. It was tight and dark, a labyrinth of connecting warren-like tunnels that became tighter and darker and darker. I felt the pressure of the earth on and all around me. I could not breathe and I was paralysed by fear – too frightened to go on and too frightened to stop. I had experienced vertigo as a child and it reminded me of this. Nevertheless, I knew that I had to go on, and as I crawled the tunnel got tighter and tighter and I lost my skin; it was stripped off me, like a snake's. I felt myself come to an opening in the tunnel, a round space ... I felt freer and found myself swimming in water in the round opening, but I felt the need to go on. This time the tunnel was narrow but I could swim and it seemed to be a straight line ... As I swam I felt the rest of me disintegrate and slip away, until I reached another space – an opening. I stopped and looked down on myself. I was a pile of bones. My bones were being picked over by a large black crow ... As I approached it looking for its meaning, to my surprise it turned into a large white owl, a large white snow owl, and she let me nestle in her warm feathers and we tried to fly. We hopped around my bones, flying for a few wing beats until we took off into the sky before I had had enough and my awareness returned fully to my body lying on the floor of the workshop (see Greenwood 2005).

Dan Noel, the workshop leader, had trained with anthropologist Michael Harner and learned his technique of journeying as a form of active meditation to the beat of a drum. Harner describes the type of experience that can be gained from such journeys as an ancient human legacy, one that Westerners have been cut off from for centuries (2003: 41, 55–6). Such experiences, which are not unusual, are a feature of the human condition and typically immerse the participant in a world alive with spirits. If experiences like these were a human legacy then I should be able to write about my experience in my research; however, this presented me with a methodological dilemma – I was not supposed to 'go native', to admit to having an emotional experience such as this, but how could I not and retain any spiritual authenticity? As an anthro-pologist I was expected not to blur the boundaries between researcher and informant, and while it was acceptable for my informants to have such experiences with spirits, it was not something that an anthropologist should admit to – it would appear to threaten her objectivity. I decided to tackle the problem head on and took a subjective/experiential methodological approach to my work by deciding to examine my own experience as well as that of my informants (see Greenwood 2000, 2005, 2009).

The next issue I had to face was how to analyse such magical experiences as a form of knowing without losing either the authenticity of the spirit connection or academic analysis. I searched for theories that did not make the direct experience of magic invisible. Nineteenth-century anthropologist Edward Tylor defined religion as a belief in spirit beings and his use of the term 'animism', to describe an inspirited world, put an emphasis on the soul, as the spiritual aspect of a person, to the forefront of early anthropological discussions on the origins of religious beliefs. Tylor thought that beliefs about spirits would gradually be replaced by science in the evolution of human thought, thus rendering such notions obsolete. This evolutionary view is now outmoded; however, its legacy still lingers on in anthropological understandings of spirit. Hence, most theories of magic seek explanation in the social effects of magical beliefs, or within individual psychological thought processes.

In my search for a theory I discovered a debate on 'mystical mentality' that had occurred nearly a hundred years ago between French philosopher Lucien Lévy-Bruhl and English anthropologist Edward Evans-Pritchard. In particular, I found helpful Lévy-Bruhl's use of the philosophical notion of *'participation'* to describe an emotional holistic orientation based on contact with a non-ordinary spirit reality, and I used this to develop my concept of magical consciousness. Participation seemed to sum up my emotional connection with the spirit owl that had occurred during my workshop neo-shamanic journey. In a participatory magical orientation a spirit is both non-material and material because spirit resides in all phenomena, invisible and visible. By contrast, in everyday Western thought the individual and the spirit, if it is acknowledged at all, is as separate as mind and body.

When I had been lying on the floor of the workshop I was the owl. In magical consciousness the owl and I were a single spirit entity; there was a mutability of subtle bodily boundaries in time and space. In a contemporary shamanic perspective, as well as perhaps in all shamanic world-views, the body is potentially porous to spirit intrusion, whether considered good, as in my case with the bird, or harmful as the cause of loss of well-being or illness. The body's boundaries are not discrete and it is of considerable importance to have control over which spirits have access in and out. This is one of the most essential keys to understanding shamanic practice; it is also of vital importance in shamanic healing, the essence of which is either to remove a hurtful or injurious spirit or to retrieve a missing spiritual component of a person.

Lévy-Bruhl's ideas on participation greatly assisted me in understanding what had happened during my first neo-shamanic encounter with a spirit being. I experienced what it was like to become a bird, in particular to fly and have a different perspective because I had let go of my commitment to a human form and had imagined myself as a bird. I gained insight into an inspirited participatory worldview, but I had to rediscover the philosopher's work.

As an undergraduate I had learned to be suspicious of Lévy-Bruhl, as Evans-Pritchard had supposedly robustly set Lévy-Bruhl right on his erroneous thinking during the mystical mentality debate. There was a certain negative mythology surrounding the philosopher due to his use of the term 'pre-logical' to describe mystical mentality. Lévy-Bruhl's use of this term to refer to native thought had led to a heated exchange among anthropologists; the essence of which accused the philosopher of the racist assertion that native thinking was mystical in comparison to that of rational Westerners. However, my search of the correspondence between Lévy-Bruhl and Evans-Pritchard showed much respect between the two men, rather than the assumed hostility of the myth version. It was clear that the essence of agreement between them – and the central point of the debate on mystical mentality – was that all humans, both native and so-called civilized, could think both mystically and rationally.

The philosopher later retrenched from his concept of pre-logical thought, agreeing that it caused too much misunderstanding, but he continued working until his death with the notion of participation to explain mystical mentality. Why was there such a seeming ambivalence to Lévy-Bruhl's work among anthropologists? Perhaps it represents too much of a challenge to the rationalized canon of theory. To understand why this might be the case, it is in order to examine some Western assumptions about spirits.

## Questioning Western assumptions about spirits

'Spirit' is a term with diverse meanings in Western thought – it can refer to the inward non-material part of a person or 'soul'; a being not connected with a material body, a disembodied soul, or an incorporeal being such as my spirit bird, or an elf or fairy; or it can indicate the innate quality or essence of a person, such as when we say that a person has courage, vivacity, or indeed 'spirituality', or they may lack vigour and be called 'despirited' or spiritless. Spirits are minimal creatures, shadows, the unfocused – things that are hard to grasp by analytic reason (Lambek 1996: 238–9). In most cultures various categories of phenomena are distinguished from commonsense reality. These categories are associated with a realm of uncanny mind-bearing beings whose power, logical status and relationships to space and time are different from those of humans in the ordinary social world (Mageo and Howard 1996: 12). 'Spiritual' implies non-materiality as in the Cartesian division between mind (spirit) and body (matter). Spiritual represents the opposite of material existence – a more subtle mode of corporeal existence that cannot usually be seen except under certain conditions and in trance, as in my transformation into an owl (Lowie, cited by Levy in Mageo and Howard 1996: 12).

Experiencing spirits as real can be disorientating for Westerners versed in scientific rationalism, and the experience is often denied, as Lévy-Bruhl has pointed out: 'our mind experiences discomfort, confusion and perplexity: what is a world which is not rational and intelligible? And it gets out of it by saying: it is a world which is not real (imaginary, arbitrary, fabulous, like fairy stories)' (cited in Willis and Curry 2004: 120). Although perhaps for the general population a spiritual world is never very far away – for example, in newspaper astrological predictions or 'stars', and a whole range of alternative therapies such as spirit healing and homeopathy – for most social scientists versed in rationalistic discourses and theories such a world is remote, if not non-existent.

In Western cultures the analytical mode of thinking asks questions about whether spirits are real or not, and this is of interest in itself in relation to their social and psychological effects, but it does not help us understand the nature of reality and how our conception of spirits might fit into that. How can we develop our understanding of spirit without losing scientific objectivity? A key to answering that question lies in understanding magic as a mode of consciousness. To do this we have to step outside of the dominant Western view of reality that dismisses the idea that spirits are real.

Before we can do this, however, we need to understand two key underlying factors that shape Western assumptions about the nature of reality. The first shows how the historical development of science in the seventeenth century came to exclude a spirit world by co-opting the practical and experimental aspects of magic and rejecting its spiritual dimension; and the second outlines the Cartesian philosophy of the separation of spirit and matter whereby the living world came to be seen in mechanistic terms.

## The irrationality of magic

In the seventeenth century, during what has come to be termed the scientific revolution, the practical experimental aspects of magic were absorbed into science leaving other spiritual features of magic to be denounced as irrational. The shift from a magical view, in which there was no division between spirit and matter, to a rational pursuit of science involved the material and immaterial aspects of natural philosophy becoming separated. Natural philosophy was a complete system that incorporated spirit and matter – with disciplinary traditions ranging from astronomy, mechanics, anatomy, medicine, metaphysics, pharmacology, cartography, mining and metallurgy to optics, music and physiology among others – that aimed to describe the entire system of the world. At the time of the scientific revolution there was no concept of 'science'; the present use of the word was first coined in the nineteenth century (Henry 1997: 172).

The scientific world-view developed partly out of a wedding of natural philosophy and the pragmatic and empirical tradition of sympathetic magic. Natural philosophy, as defined by Galileo Galilei (1564–1642), an Italian physicist, astronomer and philosopher, Auguste Comte (1798–1857), a French philosopher, and the English naturalist Charles Darwin (1809–1882), concerned a pursuit of objective knowledge of phenomena (Faivre 1989: 24). Based on an assumption that certain things had hidden or occult powers to affect other things, natural magic was dependent on a profound knowledge of how to use these powers to achieve a desired outcome. A reforming natural philosophy denounced magic and at the same time took what was useful (Henry 1997: 43–4).

Francis Bacon was one of the first natural philosophers to advocate the experimental method as the most reliable way of acquiring knowledge of the natural world. Rationalist and speculative natural philosophy and experimental natural magic had once been completely separate traditions, but Bacon advocated the use of the experimental method of the magician in a reformed natural philosophy. The good ideas in magic were silently incorporated into the reformed natural knowledge, while the bad ideas were used to denounce magic as a sink of false and ludicrous beliefs (Henry 2002: 5, 64, 79).

Magical traditions played an important part in the major shift from scholastic natural philosophy to the new more practically useful empirical natural philosophy of the scientific revolution. As historian John Henry notes, 'The history of magic since the eighteenth century has been the history of what was left of that tradition *after* major elements of natural magic had been absorbed into natural philosophy.' Natural magic disappeared from the Western conception of magic due to its most fundamental aspects being co-opted. This had a major impact on how magic is viewed in academia, even among historians of science, a number of which have, according to Henry, 'refused to accept that something which they see as so irrational could have had any impact whatsoever upon the supremely rational pursuit of science'; their arguments 'seem to be based on mere prejudice, or on a failure to understand the richness and complexity of the magical tradition' (1997: 42).

During this period the course was set for the advancement of causal logic over magical thinking, and these ideas reached their full expression during the eighteenth-century Enlightenment, a time when occult phenomena were no longer significant as a form of explanation and were deemed mere superstition, a relic of a dark and primitive past. As the term suggests, the period saw greater light shed on the conduct of human affairs: the dark mysteries of traditional attitudes in religion and political life were pushed back, and in their place a new outlook grew up, informed by reason and the power of scientific research and discovery (Vesey and Foulkes 1990: 98). God had created the world as a perfect, rational machine. Humans could become part of this rationality through the knowledge of the self-perfection of God's design; if God's laws of nature were rational, then it was through reason that people could discover them. The global effort of the Enlightenment was to explain other religions as false, and the beliefs of other societies were seen as primitive, backward and unenlightened (Rapport and Overing 2000: 273).

## Separating spirit from matter

Much of this view of science derives from the work of seventeenth-century philosopher René Descartes (1596–1650), who had an ecstatic visionary experience during which the nature of the universe was revealed to him. Rather ironically, Descartes became convinced that his mission in life was to seek truth by reason. Putting an emphasis on reason as the basis of analytic knowledge, he argued that truth was derived from rational reflection rather than from experience and observation of the senses. A mathematician at the outset of his career working on music, optics and mechanics (Henry 1997: 19–20), Descartes is famous for his '*cogito*': 'I think, therefore I am'. Descartes thought that ideas came from thinking itself: the mind produced ideas out of its own processes of rational reflection on the world. It is ideas such as this that often have an unconscious impact, and this *cogito* shapes an attitude of 'mind over matter', meaning that it is important to 'rise above' the experience. If you know this maxim, you know Descartes' main idea. He separated the thinking mind, which had a soul, from mechanistic soul-less matter. The mind for Descartes was a thinking substance with an immaterial soul capable of self-consciousness. By contrast, the body was material and part of the mechanistic universe; it had no soul and no consciousness and it was under the control of its emotions and external stimuli. A soul without a body would have consciousness, but only of innate ideas lacking sensory impressions of the world (Morris 1991: 6–14).

Unifying maths and physics, Descartes sought to show how the new philosophy could explain the forms, functions and vital process of living creatures through mechanistic accounts. His starting point was to draw on William Harvey's work on the heart and blood and excise it of its vitalistic elements (Henry 1997: 67–8, 75). Descartes' mechanical philosophy was highly influential and it was forged out of his attempts to understand the world upon certainties of geometrical reasoning. Descartes' work contributed to the mathematization of the world picture, and his mechanical philosophy marked a definite break with the past and set the seal upon how science would come to be seen (Henry 1997: 4).

Descartes' legacy was the separation of spirit (mind) from matter, and this notion has had an abiding influence on Western culture – it is thought rather than experience of the senses that is valued. However, Descartes was not the first thinker in this rationalist tradition; he followed Plato's view that the senses were untrustworthy reference. The valuing of reason over experience has not been a good one for understanding magic, and the Cartesian legacy that shaped Western notions of science and its rationalism is still evident in anthropological thinking today. Magic is now contrasted with the Western style of thought that firmly locates knowledge of the world in science. A division has occurred between a rational science identified with the material world on the one hand, and on the other magic looms large as an irrational belief in spirits. Magic is misunderstood and trivialized by the belief that only the naive take it seriously, or that it is only the practice of charlatans or evildoers. These views 'fail to give the full picture of the role of magic in culture or history' (Sullivan 1989: ix). Magic has become a collect-all term for all that is unorthodox, irrational or just inexplicable. The separation of spirit from matter left a world that was despirited and this corresponded with the development of science as a rationalistic pursuit. Anthropology, as a social science, has inherited a great deal of this attitude to spirits.

## A dance of interacting parts

The study of magic takes our parameters of knowledge into new areas that are as yet relatively unexamined by modern science. Notwithstanding the potential obstacles, let me act as an advocate on behalf of the perspective of magical consciousness to suggest that we entertain the view that during the experience of magic spirits share a degree of corporeal materiality and possess mind. Accepting this proposition allows us to imagine that their minds – embodied in whatever form we might imagine, be it owl or deity – and ours can meet in a wider consciousness; or put another way, mind *and* matter have consciousness. The body, the mind and the whole eco-system are linked within a meta-pattern. As English anthropologist, psychologist and biologist Gregory Bateson has claimed, connections are made in terms of the mind, or minds, sharing stories 'whether ours or those of redwood forests and sea anemones'; the pattern created is a 'dance of interacting parts' (only secondarily pegged down by physical limits) (2000: 467).

As we have seen, historically, since Descartes associated mind with individual human reasoning, mind has been located in the brain, but consciousness is not reducible to individual brain activity. We tend to see consciousness as a product of the brain, and the brain can be scientifically studied through scans and machines that record brainwaves, for example. However, consciousness cannot be understood by examining the brain. There have been various attempts to study body consciousness (Shusterman 2008; Weiss 1999); nevertheless the dominant popular notion holds that the brain is indeed the location of consciousness. Consider for a moment another proposition: that the brain is not the originator of consciousness, as is so commonly supposed in Western cultures, but only a trans-mitter of the sense impressions and thought processes of individual, social life and spirit beings.

Molecular biologists have tackled unravelling the chemistry of the living cell, but that information does not indicate how cells interact to give life on a global scale. If a Martian were to explore an earthling's television set they could construct complex lists of its components but would not find out anything about how to watch the programmes, or what they mean to its viewers (Grof 1999: xv). If 'mind' is defined as the personal aspects of individual process, and 'conscious-ness' as an intrinsic quality of the wider universe of which individual mind is but one part, then mind and consciousness are linked. If consciousness is wider than the individual human mind, then that mind might be shared with other beings. If we understand these other beings as spirits that have a different order of existence to the material dimension of reality or invisible, but none the less real, dimensions of material reality, then it is possible to take the view that these beings also have mind. The implications of this are that we need to see beyond a purely materialist explanation of life and consciousness to see wider patterns.[2]

We are necessarily limited by our knowledge, but in terms of the mode of magical participation it is possible to overcome the anthropological dilemma of the reality of spirits by adopting an attitude of spiritual agnosticism by not believing or disbelieving in their reality. It is possible just to accept that people believe in spirits and keep an open mind as to 'belief'. When a person is 'in' that part of their awareness it makes no difference whatsoever if they believe in spirits, or if spirit communications are labelled as psychological – if they are explained as a part of their own internal thought processes – or whether they think the entities with which they are communicating are independent of them and have a being of their own. While participating in a magical aspect of consciousness the question of belief is irrelevant: 'belief' is not a necessary condition to communicate with an inspirited world.

In this view humans create spirits in their imaginations. The subject of the imagination is a perennial one when discussing the reality of spirits. When I have led workshops and given talks on magical consciousness people often ask whether their experience of spirit communication is 'just' their imagination. My answer is that the imagination is an important tool for expanding awareness: in terms of magical knowledge it is a 'doorway' into an expanded participatory awareness. In practice, what starts as the imagination develops into something else entirely; at least that is the experience – the experience *feels* different and brings a different, and often surprising, perspective. The spirits are real when they inhabit a person's experience, or when that person inhabits the spirit's experience; or when they become a part of another awareness, or when that other awareness becomes a part of their awareness – as in the process of shape-shifting, when boundaries become less discrete allowing the transmission of insight and knowledge.

Researching magic over the years, I have adopted an orientation that can move between the analytical mode that is required by anthropology to examine the social and psychological *effects* of magical experience on people's behaviour on the one hand, and on the other, the actual experience of magic. It might appear to some people that the two orientations of the analytical mode and the participatory magical mode are mutually incompatible; however, in practice I have found that it is entirely possible to accommodate both aspects within a broader stream of awareness. We are capable of experiencing multiple sensory inputs and the bringing together of the analytical and participatory modes can be most creative, as well as provide real insight.

So, the question of the reality or non-reality of spirits appears to be unreasonable. At worst, it legitimates a denial of the experience of magic, and at best it is a distraction from the further examination of this aspect of human awareness. The best way forward so as to start to feel this aspect of consciousness is to take the phenomenological perspective of acting 'as if' – to 'bracket disbelief' – and just experience. What is essentially magical about magic is a participatory relation-ship with 'others', such as my owl, that might represent just one such relationship that connects mind in a wider pattern of consciousness.

## 'Not only, but also'

Magical consciousness, being based on participation with its emotional and embodied connection with spirit beings, is fundamentally different from the abstract analyses of science. I searched for a more inclusive scientific model, one that could incorporate magical experience that would not reduce my communication with the owl to just my imagination. There is a need to bring about a reconciliation of magic and science in a new attitude that recognizes all the characteristics of magical consciousness *and* the abstract thinking and analyses of science. This framework can be imagined as a web that encompasses multiple forms of knowledges: these can be summed up by my use of the expression 'not only, but also'.

The web allows the pioneering work of Lévy-Bruhl on emotion and spirit to be brought into analytical focus, as well as a whole variety of other social scientific theories from different perspectives. The web metaphor forms an *ideal* for multiple ways of knowing, but above all it fosters a new attitude to knowledge, one that helps us understand the experience of magic in much more depth. A new attitude is required and here I turn to Geoffrey Samuel's 'multimodal framework'. Samuel draws on Clifford Geertz's use of the web metaphor in his well-known phrase that 'man is an animal suspended in webs of significance he himself has spun' (1990: 11). Samuel notes that the web is neither purely individual, because once it is spun it can take on a life of its own, nor is it purely social because webs have individual spinners.[3] For Samuel, the web is a conceptual space in which all knowledges, including magic, have their existence. Webs can be handy things to think with – they can be used as metaphors to express a language of relationship that incorporates different forms of knowing.

Samuel observes a shift in scientific paradigm from seeing knowledge as a mirror (in which the gradual discovery of laws mirrored reality) to viewing it as a map (where certain aspects of the territory are represented, while others are ignored). In the latter conceptualization different fields of human knowledge are recognized as having different theories and each is represented (1990: 21). Each emphasizes different aspects of a situation that is too complex to be encompassed by any one of them. Samuel views a 'shamanic approach', such as my experience of transforming into an owl, as a pattern potentially present in all societies, and a pattern among other modal states in the multimodal framework that brings together different theories to link the entire human ecosystem within a series of relationships (1990: 148, 152).

The web consists of varying modes of thought that can be imagined as patterns. In order to reconcile different types of knowledge, Samuel has built on Gregory Bateson's ideas about a 'flow of relatedness', the emphasis on patterns of relationship and connectedness (Samuel 1990: 55). Bateson was drawn to cybernetics, an intellectual movement of mathematicians, neuroscientists, social scientists and engineers concerned with different levels of description that they saw as patterns of communication (Capra 1996: 51). In the following section I explore how Bateson's ideas about mental maps can contribute to a wider conception of science.

In *Mind and Nature: A Necessary Unity* (1988), Bateson tried to understand an integrated world; he tried to come to an understanding of the world by being in the world, and he sought to find a language that would describe this relationship. Thinking that logic was not suitable for the description of biological patterns, he turned to metaphor as the language of nature. Bateson looked at the nature of mental processes – of thought in the widest sense of the word. He looked at the relationship between thought and the material world, and the evolution of mental processes. Concerned with thoughts and ideas about the world, Bateson was interested in how the mind classifies and maps things through *ideation*, the term coming from 'ideate', to imagine and conceive ideas in the mind (1988: 153).

Bateson thought that we construct mental maps and organize connections and differences between things in a familiar pattern, and he was always interested in how the patterns connected. *Abduction*, on the other hand, was the intuitive process of reasoning that brings together seemingly unrelated patterns in metaphors expressed through dreams, parable, allegory, poetry, and even the whole of science and the whole of religion (1988: 153).

In seeking to articulate this model of multiple conceptions of reality, I utilize Bateson's two pivotal notions of ideation and abduction, applying them to the subject of examining 'shape-shifting', the mutability of subtle bodily boundaries. Using my example of transforming into an owl, it can be seen that the issue of spirits stands at the divide between analytical orientations and magical orientations: in the former spirits do not exist, and in magical orientations they are a central defining feature (see Table 11.1).

This model shows how magical consciousness can become one aspect of multiple orderings of reality; it thus has a place as a legitimate form of knowledge within an expanded view of science. It demonstrates how I can hold both perspectives if I shift between the analytical mode that is required by anthropology and the magical orientation that allows me to acknowledge my spirit communication with the owl. I do not have to choose between orientations; instead it is possible to accommodate both aspects and then apply which is the most appropriate to focus on at any given point in time, or for any specific situation. These two orientations are not rigidly bounded and they may weave in and out to produce a deeper anthropological understanding – a new synthesis that overcomes all opposites.

Thus a rationalistic orientation, in which spirits do not exist, can be examined together with a magical inspirited orientation. The purpose is to consider how we might understand and apply these different modes in a new manner. Here the analytical orientation and the magical orientation are presented as two patterns of knowledge that need not be seen as mutually exclusive systems of understanding separated by belief or non-belief in spirits. In an increasingly global context, this model might help to explain how people can come to hold together, and at the same time, what might appear to be conflicting beliefs in both 'science' and 'magic'.

*Table 11.1* Ideation and abduction in shape-shifting

| Ideation | Abduction |
| --- | --- |
| My shape-shifting into an owl | 1 Analytical orientation<br>• I stand outside myself observing myself lying on floor<br>• Spirits do not exist<br>• Psychology, effect of neo-shamanic beliefs<br><br>2 Magical consciousness orientation<br>• Participation<br>• Spirits exist<br>• I become owl |

Carving out this space for magical consciousness within an expanded conception of science allows for the investigation of spirit realities that would otherwise be rendered invisible. It enables a mutability of subtle-body boundaries and spirit communication to be examined in such a way that is non-threatening to canons of reason, rationality and analysis. Thus, it not only validates an area of study that cannot otherwise be readily examined, but also breaks down the division between Western and non-Western forms of knowing by helping to explain how changing, diverse and contradictory beliefs can be held at the same time in increasingly complex contexts. In today's climate of globalization I believe that this can only be a positive move that helps us look at our human commonalities in ways of thinking – of what we share – as well as our differences.

## Notes

1 Parts of this chapter were presented to the Re-Thinking Shamanisms seminar, Kastrup, Denmark on 27 May 2010. I am grateful to Hanne Veber, from the American Indian Languages and Cultures Section, Department of Cross-Cultural and Regional Studies, of the University of Copenhagen, for the opportunity; other sections are abridged from my book *The Anthropology of Magic* (2009).
2 When I am teaching this model to students I often explain it as the 'have your cake and eat it philosophy'; this helps them to remember the most important part of the idea and they always find it amusing!
3 Samuel notes the work of Bob Scholte (1984) who wrote that in state societies only a select few do the actual spinning and the majority are caught.

## References

Bateson, G. (1988 [1979]) *Mind and Nature: A Necessary Unity*. New York: Bantam.
—— (2000) *Steps to an Ecology of Mind*. Chicago: University of Chicago Press.
Capra, F. (1996) *The Web of Life: A New Scientific Understanding of Living Systems*. New York: Anchor Books.
Faivre, A. (1989) 'Speculations about nature', in L. E. Sullivan (ed.) *Hidden Truths: Magic, Alchemy, and the Occult*. New York: Macmillan.
Greenwood, S. (2000) *Magic, Witchcraft and the Otherworld*. Oxford: Berg.
—— (2005) *The Nature of Magic*. Oxford: Berg.
—— (2009) *The Anthropology of Magic*. Oxford: Berg.
Grof, S. (1999) *The Holotropic Mind*. San Francisco: HarperCollins.
Harner, M. (2003) 'Discovering the Way', in G. Harvey (ed.) *Shamanism: A Reader*. London: Routledge.
Henry, J. (1997) *The Scientific Revolution and the Origins of Modern Science*. Basingstoke: Macmillan.
Henry, J. (2002) *Knowledge is Power: How Magic, the Government and an Apocalyptic Vision inspired Francis Bacon to create Modern Science*. Cambridge: Icon Books.
Lambek, M. (1996) 'Afterword: Spirits and their histories', in J. M. Mageo and A. Howard (eds) *Spirits in Culture, History, and Mind*. New York: Routledge.
Lévy-Bruhl L. (1975) *The Notebooks on Primitive Mentality*, trans. P. Rivière. Oxford: Blackwell.

Lowie, R. (1970 [1924]) *Primitive Religion*. New York: Liveright.
Mageo, J. M. and Howard, A. (eds) (1996) *Spirits in Culture, History, and Mind*. New York: Routledge.
Morris, B. (1991) *Western Conceptions of the Individual*. Oxford: Berg.
Noel, D. C. (1997) *The Soul of Shamanism*. London: Continuum.
Rapport, N. and J. Overing (2000) *Social and Cultural Anthropology: The Key Concepts*. London: Routledge.
Samuel, G. (1990) *Mind, Body and Culture*. Cambridge: Cambridge University Press.
Scholte, B. (1984) 'Comment on Paul Shankman's "The thick and the thin: on the interpretive theoretical program of Clifford Geertz"', *Current Anthropology* 25: 540–2.
Shusterman, R. (2008) *Body Consciousness: A Philosophy of Mindfulness and Somaesthetics*. Cambridge: Cambridge University Press.
Sullivan, L. E. (1989) 'Introduction', in L. E. Sullivan (ed.) *Hidden Truths: Magic, Alchemy, and the Occult*. New York: Macmillan.
Vesey, G. and Foulkes, P. (eds) (1990) *Dictionary of Philosophy*. London: Collins.
Weiss, G. (1999) *Body Images*. London: Routledge.
Willis, R. and Curry, P. (2004) *Astrology, Science and Culture: Pulling Down the Moon*. Oxford: Berg.

# 12 Invisible, dispersed and connected

## The cultural plausibility of subtle-body models in the contemporary West

*Ruth Barcan*

'The body is a model which can stand in for any bounded system,' claimed the cultural anthropologist Mary Douglas (1984: 115), articulating a precept that is axiomatic in contemporary socio-cultural approaches to the body: that dominant conceptions of, metaphors for and experiences of the body are formed in relation to the economic, technological, ideological, symbolic and social parameters of any society.

For some time now, cultural theorists have detected subtle but fundamental shifts in the underlying metaphors of the body in the West, which may signal new possibilities in the way Westerners conceive of and indeed experience their bodies. The way that these theorists articulate and explain the shifts varies, but a number of themes recur: the late-modern model of the body is, it is often argued, becoming less solid – more fragmented, dispersed and permeable, and connected in new ways into larger networks.

This chapter focuses on one popular example of and context for this 'dematerializing' body (Fadlon 2004) – that of the subtle or energetic body as it has re-entered Western popular culture via the steadily rising prominence from the 1960s' counter-culture onwards of alternative health practices, 'Eastern'[1] practices like yoga and meditation, and New Age spirituality. The idea of a body composed of 'energy' has become increasingly familiar, to the extent where a significant portion of modern Westerners, even if they do not countenance it fully, are at least prepared to *work with* this conception of the body as it is encountered in therapeutic, yogic or spiritual practice. These practices, despite their diversity, are united in their centralization of energetic embodiment: 'the significance of energy comes close to being *hard* orthodoxy within the holistic milieu, in that without some form of belief in it one is effectively an outsider' (Partridge 2005: 34, original emphasis). Energy is the dominant term in the contemporary Western search for a popular 'equivalent' to the *chi* of acupuncture or the *prana* of yoga (Mayor 2009: 15; see also Kaptchuk 2001). Whether 'energy' is an adequate translation of concepts from subtle anatomy is debatable.[2] Acupuncturist David Mayor, for example, considers the concept of *chi* to have been 'hijacked' by Western concepts of vital energy, noting that the concept of energy is in turn beginning to filter back into Chinese acupuncture texts (2009: 15). In this chapter I use the term symptomatically – both because it is the dominant

Western translation and because its use points to one of the ways in which subtle anatomy has been made culturally and conceptually plausible to the West.

This chapter uses the increasing popularity of New Age, alternative and Eastern practices as a base for speculating about some of the underlying reasons for both the plausibility and the attractiveness of the subtle body in the popular imagination. I argue that a model that sees the body as multiple, invisible, extensive, expressive and interconnected with others is culturally plausible in the age of the Internet, social networking and mobile communications.

Underpinning this recent plausibility, however, is a much longer trajectory of thought. First, there are the distant residues of the subtle-body models as they were formulated in the ancient West – initially in Platonism and later Neoplatonism and then in a number of submerged traditions of Western esotericism (Mead 1967; Melton 1988; Hanegraaff 1998). Medieval biology continued the ancient conceptualization of the material realm as on the same continuum as the organic realm and the concomitant impossibility of a stark dichotomy between mind and body (Kaptchuk 2001: 44). In eighteenth- and nineteenth-century Europe the idea of vital energy arose in reaction to the mechanistic tenor of the new science (2001: 44). Today, the Western vitalist tradition, despite its marginalization from orthodox biomedicine, has swept up *chi* and *prana* in its wake (2001: 50) and remade them in its own image. Even so, the subtle body is most commonly understood in the West as an 'Eastern' form, via its 'importation' by the Theosophical Society in the late nineteenth century. The Theosophical and Anthroposophical conception of subtle bodies provided the direct source for the New Age (Hanegraaff 1998: 222). This importation is actually more complex than it appears at first glance: Wouter Hanegraaff, eminent scholar of the New Age, argues that the debt of Theosophy's founder, Helena Blavatsky, to an 'Oriental perspective' is 'more apparent than real' (1998: 455).[3] But the Western occult and esoteric traditions that are as much the progenitors of today's conception of the subtle body are, almost by definition, not particularly well known to most people,[4] and nor are the nineteenth-century metaphysical religions like Swedenborgianism, spiritualism or Transcendentalism that were another important source for the West (Melton 1988: 36–9; Albanese 2007).

Freudian psychoanalysis provides a more widely known conceptual antecedent. Its theories of repression and psychosomatic illness resonate with the theories of the emotional basis of illness that characterized the metaphysical religions and that are a plank of the New Age today.[5] Freudian-inspired theories of the emotional basis of disease are amenable to reframing through the lens of energetic embodiment as disruptions to the free flow of energy (for examples, see Hay 1987; Hurwitz 2001: 243–4). The diverse practices and genres of the New Age, including its spiritual, self-help and healing literatures, have played a major role in bringing subtle anatomy and the concept of energy into popular view. In sum, despite its mixed and complex lineage, subtle embodiment is best known in the contemporary popular imagination as a 'new', Eastern idea brought to us by New Age thinkers and gaining, it is argued, increasing credibility through the discoveries of cutting-edge science.[6]

The idea of the subtle body has proven attractive to those Westerners seeking alternatives to dualistic, mechanistic or secular conceptions of the body. It seems to provide a way out of a number of philosophical impasses that have been the object of both academic and popular critique from the latter decades of the twentieth century onwards, including Christian views, derived from Platonism, of the body as a hindrance to the development of the soul; Cartesian conceptions of the machine-like body; and reductionist biomedical approaches to the body. It appeals to those who seek a mysticism and/or a medicine that do not conceive of the body as machinic so much as fluid, intelligent and impregnated with – indeed, constituted by – the sacred stuff of the cosmos itself. It has found a vehicle in the New Age and a welcoming home in consumer culture, since the contexts in which Westerners are likely to encounter the subtle-body model tend to be underpinned by individualistic, often hedonistic, philosophies of individual self-fulfilment – in ironic contrast to the asceticism of the original social and spiritual contexts in which such models were usually to be found. In contemporary popular contexts, then, the subtle body is bound up in a number of the features of late modernity: popular discontent with hyper-rationalization; the search for a re-sacralized future; the 'subjective turn', with its focus on individual fulfilment (Heelas *et al.* 2005: 2–3); and the seductions of a pleasure-seeking consumer culture.

## The 'dematerializing' body: some contexts

There are several angles from which cultural theorists have approached the idea of shifts in body models in the West in late modernity. In the late 1980s, Arthur and Marilouise Kroker saw the body as fragmenting and dispersing under the commodifying forces of late capitalism. Our bodies, they claimed – rather hyperbolically – were now best known to us in alienated form as exteriorized media images (1988: 21). In the 1990s, Emily Martin argued that in high modernity, Fordist images of the body as productive, hierarchical and efficient subtly permeated biomedical and scientific writing. She saw late capitalism as ushering in new models of the body, especially when it came to imagining the immune system. These new models, she argued, befit the era of flexible labour, emphasizing the body's flexibility, responsiveness and internal interconnectedness (1992: 123). To sum up bluntly her nuanced account: 'The imagery used to describe the immune system in the body strongly evokes … descriptions of the operation of global capital' (1992: 123).

Around the same time, Jackie Stacey was also pointing to the relations between biomedical models of the body and the informational regimes of the late twentieth century. Using as a foundation the classic Foucauldian (2003) account of the increasing visibility of the body and its interiors in modernity, she understood the contemporary Western body to be thoroughly bound up with what she calls 'informational cultures' (1997: 231) and their logics, particularly 'imperatives of self-knowledge' (1997: 26): 'The visualizability of the healthy body as a system of information units that connect different aspects of the self (spiritual, emotional, physical) is an increasingly commonplace image in contemporary culture'

(1997: 166). Stacey noted, moreover, 'the emergent overlaps' between the cultures of biomedicine and those of alternative therapies in this regard (1997: 22).

The subtle-body model provides another, perhaps surprising, point of overlap between biomedicine and Complementary and Alternative Medicine (CAM). Judith Fadlon has argued that the subtle-body model's emphasis on 'energy, chakras, auras, and the vital force' (2004: 72) brought CAM and biomedicine into a form of convergence, since biomedicine itself is operating with an increasingly 'virtual' conception of the body. She considers both the subtle body of alternative medicine and the increasingly 'transparent' body of biomedicine to be part of a 'dematerialization' of the body that points to 'a new phase in the relation between body and society' (2004: 73) – the advent of postmodern hyper-reality.

More could, I think, be asked about whether this energetic conception of the body is really best thought of as a 'dematerialization' or as a different, non-dualistic, conception of materiality itself (Johnston 2008). Here, though, I want to place these different accounts of body models, which all focus in one way or another on bodily metaphors for social processes of production and exchange, in a broader socio-cultural context that includes shifts in belief systems and new forms of everyday body practices. The development of new images for the body can be seen, for example, as part of what Colin Campbell (2007) calls the 'Easternization' of the West, including the rise of immanent, monistic philosophies and the popularization of practices in which they are enmeshed, such as yoga and meditation (see also Stacey 2000). This 'Easternization' is itself part of a broader cultural turn in the West – the rise of a discourse of spirituality including, but not limited to, New Age spirituality. Though claims of a so-called 'spiritual revolution' may well have been overstated (Heelas *et al.* 2005), the individualization of religion (Carrette and King 2005: 14) and the rise of 'spirituality' as an increasingly popular way of rethinking the sacred are unquestionable contemporary phenomena (Carrette and King 2005). The New Age has been a particularly potent instrument of this phenomenon and one of the dominant vehicles for the uptake, cultural translation, dissemination and popularization of energetic body models (e.g. Gawain 1978; Brennan 1988). Through these intertwined phenomena – globalization, alternative therapeutic practices, the spiritual 'revolution' and the New Age – an energetic model of the body has permeated Western popular culture to the extent where it now has a place in the popular concept bank.

In making the case that the subtle-body model has become not only plausible but attractive, it should be evident, I hope, that I am not suggesting that subtle-body models are accepted or even known by *all* modern Westerners. It is quite possible to participate in practices based on subtle anatomy without realizing it or without accepting the model intellectually. In any case, the concept of the multiple, energetic body is often met by scientific scorn and popular cynicism or derision. While for some it is a new and exciting way of imagining the body, for others it is not only implausible but dangerous – one of the many signs that scientific rationality is under threat (see Barcan 2009). Nonetheless, given the sheer reach of New Age popular culture and of alternative health practices – in the US, there are more visits annually to alternative therapists than to orthodox primary carers (Institute of Medicine 2005: 34) – it must now be acknowledged that the subtle body has re-entered the late-modern Western concept bank.

## The contemporary cultural plausibility of the subtle-body model

The idea of a body composed of multiple, interpenetrating 'sheaths' of energy, most of which are invisible to ordinary perception and extend beyond the limits of the physical body, is, as I have sketched out, not foreign to the Western tradition. It has played a minor role, however, in contrast to the philosophies of much mainstream Western science, medicine, religion and academic philosophy, whose emphasis has typically been dualistic, insisting on a distinction – even a struggle – between mind and matter or soul and body. Why, then, its contemporary popular renaissance?

One reason is, quite simply, that its core components seem newly plausible in relation to contemporary technological and economic life. Fluidity, dynamism, flow, multiplicity and interconnectedness are the stuff of daily communication technologies and hence increasingly of the cultural imaginary. Every day, modern Westerners communicate with distant and unseen others with whom they feel themselves to be connected, even interconnected, to varying degrees. The idea of the body as a hierarchically organized multiplicity thus has a certain cultural resonance. For those people whose daily life involves multiple log-ons, different online presences, the creation of alternative identities or avatars, and the movement between different virtual worlds, the idea of the body as multiple may not involve much of an imaginative leap.

Even those with less active online lives may still find the idea of an interrelated multiplicity familiar as a way for thinking about the self, given the contemporary tension between the venerable idea of an authentic singular self and the postmodern emphasis on the multifaceted and fluid nature of identity and on the ability to refashion our bodies through clothing, body modification, diet or surgery. It is, after all, a cliché of postmodern advertising that we can 'be whoever we want to be' or that buying a new product or trying on a new dress allows us to be a different person. The idea of the authentic self sits paradoxically alongside that of the multiplicity and malleability of the self, and the two ideas are often found together, even within the one set of discourses (New Age thought being a good example). Moreover, the mode in which subtle anatomy has been popularized in New Age discourse – where its multiplicity is often reduced to a much more familiar dualism via reflective theories of the mental or emotional causes of illness – also domesticates the potential strangeness of the idea of the body as multiple. For example, Louise L. Hay, a leading proponent of metaphysical theories of illness, subscribes to an energetic conception of the body and the universe, yet her accounts of illness and her suggestions for its remediation are thoroughly and familiarly Cartesian, with the body figuring as a screen on which our inner dramas are played out. Indeed, in the following affirmation (1987: 189), she even refers to the body as a machine, an 'it':

I love and approve of my body.
I feed it nourishing foods and beverages.
I exercise it in ways that are fun.
I recognize my body as a wonderous [*sic*] and magnificent machine, and I
feel privileged to live in it.

This conflict between a non-dualistic philosophy and its highly dualistic articulation
can be accounted for not only by the ongoing influence of binary thinking as a
cultural dominant but also by the roots of New Age doctrine in, among other
things, US metaphysical religions, which were themselves influenced by Freudian
accounts of repression and the influence of mind on body (Albanese 2007:
426–7). Louise Hay's philosophy was formed within one such church – the
Church of Religious Science, founded by Ernest Holmes, who had read Freud, as
well as texts from Eastern mysticism, such as the Bhagavad Gita, and Western
hermeticism (2007: 426–7).[7]

So, dualism and multiplicity co-occur as contemporary cultural dominants.
Modern subjects are, in sum, used to thinking of ourselves as individuals with a
deep, complex interiority that is intimate yet invisible to us, familiar yet beyond
our reach, and we are also increasingly used to thinking of that complex self as
both multiple and malleable. The subtle body pushes further the idea of identity
as complex and multifaceted by extending multiplicity to the body itself. Now we
are invited to imagine ourselves as having not only a complex hidden interior or
a set of different selves but also a complex invisible extension 'outwards' into the
space around us.

The idea of our own extension through space tallies with the phenomenological
dimensions of online navigation, where local actions (the press of a key, the click
of a mouse) give us the sense of direct influence on spaces unseen and distant.
The computer or touch-screen's tactility has a proxy effect, providing us with
textures, resistance and counter-forces that strengthen the sensory illusion of
acting over distance. As new forms of interface develop, this sense of bodily
extension through space will undoubtedly increase and become more central and
more modulated. In a study of tactility as mediated through computers and other
devices, Mark Paterson discusses the development of technologies of 'haptic
interaction', which produce a sense of so-called 'telepresence' or 'copresence'
and are increasingly attempting to give the sensation of direct touch (2006:
691–3). These new forms of tactility-at-a-distance are currently being developed
and trialled in areas as diverse as 'military training, long-distance keyhole
surgery, mine clearance, Internet sex, undersea and interplanetary exploration,
and, most commonly, video games' (2006: 692).

Clearly, the growth of a model of multifaceted, extensive embodiment is itself
an embodied phenomenon, involving new expectations and experiences of space,
time and sensory perception. Such experiences often operate at the level of an
unconscious bodily schemata. This 'primordial layer' of being, as the phenome-
nologist Maurice Merleau-Ponty termed the repertoire of preconscious bodily
knowledge (1962: 219), sets the stage for a potential acceptance of new conscious

beliefs about the body, allowing them, for some people at least, to resonate as already familiar, plausible, or attractive.

For the subtle body also comes into being as a set of propositions about the body. How have such beliefs come to be newly plausible? One answer is that various fields of knowledge have been able to act as bridges. A number of knowledge systems have been able to do this – Freudian psychoanalysis being one example – but in this chapter I look at just one arena: the interface between New Age and alternative health literature and contemporary science.

Science is a 'major vehicle' (Melton 1988: 36) for the development and promulgation of New Age ideas. It provides both a set of bridging concepts and discourses and a form of legitimation. In contrast to those who see the New Age as the epitome of irrationality – the *opposite* of science (as, for example, in Robert Basil's claim that the New Age involves 'a large-scale renunciation of science' (1988: 21)) – it is much more accurate to note how New Age/alternative health discourse selectively takes up themes from contemporary science as a means to legitimate its own conceptions of the body and the world. Science is understood to be both the harbinger and the bearer of a non-dualistic (holistic) future and a retrospective endorsement of earlier bodies of knowledge. In many accounts, contemporary science is understood as verifying ancient wisdom – not, in a sense, *discovering* anything, but belatedly playing catch-up: 'Science is only now verifying what humankind has known intuitively since the dawn of history' (Ferguson 1980: 152). Moreover, this interface with science is undoubtedly a two-way street: the enormous popular reach of New Age thought, especially in the US, means that it cannot help but have influenced scientific thinking.

Quantum physics is the most frequent scientific bridge used in New Age/ alternative discourse. It is almost ritually cited in popular accounts as providing scientific proof of the correctness of ancient Eastern monism and of the view that everything is energy vibrating. The medical doctor, Ayurvedic practitioner and New Age figure Deepak Chopra has cemented this connection into the popular literature through his coinage of the term 'quantum healing' (1989: 17). Our bodies, states Chopra, 'appear to be composed of solid matter that can be broken down into molecules and atoms', but 'quantum physics tells us that every atom is more than 99.9999 per cent empty space, and the subatomic particles moving at lightning speed through this space are actually bundles of vibrating energy' (cited in Partridge 2005: 35–6). Quantum physics provides the bridge between energy as vital force and energy as scientific principle: 'Our physical universe is not really composed of any "matter" at all; its basic component is a kind of force or essence which we can call *energy*' (Gawain 1978: 5, original emphasis). It is also used as proof of the deep interconnectedness of all things: 'At the quantum level *no* part of the body lives apart from the rest' (Chopra 2001: 14).

Arguments for holism find a second avenue for scientific legitimation in the emerging medical science of psychoneuroimmunology (PNI), which takes as its starting point 'the fundamental unity of the organism' (Daruna 2004: 1). PNI focuses on the interplay between the brain/mind and the immune system.

The physiotherapist Carol Davis considers PNI to be 'a foundational challenge to Cartesian separatist thought' – 'the bridge to the coexistence of two paradigms', a possible way to span the 'seemingly uncrossable void' between reductionism and holism (2009: 19–20). Again, this is a two-way street. The popular demand for and usage of CAM therapies is one of the drivers of scientific and biomedical research into new, scientific ways of thinking about biological holism, and is prompting advances in theoretical biology (Hankey 2005).

Other forms of scientific and medical research into the links between brain and body include the new science of neuroplasticity, popularized by Norman Doidge in *The Brain that Changes Itself* (2008). The science of neuroplasticity examines the ability of the brain to 'rewire itself' in response to changed circumstances – most easily in childhood, but even in adults to a much greater extent than was once believed. Cultural practice, it is now recognized, changes the structure of the brain, and this goes for 'every sustained activity ever mapped', including not just physical activities but also 'learning, thinking and imagining' (2008: 288). Thus, neuroplasticity has been used to provide an explanation for the effect of emotions and thoughts on bodily states and health, providing, in effect, a modern brain-based explanation for phenomena that are accounted for in energetic theories as a trickle-down process in which illness is understood as a 'distortion' transmitted gradually through all seven auric bodies before finally manifesting in the physical body (Brennan 1988: 141ff.). Given that this energetic body is, as I have noted, often popularized in dualistic form (as a mind-over-matter orthodoxy), it resembles all the more the neuroplastic account of the impact of thoughts and feelings on embodiment. This bridge between popular culture and science was one of the features that made Doidge's book popular. A review in the *New York Times* (reproduced on the book's cover) declared that the book 'straddles the gap' between science and self-help and that it marks the moment when 'the power of positive thinking finally gains scientific credibility' (Zuger 2007).

A fourth bridging science is epigenetics, the fledgling science of the interactions between genes and the environment. The discovery that genes are switched on and off, including in response to environmental conditions, pollutants and so on, but also to stress, emotion and possibly even thoughts (BBC 2006; Rothstein *et al.* 2009; Church 2007), is beginning to prove a conceptual goldmine for New Age/alternative health advocates. The prospect that 'our genes dance with our awareness' (Church 2007: 32) has opened up the possibility that repeated thoughts and feeling states alter not only our brain but even our genes, and thus have potentially transgenerational effects. For Dawson Church, this understanding is the beginning of a 'new biology of intention':

> scientists are discovering the precise pathways by which changes in human consciousness produce changes in human bodies. As we think our thoughts and feel our feelings, our bodies respond with a complex array of shifts. Each thought or feeling unleashes a particular cascade of biochemicals in our organs. Each experience triggers genetic changes in our cells.
>
> (2007: 25)

Cyndi Dale explicitly links this to subtle anatomy. She claims that the science of subtle energy fields is able to deepen and enrich research into epigenetics, asserting that subtle energy fields, channels and bodies provide information for the epigenomes' (2009: 44).[8] Here, then, is yet another mechanism for explaining the influence of thoughts and feelings. In sum, a range of new scientific fields enable advocates of energetic embodiment and medicine to assert the legitimacy of both a 'new' theory of materiality and a new, scientific holism in which all levels of bodily being are in communication: 'Beliefs become biology – in our hormonal, neural, genetic, and electromagnetic systems plus all the complex interactions between them' (cited in Church 2007: 33).

These connections between various branches of contemporary science and popular, esoteric, or technical accounts of the energetic body occur in part through the actions of particular figures who in one way or another manage to span or traverse boundaries between different knowledge systems or fields of practice. The diverse CAM field is full of such figures (see Barcan 2011): a yoga master who is also a molecular biologist and practising physiotherapist (Simon Borg-Olivier); an oncologist who uses Tibetan crystal bowls (Gaynor Mitchell); a medical doctor, Ayurvedic practitioner and New Age figure (Deepak Chopra). Some of these boundary-crossings are really quite remarkable: Mona Lisa Schulz, for example, is a medical doctor with a PhD in behavioural neuroscience who practises as a medical intuitive[9] and has become a well-known figure in the US and beyond. Barbara Brennan is a mechanical engineer who was a NASA physicist and now, like Schulz, works as an energy healer and medical intuitive. The medical intuitive Caroline Myss has a long-standing professional partnership with the physician Norman Shealy. Such cross-over figures appeal to many a contemporary mind desperately seeking synthesis among the welter of competing belief systems that characterize postmodernity.

This desire for synthesis is not, however, purely postmodern, but a structural feature of modernity itself, which ushered in deep oppositions: between the modern and the traditional, science and religion, and medicine and religion, to name just three. It is hardly surprising, then, to read the Theosophist G. R. S. Mead claiming as early as 1919 that the modern scientific research of his day would gradually reveal the subtle-body notion to be 'a fertile working hypothesis to co-ordinate a considerable number of the mental, vital and physical phenomena of human personality which otherwise remain on our hands as a confused and inexplicable conglomerate' (1967: 1–2).

The persistence of the idea that science is on the cusp of proving the correctness of subtle anatomy hints, perhaps, that it is underpinned by a structure of desire and fantasy with quite enduring qualities. The subtle body is, it seems, more than just culturally *plausible*; for many people, it is desirable and attractive. So in the next section, I consider not just why people *can* find subtle anatomy to be true, but also why people might *want* it to be true. With what desires, fantasies and pleasures is it bound up?

## The attractiveness of the subtle-body model

To open out this question I want to touch on a discussion of ideology by the film critic Robert Ray. Drawing on the anthropologist Claude Lévi-Strauss's conception of myth as a symbolic way of reconciling oppositions, Ray argues that classic Hollywood cinema functioned to overcome dichotomies (1985: 58), using a 'reconciliatory pattern' (57) that was deeply ideological in its disavowal of ideology (61). This, he claims, was a classic pattern of American mythology: 'the denial of the necessity for choice' (63). Ideology, like myth, was a way of symbolically reconciling contradictory beliefs or traditions, while seeming not to do so, and this is a large part of its power to please and reassure. Myth allows us to have it both ways, and to remain blithely unaware of the contradictions. Cinema is, as Ray demonstrates, a powerful mythic vehicle; so too is the body. Indeed, the sociologist Bryan Turner claims that the body is 'the dominant means by which the tensions and crises of societies are thematized' (1992: 12). Extending this, it is also a potential vehicle for the symbolic *reconciliation* of these tensions.

The pleasure and reassurance involved in the reconciliation of contradictions and paradoxes provides a useful lens through which to consider the subtle-body model. What contemporary contradictions does it seemingly resolve? What gaps does it seem to close, what reconciliations does it allow? How might it satisfy a deep-seated cultural longing for wholeness? In asking this question, I am positing wholeness as simultaneously an ideological mechanism, an object of desire and a cultural fantasy. But it is also, of course, a key *theme* in New Age/alternative discourse and thought. In that sense, then, holism is both a mechanism of thought (a desire or fantasy) and an object of thought (a consciously held principle). In making this account of the subtle body as a vehicle for the reconciliation of opposites, it is interesting to note again that earlier writers saw it similarly. Mead understood subtle embodiment as a kind of mediator – a reconciliation of philosophical opposites like realism and idealism, matter and spirit (1967: 2).

Today, the subtle body continues to act as a bridge between a number of oppositions that are deeply resonant in the contemporary West. Its mythic work is the symbolic reconciliation of many of the foundational ruptures ushered in by modernity. First, it enables a reconciliation of the present with the past – it is both a 'new' body model (having been popularized in the contemporary West only in recent decades) and an ancient one. Alternative health/New Age discourse typically invokes it as an ancient form of wisdom that the West is only now rediscovering. A sense of rupture with the past is one of the hallmarks of modernity: the invention of the traditional is among the 'necessary counterpoints to the invention of the modern' (Stacey 2000: 115). The subtle body can be seen to 'heal' this foundational rupture between past and present, new science and ancient wisdom.

This temporal reconciliation (past with present) is also aligned with a notional spatial one – the subtle-body model is seen to unite 'East' and 'West'. As Jackie Stacey has astutely argued, this mapping of the temporal onto the spatial is a characteristic modern move: 'what the West has lost can be rediscovered elsewhere' (2000: 112). This locating of the Western past in the non-Western present is, she argues, complicit with a host of ideologically and politically loaded fantasies. In particular, it articulates to a 'new fantasy of panhumanity' (125) that has arisen as a result of globalization. This fantasy of the global is underpinned by a 'desire for a dissolution of boundaries' (105) which, according to critics like Stacey, is not a welcome transcendence of differences but rather a philosophy or ideology that preserves and masks dominant economic and social power relations (125). According to this analysis, then, the uptake of the subtle-body model occurs interior to the logic of 'the marketability of the global' (Stacey 2000: 98) – that is, it is bound up in webs of consumerist cultural practices and ideologies of holism and interconnection that allow Westerners the privilege and pleasure of imagining themselves as 'belonging to a global community' (99) but whose economic and cultural logic remains largely one of appropriation.

Another foundational rupture bridged by the subtle body is that between technology and nature, thanks to the rich connotations of the term 'energy', which might equally well describe electricity or *chi*. Connecting technology and nature also aligns with another potential bridge – that between science and various forms of pre-modern knowledge, including magic. For many contemporary scientists and doctors, this bridge between modern science, vitalism, non-Western or pre-modern knowledge systems is much to be feared; it is, precisely, the undoing of all the gains made by modern medicine, a symptom of the contemporary rise of unreason. Dr Arnold S. Relman, editor in chief of the *New England Journal of Medicine*, put that view starkly in a public debate: 'integrating alternative medicine with mainstream medicine would not be an advance but a return to the past, an interruption of the remarkable progress achieved by science-based medicine over the past century' (Relman and Weil 1999: 2122).

Others try to counter such evolutionary thinking, in which modern science supersedes pre-modern knowledge, by refusing the modern rupture between science, mystery and magic, arguing that nonsense has always lain at the centre of the scientific method itself. Marilyn Ferguson's book *The Aquarian Conspiracy*, with its self-consciously modern subtitle (*Personal and Social Transformation in the 1980s*), uses a discussion of Thomas Kuhn and paradigm shifts to argue for the inevitability – indeed the *necessity* – that ex-paradigmatic elements will appear ridiculous. Scientific advances, she notes, occur only because certain individuals are courageous enough to challenge orthodoxy: 'If we stubbornly refuse to look at that which seems magical or incredible, we are in distinguished [scientific] company' (1980: 151). Science is based on ruptures of consensus. She emphasizes this by quoting from a number of modern Western scientists (including, again, quantum physicists such as Niels Bohr) as proof that mystery, magic or nonsense can, in fact, be truth masquerading as folly: 'There is no hope, Bohr said, for any speculation that does not look absurd at first glance' (1980: 151). In similar vein, of an idea by the quantum physicist Werner Heisenberg, Bohr allegedly said: 'It isn't crazy enough to be true' (Ferguson 1980: 151).

This relativizing of reason is another way in which temporal disjunctures are bridged: today's (or tomorrow's) wisdom is yesterday's heresy. Thus, madness and insight, wisdom and folly, nonsense and orthodoxy, the thinkable and the unthinkable are made to function as temporal categories as much as epistemological ones.

I want to close with one final example of a conjoining made possible by the subtle body, one that is particularly important in the context of contemporary consumer culture and that is especially bound up in bodily *practices*: the conjoining of spirituality, medicine and bodily pleasure. While some Westerners first come across the idea of an energetic body through the New Age literature, they are equally if not more likely to encounter subtle anatomy through a set of pleasurable body practices, such as massage, yoga, reiki or meditation. Such practices appeal to those seeking an antidote to the perceived ills of modernity, providing experiences of holism instead of segmentism, silence instead of noise, and touch and connection instead of separation. They satisfy late-modern consumers in their promise of a spirituality located in the body rather than in repudiation of it. In the context of mainstream contemporary culture they take shapes that are remote from the asceticism of puritanical religions and compatible with the hedonism of consumerism.

In typical late-modern fashion, the search for meaning meshes with the desire for pleasure. These pleasures may be encountered as a rarity – the exceptional moment of transcendence, peace or exquisite sensory pleasure (e.g. the transformative meditation or the treat of having a massage) – or they may be patterned more regularly into the everyday (e.g. the weekly yoga class). Either way, they embody and seem to reconcile many of the paradoxes that typify modernity, while giving free rein to all its current characteristic expectations, desires, aspirations and pleasures – the right to choose, the right to know, the right to see, have and buy, the right to happiness, the fight against mortality, and the model of the individual as goal-setting, rights-holding and pleasure-seeking. In their current formation, these practices are, then, a mythic performance in a bodily register, allowing us seemingly to have it all without contradiction. This hope for wholeness and restoration is, to adapt an argument from John Frow, a 'myth of resurrection' (1995: 97).[10]

If it is true that the body is, in Turner's words, 'the principal field of political and cultural activity' in late-modern, 'somatic' societies (1992: 12), then the rise of practices predicated on and conducive to new experiences of embodiment and the uptake among a sizeable constituency of a new model of the body are phenomena of some significance. The contention of many cultural theorists that the dominant image of the body is dematerializing needs to be rethought somewhat in order to recognize the increasing number of people who seek to use the body as a means of *countering* experiences of fragmentation, alienation and rupture. Fragmentation and the search for holism are, of course, two sides of the same coin: the more we think of ourselves as dispersed across space, the more we might seek bodily experiences that bring us back into a more grounded experience of the body. The subtle body thus speaks both to our passion for the virtual and our pleasure in rootedness. That Westerners' sense of wholeness and ground-edness relies all too often on 'the incorporation of the other' (Frow 1995: 97) is a significant political fact. Any serious study of the changing body models and practices of the modern West needs to be able to bridge this unpleasant political reality with that of the undoubted pleasures and consolations this groundedness can bring to individuals. Such a difficult bridging act is needed to help bring greater understanding and equity to the potential futures of subtle embodiment.

## Notes

1  I use this term, politically and conceptually problematic though it is, both as a short-hand and because its fantastical and ideological dimensions are, in fact, part of the phenomenon I am exploring in this chapter. Henceforth, it is written without scare quotation marks, but the term is not to be understood unproblematically.
2  Mayor (2009: 15) dates the translation to the 1920s, when acupuncture surfaced in Europe. Even at the time, he says, there were concerns about the adequacy of the trans-lation. *Chi* is, he says, neither substance nor energy nor even matter-energy.
3  Hanegraaff claims that the Theosophical Society took up 'Eastern' conceptions of the subtle body at one remove (1998: 455). Moreover, their uptake of concepts from Buddhism and Hinduism was, he claims, selective and eclectic.
4  Mead accuses the alchemists of having so deliberately obfuscated their knowledge practices that their underlying doctrines were lost to the West in a 'fog of misconception' (1967: 17).
5  Despite the similarities, there are also significant differences between Freudian theories of repression and New Age metaphysical accounts of illness (see Stacey 1997: 112–21).
6  Though it is beyond the scope of this chapter, it is also important to note that it appears in shadowy form in some currents of twentieth-century Western philosophy (Johnston 2008; Johnston and Barcan 2006). The feminist philosopher Elizabeth Grosz suggests that the phenomenological concept of the body image can be considered a modern descendant of the subtle body (1994: 62–3).
7  Interestingly, early in the twentieth century the Theosophist G. R. S. Mead, in his study of the history the subtle-body doctrine in the West, was keen to distinguish nuanced accounts of the subtle body from what he saw as cruder dualistic forms, which he associated with 'primitives' (1967: 4).
8  Dale defines epigenomes as 'the chemicals and switches that instruct the genes' (2009: 43).
9  A medical intuitive is a term for a healer who uses intuition – clairvoyance – to diagnose health or medical issues.
10  Frow's argument refers to the global trade in body parts, in which those privileged enough to afford organ transplants can indulge a fantasy of restoration that requires the unequal participation of less fortunate others.

## References

Albanese, C. L. (2007) *A Republic of Mind and Spirit: A Cultural History of American Metaphysical Religion*. New Haven, CT: Yale University Press.
Barcan, R. (2009) 'Intuition and reason in the New Age: a cultural study of medical clair-voyance', in D. Howes (ed.) *The Sixth Sense Reader*. Oxford: Berg.

—— (2011) *Complementary and Alternative Medicine: Bodies, Therapies, Senses*. Oxford: Berg.

Basil, R. (1988) 'Introduction', in R. Basil (ed.) *Not Necessarily the New Age: Critical Essays*. Buffalo: Prometheus.

BBC (2006) 'The Ghost in your Genes', *Horizon*, television programme dir. N. Paterson. London: BBC Worldwide Ltd.

Brennan, B. A. (1988) *Hands of Light: A Guide to Healing Through the Human Energy Field: A New Paradigm for the Human Being in Health, Relationship, and Disease*. Toronto: Bantam.

Campbell, C. (2007) *The Easternization of the West: A Thematic Account of Cultural Change in the Modern Era*. Boulder, CO: Paradigm.

Carrette, J. and King, R. (2005) *Selling Spirituality: The Silent Takeover of Religion*. Abingdon: Routledge.

Chopra, D. (1989) *Quantum Healing: Exploring the Frontiers of Mind/Body Medicine*. New York: Bantam.

—— (2001) *Perfect Health: The Complete Mind Body Guide*, revised edn. Sydney: Bantam.

Church, D. (2007) *The Genie in Your Genes: Epigenetic Medicine and the New Biology of Intention*. Santa Rosa, CA: Elite Books.

Dale, C. (2009) *The Subtle Body: An Encyclopedia of Your Energetic Anatomy*. Boulder, CO: Sounds True.

Daruna, J. H. (2004) *Introduction to Psychoneuroimmunology*. Amsterdam: Elsevier Academic Press.

Davis, C. (2009) 'Psychoneuroimmunology: the bridge to the coexistence of two paradigms', in C. Davis (ed.) *Contemporary Therapies in Rehabilitation: Evidence for Efficacy in Therapy, Prevention, and Wellness*, 3rd edn. Thorofare, NJ: Slack.

Doidge, N. (2008) *The Brain that Changes Itself: Stories of Personal Triumph from the Frontiers of Brain Science*. Carlton North, Vic.: Scribe Publications.

Douglas, M. (1984 [1966]) *Purity and Danger: An Analysis of the Concepts of Pollution and Taboo*. London: Ark Paperbacks.

Fadlon, J. (2004) 'Meridians, chakras and psycho-neuro-immunology: the dematerializing body and the domestication of alternative medicine', *Body and Society* 10(4): 69–86.

Ferguson, M. (1980) *The Aquarian Conspiracy: Personal and Social Transformation in the 1980s*. Los Angeles: J. P. Tarcher.

Frow, J. (1995) 'Private parts: body organs in global trade', *UTS Review* 1(2): 84–100.

Gawain, S. (1978) *Creative Visualization*. New York: Bantam.

Grosz, E. (1994) *Volatile Bodies: Towards a Corporeal Feminism*. St Leonards: Allen & Unwin.

Hanegraaff, W. J. (1998) *New Age Religion and Western Culture: Esotericism in the Mirror of Secular Thought*. Albany: State University of New York Press.

Hankey, A. (2005) 'CAM modalities can stimulate advances in theoretical biology', *Evidence-based Complementary and Alternative Medicine* 2(1): 5–12.

Hay, L. L. (1987) *You Can Heal Your Life*. Concord: Specialist Printing.

Heelas, P., Woodhead, L. *et al.* (2005) *The Spiritual Revolution: Why Religion is Giving Way to Spirituality*. Malden, MA: Blackwell.

Hurwitz, W. L. (2001) 'Energy medicine', in M. S. Micozzi (ed.) *Fundamentals of Complementary and Alternative Medicine*, 2nd edn. Philadelphia: Churchill Livingstone.

Institute of Medicine of the National Academies (2005) *Complementary and Alternative Medicine in the United States*. Washington, DC: National Academies Press.

Johnston, J. (2008) *Angels of Desire: Esoteric Bodies, Aesthetics and Ethics*. London: Equinox.

Johnston, J. and Barcan, R. (2006) 'Subtle transformations: imagining the body in alternative health practices', *International Journal of Cultural Studies* 9(1): 25–44.

Kaptchuk, T. J. (2001) 'History of vitalism', in M. S. Micozzi (ed.) *Fundamentals of Complementary and Alternative Medicine*, 2nd edn. Philadelphia: Churchill Livingstone.

Kroker, A. and Kroker, M. (1988) *Body Invaders: Sexuality and the Postmodern Condition*. Basingstoke: Macmillan Education.

Martin, E. (1992) 'The end of the body?', *American Ethnologist* 19(1): 121–40.

Mayor, D. (2009) 'Reinterpreting *qi* in the 21st century', *European Journal of Oriental Medicine* 6(2): 12–20.

Mead, G. R. S. (1967 [1919]) *The Doctrine of the Subtle Body in Western Tradition: An Outline of What the Philosophers Thought and Christians Taught on the Subject*. London: Stuart and Watkins.

Melton, J. G. (1988) 'A history of the New Age movement', in R. Basil (ed.) *Not Necessarily the New Age: Critical Essays*. Buffalo: Prometheus.

Merleau-Ponty, M. (1962) *The Phenomenology of Perception*, trans. C. Smith. London: Routledge.

Partridge, C. H. (2005) *The Re-Enchantment of the West: Alternative Spiritualities, Sacralization, Popular Culture, and Occulture*. London: T & T Clark International.

Paterson, M. (2006) 'Feel the presence: technologies of touch and distance', *Environment and Planning D: Society and Space* 24: 691–708.

Ray, R. B. (1985) *A Certain Tendency of the Hollywood Cinema, 1930–1980*. Princeton, NJ: Princeton University Press.

Relman, A. S. and Weil, A. (1999) 'Is integrative medicine the medicine of the future? A debate between Arnold S. Relman, MD, and Andrew Weil, MD', *Archives of Internal Medicine* 159, 11 October: 2122–6.

Rothstein, M. A., Cai, Y. and Marchant, G. E. (2009) 'The ghost in our genes: legal and ethical implications of epigenetics', *Health Matrix* 19(1): 1+ *LegalTrac*. Web. 23 June 2010.

Stacey, J. (1997) *Teratologies: A Cultural Study of Cancer*. London: Routledge.

—— (2000) 'The global within', in S. Franklin, C. Lury and J. Stacey (eds) *Global Nature, Global Culture*. London: Sage.

Turner, B. S. (1992) *Regulating Bodies: Essays in Medical Sociology*. London: Routledge.

Zuger, A. (2007) 'The brain: malleable, capable, vulnerable', review of Norman Doidge, *The Brain that Changes Itself*, *New York Times*, 29 May. Online at: www.nytimes.com/2007/05/29/health/29book.html?_r=1 (accessed 23 September 2010).

# 13 Subtle subjects and ethics

## The subtle bodies of post-structuralist and feminist philosophy

*Jay Johnston*

> For materiality is always something more than 'mere' matter: an excess of force, vitality, relationality, or difference that renders matter active, self-creative, productive, unpredictable.
>
> (Coole and Frost 2010: 9)

Dynamic subtle bodies can be found in numerous discourses and activities of Western popular culture: perhaps most noticeably in Complementary and Alternative Medicine (CAM) (Barcan 2011), New Age and self-directed spiritual practices. However, their nebulous form can also be glimpsed in contemporary philosophical discourse. Examples include conceptualizations of intersubjectivity that have drawn on Bergsonian and phenomenological ideas of matter and consciousness, and may also be found in feminist philosophy of religion, particularly where a Buddhist concept of non-duality to rethinking has been applied to rethinking the sharp matter–consciousness dualisms upon which dominant Western philosophical categories are founded. Further, the recent 'turn' and interest in 'new matter' (e.g. Coole and Frost 2010; Bennett 2010) has taken these issues into more 'mainstream' academic spheres (especially cultural studies, human ecology and political science), proposing a rethinking and reformulation of 'matter' that is strongly analogous to the variety of ways in which subtle matter (as the ontological constituent of subtle bodies) has been formulated, especially in the – historically less credible – esoteric discourses (Johnston 2008). This chapter traces significant antecedents to this now prevalent and popular questioning of materiality and its agency, and details selected concepts proposed by Gilles Deleuze, Félix Guattari and Luce Irigaray that provide analogous forms of 'body' and 'self'. Further, to close, the chapter considers the way in which feminist Buddhist scholars have incorporated such concepts in their exploration of gender and embodiment.

It will be proposed herein that subtle-body forms of subjectivity (referred to as the subtle subject) are a radical form of intersubjectivity that implicitly renegotiates the dualisms of normative Western discourse. These dualisms include the perennially thorny debates of mind–body relations as well as those of self–divine and I–Other. These pairs build upon a foundational matter–consciousness division, and my argument here is that subtle subjectivity undermines such dualisms in exciting and seditious ways. In short, subtle bodies constitute a radical form of intersubjectivity; a conceptualization that renders some of the most expansive philosophical propositions about the nature of subjectivity to appear tame in comparison.

## Ontological matter–consciousness: tracing a conceptual heritage

Contemporary propositions regarding subtle bodies have been clearly influenced by the version of the subtle body developed by the Theosophical Society's members in the late nineteenth and early twentieth centuries (Johnston 2008; Barcan 2011). A feature of these Theosophical schemas was the melding of ideas from the Western Esoteric tradition (for an overview of the corpus see Faivre 1994; Stuckrad 2005) and those found in Yogic and Tantra traditions (see the chapters in Parts One and Two of this volume). Most certainly the Theosophists borrowed Sanskrit nomenclature even if the degree of direct conceptual influence of the traditions from Asia is debated (Hanegraaff 1998: 454). Theosophical subtle bodies were deeply interwoven with their cosmology and ideas of spiritual evolution, as rigorously detailed by Blavatsky in *Isis Unveiled* (1877) and *The Secret Doctrine* (1888). As extended aspects of the self, these ephemeral and energetic bodies linked the physical world to the most refined realm of spirit (and to the five other levels proposed to range in between: seven 'planes of perception' and subtle bodies in total), making the individual an embodied bridge between 'gross' matter and 'refined' spirit (or consciousness). Individuals via their subtle bodies comprised varying degrees of matter–consciousness/spirit and their spiritual development was tied to the refinement and apprehension of this subtle substance. Significantly, even 'gross' matter – or physical materiality – was understood, ontologically, to be composed of subtle matter; it was just a denser manifestation, that 'vibrated' at a slower pace. Indeed, in Theosophical schemas the seven subtle bodies that interpenetrated one another in the physical realm were differentiated by their texture and rate of vibration, not by any ontological difference.

The physical body and the 'highest' body of 'pure' spirit were posited as different only in the activity and density of their substance, not in the *kind* of substance of which they were considered to be comprised. Their difference could be characterized, as in the now well-known maxim of the French philosopher Henri Bergson (1859–1941), as a difference in degree, not in kind. Bergson proposed a specific concept of time – *durée* – as ontological (and also as a type of consciousness; 1996: 235) and this was not clearly demarcated from matter in his system. In Theosophical discourse we also find 'matter–consciousness': an animated, processural and ontological 'substance' designated as the constituent of physical as well as subtle bodies.

In passing it should be noted that the figure of Henri Bergson also evokes another type of 'boundary' inquiry located between empirical science and spiritual experience, that of parapsychology. A much maligned 'science', its ambit is the study of experiences that cannot be explained in terms of direct causality by scientific knowledge. The existence and effects of subtle bodies – and the extra-sensory perception required to apprehend them – would therefore be a suitable object for its study. Henri Bergson played a very public role in the parapsychology organizations of his day, including acting as President of the Society for Psychical Research in Cambridge. This was a brave position, considering that even in the early twentieth century parapsychology was far from being an accepted research area, with many scholars avoiding association with its institutes for fear of damage to their credibility and reputation (Grogin 1988: 44–5). Such associations have enabled readings of Bergson's philosophical work as both critiquing materialist forms of science and promoting a form of vitalism (*élan vital*), as well as championing epistemologies other than those of reason, for example intuition. Indeed, as I have noted elsewhere, Bergson was no stranger to the agendas of modern occult groups as his sister was married to a most notorious leader of the Hermetic Order of the Golden Dawn, Samuel MacGregor Matthews (Grogin 1988: 75; Johnston 2008: 57). Grogin comments in relation to Bergson that

> from his highly influential chair at the Collège de France he was uniquely positioned to lead the attack against mechanistic science and to transmit occult ideas on mysticism and vitalism to the public at large. From this platform of respectability Bergson could transmit those ideas to the public in terms that carried prestige ...
>
> (1988: 98)

The concept of matter–consciousness that Bergson proposed in his philosophical texts, most notably *Matter and Memory* (1896), presented close conceptual analogies to the type of ontological framework that supports the Theosophical concepts of subtle bodies. For Bergson, pure matter and pure spirit are idealized states (virtual), between which is a lived continuum of mutually imbricated matter–consciousness (actual). This conceptualization was to furnish one of the most influential contemporary post-structural propositions of intersubjectivity, the Body Without Organs (BwO) proposed by Gilles Deleuze and Felix Guattari.

## Bodies without organs and matter beyond flesh: intersubjectivity and subtle subjectivity

Intersubjectivity is a term employed to signal the deep mutual imbrication of subjects. Philosophically, the work of Emmanual Levinas is often given as an exemplar of this type of relationality considered from an ontological perspective. For Levinas the I and the Other were (ontologically) mutually interdependent: indeed the Other called the I into being, hence ethics as first philosophy (1974). As can be seen in the discussion below, Luce Irigaray applies Levinas' idea of this ontological relation in her own interpretation of metaphysics and subtle substance. At a very basic level, the concept of intersubjectivity challenges a 'modernist' self: that is, the concept of an individual singular 'I' that is entirely self-sustaining. Intersubjectivity emphasizes the profoundly interrelated – onto-logically, materially, politically – nature of being. Deleuze and Guattari's inter-subjective propositions have been vastly influential in contemporary Continental philosophy, cultural studies and related fields. One particular 'schema' is the BwO that seems to hold – with its base in Bergsonian ontology – strong corollaries with subtle-body concepts of embodiment:

> Not man [*sic*] as the king of creation, but rather as the being who is in intimate contact with the profound life of all forms or all types of beings, who is responsible for even the stars and animal life, and who ceaselessly plugs an organ-machine into an energy-machine.
>
> (1983: 4)

Deleuze and Guattari proposed a radically extensive form of subjectivity that exceeded organic form (like subtle bodies): the Body without Organs. This subjectivity was made from a type of ontological desire, which was mobilized through the ceaseless relations that constituted the self. The ontological, productive 'desire' of which it is comprised is presented as drawn from 'the field of imma-nence': a 'plane of consistency'. Although debates about this terminology are lengthy, the 'field of immanence' can perhaps be considered as akin to the Buddhist concept of co-dependent arising (*pratītya–samutpāda*). Its nature is that of immanence and its existence cannot be derived from any eternal or universal substance. Indeed, it is to the *Tao* that Deleuze and Guattari turn in *A Thousand Plateaus* to explicate the nature and operations of 'the field of immanence' (1987: 156–7).[1] Crucial to thinking about its relation to concepts of the subtle body is the way in which it is conceived of as both an ontological stratum *and* an actual constituent of subjectivity. As an ontological stratum, the 'field of immanence' resembles the Theosophical 'planes of perception', and indeed, in *A Thousand Plateaus* the BwO is presented as comprising several plateaus ('A plateau is a piece of immanence'; 1987: 158).

The type of subjectivity proposed by Deleuze and Guattari as a BwO is also akin to that associated with subtle-body concepts. It is highly processural, 'disem-bodied' (in a narrow corporeal sense) and, always, intimately interrelated with the wider cosmos. The BwO is featured for its role as 'passage' (although there is no transcendent aim as in Theosophical subtle bodies): it puts different 'plateaus' in relation to one another while simultaneously being composed of them (1987: 158). In contradistinction to Theosophical subtle bodies, however, Deleuze and Guattari's BwO resists schematization: indeed, this resistance is its very concep-tual reason to be. The BwO is a concept of self – of subjectivity that resists not organs *per se* but organization, it is not 'opposed to organs but to that organiza-tion of the organs called the organism' (1987: 399). Here is an emphasis on the ontological capacity of productivity, of dynamic exchange, of relation rather than on a body defined by its material (in narrow sense) organization.

While subtle-body schemas extend the boundaries of the self in similar elusive, productive, dynamic and relational ways, their articulation in a range of discourses ties them to often intricate, but fixed, pathways and plans. *Cakras* and *nadis* are plotted in relation to, within and alongside the corporeal organism. The BwO is more anarchic; it resists a tabulation of its dynamism, yet its forces and fluxes are not in this particular conceptualization subject to the perceptive cultivation that is a feature of both Eastern and esoteric forms of the subtle body. When Luce Irigaray takes up radical, processural intersubjectivity this crucial role of perception is more centrally figured.[2]

## Dual subjectivity and subtle bodies

While Deleuze and Guatarri's subjects are radically multiplicitous, Luce Irigaray's work on dual subjectivity in the text *To Be Two* (2000) presents a critique of the singular ontology of Western philosophy with the proposition of a *dual* subjectivity. It is in the exchanges between the dual (two) subjects of onto-logical difference that the subtle body as a form of subjectivity can be glimpsed. The subtle body is taken up more directly in her following book, *Between East and West: From Singularity to Community* (2002), in which Irigaray discusses her own yoga practice and understanding of Yogic philosophy. In *To Be Two* a subtle-body form of embodiment seems to comprise, and indeed enable, the rela-tions between the two subjects of sexual difference she proposes: 'Each, faithful to him or herself, would bring to the other his or her own energy and his or her manner of cultivating it' (2000: 55), without her making any direct reference to 'Eastern' philosophy–religion.

Ontology is *dual* (not singular) for Irigaray; but this dualism is an intersubjec-tivity with each subject of radical difference being intimately intertwined with one another: ceaselessly slipping and permeating the boundaries of individual subjectivity.

> To be two would allow us to remain in ourselves, and would permit gather-ing ... neither mine nor yours but each living and breathing with the other. I would refrain from possessing you in order to allow you to be – to be in me, as well.
>
> (2000: 16)

Following Levinas, Irigaray proposes that this ontological intersubjectivity – the relation between dual subjects – is the 'space' in which both are cultivated, and in which both come into being (see further Johnston 2008: 11–13). Although each of these subjects is understood as radically different (alterity) from one another, and gendered using a dimorphic model, the intimate, ephemeral, 'energetic' exchanges that take place between them enable becoming.[3] In this way difference (the radical difference between the I and the Other) is presented as enabling inter-subjectivity, rather than delineating the boundaries of the single, individual subject. This is an ontologizing of difference that is also a characteristic of the work of Gilles Deleuze. Therefore, Irigaray's concept of dual subjectivity is premised upon a relational ontology: each subject calls one another into being and shares to a certain degree interrelated ontological 'matter'. It is in the conceptualization of this 'matter' (matter–consciousness) that one meets corollaries with subtle bodies.

Subjectivity for Irigaray is implicitly tied to the lived body (phenomenological) and, considering her earlier work on feminine subjectivity, it is also, always, gendered. She has drawn sharp criticism for being essentialist in her attitude towards feminine subjectivity, although counter-readings also refute such charges from a philosophical basis (Chanter 1995). In proposing dual subjectivity, Irigaray suggests that the gender difference is played out not in terms of corporeal attributes or socio-cultural construction but by an ontological *energy*. This is an irreducible substance that cannot readily be perceived by the five senses. Termed an 'irreducible invisible' by Irigaray, this aspect of alterity, while always slipping beyond full comprehension, can be known, recognized and respected. Therefore, her call for individuals to become aware of this intersubjective, interrelating substance via perception finds parallels with Eastern body–mind cultivation practices – such as breathing techniques and meditation practice – that are employed to bring to conscious awareness one's own subtle matter–consciousness. Such practices are not advocated or referenced by Irigaray in *To Be Two*, but the cultivation of the breath is a focus of *Between East and West*. However, the ability to apprehend subtle aspects of another's subjectivity is central to the relations of dual subjectivity that Irigaray is proposing in *To Be Two*. These are relations that are founded on the presumption that one can develop an awareness of one's own subtle bodies and an apprehension of the dynamics of another subject's subtle energy: 'the other, because he is not mine, remains mobile in me, an energy tied to him but free between us: an energy linked by an inclination and by a "not"' (2000: 52).

## The between: ethics and the subtle body

The 'space' between each dual subject is for Irigaray where relations of radical difference are played out: 'the absolutely inaccessible other is, above all, here and now between us' (2000: 43). There is attributed to both subjects a 'mystery' (radical difference) that will always slip beyond full comprehension, but can at least be glimpsed. It is an intersubjective mystery, which is presented as constitutive of both self and other and enables connection between the dual subjects. The mystery is figured by Irigaray as an energetic dynamic, in the same way that subtle bodies are distinguished by their quality of energy, their dynamism. The perception of both is slippery and elusive:

> The between Irigaray advocates is an idealized 'pure' space. As previously noted, the dual subjectivity model of intersubjectivity she proposes is based on the cultivation of energy: energy emanating from bodies, and constitutive of self and other and their relation/interrelation. Even though this energy is

presented as inhabiting the between, but emanating from individuals, it is presented by Irigaray as distinguished from previous experience. The energy understood to 'be in' the space between is constructed as *tabula rasa*.

(Johnston 2008: 93)

This 'blank' space of energetic exchange is problematic. For unlike Deleuze and Guattari's BwO, these two energetic subjects of ontological difference do not interact with any other subtle forces: environmental, cosmological, or socio-cultural. Irigaray denies such phenomena an energetic dynamic. This third space, the 'between' of Irigaray's dual subjects, is troubling, and not in particularly productive ways, unless it is attributed an 'agency' of its own that is simultane-ously both of and not of dual subjectivity. This is especially important, considering that it is in this 'between' space that Irigaray figures potential transcendence, what she terms a 'horizontal transcendence' affected by the (energetic) perception of radical alterity (which for her is a radically other subject of sexual difference). This subject is one that is both embodied and disembodied.

## Western feminist Buddhism: sexual difference and subtle bodies

In very general terms, the experience of embodied transcendence (relations between subjects with subtle bodies), in the sense of a meeting with radical alterity (including divinity), is a feature of Hindu and Buddhist Tantric traditions. These traditions include practices for the mutual co-cultivation of a couple's subtle bodies. Within these practices, the relation between each subject can be considered as analogous to Irigaray's relation of 'horizontal transcendence'. This final section discusses two Western feminist Buddhist interpretations of the way in which ontologies of the subtle body refigure the sexual difference relation. The shift is from a relation of binary opposition to one of non-oppositional difference.

In *Buddhism After Patriarchy: A Feminist History, Analysis, and Reconstruction of Buddhism* (1993) Rita M. Gross identifies the Vajrayāna Buddhist tradition as centrally concerned with gender relations. However, she emphasizes that this is not a clearly dimorphic and oppositional relation. Indeed, she perceives relations between masculine and feminine as 'distinctive complements' within a non-dual matrix' (1993: 199). For Gross, masculine and feminine are not distinct subject positions or definitive gender ascriptions, but rather are 'principles' that all subjects – whatever their gender identity – work to develop through various culti-vation techniques in Tantric practice. Gross argues:

> Women and men both equally strive to develop both wisdom and compas-sion, accommodation and activity. An enlightened being will manifest both qualities and enlightenment is not different in a man or a woman. Therefore, it would be ludicrous to claim that women will be more spacious, men more active, in their enlightened manifestation. On the path, men and women both

are given practices including visualizations, in which they identify with both
the feminine and the masculine principles, and with both simultaneously.

(1993: 202)

While Gross does employ a dimorphic sense of subjectivity in the above
quotation – 'women and men' could be interpreted as gender stereotypes – her
overall argument regarding Tantric practice is that central to the practice itself is
a respect for gender difference and a commitment to learning about the Other.
Accompanying this is an exploration of the role that the breath/energy (subtle
matter–consciousness) plays in such intersubjective exchange. She argues that
phenomena of the work can be both *specific* and interrelated, and that part of
recognizing this is becoming aware of the activity of 'space' and emphasizing
relation of non-duality (1993: 203).

Gender relations of non-duality are built upon the Buddhist Two Truths
perspective. One truth would be gender difference and distinction; the simultaneous
other truth, the undermining of any stable or 'fixed' ontological category, principle
or characteristic (i.e. gender, like any other category, is void of any self-sufficient
'substance'). In Tantric relations as Gross interprets them, women and men are
not positioned in relations of sharp opposition, even though difference and
distinction are recognized and acknowledged. A Tantric framework allows Gross
to posit that such gender differences exist in a 'non-dual' framework (*śūnyatā*).
In turn, as an integral aspect of subjectivity these differences, as cultivated
through interpersonal relations in Tantric practice, enable embodied practitioners
to cultivate (co-cultivate) their subtle bodies.

This emphasis on the process of perceptive cultivation is also key to Anne
Carolyn Klein, scholar and practitioner of Tibetan Buddhism. For Klein, it is the
practice of Mindfulness that provides a 'third' way of thinking about subjectivity
(rather than just as either constructivist or essentialist: the two dominant positions
in much Western discourse):

> Mindfulness facilitates a centredness and internal coherence akin to 'essen-
> tialist' forms of strength and at the same time is compatible with construc-
> tionist or postmodern sensibilities because of its intense awareness of the
> flow that constitutes mind and body, including itself. In this way, mindfulness
> and its associated states can ameliorate the tension between essentialist and
> postmodern perspectives in feminist contexts. Buddhist theories and prac-
> tices envision a subject for whom groundedness and a sense of the constructed
> nature of self can be simultaneous, so that there is never a necessity to 'choose'
> strategically between them. There is a place and possibility for both.
>
> (1995: 68–69)

Here are elements of a recognition of a radical difference (alterity) existing
between subjects as well as an intersubjectivity: the fluxes and flows that constitute, for example, Deleuze and Guattari's BwO or Irigaray's 'horizontal' relations
between subjects of ontological difference. Both positions as articulated by Klein

place emphasis on the body and its perceptive capacities as central to subjectivity. The cultivation between subjects, from these energetic and perceptive foundations, can be considered as a mutual cultivation of subtle subjects. Although this may take into account the more ephemeral, 'energetic' subtle-body attributes of an individual, it in no way ignores their lived, fleshy, phenomenological reality; indeed, their corporeality is integral to the process.

## Conclusion

While the last section has just touched upon one way in which feminist scholars of Buddhism have considered post-structural forms of subjectivity in relation to Buddhist practice, it has hopefully been evident that the way in which they think dualisms (I–Other; male–female; matter–consciousness) provides both suitable and insightful models for rethinking the *relations* between terms more usually (in Western epistemology) considered as oppositional. There is a shared concern among these thinkers to acknowledge that the radically different can be respected *and* considered as intimately interrelated with the self (even if it can never fully be known). The concept of subtle bodies, especially as it is being rethought by feminist scholars of religion, provides a concept of matter–consciousness that supports (at an ontological level) these types of intersubjective relations. In characterizing the proposition of 'new materialism', Coole and Frost argue that one of the traits of this 'movement' is 'its antipathy towards oppositional ways of thinking' (2010: 8) and further, that 'it conceives of matter as lively or as exhibiting agency' (2010: 7). The ontological presuppositions of subtle matter–consciousness have been built upon both such traits and, I would argue, have a lot to offer in new materialisms investigation of 'matter'. Indeed, considering the corollaries to post-structuralist and feminist philosophy considered herein, I would conjecture that 'new matter' is subtle matter–consciousness. Subtle bodies by their very proposed constituents evoke ethically complex questions; such questions open out and can potentially reconfigure both dualist logic and the very conceptualization of both matter–consciousness.

## Notes

1 For an extended discussion see Johnston 2008: 136–43.
2 This is not to say that perception does not take a central role in Deleuze and Guattari's work; especially with regard to concepts of affect. See, for example, Deleuze on Francis Bacon (2003 [1981]).
3 'We are irreducible in us, between us and yet so close. Without this difference, how do we give each other grace, how do we see each other, the one in the other?' (Irigaray 2000: 10).

## References

Barcan, R. (2011) *Complementary and Alternative Medicine: Bodies, Therapies, Senses.* London and New York: Berg.

Bennett, J. (2010) *Vibrant Matter: A Political Ecology of Things*. Durham, NC: Duke University Press.

Blavatsky, H. P. (1972 [1877]) *Isis Unveiled: Collected Writings*. London, Adyar and Wheaton: Theosophical Publishing House.

—— (1995 [1888]) *The Secret Doctrine*, electronic book edn. Quezon City: Theosophical Publishing House.

Bergson, H. (1996 [rev. edn 1908]) *Matter and Memory*. New York: Zone Books.

Chanter, T. (1995) *Ethics of Eros: Irigaray's Rewriting of the Philosophers*. New York and London: Routledge.

Coole, D. and S. Frost (2010) 'Introducing new materialisms', in D. Coole and S. Frost (eds) *New Materialisms: Ontology, Agency, Politics*. Durham, NC and London: Duke University Press.

Deleuze, G. (2003 [1981]) *Francis Bacon: The Logic of Sensation*, trans. D. W. Smith. London and New York: Continuum.

Deleuze, G. and Guattari, F. (1983 [1972]) *Anti-Oedipus: Capitalism and Schizophrenia*, trans. R. Hurley, M. Seem and H. R. Lane. Minneapolis: University of Minnesota Press.

—— (1987 [1980]) *A Thousand Plateaus: Capitalism and Schizophrenia*, trans. B. Massumi. London and New York: Verso.

Faivre, A. (1994) *Access to Western Esotericism*. Albany: State University of New York Press.

Grogin, R. C. (1988) *The Bergsonian Controversy in France 1900–1914*. Calgary: University of Calgary Press.

Gross, R. M. (1993) *Buddhism After Patriarchy: A Feminist History, Analysis and Reconstruction of Buddhism*. Albany: State University of New York Press.

Hanegraaff, W. (1998) *New Age Religion and Western Culture: Esotericism in the Mirror of Secular Thought*. Albany: State University of New York Press.

Irigaray, L. (2000) *To Be Two*, trans. M. M. Rhodes and M. F. Cocito-Mondoc. London and New Brunswick: Athlone Press.

—— (2002) *Between East and West: From Singularity to Community*, trans. S. Pluhacek. New York: Columbia University Press.

Johnston, J. (2008) *Angels of Desire: Esoteric Bodies, Aesthetics and Ethics*. London and Oakville, CT: Equinox.

Klein, A. K. (1995) *Meeting the Great Bliss Queen: Buddhists, Feminists, and the Art of the Self*. Boston, MA: Beacon Press.

Levinas, E. (1974) *Autrement qu'être ou au-delà de l'essence*. The Hague: Martinus Nijhoff.

Stuckrad, K. von (2005) *Western Esotericism: A Brief History of Sacred Knowledge*, trans. N. Goodrick-Clarke. London and Oakville, CT: Equinox.

# 14 Subtle-body processes

## Towards a non-reductionist understanding

*Geoffrey Samuel*

As a whole, this book has been concerned with the history of subtle-body concepts and with their social contexts in Asian and Western societies. Much of the discussion in Parts One to Three has necessarily treated subtle-body concepts and practices as somewhat 'exotic' in nature, as relating to people long ago and far away, although a number of chapters, for example those by Janet Chawla (Chapter 3) and Alejandro Chaoul (Chapter 6), raised the issue of what working with the subtle body might mean in a contemporary context. The chapters of Part Four, which explore the role of the subtle body within contemporary European societies, have necessarily made this question more salient, and the previous three chapters have looked explicitly at the interplay between subtle-body practices and contemporary thought. Ruth Barcan explored in Chapter 12 the attractiveness of subtle-body practices in a wide range of contemporary contexts, academic as well as 'New Age'. In Chapter 13, Jay Johnston examined a variety of movements in the contemporary humanities which have developed concepts similar to those associated with the subtle body. The willingness of significant contemporary thinkers to take these concepts seriously suggests that in ignoring the subtle body as a relic of obsolete modes of thought, or as a marginal fantasy of occult and New Age writers, we may be missing something of real value.

The present chapter takes up this possibility, along with Susan Greenwood's suggestion in Chapter 11 that experiences of the non-material realm are not necessarily incompatible with an expanded conception of science. It looks to the social and natural sciences as well as to the humanities for intellectual resources that might illuminate the value of subtle-body concepts and practices. The emphasis on *practices* as well as concepts here is significant. It is often productive to think of the subtle body not merely as a philosophical or religious concept but in terms of what the practices regarding the subtle body are meant to accomplish for those who use them.

As the previous chapters have shown, the various concepts and practices for which we have used the generic label 'subtle body' in this book come in a wide variety of forms. It is difficult to arrive at a clear picture of what might be included within this class, and uncertain perhaps whether it can usefully be considered as a single class. I am most familiar myself with the subtle-body practices associated with Indian and Tibetan Tantra, both Buddhist and Śaiva, and the remarks here apply most centrally to these. Much of what I say also refers to the Chinese tradition of self-cultivation and 'inner alchemy' (*yangsheng, neidan, qigong*, etc.), which has similarities to and possibly also a historical relationship with the Indian and Tibetan material. I exclude Vedantic concepts of the subtle body (the five 'sheaths'; for example, see Chapter 2), although many of my suggestions probably apply to them as well. I am not familiar enough with Neoplatonic and Sufi subtle-body concepts to comment on them in detail. As for Theosophy and the New Age, there are obvious historical derivations to Indic and East Asian material, and much of my analysis may well apply in this area. From a methodological point of view, however, it is probably better to exclude these from an initial approach to the material, since, as John Bramble demonstrated in Chapter 10, these contemporary Western versions of the subtle body have already been reworked extensively in terms of Western modes of thought and practice.

The subtle body in the Indic and Tibetan Tantric contexts, as we saw in Chapter 2, consists of a visualized internal structure to the human body, consisting of channels (*nāḍī*) and junction points (*cakra*), through which flow a substance (*prāṇa, bodhicitta*, etc.) that is closely related to breathing, the mind, and sexual energy. The Chinese version described by Livia Kohn in Chapter 1 has many similarities, again involving channels (*mai*) through which a substance (*qi*, etc.) flows. Both Indic/Tibetan and Chinese practices involve directing, refining and purifying the *prāṇa* or *qi*, a process that is both spiritual and physiological. These *cakra* are the origin of the 'chakras' popularized by the Theosophists and the New Age. *Qi* (*ch'i, ki*, etc.) has also become a staple of New Age thought.

Given this initial delimitation of the focus of this chapter, a general statement can be made: the Indic and Chinese subtle-body concepts are intended to direct our attention to aspects of our experience and behaviour of which we are, for the most part, not normally fully aware. They do this not so much because the people who originated these texts and practices saw it as important to *describe* these aspects, but because they wanted people to do something in relation to them.

This gives us an initial take on what these subtle-body concepts were about. Whatever the subtle body might have been for the people who developed these practices, it was something that these practices intend to shape, to form, to bring under control. This process was – and still is by contemporary practitioners in these traditions – regarded as desirable and beneficial, both for the individual and perhaps also for society as a whole. In other words, it forms part of a process of self-development, or, if one prefers, a spiritual path.

## A possible model

But what is it that the subtle-body processes are attempting to shape? Here we immediately run into the problem of translation, since the technical vocabulary within which Indo-Tibetan[1] and Chinese subtle-body concepts is embedded does not have any easy one-to-one correspondence with contemporary Western concepts. While aware of the risk of the inappropriate importation of a Western psychological vocabulary, we could nevertheless speak initially here of the realm of barely conscious drives and desires, of the subtle levels of attraction and repulsion between people, the impulses, below or beyond individuals' conscious awareness, that lead them to behave in the ways that they do. To put this in other words, the subtle-body concepts map the area of the Freudian or Jungian unconscious, an equation plausibly made by Alex Comfort in his book *I and That* (see 1979: 104–24). 'Map' here has the sense both of description and of picturing and diagrammatic representation. By mapping this region, and so providing a handle on it, they also give us a possibility of bringing it under control, of domesticating it. This is the core of the explanation offered within this chapter, though further discussion is needed to elaborate and justify what it might mean.

To begin with, as a social scientist I would add that in any given social or historical context the unconscious is not just individual; it has an intrinsically social character. As Jay Johnston argued in Chapter 13, much of what the subtle-body language refers to can be seen in terms of subtle aspects of the interaction and relationships between individual human beings. I would suggest that the subtle-body vocabulary is also used to imply aspects of our relationship to our wider social and ecological context. Many of the ways in which society structures and directs our feelings, drives and ambitions operate at a subconscious or unconscious level, that of taken-for-granted assumptions about the nature of human life. These taken-for-granted ways of feeling, thinking and behaving are part of what subtle-body practices are intended to act upon. If this is so, then making sense of the area of the subtle body will require the elaboration of a theoretical language that can cope with the complex nature of the interaction between the social and the individual.[2] It will also involve confronting some of the reasons why the very idea of such an approach has generally been dismissed or seen as inappropriate. Both of these issues receive some discussion in this chapter.

First, though, I return to our initial point: subtle-body concepts, at least in the Indic and East Asian traditions, developed historically as part of a set of techniques intended to detach us from, to raise us above, the situation of collective conditioning within which we ordinarily live.[3] The precise way in which the aim of this process was and is defined varies. It may be phrased primarily in terms of health or improved human functioning, as with many Chinese self-cultivation practices, or more explicitly directed at Buddhahood, as with Buddhist practices in India and Tibet, or at union with God, as with Śaiva practices in India. Even where there is an immediately pragmatic component, however, as with *qigong* practices or in the Tibetan longevity yogas, there is a goal that involves a more radical transcendence of everyday life. A Daoist Immortal is not simply an ordinary being who has somehow acquired an expanded life-span, and a Tibetan yogin who takes on a serious commitment to Tibetan longevity practices is expected to do so with more elevated aims than that of merely improving his or her health and adding a couple of years to his or her life-span.

The general assumption of the Indic and East Asia subtle-body practices is that the subtle levels in their ordinary form both drive and direct us, and also limit us. This may be phrased, as in the Indian system, in terms of knots and obstructions that have to be cleared and untangled to enable a free flow of *prāṇa* through the system of subtle channels. At any rate, it is generally an accepted goal of these practices that we should seek to go beyond the limited and ordinary state of functioning of the subtle body. This goal can be described both in terms of a better working of the subtle body, and also in terms of a more expanded sense of identity, personality and self. It is explicit within these traditions that there is a process of training that will aid us in doing this. As part of this training, the practitioner becomes aware of the subtle levels, and learns to work with them.

As conceptualized within these traditions, the subtle body encompasses aspects of the body as well as of the mind, and this leads to the question of what the subtle body might correspond to in terms of bodily processes. Again, if we keep our initial formulation of unconscious and subconscious drives, attitudes and processes, we can think of how these express themselves through the body. There is a very wide range of potentially relevant aspects here, from bodily posture, patterns of muscle tension and relaxation, appetite or lack of it for food or sensory experience, vocal tone, perhaps also aspects of the operation of the immune system. We might, though, think of two areas as particularly critical: the central nervous system with its patterns of electrical activity, and the endocrine system and its patterns of hormonal flows and distributions.

Thus we might look at subtle-body practices as being involved with learning how to gain control over the normally autonomous functioning of these aspects of the mind-body's activities. The most dramatic examples here are the various extraordinary powers associated with yogic practice, such as the ability to survive extremely cold conditions through the generation of heat within the body, to withstand extreme heat, or to survive for long periods with little or no food. These powers are also significant as a demonstration to the wider social group that the results of the practices are real, and they link to the association between subtle-body practices and the central spiritual goals of the society in question. They are, in other words, a demonstration of spiritual power, and so also a claim to the status that is justified by that power, and perhaps also a claim to the community's economic and material support for the practitioners.

This reminds us again that subtle-body processes are intrinsically social as well as individual. They are learned in a social context, the goals and concepts involved are shared and derived from that context, and the meanings given to the powers achieved are also social. More generally, work with the mind-body complex is intrinsically social in that it affects, and is affected by, the interactions between human beings.

## Objections

The above is meant only as an initial formulation, and it is itself in several ways problematic and in need of further elaboration.[4] However, before going much further it is necessary to say something about two positions from which there is no problem. These two positions, both extremes, have dominated writing in this area: I refer to them as naive materialism and naive idealism.

*Naive materialism* is the materialist-empiricist reduction according to which all reality must be physical and material. Such views see consciousness, feeling and emotion as uncomplicated reflexes of brain activity. For people who accept a position of this kind, subtle-body concepts, which are generally understood as encompassing consciousness, feeling and emotion as well as the physical level, make little sense. Within the materialist perspective, there can be nothing to encompass that is not already adequately understood in purely physical terms.

The only issue of any intellectual interest in relation to subtle-body ideas, for materialist scholars of this kind, might be why such fantastic ideas exist and are taken seriously. Such an investigation might be undertaken with the aid of cognitive science of religion or cognitive anthropology. These are two branches of an approach, developed by such scholars as Dan Sperber, Pascal Boyer and Harvey Whitehouse, that looks for evolutionary explanations of religious and related phenomena (Sperber 1975; Boyer 2001; Whitehouse 2004; Whitehouse and McCauley 2005; cf. also Andresen 2001).

The general framework here is a somewhat simplistic version of evolutionary theory. It holds that if people believe in subtle bodies or other ideas that do not make immediate and literal sense, this must be because a susceptibility to such beliefs, however illusory, must at some stage have given those people, or their genetic material, an evolutionary advantage. While this approach does not absolutely require that the beliefs are illusory, it does nothing to imply that they are veridical, and most of these scholars clearly assume that they are fantastical.[5] Most versions of this approach in fact see the fantastical nature of concepts such as the subtle body as precisely as part of what needs to be explained. Thus Dan Sperber's theory of symbolism and Pascal Boyer's theory of religion rest heavily on the attractiveness to the human cognitive mechanism of counter-intuitive ideas (Sperber 1975; Boyer 2001; Boyer and Ramble 2001). Harvey Whitehouse, in a similar argument, sees the 'imagistic' mode of religion as embedded in 'episodic' rather than 'semantic' memory; the point of ritual in this mode is not to make sense, but to create a dramatic impact on the people who are experiencing it (Whitehouse 2000: 9–12). Justin Barrett's postulated 'hypersensitive agency detection device' (HADD), which, he suggested, resulted in the assumption of unseen agents as a way of making sense of ambiguous stimuli, leads to somewhat similar conclusions, since it too assumes that religious beliefs arise from a misinterpretation of minimal levels of information (Barrett 2004).

One could contest much about this cognitivist dismissal of the meaning of religious concepts.[6] One could also ask about the contemporary social and cultural forces that give it persuasiveness (Martin 2000). My main point in referring to it here is that it has been widely seen as crucial support for the materialist position, by providing an explanation of religion that negates the need to take religious statements seriously. As an explanation, it leaves much to be desired. Evolution, in the sense of the chronological development and differentiation of the natural species, is not in serious doubt, leaving aside parts of the Christian religious right and other religious groups who reject modern scientific accounts on a doctrinal basis. The meaning of evolution is another matter; it is far from clear that 'natural selection' is in fact an explanation in any real sense, or whether arguments of the kind proffered by the cognitivists have any explanatory value at all (cf. Fodor and Piattelli-Palmerini 2010).

However, I do not have any particular problem with the idea that human beings as biological entities have certain tendencies, properties and modes of operation. The difficulty with the reductionist account from the point of view of the subtle-body concepts is that it offers no space within which the subtle-body concept might be meaningful. The possibility of such concepts having meaning, except as an example of an absurd and counter-intuitive assertion, has been ruled out *a priori*. Thus all subtle-body concepts, for the materialist reduction, are by definiation equally nonsensical and meaningless.

The second position, *naive idealism*, is at the other extreme to the materialist reduction. Here, with many New Age writers, we have naive acceptance of subtle-body phenomena as 'real' in the same sense as material reality, and of needing no special understanding or interpretation. Chakras, auras, currents of *qi* (or *ch'i*) and so on, simply exist, in the same way as everything else, and we need only to develop enough sensitivity to be aware of them. This position, apparently so different from that of the materialists, is in fact subject to the same difficulty as the materialist reduction; there is no traction here on which to base any real scientific model of subtle-body processes. The blending of *qi*, *prāṇa*, auras, 'energy' and the like creates an all-purpose non-concept that is not amenable to investigation.

In reality, it seems clear that the subtle body is not simply another form of reality that anyone with appropriate training will perceive in the same way. Human beings are certainly capable of perceiving, or being under the impression that they are perceiving, subtle realities, but individuals rarely agree with any precision about what they are observing.[7] New Age healers who have learned to work with subtle energies may well be accessing something real, but the language they are using does not enable a genuine contact with science. Books such as, for example, Barbara Brennan's *Hands of Light* (1998) provide an impressively complex and detailed account of subtle realities, but the details appear almost entirely dependent on the author's personal perceptions. Brennan's students may learn to duplicate her perceptions to some degree, but other teachers and students within the general New Age milieu work with quite different models that share only the most basic features with Brennan's.

It is possible to argue, here, that the problem is not so much the inchoateness of the phenomenon as the untrained nature of the perceiver. Thus one might suggest that a group of properly trained psychic observers would produce more consistent and valid results. Alan Wallace presents a version of this position in relation to Tibetan Tantric subtle-body concepts (2003). He argues that a properly trained yogic investigator based in an authentic tradition of spiritual investigation such as Tibetan Buddhism can provide objective information about subtle-body phenomena, in much the same way as a scientific measuring instrument. As a consequence, he suggests, we can take the descriptions of subtle-body processes found in Tibetan Tantric literature as straightforward, veridical accounts of objective real-world phenomena. This position has its own problems, however, since even Tibetan Tantric literature presents a variety of different versions of the subtle-body structure. Thus the detailed structure of *cakra* (psychic centres) and *nāḍī* (channels) differs between two of the main Tantric lineages within which it is presented, the Cakrasaṃvara and Kālacakra. Within Wallace's framework, it would seem that we would have to suppose that one set of yogins got it right, and the others got it wrong. Yet how can we know which, particularly when in practice the same body of yogins may be learning to work in both traditions? There are, as we will see, more productive ways to approach the variations between these and other tantric subtle-body systems.

We should recognize that there are good, as well as less good, reasons why sensible and intelligent people have taken each of these alternatives, the materialist elimination of the subtle body or the idealist acceptance. These choices, as I have implied above, are not separable from the wider social and cultural politics of the world in which we live, and it is this that gives such conflicts a peculiarly aggressive and uncompromising character. It is this, too, that often makes it seem as if there is a black-and-white, either–or choice here; either scientific materialism, or theological literalism.

Certainly this is the way that authors such as Richard Dawkins (2006) or Christopher Hitchens (2007) have presented the issue. Their real enemy, no doubt, is the Christian right, and the real and imagined threats that it poses towards a tolerant and socially progressive society, rather than the kind of ideas we have dealt with in this book. However, the need to dismiss religion as a whole has meant that for these and similar authors anything that might be seen as somehow in the same category becomes dismissed through a process of guilt by association. Unfortunately, in uncritically assuming a global model of religion based on caricatures of Protestant Christianity,[8] and implying that the central feature of religion consists in unthinking commitment to a series of self-evident falsehoods, such authors are unable to perceive that the label 'religion' has come to include many different things. Concepts such as the subtle body do not necessarily have to be seen as, in effect, primitive and mistaken attempts at knowledge of the world, comprehensively superseded by the advances of modern science. For that matter, the understanding of science and the philosophy of science that underlie these naive attacks on religion is also generally quite unsophisticated.

It is important to recognize some of the reasons why compromise has seemed difficult across this particular intellectual divide. For the present, though, it is worthwhile attempting to approach the issue in a more moderate fashion, and to start by recognizing that should we wish to find a scientific understanding of the subtle-body question, there are major limitations to both approaches, the materialist reduction and naive idealism. In the following sections I deal in more detail with the materialist reduction, before proceeding to suggest how we might work towards a more satisfactory way of understanding the meaning of subtle-body concepts.

## Problems with the materialist reduction

We can see some of the logic and the problems with the materialist reduction if we look at one of its most popular forms today. This is the idea that mental activity can be reduced to the electrical activity of the brain and human nervous system.

The development of brain-imaging techniques within neuroscience in recent years has led to the discovery of a great deal of information regarding correlations between consciousness and electrical activity within the brain. It is by now clear that thoughts, feelings, drives and impulses within consciousness have systematic correlates in terms of brain activity as revealed by functional magnetic resonance imaging and other techniques.[9]

Some of this work is of direct relevance to our present topic. For example, as Garfield notes, brain-imaging studies have shown 'that meditation transforms the brain, and that long-term meditators experience dramatic, long-term transformations in cognitive function and neural activity' (Garfield 2012, citing among others Brefczynisk-Lewis *et al.* 2007; Khalsa *et al.* 2008; MacLean *et al.* 2010; Perlman *et al.* 2010). It is true that, as Garfield notes, this is hardly a surprising discovery to anyone who has been seriously involved with meditation, and true also that there are significant methodological difficulties and limitations to many of these studies (Garfield cites Chiesa and Serretti's 2010 systematic review in this connection), but this body of research nevertheless provides useful confirmation for radical sceptics that meditation is a real activity with real consequences.

The difficulty is to establish just what these correlations mean. To start with, it is important to note that while there are systematic correlations between areas of the brain and different kinds of mental activity, these correlations are generally presented in statistical form. Thus what we have are averages over, for example, fMRI scans of a number of individual brains involved in supposedly similar activities. The differences between individual scans are often substantial, and this leads to an important point, which is that the usual caveats against assuming genetic determinism apply strongly to these correlations (cf. Moss 2003, for example). The evidence suggests that different individuals acquire different, individual habits of brain activity, and that there is at most a degree of commonality between patterns of activity in different brains. I have avoided saying here that we each learn to use our brains in slightly different ways, since this form of wording might seem to prejudge the question of the locus of autonomy and individuality in this process, but it seems to me that the evidence for a complex interaction between genetics and environment is compelling.

The question remains, of course, of whether there is something 'beyond' the brain activity, and if so what that might be. In a sense one might say that the elephant in the room here is that there obviously *is* something beyond the brain activity, and that is consciousness itself. Mind is a basic datum of human experience. It can only really be eliminated from the picture by a kind of sleight of hand, in which it is assumed a priori that it is merely some kind of subjective transform of the brain activity. This move, which is basic to the materialist reduction, is, however, justified by that well-known old philosophical principle, Occam's razor, which states that given a number of competing hypotheses with similar explanatory power, one should select that which makes the fewest assumptions.

It needs to be understood that this is a highly suspect move. It assumes something that we are far from having established, in other words that consciousness does not have any degree of autonomy in relation to the neuronal firing that presumably[10] constitutes base level of activity within brain and nervous system. It also treats as not requiring explanation what is in fact an almost totally mysterious relationship – that between the mind and the neuronal activity. Thus any claim that the materialist reduction is a simpler and more economical theory able to account for the same phenomena is dependent on what is really an ideological commitment regarding which phenomena need to be accounted for. Occam's razor is a good methodological rule but it cannot and should not be used to define a whole body of data as imaginary and unreal.

The consequences of the materialist reduction are radical. Apart from begging a whole series of humanly deeply significant questions, such as that of free will and determinism, it implicitly reduces the whole realm of culture, in the anthropological sense, to an epiphenomenon of brain activity. The results are seen in the reductionist accounts of culture offered by Boyer, Whitehouse and their colleagues, which deny the possibility of seeing meaning or sense in much of what most human cultures throughout the ages have regarded as knowledge and practices of central importance to the business of living in the world.

## The autonomy of mind and consciousness

As I have suggested, the issue here is not really Occam's razor, but the refusal to countenance any hypothesis that might be suggestive of the religious or supernatural. A book on subtle bodies raises this problem rather directly, since subtle-body concepts tend to be posed, as many of the accounts in this book demonstrate, in the space between matter and spirit as much as in the space between body and mind.

Readers will doubtless vary in how far they are prepared to concede reality to the mind or to the spirit realm independently of the body. There is undoubtedly a substantial amount of evidence from parapsychology and related fields that points in this direction; a convenient recent summary is the volume *Irreducible Mind* by Edward Kelly and others (2009). Much of this research is substantial and extensive enough that it cannot easily be dismissed or explained away. Consider, for example, the substantial body of material regarding childhood memories of previous lives (Stevenson 2000, 2001; Kelly *et al.* 2009).[11] There are by now many thousands of published accounts from many different societies for which supporting evidence for the veridical nature of the memories has been produced. Despite extensive critical examination and testing, it is difficult if not impossible to find a purely 'physicalist' explanation of this data. Much the same is true of other bodies of data, such as that of visions by dying persons, or by people undergoing near-death experiences, of dead people of whose deaths the viewer was unaware, but which was subsequently discovered or confirmed (Greyson 2010). This is not to say that the observed data in these cases is necessarily to be understood in terms of any particular non-physicalist model (such as continuity of consciousness between lives in the first case, or a literal survival of consciousness after death in the second). There may be other possible non-physicalist explanations for both sets of phenomena. However, neither body of material appears compatible with treating consciousness as involving nothing more than the physical processes within the body. Much the same is true of other kinds of evidence given in the Kelly collection and many other scholarly sources.

The rebirth material is of particular interest because of its close relationship with Indic ideas about the subtle body; in fact, James Hartzell has suggested plausibly that Indic theorizing about the subtle body arose to a significant extent out of attempts to make sense of the process of rebirth (1997: 557–9).

Evidence of this kind suggests that the naive physicalist model has intrinsic flaws and limitations, and that we may be approaching the point where a substantial revision of our theoretical frameworks is required. What a new framework might consist of is less clear. In my own view, it is unlikely to resemble the Theosophical approach, which essentially consists of naive physicalism with a series of 'subtle' layers added on. For the present, however, incorporating evidence of this kind into a theoretical perspective on the subtle body remains highly problematic, as well as professionally risky for practising scientists.

For those who believe that science should be open to investigating whatever models and hypotheses may be required to make sense of the data, this is perhaps a regrettable state of affairs, and it is good to observe a renewed willingness among younger scholars, in the social sciences at least, to take 'anomalous experience' seriously (cf. Young and Goulet 1998; Goulet and Miller 2007; see also Greenwood, this volume). In the present context, however, I limit myself to exploring an intermediate and less radical position. How far we can recognize the autonomous status of consciousness *without* invoking concepts that are clearly non-material in nature, or assuming the existence of mind separately from the body? It is, I think, possible to outline models that are materialist in a broad sense, but are able to include a much wider range of phenomena than naive physicalism, and to account for those phenomena in a more satisfactory manner.

A central issue of here is that of *emergence*. I return here to a passage by the late Chilean cognitive scientist and neurophysiologist Francisco Varela and his colleague Natalie Depraz that I have quoted previously (Samuel 2006). Varela and Depraz point to the process of 'upward causation', by which mental imagery can be seen as a system of large-scale synchronization of neural processes, a '*transient coherency-generating process* of the organism' (2003: 212). However, they insist that this process of 'upward causation' implies a corresponding process of 'downwards causation':

> Many will accept that the self is an emergent property arising from a neural/bodily base. However … the *reverse* statement is typically missed. If the neural components and circuits act as local agents that can emergently give rise to a self, then it follows that this global level, the self, has direct *efficacious actions* over the local components. It is a two-way street: the local components give rise to this emergent mind, but, vice versa, the emergent mind constrains and affects directly these local components.
>
> (2003: 214)

The option presented here is that the self is *emergent*, in that it derives from the material basis of the neural/bodily complex as it develops through the growth and maturation of the individual. The argument here goes back to the idea in Varela's first major work, *Autopoesis and Cognition*, written jointly with his teacher and colleague at the University of Chile, Humberto Maturana, of living organisms as 'autopoetic' (self-constructing) systems (Maturana and Varela 1972). In their 2003 article, Varela and Depraz instance the ability of a person suffering with epilepsy to learn how to gain conscious control over the onset of an epileptic seizure. In fact the question of health and of the role of consciousness in healing is one of the key areas where significant evidence has appeared in recent years in relation to these questions, and I comment further on it below. First, however, it is worth looking more closely at what we might call the 'Varela model' of emergent mind.

Varela's work and the idea of an emergent structure give us a plausible picture of mind as derivative from but in some respects at least autonomous of the material level. It does not require or explicitly include the *Irreducible Mind* agenda (Kelly *et al.* 2009), of mind as existing freely from its biological base, but, as we will see, once the ecological dimension is built in, the Varela model allows for at least some elements of autonomy from the material base. It harks back in many ways to the old-fashioned idea of the hierarchy of sciences in which chemistry is built on and in some sense 'emergent' from physics, and biology has a similar relationship to chemistry. However, if we want to build on this foundation, we perhaps need to look more closely at what we are accepting.

We might begin with a key sentence in the above quotation: 'If the neural components and circuits act as local agents that can emergently give rise to a self, then it follows that this global level, the self, has direct *efficacious actions* over the local components.' Does the consequence stated in this sentence follow? Indeed, what does it mean to say that the global level 'has direct *efficacious actions* over the local components'? An unfriendly critic might comment that there is a kind of sleight of hand going on here, and it has to be admitted that the precise mechanism for the emergence of a centre of efficacy, of a consciousness that can act, still has to be specified. Perhaps, though, a lacuna is always going to remain at this point, however closely science may manage to zero in on this critical transition, and certainly the naive materialists do not have an answer at this point, only a denial that one is needed. Rather than seeing this as a necessary bar to the acceptance of Varela's model, I suggest a closer examination of the possible relationship between the two levels, the global level (the self) and the local (the neural components).

Some initial assistance can be gained from another major twentieth-century figure who like Varela worked on the interface between biology and culture: Gregory Bateson. In several of the essays reprinted in his *Steps to an Ecology of Mind* (1973), Bateson distinguishes, speaking here of living organisms in general, between two levels of learning: initially, learning and meta-learning, later Learning 1 and Learning 2 (with the possibility of a third level, Learning 3, envisaged in some of his later statements). The distinction here is between an immediate, conditioned stimulus-response reaction (the product of Learning 1), and a higher-level process of learning ('learning to learn'), which involves some kind of grouping or structuring of experience so as to enable more complex and sophisticated responses. Learning a language, learning to dance (as distinct from learning a fixed set of movements), learning a culture, all imply this kind of higher-order process, which Bateson argued was observable in a range of more complex living organisms. His own work at this time was mainly concerned with understanding disorders in the learning process (including his famous 'double bind' hypothesis) and how they might be reversed.[12]

Bateson's Learning 2 would seem to be much the same process as Varela's self emerging from the local agents. Bateson places the emergence in the context of learning theory, a move that avoids or evades the troublesome associations that link to the word 'self'. There is nevertheless a strong sense, particularly in Bateson's later work, that Learning 2 (and even more Learning 3) involves something that might be termed self-awareness, and even a spiritual dimension.[13]

An important point for both Varela and Bateson is the role of the wider context of the individual. These models are about individuals that are always already part of a wider social and natural context, and become what they are through a continuous process of interaction with that context. Neither Varela nor Bateson has any interest in denying the centrality of biology – this is one of the main reasons, perhaps, why purist scholars in the social sciences and humanities, wanting to hold on to a world in which culture is autonomous from biology, have found their work difficult to digest. Both, however, describe the emergence from the biological context of a level of functioning that appears to demand a distinctive level of description and analysis, and corresponds in some sense, at least in human beings, to our sense of the self.

Recent research in fields such as neuroendocrinology provides significant data as to the mix of social and biological factors in such interactions. As with the literature on neuronal activity referred to by Varela, there is a tendency for one direction along what is again clearly a two-way street to be emphasized, but there is also a growing literature looking at the reverse direction. As Sari van Anders and Neil Watson state:

> most studies focus on the effects of hormones on somatic or behavioural measures, and rightly so, because hormones have powerful effects on the nervous system throughout life. But there is an oft-neglected converse of this perspective. One's own behaviour, the behaviour of others, and other environmental influences can all potently alter the functioning of the endocrine system, resulting in pervasive changes in behaviour.
>
> (2005: 213)

One might look, for example, at the so-called 'winner effect', by which male animals – including, it seems, male human beings – learn to fight better as a result of winning, and conversely, one supposes, learn how to fail by losing, the shifts in both cases being associated with levels of testosterone within the body (Van Anders and Watson 2005; Oliveira 2009). One can also look at the increasing evidence for the role of oxytocin in maintaining what human beings know as love and affection, and for the social factors associated with its generation (Ross and Young 2009; Heinrichs *et al.* 2009). These hormonal changes are not simply changes in the hormones within the body at a given time. They are also associated with ongoing changes to the neural system (neuroplasticity): 'these results suggest that socially induced changes in circulating steroid hormones have the potential to sculpt the neural mechanisms underlying social behaviour' (Oliveira 2009: 425).

While most of this literature avoids explicitly engaging with consciousness, for the kind of reasons we have already explored, it is clear that for humans consciousness is part of the process; we are, after all, conscious of feelings of victory and defeat, affection and sociality.

It may be suggested that our conscious awareness of the external world, as mediated by the way in which we interpret the data received by the senses, is also generated by a complex ongoing interaction between our biological instantiation and the external world (including sensory input from our internal biological processes), mediated by hormonal and neural processes that generate but are also structured by the emergent self of which Varela speaks. We can assume that cognition, and our awareness of our surroundings more generally, is affected by short-term hormonal flows and changes, and also that the neural structures through which we perceive the world are built up interactively by processes that involve both these flows and externally given structures such as those provided by spoken and written language and by visual media.

Similarly the ways in which we perceive emotions, feelings and sensations of various kinds are built up interactively in relation to our experience, which of course includes the ways in which culture and language help to structure our awareness of emotion.[14] A further development of a model of this kind can be found in my 1990 book *Mind, Body and Culture*, which suggests how cultural and biological understandings of the human organism can be integrated into a single model that does not unduly privilege either side.

Neither Varela nor Bateson, it should be noted, assumes that the emergent self, or the structures of Learning 2, necessarily provide the organism with a full and accurate picture of the world, either external or internal to the organism. Elsewhere, in fact, Bateson argues that any representation of the world is by definition incomplete, since inevitably less complex than the world itself (Bateson 1973: 115–16). In this respect, the models of both Varela and Bateson have an affinity with the Buddhist sense that reality is somehow far more complex than the ability of any given organism to fathom, so that understanding is always partial and incomplete. This is an important point in relation to the subtle body, since one of the problems with the subtle body is precisely that it does not appear to correspond exactly to the physical structures of the material body. However, they equally do not assume that the implicit or explicit understanding of the world gained by the individual is nonsensical, as the cognitive authropologists do.

If one sees the subtle body, as I suggested earlier, as a kind of view of the brain and central nervous system from within, however, we can see it both as a partial view of reality and also as one that makes sense and is of use to the organism. What is significant about the subtle body is that when internalized as part of a regime of training it provides the organism with a way to operate with the area of inner feelings, emotions and perceptions, otherwise difficult to grasp in conceptual form.

Put otherwise, subtle-body concepts and practices can be seen as part of a conscious version of the process of autopoesis or Batesonian learning, itself generated historically through the autopoesis and learning of individual human beings, and passed on as a series of techniques for learning something seen as valuable by their cultures. The ability of subtle-body concepts and practices to do this is not compromised by their failure to match the inner structures of the body in a literal way, because this is simply not what they are meant to do.

Thus, for example, the differences between the descriptions of the subtle body in Kālacakra and in other Buddhist Tantras (Chapter 2) do not reflect different understandings of a static, universal, human body. They should rather be seen in connection with the yogic practices of which they form a part, as directional and processual, as meditational devices that are intended to move the human mindbody organism along two somewhat different pathways, in two different directions.

Here it is worth remembering that subtle-body practices in the Indo-Tibetan and Chinese traditions are not necessarily just concerned with the attainment of soteriological goals, but also with this-worldly goals such as improved health and bodily functioning. Recent work on the importance of meaning in the so-called placebo effect, and more generally on the importance of 'subjective' and cultural aspects in relation to the immune system, make it more plausible to consider such practices as, potentially at least, having a real effect (cf. Moerman 2002, Wilce 2003). Many subtle-body practices can be seen as, in effect, working on the immune system and related aspects of bodily functioning.[15] Here one might think of the Śaiva *kriyā* practices, Tibetan *'phrul 'khor* exercises (as discussed by Chaoul in Chapter 6) and contemporary Chinese *qigong* practices.

All this provides us with a picture of the subtle body as something that is relational, that is constructed, and that is nevertheless real, and that can be grounded in our best current sense of neurophysiology. It also suggests that learning to operate with the subtle body might become, were the world a little different, something other than an exotic pursuit carried out by a tiny minority of esoteric practitioners. It could rather be part of an everyday education appropriate to life on a small, heavily populated planet, where the ability of future generations to live harmoniously and productively with each other and with the planetary ecology that sustains them will be vital for human survival.

As this implies, there is a moral dimension to the subtle-body practices. This is doubtless another of the ways in which the subtle body can be, for contemporary Western modes of knowledge, an uncomfortable and difficult issue to theorize. The subtle body, in many of the versions that are discussed in this book, and certainly in the Indian and Tibetan Tantric traditions, does not only represent what is, or even what we could bring into existence should we employ the practices in question. It also represents what the tradition holds that we *should* become. The Buddhist identification of the internal flows and associated sexual and emotional impulses within the subtle body with *bodhicitta*, the compassionate motivation that is the essential driving force for the attainment of Buddhahood, makes this point particularly clearly. I will not explore this issue further here, but it is undoubtedly worth noting, and it is one of the dimensions of the subtle body that should, I believe, be confronted more directly. The subtle body does not fit easily into a value-free science, and perhaps the further investigation of the subtle body can help too in unravelling the complex ways in which our present sciences are themselves invested with explicit or, more often, implicit values.

For the present, though, the important point is that subtle-body concepts and practices deserve serious examination. It is not enough simply to exclude all consideration on the dogmatic and unscientific grounds that these concepts and practices do not fit into our current paradigms. We should at least allow ourselves the freedom to ask what they may amount to in reality, and what they may contain that could be of genuine value within the contemporary world. Perhaps most critically, we need to ask: what do these concepts allow one to do? What pathways (for cultures, religious systems, for the planetary eco-system as a whole), and what possible futures, may be opened up by a willingness to explore the possibilities of the subtle body? And what futures are being closed off by the refusal to take them seriously?

## Notes

1 'Indo-Tibetan' here is intended to include both Indian and Tibetan.
2 For a sketch of such a language, see Samuel 1990. See also Samuel 2001, 2010.
3 This is not to deny that there may have been, and almost certainly were, other components to the development of subtle-body concepts. Chapter 1 discussed some of the early Indian precursors of Tantric subtle-body concepts, and the analysis given here would not necessarily apply in these cases. To give two further examples, Elisabeth Hsu has argued for the significance of medicine and the diagnostic use of touch in the development of early Chinese concepts of *qi* (2005), and Marina Roseman has suggested that the occurrence of a range of separable 'souls' or spirit-locations in Southeast Asian tribal populations such as the Malaysian Temiar might also have contributed to the *cakra*-s and similar structures (personal communication, 1996).
4 One area that is problematic is that the phraseology I have used is essentially that of individual self-development and transformation. This individual focus is deeply built into our ordinary language usage in English, though less so in other languages such as Tibetan. Samuel 1990 develops a simple model for such processes (the multimodal framework) that does not assume the individual level as primary.
5 Justin Barrett is unusual in this group in apparently combining Christian belief with an evolutionary explanation for the mechanisms that enable humans to have such beliefs (Barrett 2004).
6 See Samuel 1990 for some early arguments against Sperber's position.

7 Of course, the same could be said about ordinary reality; three or four independent observers often have considerable trouble in providing an agreed description of the colour or shape of an object, despite having a commonly agreed vocabulary to do this with. It might be that some of the difficulty in the subtle-body case is not so much the more difficult nature of the perception as the lack of an agreed vocabulary. But this still takes us to the issue of why it has been difficult to arrive at an agreed vocabulary in this area, beyond highly general terms such as 'energy' or *qi*.

8 I am not implying that Asian religions are free from the faults that might be associated with Christianity. Asian religions have had their own role in legitimating violent, oppressive and socially conservative regimes, and for that matter Christianity, if responsible for high levels of repression and oppression throughout the ages, has surely also been an energizing force behind the growth of tolerance and social responsibility.

9 Strictly speaking, fMRI measures blood flow, which is a proxy for electrical activity; neither fMRI nor EEG, which measures electrical activity on the scalp surface, is a direct record of electrical activity in the brain. Consequently, fMRI gives a fairly general picture of activity in a brain region over a window of a few seconds. Other measures are being developed which it is hoped will provide better localization in both time and space, but we are clearly still some way from following neuronal activity in great detail.

10 The presumption here might also be open to some questioning.

11 As distinct from adult recall of past lives, which raises different methodological problems.

12 Some of this work was foundational for the anti-psychiatry movement, in which Félix Guattari was a leading figure, and so fed into some of the literature discussed by Jay Johnston in Chapter 13.

13 See the article 'Style, Grace and Information in Primitive Art' included in Bateson 1973, which deliberately uses the term 'grace' with its strongly religious associations, in this context.

14 Here we can think, for example, of the ways in which different languages visualize emotions, feelings and impulses as fluids and other substances, often associating them with real organs within the body (heart, liver, stomach) in ways that do not necessarily correspond to the biological function of that organ and vary greatly between cultures. Thus the general English and Anglo-Saxon associations of love or courage with the heart, fear with the stomach, and so on, are, in Lakoff and Johnson's terms, 'metaphors we live by' rather than accurate scientific statements regarding the inner functioning of the body (1980). I should add that there are problems with Lakoff and Johnson's wider theoretical assumptions (cf. Martin 2000). Their work nevertheless demonstrates the importance of underlying models to the structures of specific natural languages, and so of the systems of knowledge built up within them.

15 That is, assuming that their effects are real. In fact, my intention here is not to claim that the practices necessarily achieve what they are claimed to achieve, for example in relation to improved health and bodily functioning, but to suggest that such effects are plausible and possible as a result of the kinds of practice we are considering here.

# References

Andresen, J. (ed.) (2001) *Religion in Mind: Cognitive Perspectives on Religious Belief, Ritual and Experience*. Cambridge: Cambridge University Press.

Barrett, J. L. (2004) *Why Would Anyone Believe in God?* Walnut Creek, CA: Altamira Press.

Bateson, G. (1973) *Steps to an Ecology of Mind: Collected Essays in Anthropology, Psychiatry, Evolution and Epistemology*. St Albans: Paladin.

Bohm, D. (1980) *Wholeness and the Implicate Order*. London: Routledge and Kegan Paul.

Boyer, P. (2001) *Religion Explained: The Human Instincts that Fashion Gods, Spirits and Ancestors*. London: Heinemann.

Boyer, P. and Ramble, C. (2001) 'Cognitive templates for religious concepts: cross-cultural evidence for recall of counter-intuitive representations', *Cognitive Science* 25: 535–64.

Brefczynisk-Lewis, J., Lutz, A., Shaeffer, H., Levison, D. and Davidson, R. (2007) 'Neural correlates of attentional expertise in long-term meditation practitioners', *Proceedings of the National Academy of Sciences* 104 (27), pp. 11483–8.

Brennan, B. A. (1988) *Hands of Light: A Guide to Healing Through the Human Energy Field*. New York: Bantam.

Chiesa, A. and Serretti, A. (2010) 'A systematic review of neurobiological and clinical features of mindfulness meditations', *Psychological Medicine* 40: 1239–52.

Comfort, A. (1979) *I and That: Notes on the Biology of Religion*. New York: Crown.

—— (1981) 'The implications of an implicate: notes on David Bohm's *Wholeness and the Implicate Order*', *Journal of Social and Biological Structures* 4: 363–74.

Dawkins, R. (2006) *The God Delusion*. London: Bantam Press.

Fodor, J. and Piattelli-Palmarini, M. (2010) *What Darwin Got Wrong*. London: Profile.

Garfield, J. (2012) 'Ask not what Buddhism can do for cognitive science; ask what cognitive science can do for Buddhism', *Bulletin of Tibetology* 47: 15–30.

Goulet, J.-G. A. and Miller, B. G. (eds) (2007) *Extraordinary Anthropology: Transformations in the Field*. Lincoln: University of Nebraska Press.

Greyson, B. (2010) 'Seeing dead people not known to have died: "Peak in Darien" experiences', *Anthropology and Humanism* 35(2), 159–71.

Hartzell, J. F. (1997) 'Tantric Yoga: a study of the Vedic precursors, historical evolution, literatures, cultures, doctrines and practices of the 11th century Kaśmiri śaivite and Buddhist unexcelled Tantric Yogas', unpublished PhD thesis, Columbia University.

Heinrichs, M., von Dawans, B. and Domes, G. (2009) 'Oxytocin, vasopressin, and human social behavior', *Frontiers in Neuroendocrinology* 30: 548–57.

Hitchens, C. (2007) *God is Not Great: The Case Against Religion*. London: Atlantic.

Hsu, E. (2005) 'Tactility and the body in early Chinese medicine', *Science in Context* 18: 7–34.

Kelly, E., Kelly, E. W. *et al.* (2009) *Irreducible Mind: Toward a Psychology for the 21st Century*. Lanham, MD: Rowman & Littlefield.

Khalsa, S., Rudrauf, D., Damasio, A., Davidson, R., Lutz, A. and Tranel, D. (2008) 'Introceptive awareness in experienced meditators', *Psychophysiology* 45: 671–7.

Lakoff, G. and Johnson, M. (1980) *Metaphors We Live By*. Chicago and London: University of Chicago Press.

MacLean, K. *et al.* (2010) 'Intensive meditation training improves perceptual discrimination and sustained attention', *Psychological Science* 21(6): 829–39.

Martin, E. (2000) 'Mind-body problems', *American Ethnologist* 27: 569–90.

Maturana, H. R. and Varela, F. J. (1980) *Autopoiesis and Cognition: The Realization of the Living*. Dordrecht, Boston and London: Reidel.

Moerman, D. E. (2002) *Meaning, Medicine, and the 'Placebo Effect'*. Cambridge and New York: Cambridge University Press.

Moss, L. (2003) *What Genes Can't Do*. Cambridge, MA and London: MIT Press.

Oliveira, R. F. (2009) 'Social behavior in context: hormonal modulation of behavioral plasticity and social competence', *Integrative and Comparative Biology* 49: 423–40.

Perlman, D., Salomons, T., Davidson, R. and Lutz, A. (2010) 'Differential effects on pain intensity and unpleasantness of two meditation practices', *Emotion* 10: 65–71.

Ross, H. E. and Young, L. J. (2009) 'Oxytocin and the neural mechanisms regulating social cognition and affiliative behavior', *Frontiers in Neuroendocrinology* 30: 534–47.

Samuel, G. (1990) *Mind, Body and Culture: Anthropology and the Biological Interface.* Cambridge and New York: Cambridge University Press.

—— (2001) 'The effectiveness of goddesses, or, how ritual works', *Anthropological Forum* 11: 73–91.

—— (2006) 'Tibetan medicine and biomedicine: epistemological conflicts, practical solutions', *Asian Medicine: Tradition and Modernity* 2(1):72–85.

—— (2010) 'Healing, efficacy and the spirits', *Journal of Ritual Studies* 24(2): 7–20 (special issue, *The Efficacy of Rituals Part II*, ed. W. S. Sax and J. Quack).

Sperber, D. (1975) *Rethinking Symbolism.* Cambridge and New York: Cambridge University Press.

Stevenson, I. (2000) 'The phenomenon of claimed memories of previous lives: possible interpretations and importance', *Medical Hypotheses* 54: 652–9.

—— (2001) *Children Who Remember Previous Lives: A Question of Reincarnation*, rev. edn. Jefferson, NC: McFarland.

Van Anders, S. M. and Watson, N. V. (2006) 'Social neuroendocrinology: effects of social contexts and behaviors on sex steroids in humans', *Human Nature* 17: 212–37.

Varela, F. J. and Depraz, N. (2003) 'Imagining: embodiment, phenomenology, and transformation', in B. A. Wallace (ed.) *Buddhism and Science: Breaking New Ground.* New York: Columbia University Press.

Wallace, B. A. (2003) 'Introduction', in B. A. Wallace (ed.) *Buddhism and Science: Breaking New Ground.* New York: Columbia University Press.

Whitehouse, H. (2000) *Arguments and Icons: Divergent Modes of Religiosity.* Oxford and New York: Oxford University Press.

—— (2004) *Modes of Religiosity: A Cognitive Theory of Religious Transmission.* Walnut Creek, CA: and Oxford: Altamira Press.

Whitehouse, H. and McCauley, R. N. (eds) (2005) *Mind and Religion: Psychological and Cognitive Foundations of Religiosity.* Walnut Creek, CA and Oxford: Altamira Press.

Wilce, J. M. Jr (ed.) (2003) *Social and Cultural Lives of Immune Systems.* London and New York: Routledge.

Young, D. E. and Goulet, J.-G. A. (eds) (1998) *Being Changed by Cross-Cultural Encounters: The Anthropology of Extraordinary Experiences.* Peterborough, ON: Broadview.

# Index